Anxious Histories

Anxious Histories
Narrating the Holocaust in Jewish Communities at the Beginning of the Twenty-First Century

Jordana Silverstein

berghahn
NEW YORK • OXFORD
www.berghahnbooks.com

First edition published in 2015 by
Berghahn Books
www.berghahnbooks.com

© 2015, 2017 Jordana Silverstein
First paperback edition published in 2017

All rights reserved. Except for the quotation of short passages
for the purposes of criticism and review, no part of this book
may be reproduced in any form or by any means, electronic or
mechanical, including photocopying, recording, or any information
storage and retrieval system now known or to be invented,
without written permission of the publisher.

Library of Congress Cataloging-in-Publication Data

Silverstein, Jordana, author.
 Anxious histories : narrating the Holocaust in Jewish communities at the beginning of the twenty-first century / Jordana Silverstein.
   pages cm
 Includes bibliographical references.
 ISBN 978-1-78238-652-0 (hardback) — ISBN 978-1-78533-523-5 (paperback) — ISBN 978-1-78238-653-7 (ebook)
  1. Holocaust, Jewish (1939-1945)—Study and teaching. 2. Holocaust, Jewish (1939-1945)—Psychological aspects. 3. Holocaust, Jewish (1939-1945)—Historiography. I. Title.
 D804.33.S59 2015
 940.53'18071—dc23

2014033561

British Library Cataloguing in Publication Data

A catalogue record for this book is available from the British Library

ISBN: 978-1-78238-652-0 hardback
ISBN: 978-1-78533-523-5 paperback
ISBN: 978-1-78238-653-7 ebook

This book is dedicated to the
memories of my two grandmothers,
Zosia Stawski and Gladys Silverstein,
for their presences and absences in my
life, my memories and my histories.

Contents

Acknowledgements	ix
Introduction. Holocaust Historiography, Anxiety and the Formulations of a Diasporic Jewishness	1
Chapter 1. 'Don't Ever Think That It Can't Happen Again': Memories of the Holocaust, Anxieties of Difference	36
Chapter 2. 'I Think It Makes It More Real That Way': Chronology, Survivor Testimony and the Holocaust	62
Chapter 3. 'From the Utter Depth of Degradation to the Apogee of Bliss': Uncanny and Mimicking Diasporic Zionism	99
Chapter 4. 'There Is No Doubt That It Was a Jewish Experience': The Forgetfulness of a Haunting Settler Colonialism	142
Chapter 5. 'Why the Role of Women Was Any More Special Than the Role of the Rest of Them': Circumscribing Jewish Femininity in Holocaust Pedagogies	178
Conclusion. 'It's an Unusual Topic You've Chosen': Negotiating Emplacement through History-Making	207
Bibliography	213
Index	235

Acknowledgements

A work like this is never simply the labour of an individual. So many people supported me – emotionally, intellectually and financially – and it feels like a great privilege to have been able to engage with and learn from such wonderful minds.

My deepest gratitude first and foremost goes to the many schools and individual teachers in Melbourne and New York who so generously took the time to speak to me and share their curriculum documents. I thank them for their assistance and wisdom.

Esther Faye was a patient, encouraging, brilliant, generous, caring and attentive mentor throughout, and this project would not exist without her guidance and inspiring intellect. It was wonderful to have had the opportunity to study with her.

In New York, so many people ensured that my stays were productive and enjoyable: relatives and friends, old and new; the archives at the United States Holocaust Memorial Museum (in Washington, DC), and the Lillian Goldman Reading Room at the Center for Jewish History in Manhattan, and in particular the archivists at the YIVO Institute and the American Jewish Historical Society (AJHS); the Board of Jewish Education in New York, in particular Emily Witty, who provided much needed help in locating appropriate schools and shared her expertise; the women at Ma'yan, and in particular Paulette Lipton; Paul Radensky at the Museum of Jewish Heritage who took the time to speak to me about his work; Chani Maybruch provided some helpful insights; and the many people at the various synagogues and community institutions I visited who welcomed me into their communities.

In Israel, Emily Bock provided me with company and a place to stay; the incredible women of Machsom Watch, and Lydia Aisenberg at Givat Haviva took me to the West Bank and provided me with some of the most profound experiences of my trip; and Richelle Budd-Caplan at Yad Vashem and Marc Kurs at the Beit Hatefusoth Museum in Tel Aviv University shared their expertise and ideas with me. I am indebted to all these people in both countries.

In Melbourne, Sue Hampel, Frances Prince and the *madrichim* involved in March of the Living Melbourne in 2007 provided me with much assistance, while Bernard Rechter at the Melbourne Jewish Holocaust Museum and Research Centre gave me some important local knowledge. Many friends and family shared their ideas about what it is be Jewish in Melbourne today, and worked with me on various side projects, most particularly Rachel Liebhaber, Liam Neame, Dalit Kaplan, ronch willner, Leah Kaye, Max Kaiser, Jem Light, Danya Jacobs, and the rest of the Australian Jewish Democratic Society (AJDS). I am rather thankful for all their help, wisdom and encouragement.

The University of Melbourne School of Historical Studies, Faculty of Arts, and School of Graduate Research provided the funding which enabled me to go on overseas research trips, and an Australian Postgraduate Award kept me housed and fed.

My fellow postgraduates were enriching to work beside. Crystal McKinnon, David Slucki and Matthew Klugman offered me generous, incredibly fruitful and wonderfully challenging engagement; Keir Wotherspoon was the best officemate a person could hope for; Esther Jilovsky and Melissa Walsh were wonderful collaborators on various projects; and drinks and conversations with Rachel Patrick and Mark Pendleton ensured this book was completed. Gideon Reuveni helped to provide me with many important ideas. Kat Ellinghaus has been a wonderful mentor, employer and friend. Robert Reynolds and Leigh Boucher offered me support and encouragement far beyond what could possibly be expected. Mary Tomsic has been a source of endless collegiality, friendship and essential coffee breaks. Paul Bartrop gave me early inspiration for this project, while Shannon Woodcock provided much intellectual stimulation and support throughout. Patrick Wolfe has been a kind and generous supporter. Joy Damousi, Jane Carey and Clare Corbould have been mentors, friends, employers and incredibly encouraging throughout this project. I am immeasurably grateful to all of these people.

Numerous people – including many mentioned elsewhere here – read drafts of parts or all of this book at various different times. I am thankful for their suggestions and ideas, and am particularly grateful to Jonathan Boyarin and Idith Zertal, who commented on an earlier version of this manuscript, as well as the three anonymous reviewers of this manuscript for Berghahn Books. All of their ideas were invaluable, pushing me to clarify my thoughts at every turn. The editors at Berghahn Books – Adam Capitanio and Elizabeth Berg – have been wonderful indeed to work with. Thanks too to Shelley Krycer for allowing me to use her wonderful image on the cover of this book.

Previous versions of two chapters have been published as articles: J. Silverstein. 2012. '"From the Utter Depth of Degradation to the Apogee of Bliss': The Genderings of Diasporic Zionism and Jewish Holocaust Education', *Journal of Modern Jewish Studies* 11(3), 377–98.; J. Silverstein. 2012. 'Jewish Holocaust Histories and the Work of Chronological Narratives', *Journal of Jewish Education* 78(1), 58–83. I thank both journals for permission to publish them in revised form here, and the various anonymous reviewers whose insights helped me to develop those chapters.

Sara Dehm did a fantastic job of transcribing the interviews for me, and has been a truly excellent sister-out-law. Erica Millar and Claire McLisky have been splendid and loyal friends, housemates and fellow Ph.D. students. They have both strengthened and inspired me in so many ways. And then there are some of the non-historian friends who have provided me with love and support in various forms over the years: in particular Kristine Jover, Valentine, Angela Smith, Julia Dehm, Jacqui Brenner, Kelly Laing, Ania Anderst, Sian Vate, Rohan Martyres and Paul Glennie. My extended Stawski and Rosengarten families have taught me much about the joys of belonging.

Ben, my dear brother, has encouraged and inspired me, and I'm honoured to be his friend: his brilliant mind and clarity of thinking, as well as his sense of humour and gloriously good spirit, make the world an infinitely better place. My parents, Rae and Mervyn, have provided so much comfort, support, guidance and care. I am thankful for all that these three wonderful people have given me.

INTRODUCTION

Holocaust Historiography, Anxiety and the Formulations of a Diasporic Jewishness

> The premier demand upon all education is that Auschwitz not happen again. Its priority before any other requirement is such that I believe I need not and should not justify it.
> —Theodore Adorno, *Can One Live after Auschwitz? A Philosophical Reader*

> To establish a set of norms that are beyond power or force is itself a powerful and forceful conceptual practice that sublimates, disguises and extends its own power play through recourse to tropes of normative universality . . . [T]he task is to interrogate what the theoretical move that establishes foundations *authorizes*, and what it precisely excludes or forecloses.
> —Judith Butler, 'Contingent Foundations: Feminism and the Question of "Postmodernism"'

When I was at school, a game occasionally played by my friends was to ask, 'Are you a Jewish Australian or an Australian Jew?' The idea was that whatever you put first was what you prioritized. I remember my brother pointing out once that, grammatically, it was whichever one put second that was the key idea around which they organised their identity. But the terms signified for all of us that what came first was most important; and that, from a young age, we were already contemplating which came first. The two terms (or ideas, or identities), it seemed, did not sit well together; it was a competition between the two. One came first. The other was deprioritized.

Many years later I read Judith Butler's resonant words, where she writes, '[c]onsider that it may be a mistake to declare one's affiliation by stating an order of priorities: I am X first and then Y. It may be that the ordering of such identifications is precisely the problem produced by a discourse on multiculturalism which does not yet know how to relate the terms that it enumerates.'[1]

I never answered the question, as it didn't seem to make much sense to me to choose one to prioritize in that way. My brother made a seemingly semantic point to disagree with the premise of the question. Both of us refused to engage with the terms of Jewishness – or Australianness – that it offered. I was reminded of this when in Israel undertaking fieldwork for this project, and having dinner with some friends, all of whom had migrated to Israel: in the terms of the Zionist project, they had made *aliyah*, or 'ascended'. One woman commented that the 'long-lasting problem of the Diaspora Jew is choosing who to vote for in elections – does one vote based on domestic issues, or based on each party's attitudes to Israel?'[2] In her rendering, there is a split, irreconcilable, identity at work. This, she claimed, was part of her motivation for making *aliyah* – as though in Israel one could be Jewish without having any ties to a separate nation-state. As though nationalism was natural and inevitable. As though Israel and Jewishness were inseparable. And as though this split was a problem – that one could be a better Jew when one only had a sole allegiance. As though being Jewish outside Israel meant that one would always have one eye looking towards Israel.

What governs the original question, I now understand, is a network of ambivalences and anxieties. We were being asked – and we were asking each other – where we felt comfortable; where we felt at home; where we located our identities; where we belonged. Israel was probably in the question, perhaps unarticulated or conflated with the signifier 'Jewish', but some sort of presence nonetheless. The questioner, as well as the person providing the answers, was interrogating the level of anxiety over where we as Jews belong in a world made up of nation-states, and how we felt about our Jewishness and its possibilities for creating a space of syncretic belonging.

What though if the story were to be changed? Instead of Diaspora as a static, troublesome, divisive place, what if the Jewish diaspora were to be thought of as primarily a story of travel and movement, 'hither and thither', in the terms offered by Homi Bhabha.[3] What if, as David Shneer and Caryn Aviv have suggested, we conceptualise the Jewish world *not* in terms of Homeland/Diaspora, but as everywhere that Jews live being places of diaspora.[4] If Israel, for instance, was removed as the centre and we viewed Jewishness as having many places of origin and ongoing presence; and the communities in Melbourne and New York, and, indeed, everywhere, as not being shaped by a condition of centre and periphery, but rather of (dis)placement. And, more than that, of 'in-betweenness' or liminality.[5] As being about potentially moving homes, but still being able to be rooted somewhere, anywhere. As a relationship between various lands and, perhaps most importantly, interactions with different peoples and nations – as, indeed, a condition of being various. Would this lessen our anxieties about the order or affiliation of our identities? What would this do to the ways we narrate our histories?

In this book I locate this anxiety about how to live in the world, or about how to understand one's affiliations, within a body of historiography. I am interested in denaturalizing the historical narratives about the Holocaust that are being taught in a selection of Jewish schools in Melbourne, Australia and New York City, United States. By locating them within a wider body of historiographical production I explore the ideas of Holocaust history that are being formulated. In doing so I provide an understanding of the work that such narratives undertake: the work they do to create histories and identities. As I will show, the Holocaust as a profound moment of genocidal violence, horror and displacement for Europe's Jews has since served to structure many subsequent Jewish understandings of history.

Indeed, a governing concern of Holocaust pedagogy for one teacher in New York at the beginning of the twenty-first century is that 'we're dealing with how do these students live and work with this memory and what are they supposed to do about it'.[6] Memories of the Holocaust, for this teacher as for others, are something one carries with them; they require work to be understood and incorporated; and they require the carrier to undertake some action. But the carrying of these memories also makes a difficult demand on the teacher: how to formulate memories – or histories – of the Holocaust such that the students are able to live, work and *do* something with them.

This book is thus formulated around a series of questions: What work are the histories of the Holocaust that are being taught in these Jewish schools in Melbourne and New York undertaking? What lessons are being taught? What identities are being negotiated and formulated? How are the deep, terrifying horrors of the Holocaust and their after-effects being managed? What is the Holocaust being made to mean in these Jewish schools? Histories of the Holocaust taught in these conditions are not mere dispassionate histories. For many, they are not lessons of a foreign land nor a foreign people. When teachers in these Jewish schools teach their students about the Holocaust they (feel they) are teaching something of themselves and their students. This, importantly, determines what is being taught.

As this book progresses we will come to understand that there is one thread which concerns all of the teachers in various ways. This is the problem, or the anxiety, that after the Holocaust the Jews' place in the world is precarious. Indeed, this is somewhat understandable: it is difficult to teach about a world that seemingly does not want you to be a part of it, while still trying to stake a claim to a position within it. And, moreover, these teachers live in Melbourne and New York and maintain strong Zionist feelings. As such, they are deeply ambivalent about how Jews can fit in within both Jewish and non-Jewish worlds, as well as the various intersections of these worlds. This ambivalence results in an overwhelming anxiety which permeates not just these teachings but also the Jewish communities in which they are more broadly situated.

In this book I argue that teachers in the schools under consideration are anxious about how Jews can fit into the Australian, U.S. and Jewish worlds in which they live. Indeed, they are anxious about how to negotiate the ways in which these worlds interconnect and interact. This can be seen in a number of ways which I will explore in this book: for example, in the reports of the ongoing hostility of the non-Jewish world to Jews living in their midst; in the ways in which particular ideas of strength are articulated, ideas which primarily concretise around hypermasculine forms of physical strength and the creation and existence of a Jewish nation-state; in the clear delineation of particular ways in which Jewish women are to be present in the histories, segmenting them off from men and thereby working to recuperate European incarnations of Jewish masculinities; in the adoption of settler colonial ways of remembering and forgetting; and in the use of modes of history and historiographies which strive to be coherent with those utilised by the dominant societies in which the teachers and students live. In this book these various histories will be read as products of a set of anxieties.

Holocaust education in this framework functions as both a symptom of and a way of working through these anxieties. It is a working-through of the fear that Jews do not fit, that they are not allowed to live securely in these particular non-Jewish, modern, Western worlds of Australia and the United States – that it is impossible to be acceptably 'Jewish' in these places, or, indeed, outside of Israel. Importantly, the reactions to and deployments of the incarnations of modernity which exist in Holocaust education in these schools are neither stable nor unitary. Rather, they are multifarious and changing – an unease or anxiety can be detected, but it is not constant. Zygmunt Bauman describes this as ambivalence, as 'the possibility of assigning an object or an event to more than one category', which brings with it an 'acute discomfort we feel when we are unable to read the situation properly and to choose between alternative actions'.[7] There exists an ambivalent relationship on the part of diasporic Jews to these societies – they are unsure of where Jews fit, and unsure of where and how they want Jews to fit in. In part, this is what makes them diasporic. This, as will be shown, these teachers convey over and over to their students. In this book then, the ways in which this anxiety works to create a particular body of Holocaust historiography will be explored.

Methodologies of the Text

This book is in large part an excursion in critique. In it I provide a close, deconstructive analysis of a series of texts – and locate these texts within broader collections of historical literature – in order to unravel and understand a body of historical narration. As follows this project, my intention here is not to describe an objective truth, or reading, of what teachers are teaching. My intention, rather, is to open a series of questions, to complicate the narratives, and not to provide definitive answers. I am interested in how the discourses that the teachers pursue are productive: what do they say? What do they produce, or help to constitute? Some of the teachers, I should note, may not recognise themselves in my analysis of their teachings: this is perhaps an inevitable outcome of the methodologies I have used. In this text I also attempt to show the difficulties involved in constructing a narrative of the Holocaust which can be taught in history classes in schools: there are many impossibilities involved in such pedagogical pursuits.

The historical narration, or historiography, being explored in this book is predominantly based on curricula collected from, and a series of interviews with, teachers of the Holocaust in a selection of Jewish dayschools in Melbourne and New York in 2006. In this way, I am not presenting a longitudinal study of Holocaust education: this is more of a snapshot, or a glimpse at an archive captured at one year in time. Curricula were collected where available – four schools in Melbourne and three in New York supplied curricula. Interviews were conducted with teachers of the Holocaust in five schools in Melbourne and seven schools in New York.[8] Some of these schools were co-educational, and some were all-girls schools. No all-boys schools participated in the study – teachers were either too busy to participate, did not return phone calls or emails, or explained that they do not teach about the Holocaust, as they teach only 'modern Jewish history (nationhood to present)'.[9] As such, the conclusions being presented are not intended as totalizing. This book does not present information about the general state of Holocaust education today, but rather moves through some questions and ideas that arose through interactions with these twelve schools, and the fifteen teachers at the schools, involved in the research. Some of these conclusions could apply to the teaching at other schools, others may not.

The schools in New York were overwhelmingly Orthodox-oriented.[10] One non-Orthodox school participated in the study, and this was a non-denominational school.[11] To be an Orthodox school means that the school is associated with the Orthodox Jewish movement, which, in brief, entails a belief that the Torah was written by God and that it must therefore be strictly followed.[12] The schools in Melbourne included a Progressive school, two Modern Orthodox schools, one Orthodox school, and one secular school. The Progressive school is associated with the Progressive movement, which entails a particular idea of the modernization of Judaism, involving not only different understandings of the ways in which the Torah and Talmud should function, but also a belief that Judaism should be moulded to a degree with the secular societies in which it exists.[13] The secular school in Melbourne and the non-denominational school in New York both predominantly focus on Jewishness as cultural and nationalistic, rather than religious. While Jewish religious festivals are observed to a degree, the emphasis is placed on history and culture rather than religion.

The schools which participated are overwhelmingly Ashkenazi in orientation. Apart from one New York school which is predominantly Sephardi, the students and families which make up the school bodies are predominantly of Eastern European heritage. One school in Melbourne is – according to an interviewee – largely made up of families with Russian backgrounds, as is one of the schools in New York. Most of the schools in Melbourne are dominated by descendants of survivors of the Holocaust, although there are certainly also students from other national and ethnic backgrounds. In New York the schools all contain some students who are descendants of survivors of the Holocaust, however not to the same degree as in Melbourne. This is largely due to the different histories of the two cities, wherein the vast majority of Jews migrated to New York from Russia and other parts of Eastern Europe at the turn of the twentieth century, whereas Melbourne had its biggest influx of Eastern European Jews after the Holocaust.

How then, if New York and Melbourne have such different Jewish histories, can teachings of the Holocaust within their Jewish communities be compared? It is important to note that a comparison is not being made between the two communities in general. They are importantly different, not just in their histories but in their size: while New York holds the most Jews of any city in the world outside of Israel, Melbourne's Jewish population is considerably smaller.[14] But a comparison of Holocaust education in the two cities is still viable for a number of reasons. Firstly, both communities are located within settler colonial states. Here it is useful to understand that a settler colonial state entails the creation of a nation-state based on the premise that the colonizers/settlers colonize with the purpose of themselves remaining on, and possessing, the land.[15] Various forms of domination of Indigenous peoples are perpetrated as a result (as well as various forms of Indigenous resistance to this domination and attempted erasure). From the colonizer's perspective, this necessarily requires the formulation of a national identity which coalesces around the colonizer as the justifiable occupier of that land. As such, the formulation of histories which support the colonizer's place in the country is required. The specific ways in which this functions and how it impacts upon the pedagogies under consideration will be interrogated further in Chapter Four. For our purposes here, it is simply important to note that Holocaust education in both cities occurs within these settler colonial conditions.

Secondly, every teacher at every school who participated in this study expressed strong Zionist feelings and ideas as a basis for the school and their teachings, yet this Zionism is one which coexists with the maintenance of Jewish communities outside Israel. The specific formulations of Zionism which this creates will be explored in Chapter Three; again, however, it is important that at this point we consider the importance of ideas of Zionism to this Holocaust education as providing a fertile ground for meaningful comparison between teachings in Melbourne and New York. A structuring force of both of these incarnations of settler colonialism and Zionism are anxieties about the place of the protagonists in the world: this has an important impact upon the creation of group histories. As will be explored, for settler colonizers, as for Zionists living outside Israel, an anxiety about not fitting in persists. The presence of this anxiety, and the effects which it produces, makes comparison between Holocaust education in these Jewish schools in Melbourne and New York useful and meaningful. It is important to note that these systems of settler colonialism and Zionism are, to an extent, structural forces. Alongside other dominant frameworks of Western societies – capitalism and the patriarchy, to name but two of the most significant – their structuring force has a profound impact upon the teachings which I am exploring in this book. Sitting next to this is a series of political and ideological decisions that the teachers make, informed by certain understandings of history.

And so while there are considerable differences between the two histories and the various communities within the two cities, there are aspects of their current incarnations which mitigate against these differences, particularly when considering the ways in which histories of the Holocaust are formulated, narrated and taught in these Jewish high-school classrooms. This book prioritizes these similarities. Thus in this book I will consider not just the explicit ways in which Zionism and settler colonialism impact upon the histories being taught, but also the ways in which teachings about Jewish women in the Holocaust and the very structures of these historiographical forms are inflected by these larger contexts. Moreover, the focus of this book is on education in Jewish schools – rather than in schools more generally – as they are sites for the exploration of some of the ideas and histories which circulate within these Jewish communities. The question being posed, therefore, is one of how Jews represent themselves and their own histories.

My use of 'Jewish communities' here is not intended to homogenize these communities, but rather to point to the diversity within and between different individual Jews and the communities which exist. For ease and simplicity of expression 'Jewish communities' will be referred to throughout this book, but this ought not to be taken as homogenizing these diverse peoples and ideas. As the examples will show, there are differences in pedagogical approaches.

By virtue of the narrow frame of this book – an examination of Holocaust education in Jewish schools – emphasis is being placed on the role of a predominantly Ashkenazi event in formulating Jewishnesses.[16] Following the work of Ella Shohat and Ammiel Alcalay, we can understand that within Jewish historiography, the histories of European Jews maintain an institutionalized dominance over those of Jews from the Levant, Sephardi and Mizrahi Jews.[17] As Alcalay explains:

> [h]and in hand with European military, technological, financial, and political predominance has come the institutionalized transmission of European culture. The excising of references to the Levant, with its common and uncommon, Semitic and non-Semitic past . . . , from most if not all standardized versions of the European curriculum has made myths of European superiority and self-containment that much harder to dislodge.[18]

Highlighting stories of Europe's Jews in this book is not intended to reproduce this excising and the attendant power structures; rather, by specifically focusing on areas of Holocaust storytelling – its gendered aspects and its anxieties, to name two – which are rarely discussed, in a more general sense conversations which have previously been foreclosed will be opened. The intention therefore in focusing on the teaching of histories of the Holocaust is not to *over*emphasize their role. This book will problematize the ideas and histories of the Holocaust which are taught, and the identities which they in turn teach, in a manner which is hopefully attached to – and is certainly informed by – the project which seeks to dislodge hegemonic Ashkenazi histories and identities from their dominant positions within Jewish historiographies.[19]

There are some key terms around which this book is organized, and it is important therefore that we understand the meanings that they contain, and the different histories which they carry with them. Let us examine them in turn: education, anxiety, diaspora, nation-state and modernity and mimicry. Let us also remember, as we move through the critique of historiographies contained within this book, that it will appear at times that there are contradictions: that I critique the individualization of women's experiences, but also the collectivization of experiences; that I critique the use of particular languages, but also note that history has no existence independent of its representation. These, however, are not contradictions, but rather remind us that there is no truly adequate way to teach about the Holocaust. Every narrative, every system of representation, falls short in some way. The problems of representation, of containing history within a narrative or relying on a set of signifiers, forever remain. In this sense, as will become increasingly clear throughout this book, ambivalence can indeed be productive.

Education

While there are many avenues through which the anxieties under consideration are negotiated and incorporated into narrative, and many different spaces in which Holocaust historiographies are being created, a focus on Holocaust education provides a significant site through which to explore these matters. This is the case as education crystallises versions of what is thought in the present, producing them in order to ensure the ideas move into the future. By studying Holocaust education we can gain a sense of what communities prioritize in remembering the Holocaust, and the ways in which these memories and histories are produced by current political, social and cultural conditions.[20] This pedagogy is noteworthy as the teaching of the Holocaust in Jewish schools in Melbourne and New York functions primarily not just as a way of teaching students about what happened in the past, but rather, and perhaps most importantly, as a way of teaching them a collective, social history.[21] In sharing this collective past, the students are constituted as part of a broader Jewish nation, who are all invested in this history.

The histories which are taught in these schools are fashioned through the remembering and forgetting which produces national stories, myths, collective memories and histories more generally. As Jonathan Boyarin articulates it, 'what we remember to do, the way we remember things happening, is not only an academic exercise but integral to the persistence of hegemony and resistance'.[22] That is, the project of establishing which collective memories, which histories, will be privileged by the collective is not simply a question of what happened in the past – rather, it serves to dictate the future of that collective; to assist in the negotiation of hegemonic ideas, which rely on their being simultaneously asserted and challenged, in a dialectical relationship. The memories are thereby always changing, always being (re)made. In taking lessons from the past and privileging certain memories over others, while forgetting or distorting others, the collective's sense of what they are and can be is disciplined. Importantly though, I am not asserting that the creation of histories is always a conscious and coherent process. As was clear from interviews with the teachers, many of them do not make conscious decisions about every aspect of the histories, and there are many ways in which these histories are ambivalent or seemingly contradictory. What is perhaps more prevalent is an incorporation of ideas which circulate.[23] Not every step in the chain of the construction of the history is conscious, but each step serves to confirm the dominant position of a series of particular histories. At each step the histories are built upon, altered and their authority reinforced. In noting that some decisions are not made consciously, I do not wish to downplay their seriousness: instead, I am making an argument for the importance of consideration of the role of the unconscious, and for attention to be paid to the force of the normative, in the construction of historiography.

It is this idea of the creation of specific memories by the powerful within the collective, embodied in specific lieux de mémoire, for the purpose of creating a collective history and thus identity, which will guide this book through an examination of the protracted effects of anxious Jewishness(es) on Holocaust education. This education thus can be understood as a series of lieux de mémoire: as Pierre Nora explains, lieux de mémoire are the sites, monuments and memorials which a nation creates in order to remember the past.[24] By forming memorials – whether made of concrete or written on paper – memories are solidified and frozen in time. National histories, whether of a nation bounded by a state or a transnational group such as the Jews, are produced relying on these collective memories.[25]

History education is a particularly fruitful site for the discussion of group memories and histories because of its political motivations: history education involves the formulation of narratives in the present with the intent of instructing the future.[26] What we teach the children of a particular collective will inevitably influence the memories they grow up with. Anna Clark argues that 'history syllabuses and textbooks, with their capacity to define the nation's past, are central to the development of national narratives'.[27] The centrality of history education for the instruction of definitive group identities was similarly highlighted by Joyce Dalsheim. In writing about the teaching in Israel of the continuing conflict between Palestinians and Israelis, Dalsheim describes the pervasive imagining of objectivity in history-teaching:

> [s]tudents and parents also seem to take for granted that 'history' is being taught, in which history comes to stand for an accurate portrayal of the past, rather than an imagined historiography which (consciously) employs certain key terms, chooses to include and exclude particular time periods within the narrative form creating continuity and unity out of fragmentation and difference.[28]

History education, in this formulation, is imagined as not portraying what happened, but *is* what happened, in an objective, thoroughly accurate sense. The potency of this form is contained within this idea: if the history education describes the past as it really was, then its power to determine the identity of the community whose history it is, is enhanced. This conception of history will be returned to in Chapter Two.

These ideas about collective memory were first offered by Maurice Halbwachs, and have since been built upon by many others.[29] As has been explained, this book is based on a series of interviews with individual teachers, as well as explorations of their curricula. This then raises a question – if the work of individuals is being examined, how does that work to constitute group identities? The teachers rely upon each other, rather than, for instance, Yad Vashem or the United States Holocaust Memorial Museum for their information, and so it becomes important to ask: how are these curricula created in the ways in which Clark and Dalsheim suggest?[30] It is here that the work of Halbwachs becomes important. As Jonathan Crewe frames it, Halbwachs asserted that 'individual memory [is] a function of social memory, not an isolated repository of personal experience'.[31] The memories which individuals maintain are not produced by themselves in isolation from others but rather result from their place in social, cultural and political worlds – they are products of specific times and spaces. It is this question of the production of those collective memories which this book shall examine.

Historiographical practices are also important in the structuring and inscribing of group histories. As will be explored in Chapter Two, how a narrative proceeds, which events are described and whose voices are heard all fundamentally impact upon how the contents of the histories will be understood. Dalsheim argues that 'these frameworks . . . giv[e] meaning and power through moral authority to the narratives'.[32] The historical education gains its authority through the morality of the tales which are told, coupled with its foundations in and reproductions of collective memories. We can thus appreciate the centrality of historical educational narratives in formulating Jewish group identities.

Holocaust

It is important to gain a sense of what is being symbolized in the word 'Holocaust'. To what does the Holocaust refer, and why do I use that word here, instead of others such as Shoah or Churban? At its most general sense, the Holocaust refers in the Jewish imagination and historiography to the Nazi-directed programme of destruction of Jewish communities in Europe in the 1930s and 1940s.[33] But the meaning contained in this term is constantly evolving.[34] Giorgio Agamben notes that 'Holocaust' is a translation from Latin (*holocaustum*), which in turn is a translation from Greek ('*holocaustos*, which is, however, an adjective ... the corresponding Greek noun is *holocaustōma*'), and originated in the idea of a completely burnt offering to a god.[35] Shoah, the Hebrew term, Agamben explains 'means "devastation, catastrophe" and, in the Bible, often implies the idea of a divine punishment'.[36] How then to choose between these two imperfect terms, Holocaust and Shoah?[37] While teachers at times use both Shoah and Holocaust, I made a decision for this book to use the most widely recognised terminology, and that, in Melbourne and New York at least, at this point in time is Holocaust. Using this term also opens up the possibility that the destruction being discussed could involve non-Jewish victims; to use a Hebrew term seems to inevitably refer only to Jews.

What then does 'Holocaust' signify? No term is forever stable or always already established. Zev Garber argues that 'Holocaust's' deeply religious basis as signifying a sacrifice to God – which, he argues, creates a holy relationship between Jews, Nazis and God, with the Nazis as sacred beneficiaries – means that it cannot be divorced from these connotations.[38] While 'Holocaust' might carry the connotations which Garber suggests, is it true to argue that it cannot be separated from them? Particularly as, as Garber states, most people – both Jewish and non-Jewish – have no knowledge of these sacrificial connotations. If usage of a term can change its meaning, to what extent does it necessarily retain its original meanings? Most discussions of Holocaust, or Shoah, point to an understanding of an event which, while there may be some differences, is generally understood to have not been a sacred sacrifice. Sander Gilman argues that:

> any understanding of the Shoah must acknowledge that its meaning and function has changed over the fifty years since it occurred. The murder of the Jews moved from being one aspect of the crimes of the Nazis to being their central, defining aspect over half a century. Over the past decade or so, it has evolved from a specific, historical moment to the metaphor for horror itself.[39]

This is but one of many ways in which Holocaust discourses have shifted over time. Yet how can the historicity of the event be captured in a single word, or a chain of words? Surely any naming is always inadequate to the task. While the term 'Holocaust' is being utilised in this book as a descriptor of a set of events, this term does not and cannot contain everything to which it refers, nor can it hold these meanings in a stable manner. What this Holocaust means in the historiographies being negotiated and created in some Jewish schools in Melbourne and New York today will be explored throughout this book.

Anxiety

In his book *Coming Out Jewish*, in a chapter entitled 'Ghetto Thinking and Everyday Life', Jon Stratton writes that 'Fear is an important component in the lives of those of us who come from Ashkenazi and in particular Yiddish, backgrounds.' Some of this feeling, he argues, is not particular to Jews, but is present in many other migrant and minority groups. Moreover, he writes:

> What I will argue is that over many centuries the Jews of Europe evolved a way of being in the world which was premised on an assumption that the world in which they lived their everyday lives was fundamentally antagonistic to them. Fear was an adaptive defence mechanism which kept the Jews on their guard, ever watchful, ever protective of their own. The Holocaust did not produce this attitude to the world. Rather, for Jews, it was mediated through this prior existing lens.[40]

While Stratton writes of fear, I am interested in this book in approaching this particular relationship to Jewish histories, presents and futures, through the frame of anxiety.

Many teachers spend a great deal of time discussing the problems they perceive Jews face in the West today, in Melbourne and New York specifically, but in Western countries more generally too. Through this we can detect an anxiety in the manner suggested by Sigmund Freud, who wrote that 'anxiety . . . is in the first place something felt'.[41] This feeling has an 'unpleasurable character': as 'anxiety arose as a response to a situation of *danger*; it will be regularly reproduced thenceforward whenever such a situation recurs'.[42] This situation was, originally, birth, or a 'biological helplessness'; this is played out in later life as a 'psychic helplessness'.[43] That is, in this formulation which will be deployed throughout this book, anxiety results from a feeling of helplessness, or a lack of sureness about one's place in relation to the object which they desire.[44] In the particular circumstances and histories under consideration here, that object is most predominantly a safe, known and 'homely' place in the world.[45]

The anxieties over these problems find expression in numerous ways. Firstly, these teachers are anxious about the place of Jews in non-Jewish societies: we can detect an anxiety that Jews are not really welcome in these spaces. Indeed, it is taught that just as Jewish life thrived in Europe before the Holocaust and was then ruined, so too today's thriving Jewish worlds could be threatened and destroyed. Charles S. Maier, in his essay 'A Surfeit of Memory', refers to this when he speaks of Holocaust museums which are built, he argues, for Jews to teach others that they have 'suffered incredibly and want recognition of the fact'.[46] If we follow the implications of Maier's argument, we could argue that teachers teach about the Holocaust in order to remind their students that Jews have suffered at the hands of Western nation-states. This functions as a caution about being Jewish in the

West, as well as, at particular times, a caution about the West and whether or not its national systems can be trusted and embraced. The anxiety persists – will they accept us? Will we be allowed to remain civil subjects?[47] There is, as Ghassan Hage has suggested, therefore an investment in the state of the nation; in this case, both the Jewish nation and the Australian and U.S. nations.[48]

Conversely, it has been argued that the history of Jewish interactions with modernity can be understood as having reached a point, in the late twentieth and early twenty-first centuries, where Jews are in fact comfortable within the (late) modern, non-Jewish national locations in which they find themselves.[49] In this scenario, the anxiety becomes one of a *lack* of difference: how can Jews assert their difference when they are, fundamentally, the same?[50] As David Biale argues in the U.S. context, Jews are no longer a completely marginal group: through 'economic success and social integration' Jews have been made white, in distinction to the still marginalized black peoples.[51] There is, according to this idea of Jewish acceptability, the belief that Jews in these states heighten their histories of antisemitism and discrimination in order to formulate an identity which is based on discrimination and marginalization. In the face of a situation with no discrimination and no difference, these anxious Jews focus on histories of the Holocaust and its accompanying radical difference. This argument was proposed by Kerwin Lee Klein, who asserts that memory discourses arose together with identity politics: that, within Jewish history, Holocaust memory is being seized upon in order to return to older ways of narrating Jewish experience.[52] In the face of experiencing a space where no difference exists between Jews and others, the working-through of traumatic pasts which memory provides is considered a resource.[53] Memory-work in this formulation can therefore provide the ground for the narration of difference, a difference which, Klein suggests, is no longer present in the societies of the U.S. and Europe within which these memories are proposed. Indeed, this is also an argument which Maier proposes. These heightenings of a dangerous difference, as the argument goes, function to negotiate an anxiety that there is no difference.

As will become apparent as this book proceeds, the converse is being proposed as motivating the historical- and memory-work being undertaken by the teachers of the Holocaust under consideration. While it may appear that this anxiety of which Klein – amongst others – writes exists amongst Jews in the U.S., it was not evident in the discourses of Holocaust history being explored in the Jewish schools under consideration here. The anxiety persists that there is a difference, and, as Chapter One will demonstrate, this difference is a result not just of Jewish particularity but, just as fundamentally, of the specific ways in which these Australian and U.S. societies are formulated along lines of racialised difference. This, however, is not to suggest that there are not times when Jews are comfortable in Melbourne or New York, nor that the anxieties over antisemitism and the recurrence of the Holocaust are not, at times, excessive. The moments at which we can see this other anxiety, the anxiety about a lack of difference, coming through will therefore be pointed to as the book proceeds.

But if we return to the anxiety which this book is arguing is manifested and worked through in the curricula – the anxiety that these Jews do not belong in the Jewish and non-Jewish national spaces within which they desire to be – we can understand that embedded within this anxiety is the question of structures of power. Do Jews have any formal power, or are they disempowered, permanently trapped on the margins? As will be explored in greater detail throughout this book, there are numerous ways in which discourses and feelings of empowerment are actualised in Holocaust pedagogy. The importance of this interplay between power and powerlessness was explained by David Biale when he wrote that '[t]he very rapidity with which the Jews have moved from powerlessness to power has produced a crisis of Jewish ideology. . . . In both Israel and the Diaspora, a new political language is only beginning to emerge, a language for understanding both the possibilities and the limitations of Jewish political power in the modern world.'[54] This juxtaposition of power and powerlessness is part of the anxiety: in a short span of time European Jews have moved from the powerlessness of the Holocaust to being relatively empowered, whether in the U.S., Australia or Israel. Yet the story of the Holocaust is necessarily predominantly one of Jewish powerlessness (with important moments of resistance). How then to write this history of powerlessness, particularly within a Zionist framework which creates stories of specific moments of survival and endurance, coupled with instances of absolute degradation? It seems inevitable that this would create some sort of ambivalent response to the world, some anxiety about the possibilities available for Jews. This 'crisis of Jewish ideology' and the 'new political language' which necessarily must be formed are thus under exploration in this book.

We can also note that the ways in which this anxiety is manifested are gendered. By examining the anxieties through a gendered lens we can better understand the aspects of the anxieties which are produced by the governing structures of Jewish Zionist thought. As Claire Kahane has argued, representation – language, or discourse – is fundamentally gendered, and that gendering occurs through the very act of symbolization and representation.[55] That is, as Judith Butler and Elisabeth Cowie have variously explained, language is created through the same processes that create gendered systems of knowledge. Neither exists prior to the other; they are formed together.[56] Kahane is interested in exploring the question of, if representations are inherently gendered, how are Holocaust representations gendered?[57] In this book I will argue in response that, in light of the interviews with teachers of the Holocaust in Jewish schools and an examination of their curricula, these are gendered representations which are shaped by anxiety. It is an anxiety regarding the ways in which Jews, and Jewishnesses, are gendered in the aftermath of the Holocaust.

As will be explored in greater depth in Chapter Three, the gendered representations of this anxiety follow from Zionist ideas of what characterises the 'Diaspora Jew'. I use capitals here and throughout the text to denote the particularity of this figure: it is the idea of Diaspora contained in the Zionist imaginary, not that of the diasporic (which will be designated throughout by the use of a lower-case 'd'). I outline this further in the next section of this Introduction.[58] These teachers are worried that Jews will become like the supposed pre-Israel diasporic Jews: that they will become victims, powerless, dependent, lacking. In a word, that they will become feminized.[59] As Melanie Kaye/Kantrowitz articulates it, 'from a Zionist perspective diaspora signifies a frail gaping female absence where oppression and assimilation lurk, along with an attenuated identity which owes . . . Israel'.[60] These teachers feel that they must be masculine, as the feminine has, in this modern Jewish thinking, which follows much modern Western thinking, been characterised as negative. These teachers are referencing a particular masculinist conception of strength: an idea of strength as predominantly informed by militarism. And so they borrow this image of masculinity from Israel, which in turn has been borrowed, in mimicry, from the West. This is not to suggest that these Jews see themselves as possessing this type of strength, but rather that Israel, in this imagining, vouches for the strength of all the Jews. Hence, teachers standing in these spaces outside Israel are, it seems, staking their lives on the existence of Israel's masculine virility. In this imagining, the Holocaust was a slip, a moment when both Western civilization and Jews failed to be what and who they are meant to be. The current Israeli masculine strength, coupled with a belief in the re-established modern order, will ensure that this is not repeated.

This idea entails the understanding that it may be enough for Diaspora Jews to support Zionism, or to profess a Zionist ideology and politics, for them to have their strength redeemed.[61] But, in this claiming support for Zionism (or assuming the identity of the Zionist) there is a slippage. For the Diaspora Zionist is a mimic – they mimic the ideology which Israeli Zionism mimics from modernity. As such, the Diaspora Jew's masculinity is the *almost the same but not quite* of which Homi Bhabha speaks, which in turn works to produce the anxiety that this masculinity is not masculine enough – that they are *not quite* masculine.[62] I will return to Bhabha's important ideas of mimicry below.

Zionist thought today about where Jews can and should feel at home centres on Israel – that Jews can only be themselves and at home when in Israel.[63] Zionist narratives foreground ideas of centre and periphery, where the centre (Israel) is the strong, powerful (masculine) home, and the periphery (Diaspora) is the inferior, weak (feminine) site of displacement. Jon Stratton, writing about Jewishness in the West, explains that '[t]he core-periphery model is central to [Western] modernity'.[64] This notion of centre and periphery, which structures Western narratives and Zionist narratives of history, also permeates these examples of

Holocaust education, as will be shown. Yet there is a twist. These narratives of the Holocaust focus on the past in Europe, the present in the U.S. or Australia, and the imagined future in Israel. And so where then is the centre? Which country? It can be understood that, discursively, it is the U.S./Australia, which is where these Jews are today living, looking backwards and forwards to Europe and Israel. This then is another source of anxiety. Israel is meant to be the centre, yet these teachers are implicitly proposing that they and their students can be, and are, comfortable in the U.S./Australia. We can therefore understand that these teachers are thus made anxious about their own strength or masculinity, for this Western modernity stresses that the way to be a safe and secure people is to be strong (in the sense of a hyper-masculine virility), and that this can only be achieved by maintaining a nation-state as a site of self-determination, and thus as the national centre.[65]

Finally, it is crucial for me to state that I frame this book in terms of anxiety, and the creation of anxious histories, not as a way to denigrate these feelings and their effects. Instead, I hope that this book can contribute to historians – and Jews – taking these feelings and their negotiation more seriously, as we work together to understand the ways that the Holocaust continues to cast its shadows. Anxiety, as will become clear, can be incredibly productive. And given the historical circumstances – that of teaching about this moment of destruction, while remaining in the West – it is not surprising to me that it takes such a dominant place. Indeed, if the histories narrated in these conditions were calm, rational and disengaged, then we would certainly have something to worry about.

Diaspora

The teachers in this study are, it will become clear, unsure of what it means for Jews to live outside Israel, in the space commonly referred to as the Diaspora. Diasporas in this way are often written about as being a relationship – ambivalent, stressful, joyful, continuing – between people and their homeland. They are part of a thinking of a type of world that has homelands, centres and peripheries.[66] I would like to suggest, following James Clifford (amongst others), that instead of seeing people in Diaspora as connected through their mutual relationship to a central location, diaspora could be about creating worldwide communities of 'displacement'.[67] This would entail a re-evaluation of those things which have typically been understood to encompass diaspora – the presence of a central homeland from which a people has been displaced, are now in a state of exile, and maintain and exhibit longings for that homeland.[68] The presence of a site of displacement, and a lack of complete homeliness in the newfound location need not be eradicated in this model. Rather, it is the *site* of displacement that is removed from the centre of the model, and stories of movement reinscribed as central.[69]

For this reason, I use Diaspora to signify the 'Diaspora' contained in the Diaspora/Homeland binary (or the centre/periphery binary), and diaspora to signify a notion of a diaspora that does not coalesce around such binaries, but instead attains coherence through ideas of commonality expressed through history, memory and culture, as well as through movement, travel, displacement, and an embracement of multiple allegiances. By avoiding capitalization, I aim to point towards the lack of definity, or sureness, in its naming: it is not one thing, nor is its meaning easily captured and contained. This diaspora is a floating idea, not a proper noun.

As such, the idea of diaspora offered by Australian academic and 'neither Jew nor non-Jew', John Docker, becomes relevant and useful as a starting place. Diaspora, for Docker, entails movement, knowledge and history, as well as expanding and ever-evolving identities. Docker writes that diaspora provides:

> a sense of belonging to more than one history, to more than one time and place, more than one past and future. Diaspora suggests belonging to both here and there, now and then. Diaspora suggests the omnipresent weight of pain of displacement from a land or society, of being an outsider in a new one. Diaspora suggests both lack and excess of loss and separation, yet also the possibility of new adventures of identity and the continued imagining of unconquerable countries of the mind.[70]

This was reiterated and expanded on by the photographer Jason Francisco, who writes of the bringing of memories of old homelands to new places. He claims that '[i]t appears that the self-retracting trail of Jewish migrations confirms . . . a distinctive feature of the Jewish diaspora . . . : rediasporization, the centuries-old phenomenon of (imaginary) Jewish homelands having been transferred and palimpsested upon one another, "such that Cairo becomes a remembered Cordoba and the new Jerusalem a remembered Vilna"'.[71] This idea of locations being moved to and inhabited, then discarded – whether by choice or by force – and remembered, is useful.

Indeed, perhaps this is a model of Jewishness which is reinforced through Holocaust education – a model of places of inhabitation remembered and held onto, yet an identity which is reinscribed with the current places of living. A model of being located in both Melbourne/New York and Europe and Israel. For the histories of the Holocaust which are being written might be based in Zionist thought but, as will be shown in Chapter Three, they are inflected by a particularly diasporic Zionism. This is a Zionism which rests on anxiety, a Zionism which is expressed through language, history and various deeds. But not through the making of Israel a physical home. These diasporic Holocaust histories are also inflected by the histories of the U.S. and Australian nations in which they are being written. Indeed, it is perhaps their specific anxieties which renders them diasporic.

This brings us to consider the character of the diasporic Jewish people who are writing these histories of the Holocaust. For Jonathan and Daniel Boyarin, group identity – and, more specifically, Jewish identity – reaches its greatest potential when it is diasporic, or non-hegemonic. For them, 'cultures, as well as identities, are constantly being remade. While this is true of all cultures' they assert, 'diasporic Jewish culture lays it bare because of the impossibility of a natural association between this people and a particular land – thus the impossibility of seeing Jewish culture as a self-enclosed, bounded phenomenon'.[72] In the Boyarins' formulation of Jewishness, identity rests on 'family, history, memory, and practice' – on genealogy and practice, rather than 'autochthony or indigenousness'.[73] As they assert, 'we not only do these things because we are this thing, but we are this thing because we do these things'.[74] In this book it is the making and passing on of histories of the Holocaust which is 'this thing'. Histories in the Jewish diaspora thus become of fundamental importance as a means of ensuring group cohesion, a useful way of tracking the changing ideas of the group, as will become clear throughout the text. As was discussed previously with reference to history education more generally, the purpose of teaching a group about its past is to formulate that group's identity: a group in this sense is both the individual students who are being interpellated and the broader group identity of which the individuals are a part. In the diaspora this becomes all the more important for, as the Boyarins suggest, identity is based not on connection to land, but on a connection to the past and to present group practices. These histories of the Holocaust therefore are made all the more diasporic.

This interplay between history writing and diasporic thinking is explored by Bryan Cheyette in his recent book *Diasporas of the Mind*. Cheyette writes that:

> At one end of the spectrum, diaspora is on the side of impurity and hybridity (and points in the direction of emergent or lost cultures) and, at the other end, diaspora is conservative and "roots-defined" and has as its end point a return to an autochthonous (pure) space. The celebratory version of diaspora tends to foreground a transgressive imagination and precolonial histories of intertwined cultures (and is associated with Postcolonial and Diaspora Studies), whereas a victim-centred version tends to stress particular communities of exile with specific and unique histories of suffering (and is associated with Holocaust and Genocide Studies).[75]

Cheyette argues in response for an embrace of a kind of thinking – which he terms 'metaphorical thinking', as distinct from 'disciplinary thinking' – which would be able 'to make connections across histories and communities'.[76] While Cheyette makes the argument here for a distinction between how the formulation of the diaspora has been understood within these different academic fields, the work of this book is, in part, to evade these distinctions and bring postcolonial studies and Holocaust studies together. Similarly, Michael Rothberg's book *Multidirectional Memory* brings these different fields into conversation, thereby enhancing both. Thus a similar mode of understanding of the diaspora, critical thinking and the

Holocaust seems to me to inform Cheyette's, Rothberg's, as well as my own, work. All three present the possibilities that are opened up when diasporic thinking informs how we conceptualise the histories and memories of the Holocaust, or when seemingly different memories and histories are placed alongside each other, helping us to recognise that we do not make memories in isolation, or in sealed-off communities.[77]

Moreover, Jewish peoples in New York and Melbourne formulate identities not solely in response to a Zionism which describes them as lacking, or to the narratives of out-of-placeness and insecurity which are created through Holocaust education. As Paul Gilroy makes clear with reference to the African diaspora, it is necessary to consider 'how blacks [in Britain] define and represent themselves in a complex combination of resistances and negotiations, which does far more than provide a direct answer to the brutal forms in which racial subordination is imposed'.[78] In both New York and Melbourne there are many different Jewish communities and peoples formulating and negotiating living in diasporas, creating and representing Jewishness in diverse, multivalent ways. We can see this through music, writing and academia. While a fuller exploration of this does not fall within the boundaries of this book, it is important for us to remember.

Yet, a problem might still remain. Regardless of the model of diaspora deployed to understand these histories and contexts, by writing about a single Jewish diaspora, or diasporas, one risks homogenizing the diverse peoples within that group. Indeed, the very notion that there is such a group has the potential to efface difference. Ella Shohat points to this problem in her discussions of the relationship between Zionism and Sephardim and Mizrahim, asserting that the Zionist narrative of a return to a homeland 'disauthorizes' any positive attachment to a previous place of inhabitation.[79] It erases the fact that Jews in other countries – specifically, in her telling, 'the Arab Muslim world' – may have had stronger relationships and affiliations with the people with whom they once lived, rather than with other Jews. Shohat asserts that these histories are disavowed because they 'threatened the conception of a homogenous nation akin to those on which European nationalist movements were based'.[80] Moreover, in the Zionist telling, '[a]ll Jews are defined as closer to each other than to the cultures of which they have been a part'.[81] That is, these other(ed) histories threaten the narrative of national cohesion that Zionist writers and thinkers work so hard to create and perpetuate. The homogenizing work which these histories do will be considered in more detail in Chapters Three and Four.

The Nation-State and Modernity

Throughout this book, ideas of Western modernity will be invoked. There are many definitions and understandings of modernity which proliferate so it becomes important to ask, to what do these ideas refer, within the context of this book? Firstly, it is important to see the term 'Western modernity' as referring to a system of organizing of the world, and of knowledge produced about that world. It is a representational system with material effects. Dipesh Chakrabarty explains that 'following the tenets of the European Enlightenment, many Western intellectuals thought of modernity as the rule of institutions that delivered us from the thrall of all that was unreasonable and irrational'.[82] We can see here the expression of ideology through institutions. Similarly, Partha Chatterjee explains that the French Revolution has come to symbolize the classic moment of European enlightenment and modernity because of its mythic uniting 'of the identity of the people with the nation and, in turn, the identity of the nation with the state. There is no question that the legitimacy of the modern state is now clearly and firmly grounded in a concept of popular sovereignty'.[83] He is pointing here to a material result of this modernist ideology, which foregrounds national cohesion embodied in the joining together of nation and state. This symbolic aspect is central to our understandings of Western modernity.

Secondly, the teachers whose words and work are being examined in this book have a broad understanding of a world which they negotiate. While they may rarely speak explicitly of the West or of modernity, an overarching sense of these concepts and materialities inflects their ideas. The teachers articulate a vision of a world in which they want to be a part. It is, more often than not, a world based on a set of ideas of Western modernity – predominantly the conception of the importance of the nation-state and its associated structures in containing group identities – even if it is not explicated explicitly as such.[84] It is not being suggested here, or within the teachings, that Western modernity is any one thing. But we can appreciate some overarching concerns which press upon the teachings, as will be outlined next.

Where, as stated above, Chakrabarty and Chatterjee write of symbolic conceptions of modernity, it is also useful for us to consider the historical ways in which modernity has been formulated, particularly with regard to Jewish interactions with a modernizing West. Indeed, the process of Jews negotiating their place within the Western societies in which they live has a long and involved history. Jews living in European countries have sought a place within the changing social structures and processes of a modernizing Europe, and indeed have been fundamental to the development of this modernity.[85] For Jacob Katz, one of the first historians to theorize the Jewish relationship with a modernity which came both from outside and within the Jewish people, the negotiation involved a movement 'from their former distinct Jewish pattern toward the standard common in their non-Jewish surroundings'.[86] Katz describes this as a movement 'out of the ghetto', where Jewish distinctiveness was lost as part of this move which was demanded of the Jews in order to gain acceptance within non-Jewish European systems and institutions of modernity, in particular European nation-states.[87] As Jonathan

Frankel explicates it, 'it is above all, perhaps, in his [sic] analysis of two major themes in the development of the Jewish people during the nineteenth century . . . – enlightenment and emancipation – that the historian first finds himself [sic] confronted by the clash between tradition and modernity'.[88] It was the processes of European enlightenment and emancipation that brought forward the assimilatory movements of Jewishness, whose echoes are seen in the Holocaust pedagogy under consideration in this book.

Yet, as Michael Meyer explains, there are two processes of Jewish modernization: the first is 'a process whereby Jews increasingly participate in the modernization of the societies in which they dwell . . . In other words, modernization becomes a concomitant or effect of integration'.[89] The second is a more inwardly-focused, specifically Jewish process of modernization wherein it is not just Jews as individuals who are modernizing, but Jewish practices and institutions which are changing shape and modernizing.[90] It seems, however, that whether it is individuals or institutions that are changing, the process is fundamentally similar: the motivating force is one of alteration in accord with the changing modernizing non-Jewish society.

There have been various challenges to these models of Jewish interactions with modernity, and formulations of Jewish modernity. One comes from Paula E. Hyman, who has illuminated the gendered implications of these processes. Men and women, Hyman argues, experienced the beginnings of Jewish modernity differently because of their varying relationships to the public and private spheres.[91] Moreover, as she stresses, gender relations are relationships of power which are played out within Jewish communities as well as in relation to the non-Jewish European communities in which Jews have lived.[92] These gendered relationships, as was shown in the discussion of Zionism previously, have had a significant impact upon the ways in which Jews have identified and negotiated their relationships with modernity. Arnold M. Eisen provides a second challenge, wherein he accepts the basic premise of the contestations provided by the Emancipation and Enlightenment movements of the nineteenth century, but critiques the ideas of modernity which historians of Jewish modernity have relied upon. Eisen argues that Emancipation was, and is, the most significant aspect of modernity for the key question it poses: 'whether Jews of varying commitments . . . can create plausible structures of sufficient flexibility and strength to develop and hold their various allegiances to Jewish traditions'.[93] These structures have involved both the secular and the sacred, although, as Eisen suggests, these categories cannot be simplistically divided into modernity and Judaism, respectively. Rather, 'Judaism in the modern period should not be viewed as a set of beliefs concerning revelation, chosenness and God, but as a set of actions and beliefs, such actions in the nature of the modern case being defined primarily as ritual but including communal, political and professional activities'.[94] In short, Jewish interactions with broader systems of modernity have not simply been a one-way force, with Judaism and Jewishness irrevocably changed. Instead, this modernity and Judaism have impacted upon each other, changing the ways in which both modernity and Jewishness are, and can be, thought about.

There are numerous specific examples of Jewish traditions and practices being shaped around the practices which existed in the broader non-Jewish communities, in order to aid in 'establishing [a] claim to Western norms of civilization'.[95] One important one is the Wissenschaft des Judentums movement, which, as Michael Meyer and Yosef Yerushalmi explain, sought to express Jewish history within the dominant scientific method that pervaded Western modernist historical practices in the nineteenth century.[96] In these various examples, which only account for a minute sample of the full range of aspects of Jewish practices which were affected by similar processes, we can appreciate that an important aspect, historically and contemporarily, of Jewish modernity and relations with non-Jewish modernity is the changing shape of Jewishness. Obviously, the two systems of modernity – Jewish and non-Jewish – are not discrete, as various incarnations of modernity have impacted upon each other to create the diverse range of systems which continue to shift and evolve. But the changes which we can identify have occurred in order to negotiate a place for Jews within these broader societies and systems of knowledge.

How then do these various processes of modernization impact upon the histories of the Holocaust and the ways in which we can interrogate them? Primarily it is through a consideration of the importance of the commingling of nation and state which has become so fundamental to Western ideas of modernity and has been adopted within Jewishness, coupled with the histories of Jewish negotiations with/in that model. As Jon Stratton makes clear, the 'production of the Jews as Other took place in the context of a transformation in the understanding of space, particularly in the experience of "place" and the primacy given to place. One of the characteristics of the modern world was that place became the site on which national identity was formed'.[97] That is, some important forms of difference are produced through the organization of modern nation-states. These modern differences – many different forms of which will be discussed throughout this book – are always created together in conversation. Belonging can only be constituted through the simultaneous formulation of not-belonging.

Moreover, the modern nation-state is figured, according to Ghassan Hage, within conceptions of home. Control of the nation-state is the ultimate prize, and the fulfilment of national desires, for the modern nation. The nation-state is seen by those with power in the state – writing in an Australian context he described this as whiteness, and the ability to gain whiteness – as their domain to control: they imagine themselves as having 'a managerial capacity over [the] national space'.[98] In the modern nation-state those not in the position of 'managing' the nation are seen as inferior and able to be excluded. Hage's focus on the discourse of home is most useful here. For in narrating these histories of the past – particularly histories of the Holocaust, a moment when European Jews were not sure what home was – one conjures up ideas about home. Moreover, if Jews do not always have the capacity to be a part of the managerial class – those people who, in Hage's description, have proprietal control over the nation – feelings of anxiety will result. It is these anxieties which lead to the concern that Jews do not belong in these modern nation-states.

Modernism and nationalism, as Hage describes them, are based on ideas of exclusivity and the battle for homeliness that comes with that. How then is this negotiated within modernist Jewish thinking? Perhaps this is the role which Israel fulfils, and why, to return to the question I described previously, people are so concerned to articulate their relationship to both the country in which they live and the 'Jewish homeland'. Israel, as the so-called homeland, then, is the projected site of these modern, diasporic anxieties over who fits in and has control, and who should be excluded. We can thus understand that Israel is the anxious site for the affirmation of the Jews as a part of modernity, because it is the site for the articulation of a Jewish home in this tradition of Western modernity.[99] And the histories created – in this case, the histories of the Holocaust – serve as a buttress for that potential homeliness.

Mimicry

In the histories of the Holocaust being taught in the Jewish schools under examination here, as I have raised at various points, we can identify mimicry at work. Zionists gaze upon the West, upon the Western idea of the modern nation-state, and how one would narrate that history; Holocaust educators in Melbourne and New York gaze upon Zionism, upon Israel, for ideas of how to narrate the recent past. In this gazing, what they each see is distorted. And thus they mimic, in the manner Homi Bhabha describes as being '*almost the same but not quite*'.[100] In this formulation 'the discourse of mimicry is constructed around an *ambivalence*; in order to be effective, mimicry must continually produce its slippage, its excess, its difference'.[101] We can understand Zionism here as a mimicry of Western modernity, and diasporic history-telling as a mimicry both of that Zionism and of Western modernity more generally. The slippage, excess and difference is evident in the history-telling about the Holocaust – the mimicry occurs in the ways in which these histories are narrated, mimicked from Zionist narrations. Moreover, this mimicry is a means of dealing with the teachers' anxieties – they attempt to replicate the ways that the West narrates history in their attempt to be a part of the West. But it is mimicry, not perfect replication, and it is responded to as such by the West. This serves to create a further anxiety, produced by the lack of authenticity of the mimicry. This Bhabha identifies as part of the 'final irony of partial representation': that there is a 'desire to emerge as "authentic" through mimicry – through a process of writing and repetition' that can never be an authentic, exact replication.[102] Nor does this mimicry ever deal with the fact that, as Bhabha suggests, the mimicry unsettles the colonial discourses which are being mimicked. The mimicry is thus both a way of dealing with the anxieties and a source of anxiety: it tries to replicate that which it undoes in its very act of replication.

Daniel Boyarin picks up on this point in his discussion of Herzlian Zionism as an attempt at colonial mimicry. He explains that 'the parodists too often do not themselves see how their mimicry disarticulates the colonialist text and thus find themselves trapped within the imaginary of its articulation'.[103] Two instances of mimicry jump out from Boyarin's text as instructive. Firstly, he describes how '[a]mong the first acts of [Herzl's] enactment of Zionism was the foundation of "the Jewish Company" – precisely under that name and in London. Herzl had finally found a way for the Jews to become Europeans; they would have a little colony of their own.'[104] That is, Herzl mimicked modernity's (capitalist) institutions by founding a colonial company. Secondly, Boyarin discusses participation in acts of physical violence as necessary, arguing that the enactor of violence is considered the superior. He suggests that:

> it is also true that the seemingly most forceful resistance can turn into the most efficient complicity with the cultural project of the colonizer, by becoming just like him, sometimes even more than he is himself, and that this is what we need to understand about Zionism. The socialist cocommander of the Warsaw revolt, the anti-Zionist Marek Edelman, who [until his death in 2009] remain[ed] in Poland as a Diasporic Jewish (Yiddish) nationalist and member of Solidarity, saw this very clearly: "This was a revolt!? The whole point was not to let them slaughter you when your turn came. The whole point was to choose your method of dying. All of humanity had already agreed that dying with a weapon in the hand is more beautiful than without a weapon. *So we surrendered to that consensus*".[105]

These words from Edelman draw attention to the discursivity of violence – that it is widely agreed upon within Western modernity that to die while violently retaliating is better than dying 'without a weapon'. In Zionist narratives of the Holocaust, both within and outside Israel, those who violently rose up are seen as a separate, superior, group. This is the 'parodic performativity' which Bhabha describes.[106] It is the mimicking of Western, modern ways of writing into history the past and the present, as Bhabha discusses, in which there is an ambivalence and an uncertainty over whether these are the best ways of representing Jewishness and indeed of *being* Jewish. This mimicry is therefore both an attempt at the resolution of anxieties as well as productive of further feelings of anxiety.

Framing the Text

This book is broadly divided into two parts. Chapters One and Two, which map the borders of the historical narratives being produced, and Chapters Three, Four and Five, which fill in the contours and expand on what these histories contain. My intention throughout is to denaturalize – and thus destabilize – those forms which are considered to be the most obvious ways of narrating a history of the Holocaust. Chapter One locates the anxiety under consideration in this book as arising from a concern about the place of Jews in the U.S. and Australia, these settler colonial, modern, Western nation-states. The outlines of the anxiety, as expressed by the teachers, will be sketched, as will the ways in which these are nation-states founded on, and depending upon, difference. This chapter asks how this (diverse) diasporic group is negotiating its liminal place in relationship to nation-states which define themselves through difference and exclusion.

Chapter Two will foreground questions of historical methodology. It will examine the ways in which chronological narratives and survivor testimonies are used by teachers in an effort to make the Holocaust coherent and knowable for the students. This chapter problematizes the ideas of history and truth contained in these examples of Holocaust education. Here I ask, why do the teachers follow these modes of historical narration? There are a number of explanations, the most significant of which is that they are following the dominant Western modes of historical narration. The adoption (or mimicry) of these modes of narration is part of the project which is being described throughout this book: that of attempting to manage the anxiety over the place of the Jews in these modern, Western societies through the adoption of modern, Western forms of historical understanding.

Chapter Three turns to questions of the influence of Zionist ideas of the Holocaust upon these histories. I argue that the Zionist positioning of Israel as the masculine subject to the Diaspora's feminine subject has had a large effect on the politics of the narratives which are being taught. This chapter will explore the various manifestations of this influence in the curricula and interviews, and the ways in which this occurs as a negotiation of the anxieties about the place of Jews within the Jewish world.

Chapter Four will locate these histories within their nation-state contexts – the U.S. and Australia – through an exploration of the influence of settler colonialism. It will be argued that these teachings carry within them an implicit settler colonial quality. It is not that the teachers explicitly formulate their histories based on settler colonial historiographical principles, but rather that settler colonialism haunts these histories of the Holocaust. This occurs most predominantly in the form of forgetting, and the prioritization of Jewish histories of the Holocaust. This works, I argue, in order to negotiate a place for Jews within these settler colonial societies: by mimicking these settler colonial histories the histories, and the historians, are located on the side of the colonizer, rather than the colonized. This is undertaken in order to relieve these anxieties.

And finally, Chapter Five will examine the ways in which Jewish women's experiences of the Holocaust are written into these histories. I will argue that there are a series of very specific ways in which women are included in these histories. This

26 | *Anxious Histories*

is most predominantly as a group, yet at times individual women are drawn upon to illustrate particular points and ideas. I will show that this occurs in order to, in the face of Zionist ideas of Jewish Diasporas, recuperate Diasporic masculinity. If Jewish womanhood can be segmented off and given the responsibility for femininity, then masculinity can perhaps be redeemed. Anxieties about the perceived femininity and masculinity of Jews in Melbourne and New York can thereby be partially relieved. While what it means to be a Jewish man in this context is also important to examine, in this book I am interested in examining that which is excised from the histories. To examine the boundaries of Jewish manhood as presented through these teachings is therefore outside its scope.

One teacher at a school in Melbourne explained in an interview that she tells her students from the start of the subject that although she is not very religious she has:

> a very strong Jewish identity, and sometimes when I'm cooking for Shabbat on a Friday afternoon, or when I'm in [synagogue], and I think, even if I wanted to stop doing it, I just don't think that I could because of the obligation to keep it going after what happened. And I think that's okay, you know. I think that that's a part of it but partly we're teaching it so they know, but also partly because of the *mitzvah* of *zachor* [remembrance].[107]

The ways that the histories of the Holocaust which are created in these high schools function to create new Jewish historiographies, and in doing so act as these (anxious) memorials, is the focus of this text. By foregrounding the teaching of a pivotal moment in Western Jewry's interactions with modernity – the Holocaust – I am arguing that we can learn much about Jewish identities in Melbourne and New York today. Moreover, by examining these new histories and historiographies being created we can understand much about how migrant groups, and post-genocide groups, negotiate their marginality, how diasporic identities are (re)made, and how we can thus grasp some of the pain – and some of the possibilities – imbricated in such marginality.

Notes

> Part of the project of this book is to point to the multiple, ambivalent, complex, liminal and multi-layered ways in which Jewish identities are lived today. As will become clear throughout this book, this is an important element of what is being understood as a diasporic excess: an overflowing of meaning, which cannot, and should not, be easily contained. For that reason, the endnotes – as a (literally) marginal site – herein at times become an important site for the elaboration and contestation of the ideas addressed in the main body of this book. They are also a space for the expansion of the discussion of the literature which has been produced on the matters and ideas which are discussed in the main text of this book. As such, the endnotes here are a vital part of an ongoing and ever-evolving conversation between peoples and literature.

1. J. Butler. 1996. 'Universality in Culture', in J. Cohen (ed.), *For Love of Country: Debating the Limits of Patriotism*, Boston: Beacon Press, 45.
 2. This was echoed in a posting on a Melbourne Jewish blog called *The Sensible Jew*. Liss, 'My Cousin Sammy (OR: The Single-Issue Voter: A Portrait)'. Retrieved 24 June 2009 from http://sensiblejew.wordpress.com/2009/06/23/my-cousin-sammy-or-the-single-issue-voter-a-portrait/; Retrieved 2 January 2014 from http://galusaustralis.com/2009/06/261/my-cousin-sammy-or-the-single-issue-voter-a-portrait/. Author now listed as 'The Hasid'.
 3. H.K. Bhabha. 1994. *The Location of Culture*, London: Routledge, 12.
 4. C. Aviv and D. Shneer. 2005. *New Jews: The End of the Jewish Diaspora*, New York: New York University Press, 1–25. This is the model that I will follow in this book. With that said, a particular idea of the 'diaspora' is constructed within the Zionist imaginary. At times in this book I will refer to this as the Diaspora, not to endorse the distinction between Israel and Diaspora, but rather to make clear how this idea of Diaspora is constructed and narrated. This idea of Diaspora will be rendered with a capital D; the diasporic with a lower-case.
 5. See generally Bhabha, *The Location of Culture*, 1–18.
 6. Interview with Teacher A at School NYA. To protect the anonymity of teachers and schools, they are referred to throughout by anonymous acronyms. 'NY' indicates a school in New York, while 'M' indicates a school in Melbourne.
 7. Z. Bauman. 1991. *Modernity and Ambivalence*, Cambridge: Polity Press, 1.
 8. While there are countless Jewish schools in New York, there are only seven in Melbourne that teach at a high-school level. For that reason, a comparative number of schools in New York were involved in this study.
 9. Email from Principal A at School NYH, 28 November 2006.
10. This is representative of the composition of Jewish schools in New York and the U.S. more generally. Marc Lee Raphael explained that 'in 2005, approximately 205,000 students were enrolled in 760 schools (elementary and secondary) – about two-thirds in New Jersey and New York – an increase of more than 10 percent in the past five years. Of these students … more than 80 percent are affiliated with Orthodox institutions, and Orthodox-affiliated schools are growing at a slightly faster rate than the non-Orthodox schools. This is in part the result of an insistence in most Orthodox synagogues today that boys and girls attend Jewish day schools as well as of a higher fertility rate among the Orthodox.' M.L. Raphael. 2008. 'Introduction', in M.L. Raphael (ed.), *The Columbia History of Jews and Judaism in America*, New York: Columbia University Press, 11.
11. There are schools in New York which are organized by the Conservative movement, but they did not participate in the study.
12. Riv-Ellen Prell provides a history of the Orthodox movement in the U.S., and particularly New York. See R.-E. Prell. 2008. 'Triumph, Accommodation, and Resistance: American Jewish Life from the End of World War II to the Six-Day War', in M.L. Raphael (ed.), *The Columbia History of Jews and Judaism in America*, New York: Columbia University Press, 124–6. Andrea Gotzmann and Christian Wiese explain that Orthodox Judaism 'attempts to dissociate the interpretation of law and thus also the history of law from historical and even natural processes. At the same time, even for those who embraced this dynamic model of interpretation, history served as a means of defining meta-historical contents. These range from securing religious contents as fixed points of orientation in the historical flux, through to ideologized constants of Jewish tradition and of communal life.' A.G. Gotzmann and C.W. Wiese. 2007. 'Introduction', in A. Gotzmann and C.W. Wiese (eds), *Modern Judaism and Historical*

Consciousness: Identities, Encounters, Perspectives, Boston: Leiden, xix. For histories of and debates within Orthodox Judaism see J. Neusner (ed.). 1993. *The Alteration of Orthodoxy*, New York: Garland Publishing, Inc.

13. Dana Evan Kaplan provides an overview of Progressive and Reform Jewish beliefs. See D.E. Kaplan. 2003. *American Reform Judaism: An Introduction*, New Brunswick: Rutgers University Press. Alan T. Levenson provides a description of the U.S. Reform movement, which informs the Australian Progressive and Reform movement to a great degree. See A.T. Levenson. 2008. 'Contemporary Jewish Thought', in M.L. Raphael (ed.), *The Columbia History of Jews and Judaism in America*, New York: Columbia University Press, 409–10. For the perspective from the organisation's roof-body see 'History: World Union for Progressive Judaism'. Retrieved 31 March 2014 from http://wupj.org/About/history.asp. On histories of and debates within this stream of Judaism see J. Neusner. 1993. *The Reformation of Reform Judaism*, New York: Garland Publishing, Inc.

14. According to a survey conducted in New York by the United Jewish Appeal (UJA)-Federation of New York, there are 643,000 Jewish households in the New York area and 'over 1,412,000 Jews reside in these households – adults who consider themselves Jewish, and children being raised as Jews.' UJA-Federation of New York. October 2004. *Jewish Community Study of New York: 2002*, 24. Retrieved 21 June 2009 from http://www.ujafedny.org/atf/cf/%7BAD848866-09C4-482C-9277-51A5D9CD6246%7D/JCommStudyHouseholdandPopulation.pdf. According to the Melbourne B'nai B'rith Anti-Defamation Commission there are approximately 45,000 Jews in Melbourne, out of a total of approximately 100,000 Jews in Australia. Information taken from B'nei B'rith Anti-Defamation Commission Inc., *Jews in Australia*. Retrieved 21 June 2009 from http://www.antidef.org.au/www/309/1001127/displayarticle/1001458.html.

15. See P. Wolfe. 2000. 'Logics of Elimination: Colonial Policies on Indigenous Peoples in Australia and the United States', *University of Nebraska Human Rights and Human Diversity Initiative Monograph Series* 2, no. 2.

16. 'Ashkenazi' refers to Jews who themselves or whose ancestors are from Western and Eastern Europe. 'Sephardi' refers to Jews who themselves or whose ancestors are from the Iberian Peninsula. 'Mizrahi' refers to Jews who themselves or whose ancestors are from the Middle East and North Africa. For a brief explanation see M. Kaye/Kantrowitz. 2007. *The Colors of Jews: Racial Politics and Radical Diasporism*, Bloomington: Indiana University Press, 69.

17. See E. Shohat. 2006. 'Taboo Memories, Diasporic Visions: Columbus, Palestine, and Arab-Jews', in *Taboo Memories, Diasporic Voices*, Durham, NC: Duke University Press, 201–32; E. Shohat. Autumn 1988. 'Sephardim in Israel: Zionism from the Standpoint of Its Jewish Victims', *Social Text* no. 19/20, 1–35; A. Alcalay. 1993. *After Jews and Arabs: Remaking Levantine Culture*, Minneapolis: University of Minnesota Press. See also S. Lavie. Spring 2002. 'Academic Apartheid in Israel and the Lillywhite Feminism of the Upper Middle Class', *Women in Judaism: A Multidisciplinary Journal*; S. Lavie. 2014. *Wrapped in the Flag of Israel: Mizrahi Single Mothers and Bureaucratic Torture*, New York: Berghahn Books.

18. Alcalay, *After Jews and Arabs*, 3.

19. This project of dislodging hegemonic histories echoes Dipesh Chakrabarty's work of 'provincializing Europe'. See D. Chakrabarty. 2008. *Provincializing Europe: Postcolonial Thought and Historical Difference*, Princeton: Princeton University Press. Ella Shohat, writing with reference to the use by European Jews of the texts of the Cairo Geniza – that great storehouse of Egyptian Jewish life and culture, which was emptied out and its contents taken to England – writes of the 'asymmetrical power relations' that exist

between the Egyptian worlds that are documented in these texts, and the European scholars who use the texts to write histories. She claims that '[w]ithin these asymmetrical power relations, Euro-Jewish scholars infused the colonized history with national meaning and telos, while, ironically, Arab-Jews were simultaneously being displaced and, in Israel, subjected to a school system in which Jewish history textbooks featured barely a single chapter on their history.' Shohat, 'Taboo Memories, Diasporic Visions', 227. For further discussion of the Cairo Geniza, see A. Ghosh. 1993. *In an Antique Land*, New York: A.A. Knopf; Alcalay, *After Jews and Arabs*, 128–43; J. Docker. 2001. *1492: The Poetics of Diaspora*, London: Continuum, 1–19.
20. Marianne Hirsch's ideas of postmemory can be usefully deployed here to aid our understanding of the work which Holocaust pedagogy is undertaking. Postmemory here 'characterizes the experience of those who grow up dominated by narratives that preceded their birth, whose own belated stories are evacuated by the stories of the previous generation shaped by traumatic events that can be neither understood nor recreated.' Moreover, 'postmemory is distinguished from memory by generational distance and from history by deep personal connection. Postmemory is a powerful and very particular form of memory precisely because its connection to its object or source is mediated not through recollection but through an imaginative investment and creation.' The teachings, therefore, carry this postmemory. See M. Hirsch. 1997. *Family Frames: Photography, Narrative and Postmemory*, Cambridge, MA: Harvard University Press, 22.
21. For explorations of the ways in which histories of the Holocaust are taught in Israel see, for instance, Y. Auron. 2005. *The Pain of Knowledge: Holocaust and Genocide Issues in Education*, trans. Ruth Ruzga, New Brunswick: Transaction Publishers; Idit Gil. Summer 2009. 'Teaching the Shoah in History Classes in Israeli High Schools', *Israel Studies* 14(2), 1–25. While it is different to teach a national history of the Jewish people in Israel (where the nation is attached to a state) and outside of it, some of the considerations are similar.
22. J. Boyarin. 1992. *Storm from Paradise: The Politics of Jewish Memory*, Minneapolis: University of Minnesota Press, xx.
23. 'Identities and memories', John R. Gillis argues, 'are not things we think *about*, but things we think *with*. As such they have no existence beyond our politics, our social relations, and our histories'. J.R. Gillis. 1994. 'Memory and Identity: The History of a Relationship', in J.R. Gillis (ed.), *Commemorations: The Politics of National Identity*, Princeton, New Jersey: Princeton University Press, 5. See also J.E. Young. 1993. *The Texture of Memory: Holocaust Memorials and Meaning*, New Haven, CT: Yale University Press, 6.
24. P. Nora. Spring 1989. 'Between Memory and History: *Les Lieux De Memoire*', *Representations*, no. 26, 7–24.
25. See N.Z. Davis and R. Starn. Spring 1989. 'Introduction', *Representations*, no. 26, 1–6; Y. Zerubavel. 1995. *Recovered Roots: Collective Memory and the Making of Israeli National Tradition*, Chicago, IL: University of Chicago Press; M. Bal, J. Crewe and L. Spitzer (eds). 1999. *Acts of Memory: Cultural Recall in the Present*, Hanover, NH: University Press of New England; C. Bold, R. Knowles and B. Leach. Autumn 2002. 'Feminist Memorializing and Cultural Countermemory: The Case of Marianne's Park', *Signs* 28(1), 125–48. Yosef Yerushalmi and Amos Funkenstein discuss this question of memory and history from within specifically Jewish contexts, albeit starting from very different ideas about the relationship between memory and history. See Y.H. Yerushalmi. 1982. *Zakhor: Jewish History and Jewish Memory*, Seattle: University of Washington Press and A. Funkenstein. 1993. *Perceptions of Jewish History*, Berkeley: University of California Press, 3–21.

26. A. Clark. 2004. 'Teaching the Nation: Politics and Pedagogy in Australian History,' PhD Thesis, University of Melbourne, 21–22. The words of Chris Healy echo this: '[s]ocial memory is not the only effect of history in schools, but it is certainly one of them. The teaching of history in elementary schools is precisely one of those moments when histories are performed.' C. Healy. 1997. *From the Ruins of Colonialism: History as Social Memory,* Cambridge: Cambridge University Press, 109.
27. Clark, 'Teaching the Nation', 6.
28. J. Dalsheim. 2004. 'Settler Nationalism, Collective Memories of Violence and the "Uncanny Other"', *Social Identities* 10(2), 155. See also E. Podeh. Spring/Summer 2000. 'History and Memory in the Israeli Educational System: The Portrayal of the Arab-Israeli Conflict in History Textbooks (1948-2000)', *History & Memory* 12(1), 65.
29. M. Halbwachs. 1992. *On Collective Memory,* trans. Lewis A. Coser, Chicago, IL: University of Chicago Press.
30. The teachers were all asked where they get their information from: predominantly it was from other teachers, or their own research and work. Yad Vashem, the United States Holocaust Memorial Museum (USHMM), and the Jewish Holocaust Museum and Research Centre were not really relied upon by these teachers.
31. J. Crewe. 1999. 'Recalling Adamastor: Literature as Cultural Memory in "White" South Africa', in M. Bal, J. Crewe and L. Spitzer (eds), *Acts of Memory: Cultural Recall in the Present,* Hanover, NH: University Press of New England, 75.
32. Dalsheim, 'Settler Nationalism, Collective Memories of Violence and the "Uncanny Other"', 155–56.
33. Zev Garber points out that while Holocaust with a capital H refers to this, holocaust (with an uncapitalized h) is used to describe genocides more generally. Z. Garber. 1994. *Shoah: The Paradigmatic Genocide. Essays in Exegesis and Eisegesis,* Lanham, MD: University Press of America, 52. He also argues that Holocaust typically refers to, as stated above, the destruction of Jewish communities and the killing of six million Jews. But this works to remove the deaths of the five million others who were killed in Nazi concentration and death camps, which 'seems to imply that Gentile deaths are not as significant as Jewish deaths.' Ibid., 63.
34. V.M. Patraka. 1997. 'Situating History and Difference: The Performance of the Term *Holocaust* in Public Discourse', in J. Boyarin and D. Boyarin (eds), *Jews and Other Differences: The New Jewish Cultural Studies,* Minneapolis: University of Minnesota Press, 54.
35. G. Agamben. 1999. *Remnants of Auschwitz: The Witness and the Archive.* New York: Zone Books, 28. Garber expands on the connotations of Holocaust as signifying a burnt whole. 'Why Do We Call the Holocaust 'The Holocaust?'' An Inquiry into the Psychology of Labels' in Garber, *Shoah,* 53–54.
36. Agamben, *Remnants of Auschwitz,* 31.
37. There are many historians and theorists who engage with this question of which name to use. For discussions of this see H. Kellner. 1998. '"Never Again" Is Now', in B. Fay, P. Pomper and R.T. Vann (eds), *History and Theory: Contemporary Readings,* Massachusetts: Blackwell Publishers, 234–35; A.-V. Sullam Calimani. October 1999. 'A Name for Extermination', *The Modern Language Review* 94(4), 978–99; J.E. Young. 1988. 'Names of the Holocaust: Meaning and Consequences', in *Writing and Rewriting the Holocaust: Narrative and the Consequences of Interpretation,* Bloomington: Indiana University Press, 83–98.
38. 'Why Do We Call the Holocaust "The Holocaust?"', in Garber, *Shoah,* 55–6. Garber explained that the term was enforced by Elie Wiesel, who based it on a reading of the biblical story of the *Akedah,* the binding of Isaac. Ibid., 59–62.

39. S.L. Gilman. Winter 2000. 'Is Life Beautiful? Can the Shoah Be Funny? Some Thoughts on Recent and Older Films', *Critical Inquiry* 26(2), 281.
40. J. Stratton. 2000. *Coming out Jewish: Constructing Ambivalent Identities*, London: Routledge, 84. Stratton later goes on to distinguish fear from anxiety; however, the way he characterises fear in the quote above has important parallels, I think, with what I am here characterizing as anxiety.
41. S. Freud. 1936. *The Problem of Anxiety*, trans. Henry Alden Bunker, M.D., New York: The Psychoanalytic Press and W.W. Norton & Company Inc., 69.
42. Ibid., 69, 72. Emphasis in original.
43. Ibid., 71–2, 77.
44. Ibid., 83–4.
45. I take this idea of the 'homely' from Ghassan Hage, and will return to it in my discussion of the nation state and modernity below.
46. C.S. Maier. Fall/Winter 1993. 'A Surfeit of Memory? Reflections on History, Melancholy and Denial', *History & Memory* 5(2), 145.
47. There is an additional source of anxiety: what will be the costs of being accepted? To what extent will Jewish difference (as elastic as such a concept is) be acceptable, and to what extent will Jewish differences be rejected? That is, at what point do the movements of mimicry and assimilation which this book is describing become mandatory? Further exploration of these questions – which can only be answered through a thorough exploration of U.S. and Australian nationalisms – is outside the scope of the book.
48. G. Hage. 2003. *Against Paranoid Nationalism: Searching for Hope in a Shrinking Society*, Annandale, NSW: Pluto Press, 1–3.
49. Robert Seltzer points out that this has been part of the process of a generalized Americanization of Jews and Jewishness: there has been a 'paradoxical effect of the Americanization of the Jews: America undermined and energized Jewish commitment. Much was discarded and much was saved'. R.M. Seltzer. 1995. 'Introduction: The Ironies of American Jewish History', in R.M. Seltzer and N.J. Cohen (eds), *The Americanization of the Jews*, New York: New York University Press, 5. Michael Galchinsky explores the ways in which Jews in the U.S. have seen themselves as relatively comfortable, particularly through a reading of Philip Roth's *Operation Shylock*. M. Galchinsky. 1998. 'Scattered Seeds: A Dialogue of Diasporas', in D. Biale, M. Galhinsky and S. Heschel (eds), *Insider/Outsider: American Jews and Multiculturalism*, Berkeley: University of California Press, 203–9.
50. As Ruth R. Wisse makes clear, a lack of difference entails Jews in the U.S. giving up something of themselves, of their Jewish identity. R.R. Wisse. 1995. 'Jewish Writers on the New Diaspora,' in R.M. Seltzer and N.J. Cohen (eds), *The Americanization of the Jews*, New York: New York University Press, 66–67. When we consider that the Jews under consideration in this book are involved in formal Jewish dayschool education, we necessarily identify a disjuncture between this argument about anxiety and that which the book is pursuing: the Jews under consideration evidently, to some degree, foreground their particular, and different, Jewish identities.
51. D. Biale. 1998. 'The Melting Pot and Beyond: Jews and the Politics of American Identity,' in D. Biale, M. Galchinsky, and S. Heschel (eds), *Insider/Outsider: American Jews and Multiculturalism*, Berkeley: University of California Press, 28. The question of the racializing of Jews will be taken up in Chapter One. For further exploration of the idea that the U.S. has been a welcoming place to Jews, who have found a comfortable place there, because of their relative whiteness but also because of their development of 'multiple identities', see D. Biale, M. Galchinsky and S. Heschel. 1998. 'Introduction:

The Dialectic of Jewish Enlightenment', in D. Biale, M. Galhinsky and S. Heschel (eds), *Insider/Outsider: American Jews and Multiculturalism*, Berkeley: University of California Press, 1–13.
52. K.L. Klein. Winter 2000. 'On the Emergence of Memory in Historical Discourse', *Representations* 69, 143.
53. Ibid., 145.
54. D. Biale. 1986. *Power & Powerlessness in Jewish History*, New York: Schocken Books, 4.
55. C. Kahane. 2001. 'Dark Mirrors: A Feminist Reflection on Holocaust Narrative and the Maternal Metaphor', in E. Bronfen and M. Kavka (eds), *Feminist Consequences: Theory for the New Century*, New York: Columbia University Press, 161–88.
56. See J. Butler. 1990. *Gender Trouble: Feminism and the Subversion of Identity*. New York: Routledge, 1–15, and E. Cowie. 1990. 'Woman as Sign,' in P. Adams and E. Cowie (eds), *The Woman in Question: M/F*, London: Verso, 117–33.
57. Kahane, 'Dark Mirrors,' 162.
58. In Lee Edelman's discussion of the figure of the Child in relation to reproductive futurity he writes about 'the image of the Child, not to be confused with the lived experiences of any historical children'. L. Edelman. 2004. *No Future: Queer Theory and the Death Drive*, Durham: Duke University Press, 11. I am arguing that something approximately similar is the case for the Diaspora Jew in the Zionist imagination, as I will explain in more detail in this introduction, in the section entitled 'Diaspora'.
59. Jean Radford writes about a similar relationship between Jews and women in Otto Weininger's writing: that they are both situated as disempowered and lacking. J. Radford. 1998. 'The Woman and the Jew: Sex and Modernity', in B. Cheyette and L. Marcus (eds), *Modernity, Culture and 'the Jew'*, Cambridge: Polity Press, 91–92. Anxieties about national identity and gender differences is a thread which runs throughout this book.
60. Kaye/Kantrowitz, *The Colors of Jews*, 195.
61. Daniel Boyarin makes this point with regard to Freud's ideas of his own Zionism, which entailed the belief that 'merely being a stalwart Zionist was enough to transform the Jewish man from his state of female degeneracy into the status of [a] . . . mock Aryan male', thereby solving 'the Jewish problem'. D. Boyarin. 2000. 'The Colonial Drag: Zionism, Gender, and Mimicry', in F. Afzal-Khan and K. Seshadri-Crooks (eds), *The Pre-Occupation of Postcolonial Studies*, Durham: Duke University Press, 236.
62. See 'Of Mimicry and Man' in Bhabha, *The Location of Culture*, 85–92.
63. This is bound up in the Hebrew idea of Diaspora as *galut*, or exile: as Howard Wettstein argues, '[t]o view one's group as in *galut* is to suppose that what is in some sense the proper order has been interrupted'. H. Wettstein. 2002. 'Coming to Terms with Exile', in H. Wettstein (ed.), *Diasporas and Exiles: Varieties of Jewish Identity*, Berkeley: University of California Press, 47. For religious settlers in the West Bank and East Jerusalem the belief that Israel is the only possible home for Jews has biblical origins. Jacqueline Rose describes how 'many settlers insist, that Israel is the land God promised to the Jews'. J. Rose. 2005. *The Question of Zion*, Carlton, Victoria: Melbourne University Press, 98. For a thorough exploration of settlers see I. Zertal and A. Eldar. 2007. *Lords of the Land: The War Over Israel's Settlements in the Occupied Territories, 1967-2007*, New York: Nation Books. For explorations of the idea of 'Zionism as Messianism' in more detail, see Rose, *The Question of Zion*, 1–57. Erich S. Gruen expands on these biblical histories of the relationship between the Jewish Diaspora and a Jewish homeland centred around Jerusalem. See E.S. Gruen. 2002. 'Diaspora and Homeland', in H. Wettstein (ed.), *Diasporas and Exiles: Varieties of Jewish Identity*, Berkeley: University of California Press, 18–46.

64. Stratton, *Coming out Jewish*, 117.
65. See T. Mayer. 2000. 'From Zero to Hero: Masculinity in Jewish Nationalism', in T. Mayer (ed.), *Gender Ironies of Nationalism: Sexing the Nation*, London: Routledge, 282–303.
66. S.L. Gilman. 1999. 'Introduction: The Frontier as a Model for Jewish History', in S.L. Gilman and M. Shain (eds), *Jewries at the Frontier: Accommodation, Identity, Conflict*, Urbana, IL: University of Illinois Press, 1.
67. J. Clifford. 1997. *Routes: Travel and Translation in the Late Twentieth Century*, Cambridge, MA: Harvard University Press, 249–50.
68. See R. Cohen. 1997. *Global Diasporas: An Introduction*, London: UCL Press for explanations of different models of diaspora. Michael Galchinsky similarly examined 'traditional Jewish' ideas of diaspora against more recent postcolonial approaches. See Galchinsky, 'Scattered Seeds', 185–211.
69. Perhaps though this model is similarly problematic, as it still relies on there being a centre. But, then, what model of identity does not rely on a centre, or commonality, which is produced by and productive of the group?
70. Docker, *1492*, vii–viii.
71. J. Francisco. 2006. *Far from Zion: Jews, Diaspora, Memory*, Stanford, CA: Stanford University Press, 97.
72. D. Boyarin and J. Boyarin. Summer 1993. 'Diaspora: Generation and the Ground of Jewish Identity', *Critical Inquiry* 19(4), 721.
73. Ibid., 714.
74. Ibid., 705.
75. B. Cheyette. 2013. *Diasporas of the Mind: Jewish and Postcolonial Writing and the Nightmare of History*, New Haven, CT: Yale University Press, 6.
76. Ibid., 264.
77. Michael Rothberg describes this through his framing of 'multidirectional memory' and writes that 'pursuing memory's multidirectionality encourages us to think of the public sphere as a malleable discursive space in which groups do not simply articulate established positions but actually come into being through their dialogical interactions with others; both the subjects and spaces of the public are open to continual reconstruction . . . Memories are not owned by groups – nor are groups 'owned' by memories. Rather, the borders of memory and identity are jagged; what looks at first like my own property often turns out to be a borrowing or adaptation from a history that initially might seem foreign or distant.' M. Rothberg. 2009. *Multidirectional Memory: Remembering the Holocaust in the Age of Decolonization*, Stanford, CA: Stanford University Press, 5.
78. P. Gilroy. 2002. *There Ain't No Black in the Union Jack: The Cultural Politics of Race and Nation*, London: Routledge Classics, 204.
79. Shohat, 'Taboo Memories, Diasporic Visions', 222–23.
80. Ibid., 225.
81. Ibid., 215.
82. D. Chakrabarty. 2002. *Habitations of Modernity: Essays in the Wake of Subaltern Studies*, Chicago, IL: University of Chicago Press, xix.
83. P. Chatterjee. 2004. *The Politics of the Governed: Reflections on Popular Politics in Most of the World*, Delhi: Permanent Black, 27.
84. Sanjay Seth traces a similar process of the adoption of colonial, modern western knowledge through education in India. He argues through this that 'the status of modern western knowledge – the assumption that it is not merely one mode of knowledge but is knowledge "as such," . . . – is questionable, and needs to be rethought.' S. Seth.

2007. *Subject Lessons: The Western Education of Colonial India*, Durham, NC: Duke University Press, 3.
85. For explorations of the many different ways in which Jews in different parts of Europe, the Ottoman Empire, the Middle East and the U.S. participated in, and were an essential part of the development of, modernity, see the chapters in 'Part Three: Modern Encounters' of D. Biale (ed.). 2002. *Cultures of the Jews: A New History*, New York: Schocken Books, 725–1146.
86. J. Katz. 1973. *Out of the Ghetto: The Social Background of Jewish Emancipation, 1770-1870*, Cambridge, MA: Harvard University Press, 2.
87. Paula E. Hyman and Arnold Eisen characterize this as the master narrative of Jewish modernity and Jewish relationships with non-Jewish modernities. See P.E. Hyman. 2002. 'Gender and the Shaping of Modern Jewish Identities', *Jewish Social Studies* 8(2–3), 153–4; A.M. Eisen. Fall 1994. 'Rethinking Jewish Modernity', *Jewish Social Studies* 1(1), 1–2.
88. J. Frankel. 1992. 'Assimilation and the Jews in Nineteenth-Century Europe: Towards a New Historiography?', in J. Frankel and S.J. Zipperstein (eds), *Assimilation and Community: The Jews in Nineteenth-Century Europe*, Cambridge: Cambridge University Press, 6. Zygmunt Bauman focuses on the question of assimilation and the various processes which occurred in order to shape Jewish political movements, particularly those of socialism and communism, within Western societies. See Z. Bauman. Fall 1988. 'Exit Visas and Entry Tickets: Paradoxes of Jewish Assimilation', *Telos* 77, 45–78, and Bauman, *Modernity and Ambivalence*, 102–59.
89. M.A. Meyer. 1998. 'Reflections on Jewish Modernization,' in E. Carlebach, J.M. Efron and D.N. Myers (eds), *Jewish History and Jewish Memory: Essays in Honor of Yosef Haim Yerushalmi*, Hanover, MA: Brandeis University Press, 370.
90. Ibid., 371–3.
91. Hyman, 'Gender and the Shaping of Modern Jewish Identities', 154.
92. Ibid., 159.
93. Eisen, 'Rethinking Jewish Modernity', 10.
94. Ibid., 18.
95. Hyman, 'Gender and the Shaping of Modern Jewish Identities', 155.
96. M.A. Meyer. 1991. 'The Emergence of Modern Jewish Historiography: Motives and Motifs', in A. Rapoport-Albert (ed.), *Essays in Jewish Historiography*, Atlanta, GA: Scholars Press, 160–75; Yerushalmi, *Zakhor*, 84–88.
97. J. Stratton. 2008. *Jewish Identity in Western Pop Culture: The Holocaust and Trauma through Modernity*, New York: Palgrave Macmillan, 10.
98. G. Hage. 1998. *White Nation: Fantasies of White Supremacy in a Multicultural Society*, Annandale, NSW: Pluto Press, 20, 42. Hage follows Pierre Bourdieu's conception of whiteness as a form of cultural capital, able to be accumulated. See Hage, *White Nation*, in particular 52–5 and Chapter 2 (48–77) more generally.
99. Jon Stratton presents a similar consideration of Jewish relationships with homelands. See Stratton, *Coming out Jewish*, 53–83. Daniel Schroeter problematizes this idea of Israel as the Jewish home, as, he argues, Jews often had a stronger relationship with the countries in which they are located, rather than to Israel: this entailed the existence of 'a Diaspora culture that transcends national boundaries'. D.J. Schroeter. 2002. 'A Different Road to Modernity: Jewish Identity in the Arab World', in H. Wettstein (ed.), *Diasporas and Exiles: Varieties of Jewish Identity*, Berkeley: University of California Press, 150. Daniel Boyarin critiques the gendered, imperial ideas of home which are encompassed in Theodor Herzl's writings of the need for a Jewish home. This is part of the mimicry which is now to be discussed. See Boyarin, 'The Colonial Drag', 252.

100. Bhabha, *The Location of Culture*, 86. Emphasis in original.
101. Ibid. Emphasis in original.
102. Ibid., 88.
103. Boyarin, 'The Colonial Drag', 257.
104. Ibid., 253.
105. Boyarin, 'The Colonial Drag', 255. Emphasis in Boyarin. Marek Edelman quote is originally in I. Zertal. Spring 1994. 'The Sacrificed and the Sanctified: The Construction of a National Martyrology', *Zemanim* 12(48), 38.
106. Boyarin, 'The Colonial Drag', 255.
107. Interview with Teacher A at School MC.

CHAPTER 1

'Don't Ever Think That It Can't Happen Again'
Memories of the Holocaust, Anxieties of Difference

> Living cultures have other dynamics. Culture as a way of life is a form of resistance. We resist through culture the homogenising categories of our ideological forms, once they get powerful and institutionalised.
> —Ashis Nandy, 'The Limits of the Diaspora: A Conversation with Ashis Nandy'

> The issue of who belongs to a nation and in what ways, who are citizens and who are subjects, is one which is never concluded, for the process of nation formation is indeed that, a process. Nations are not made once and for ever. Rather they are constantly re-made and re-imagined, the boundaries redrawn.
> —Catherine Hall, 'Gender, Nations and Nationalisms'

After the Holocaust the vast majority (although certainly not all) of the small number of Jews remaining in Eastern Europe left, moving to Australia, the U.S., Palestine, Brazil, Argentina, South Africa and a number of other countries.[1] In these new locations they attempted to start new lives: to raise families, build organizations (such as synagogues, Jewish Community Councils, Jewish schools, Zionist youth groups), and create cultural institutions (for example, Yiddish theatre societies, music groups, bookshops, cafes). Outside of the Jewish communities they worked, to varying degrees, to become a part of the societies in which they were living. This dual idea of maintaining separate Jewish institutions and communities while also trying to be a part of the broader society has been, at times, difficult. This difficulty, and – in the terms of this book – the anxieties it creates, has been negotiated in a multitude of spaces and places. My focus here will specifically be on the negotiations which take place in Holocaust education, in the writing of Jewish histories, in Jewish schools, newspapers and organizations. That is, I am interested in the problematic of how being a diasporic people – feeling permanently in some way slightly but dangerously out of place and simultaneously ambivalently at home, in the non-Jewish Western societies in which these people live – is contemplated in these examples of Holocaust education, as well as in broader Jewish social discourses. This, it can be understood, is not a problem just of the Jews, but more significantly, a problem of modernity itself, and in particular of Western, and European-influenced, modernity. Following Jacques Derrida, Jon Stratton argues that:

> [e]xpelled . . . during the formation of 'Europe,' the Jew is allowed to return but remains, always, a stranger in the ideally homogeneous European nation-states. . . . [T]he Jew becomes the defining moment of the production of modernity – defining in the first instance at the time of Jewish expulsion but, then, defining when the Jew is allowed to return not, though, as a member of the European community of national citizens but as a stranger, tolerated but not thought of as really European.[2]

While Stratton writes of Europe, we can understand these ideas as travelling beyond the geographical confines of Europe to nation-states which have adopted these central ideas of European modernity, including the U.S. and Australia. We need to remember here though – as Stratton reminds us – that this 'stranger-ness' is most definitely historically produced: it exists differently in different times and places. And while Stratton writes of 'the Jew', that Jew cannot be equated to all Jews, always (or even all European Jews, in all European locales). It is important not to fetishize or naturalize outsiderness.

In this chapter I explore the ways in which histories and descriptions of Jewishness contain this anxious element. The purpose here is to come to an understanding of the ways that these anxieties surrounding the place of Jews in the non-Jewish West are formulated, and then also how these discourses are part of a long history of Jewish impact upon, and formulation and negotiation of, modernity in Western societies. The idea of modernity that I want to deploy here is that which was articulated in the Introduction: it coalesces around the importance of the nation-state in the formulation of group identities, and the ways it is possible to understand and narrate a group's history within this. It is, moreover, a question of how nation-states manage internal differences amongst their populations: how do those in control establish the parameters for belonging? Importantly, these are racialized nation-states, wherein, as will be explored later, racialization is a primary axis of inscribing difference within them. Jewish difference is thereby, to a large degree, fitted in to a pre-existing schema.[3] This modernity is therefore simultaneously something which is outside of Jewish communities, and which has been formulated by and in response to the presence of Jews and others.

It is important to any discussion of the problematics of finding one's place in a new national home to reflect on the characteristics of the 'homely' nation. This is the idea of the Western nation-state which Ghassan Hage has articulated.[4] As such, the ways in which both Australia and America are nations largely defined by racialized difference, and its accompanying exclusions and projects of homogenization, become important for us to consider. National projects of assimilation have been central to dictating the experiences of Jews in the United States and Australia.[5] In both countries assimilation into the nation has involved not just the changing of behaviours but also has a racialized undercurrent. This racialization can be seen to extend to another element that structures the teachings here: Zionism and its accompanying belief that difference is a problem. For the Zionism that is displayed at times – as we shall see throughout the remaining chapters – helps to formulate a national group that permanently looks towards Israel, distrusting non-Jewish countries. In this way, the anxiety persists: the Holocaust could be repeated, and difference – in its various forms and incarnations – is a source of concern. The fear of persecution exists as these Jews do not feel they truly belong in Australia or the U.S., or indeed in Israel. This lack of true belonging feels hazardous. And, perhaps, in a sense they never can fully fit within these particular systems. We can see overwhelmingly in social histories of U.S. or Australian Jewry that examine the place of Jews within the racial systems of these countries that Jews present a challenge to these systems by virtue of their in-betweenness. There is a perceived inability of these systems to find a place for the Jews, who are variously considered to be a racial, national, ethnic or religious group, and yet simultaneously not quite any of these.[6] As will become evident through this chapter, there is a deep ambivalence about the place of Jews, and what constitutes a (Zionist) Jew outside Israel today.

In this chapter I will briefly explore the different ways in which American and Australian national histories have constructed ideas of a racialized citizenry, and, as such, how Jews have negotiated a place within these societies. We will then turn to the teachings under consideration in an effort to explore more fully the anxieties expressed by teachers about the place of Jews in these worlds. It will become evident that, through an examination of Jewish histories and Holocaust pedagogy in Melbourne and New York, we can identify what we could call a transnational anxiety about the place of Jews in locations within the U.S. and Australia today. This anxiety, as I explained in the Introduction, is based on an uncertainty about an originary place: that is, how is emplacement threatened by (potential) discrimination and alienation? Or, to put it another way, how are some Jews negotiating a history and imagined future shaped by antisemitism, and its attendant displacements? This negotiation, it almost seems self-evident, in turn is ambivalent and productive of anxiety.

U.S. Considerations

As we will come to see, Jewish ambivalences and anxieties over the place of Jews in the U.S. are negotiated in numerous different ways. One important manner is in the ways Jewish communities identify with the state. There are examples of this in seemingly everyday life, as I noticed while conducting my research. For instance, we can identify this in words spoken by a rabbi at a Friday night (*Shabbat*) service at a Reconstructionist synagogue in New York which I attended in 2009.[7] The rabbi, towards the end of the service, read the names of the U.S. soldiers who had been killed in Iraq and Afghanistan in the previous week. She explained to the congregation that this reading of names had been taking place for the previous three and a half years, since the beginning of the U.S. invasion of Iraq. She further explained that the names of the U.S. soldiers were read but not those of the Iraqis and Afghanis who had died because information about the latter was not available.[8] Moreover, she told the congregation, her reading these names 'is not political – it's about remembering'. In making this claim she was screening out the politics involved in the deaths of the soldiers and in their remembrance.[9] More importantly, however, by remembering the U.S. soldiers and not the Iraqi and Afghan civilians by name, the rabbi positioned herself and her congregation as remembering through the lens of the state rather than of the victims of state violence. This teaches the members of the congregation that they should identify with the state – they should mourn the deaths of the soldiers, rather than the civilians. Indeed, dying for one's country has been highlighted by Benedict Anderson as a fundamental aspect of modern nationalism, carrying with it a 'moral grandeur'.[10] It is notable therefore, although perhaps unsurprising, that the rabbi did not make mention of non-American soldiers who were killed. A close relationship between the Jewish members of the congregation and U.S. imperialism was thereby reinforced.

Similarly, when visiting the United States Holocaust Memorial Museum (USHMM) in Washington, D.C. in the first week of November 2006, I enquired at the information desk: how were they were memorializing *Kristallnacht* (the anniversary of which is on 9–10 November)? The employee stated that the USHMM was not marking *Kristallnacht*, as, *instead*, Veterans Day was being remembered. Veterans Day is a U.S. national holiday which takes place on 11 November and serves to honour and remember U.S. war veterans. To mark Veterans Day, the USHMM was displaying the flags of the army units which liberated the Nazi death and concentration camps. Again, we can see here the alliance of Jewish remembering with the U.S. state, rather than with (Jewish) victims. Although the USHMM is not a Jewish institution, and makes no claim to be, it presents a narrative of what is shown to be a Jewish event.[11] While the emphasis of the narrative in the museum is certainly on the role of the U.S. and its soldiers[12] – and therefore the remembering of Veterans Day is not inconsistent with the overall message of the museum – it is significant that there is not room in the memorial activities of the museum to remember *both* Veterans Day and *Kristallnacht*. In choosing to remember Veterans Day, to the exclusion of *Kristallnacht*, the museum is aligning itself with the (American) state, rather than with the victims of (German) state violence. It is presenting the matter as a zero-sum game: as one or the other. These two incidents – as minor as they may seem – can be understood to represent a much larger project of negotiation.

We can see a similar relationship of (tense) negotiation surrounding the identification with the markers of acceptability in the U.S. in the writings of Karen Brodkin. Brodkin writes of the intergenerational differences amongst Jews in the U.S., and the ways that this is indicative of a changing relationship over generations between Jews and U.S. society more generally. There are, she argues, also continuities in these relationships, which are mostly centred on the uneasiness felt in living in the U.S., amongst non-Jews. She focuses most predominantly on Ashkenazi Jews in New York,[13] explaining that:

> the trial and execution of the Rosenbergs in 1953 heightened our sense of difference. It was a terrifying thing and discussed in the same hushed tones that the Nazi genocide was talked about in our house . . . My parents talked about these things with their friends, but I do not think they discussed them with our non-Jewish neighbours. I believe this was out of a fear that to do so might evoke an anti-Semitism they suspected our white neighbours harbored but which they didn't want to know about.[14]

According to Brodkin, 'being a Jew [in this world] . . . meant standing somewhat apart from the white world, being bicultural in a way that Jews shared with other upwardly mobile European ethnics'.[15] She explains that her family 'also embraced the white world, especially its middle-class aspects'.[16] It was this seeking out and eventual partial materializing of upward mobility that, according to Brodkin, enabled Jews to become 'white', or to participate in society as non-Jewish white people do. This whiteness is, in an important sense, equivalent to acceptance within and by the state, as Ghassan Hage describes.[17] Brodkin thus locates whiteness in the U.S. in class.[18] This, however, was not an issue which teachers of the Holocaust in New York schools showed widespread consciousness of, nor was it raised by most of them in their teaching.[19] Teachers, it seemed, were more concerned by Jews being excluded on ethnic, religious or political grounds from the nation-states in which they were living.[20]

David Biale's descriptions of Jewish assimilation in the U.S. are also useful in helping us understand the seemingly precarious position of Jews in this world today.[21] For Biale, European Jews figure as the once paradigmatic minority group. He explains that in Europe, prior to their nineteenth century migration to the U.S – the *goldene medina*, or the site posited as a Jewish homeland – Jews had been 'the defining opposite of what is now called "white"'.[22] Other internal minority groups in Europe had been treated in accordance with how Jews were treated. This, he explains, was carried over into the U.S. in the early twentieth century with the constructions of Jewishness, Otherness, and the ability of groups to assimilate being depicted in such plays as Israel Zangwill's *The Melting Pot*.[23]

But Biale also argues that Jews in the U.S. are perhaps not as unable to assimilate and become accepted and acceptable as they have thought. This is evidenced, he suggests, by the mainstream success of both *The Melting Pot* and the USHMM in Washington. Both this play and the Museum point to past histories in Europe of persecution, and a present of stability and acceptance in America.[24] Indeed, we can understand that the feelings of acceptance in America *rely* on histories of persecution in Europe to make sense: the U.S. present and future cleans up the mess made by the European past. In this story – which is a narrative whose basis I will return to in Chapter Four – the U.S. is never the site for persecution, but rather is the site for redemption. As such, these cultural products efface any positive Jewish involvement in European life. This in turn complicates the ideas which are under exploration in this book – why is there a recurrence of feelings of anxiety in America that the Holocaust will be repeated? If this work is being undertaken, at times, to demonstrate that the U.S. is a safe haven, why is this not always felt? Firstly, as will be shown, the fears and anxieties expressed by the teachers extend beyond the borders of the U.S.: they are often more widespread anxieties about the place of Jews in relation to non-Jewish systems in general. Secondly, it is perhaps inevitable that any migrant group will, to an extent, feel that they are outsiders in a new country, and this is perhaps even more so in the context of a post-genocide community. Thirdly, as I am outlining here, Jewish life in the U.S. is often experienced by some Jews as precarious.

This importance of the past to possibilities of assimilation – to finding a solid place in the U.S. through the alteration of both American and Jewish identities – was raised in a 2009 article in *Vanity Fair*. Writing about a group of New York-based fiction authors he labels the 'New Yiddishists' – such as Jonathan Safran Foer, Nicole Krauss, Michael Chabon and Nathan Englander[25] – David Sax points to the ways in which these authors engage with both the past and present in their writings in order to ask how to remain Jewish in a multicultural world: where is the place of Jews in the American world?[26] He writes that:

> The New Yiddishists aren't avoiding the present because it's boring. Jewish literature, from the Talmud to contemporary fiction, has always relied on interpreting the prickly contradictions of life through the past. Many of the stories of the New

Yiddishists jump back and forth between generations of Jewish families, showing how the questions that we struggle with today are the same ones that Jews have dealt with before: How do we stay true to our heritage while living in a multicultural society? Are we Jews, Americans, or both? What is our place in this world?[27]

Indeed, even in the terminology he utilizes – New Yiddishists – there is an interplay of time. Yiddish, overwhelmingly, is a language which is in a post-vernacular phase, its usage here pointing more towards an ethic and style of writing, rather than the language itself.[28] Histories, or generations, of families interplay with histories of the broader communities, which in turn interplay with those of the larger societies, all working to negotiate an anxious uncertainty about where Jews are placed within these varyingly multicultural societies.[29]

It is useful here to return to a discussion of whiteness, and to combine it with these ideas of the relevance of history and the past in defining these anxious identities. After the end of World War II, and with the beginning of the Civil Rights movement, race became the central aspect of assimilation discourses; groups were considered on the basis of their whiteness or the lack thereof. As Biale articulates it, drawing our attention once again to the interrelationship between class and race

> as anti-Semitism and formal discrimination waned in the post-World War II years and as Jews became economically successful, they found themselves for the first time in modern history as doubly marginal: marginal to the majority culture, but also marginal among minorities.[30]

Their relative acceptance in class terms did not completely erase their marginality. Yet, as Sander Gilman argues, '[i]n the past decade, the "Jews" have been imagined as a successful minority. This perceived success came at exactly the time, as Peter Novick has noted, when the Shoah had become the touchstone for all histories of persecution and genocide.'[31] As Jews have lost their marginal status, so too in one sense have their histories. Instead, histories of Jewish persecution (and marginality) – pre-eminently, the Holocaust – have become the dominant ways of understanding minority persecutions. This, according to Biale, also marked the first time in the U.S. when Jews were being assessed on a basis of blood, in a hierarchy that was developed around a different minority group – African-Americans.[32] But, just as importantly, the marginality of Jews has not ceased.

Biale further asserts that Jewish 'culture may well have prepared them better than most immigrant groups for success in America. Thus, not only economic success and social integration but also an intrinsically different history divided the Jews from American blacks. Whether they liked it or not (and usually they did), the Jews in postwar America had become white.'[33] In talking about the USHMM he explains that it 'is an example of how Jews seek to be marked at once as part of the majority culture, by linking their history to the institutions of America, and as different, by insisting on the particularity of their history as a persecuted minority'.

It is the connecting of a 'negative European Jewish narrative with the positive image of America, as a kind of brief for Jewish integration' in a manner which Biale argues has been occurring since the beginning of the twentieth century.[34] This change in position for Jews has been, Biale contends, a source of anxiety. And this anxiety about a lack of difference, Biale and Novick argue, has been resolved through the foregrounding of this specific narrative of persecution. It is useful for us to shift the frames here to understand the work which they are suggesting is being done. For it is the racializing of identity in the name of maintaining Jewish particularity which provides the very conditions of possibility for the continuing anxiety about the place of Jews in a non-Jewish world. That is, the anxiety results from the production and utilization of narratives which point to the racial basis of the Holocaust. In the moment when narratives of the Holocaust are brought forth in order to produce difference, the anxiety is also produced. And this anxiety, I am arguing here, is an anxiety that Jews, in these modern, racialized spaces, do not fit *because* of the racializing of difference. And, of course, the Holocaust is an example of this not-fitting. We can thus understand the problem at the centre of the arguments which Biale and Novick propose, and move forward with an understanding of the ways in which this racializing of the events of the Holocaust, and the continuation of the racializing of difference in modernity, work together to create an anxious space which requires negotiation.

How then does history-writing fit into these negotiations of the place of Jews? This is a question explored by Susannah Heschel, who argues that Jewish Studies in America has provided a counterhistory. She explains that the Wissenschaft des Judentums (or the creation of Jewish Studies as a scientific inquiry) in Germany in the nineteenth century was created to demonstrate that Jewish history surpassed Christian or Muslim histories – that Jews were superior, and that modernity (which was understood as positive) was a Jewish movement.[35] That is, the Wissenschaft was positing Jewish history as being apart from and prior to Christian histories, rather than as the same movement. This relationship between modernity and Jewishness therefore is not predicated on anxiety, but rather modernity and Jewishness are seen as fundamentally intertwined in a way not replicated in the Holocaust education under examination in this book.

This is somewhat contradicted in the work of John Efron who, in a discussion of the Jewish Orientalism which was a part of the larger Wissenschaft movement, argues that the German Jewish Orientalists took a colonial approach towards Eastern European Orthodox Jews, demonstrating a contempt for them that, he suggests, 'was a contempt that was bred by familiarity and fear that German Jews, on the eve of emancipation, would be viewed as equally incorrigible as their Russo-Polish coreligionists'.[36] We can understand in this reading that there was a strong desire on the part of these new Jewish historians to be a part of the Enlightenment European state, and hence a desire to reject those Jews who did not seek the same. This, however, was founded in a Jewish movement – that of the Wissenschaft.

Jewishness was acceptable and desired, to a degree. Similarly, incorporation within the German state was acceptable and desired, to a degree. This ambivalence recurs throughout the histories being described in this book.

To return to Heschel's characterization of the Wissenschaft movement, she argues that in the U.S. this potentially radical movement of Jewish studies was lost, as

> it is [in America] that Jewish studies became transformed into a conservative field whose goal was the incorporation of Jewish history into the larger framework of Western civilization ... Jewish studies, its proponents argued, deserved a seat at the banquet because of its contributions to the West, not because it unsettled any established understandings of the West.[37]

This can be identified as part of a project of Jewish assimilation: as we will see throughout this book, histories are made to be the same, to reflect the same inquiries and concerns, just as the rabbi at the beginning of this section strove to demonstrate that she maintained the same concerns as those of the American state. It is significant that this occurred in the U.S., a site under examination in this book as exemplary of the ambivalences and anxieties which have been a part of this project of Jewish assimilation. However, in a larger categorization of the Christian West, Heschel argues that Jews are outsiders, occupying 'a position of ambivalence and ambiguity that functions as a kind of counterhistory to the multicultural account of the West: not all white Europeans are Christians'.[38] Jews in this telling function as a potential reminder of difference, thereby complicating not just their own histories but also the histories and identities of the societies in which they live. This will, and does, unsurprisingly, cause consternation.

From here it is useful to turn to the histories under examination: those contained within Holocaust pedagogies in New York. In the teachings of the Holocaust under consideration it is Jewishness as a racial and national descriptor which comes to the fore. These bases for Jewishness were expressed repeatedly as a source of anxiety for teachers of the Holocaust, based on a fear that the Holocaust could be repeated: that Jews could again be targeted for being Jews. This fear then leads into a more generalized anxiety that Jews and Jewishness do not have a place in the world. This was manifested in a number of different expressions in the interviews conducted, which will now be discussed: that engaging with non-Jewish world systems is problematic; that democracy itself is not a system to be trusted; and that there is a history of persecution of Jews which (inevitably) recurs over and over again.

Holocaust Pedagogy in New York

In interviews with teachers of the Holocaust in New York, there were a number of moments when teachers expressed anxieties about interactions with others, and of living in non-Jewish countries and having to engage with non-Jewish systems of governance quite directly. The nationalizing and racializing of both Jewishness and Americanness has meant that Jews are, as was explicated above, figured as both an internal and external Other. This has, unsurprisingly, been taken on by many teachers. A teacher at a school in Manhattan explained that she:

> discuss[es] the attitude of non-Jews towards Jews and how it's unpredictable at times and how Jews are normally subjected to a double standard whereas – you know, let's say, for example, in Middle Eastern conflicts, the Arabs can use certain methods of terrorism and afflict others in various ways, but when the Jews use firearms, the UN [United Nations] enacts a resolution against their use of firearms and so on. So there's a double standard, and the double standard has always been prevalent in Jewish history and in the Holocaust, talking about the build-up or rise of Nazi Germany and how the Jews were subjected to double standards in the Nuremberg Laws and how . . . the propaganda led the Germans to believe they were actually true.[39]

Here we can see a reflection on the idea that Jews hover on the margins, at any moment able to be pushed outside. Jewishness is constituted by a history of subjugation by other national and international entities. Importantly, at the forefront of this statement sits a governing concern about antisemitism – what links the UN with Nazi Germany in this teacher's imaginary is that they are both dominated by, and fundamentally constructed by, antisemitism. There is the direct equation of the two, through their treatment of Jews. This comparison relies on a deep suspicion and distrust of non-Jewish institutions, for the implications of her statement are broader than just Nazi Germany and the UN – there is the idea that everyone is (potentially) hostile to 'Jewish interests'. Yet there is ambivalence: we must also remember that she makes this claim *while continuing to live and teach in the U.S.* It must be concluded therefore that she has *some* faith in non-Jewish institutions. This point is crucial to understanding the anxiety I am sketching.

Moreover, this teacher positioned Arabs as dominant in the world in the same way as the Nazis were. An important connection between the two groups is that they currently figure in a Zionist imaginary as the leading proponents of antisemitism – Nazis as the perpetrators of the Holocaust and 'Arabs', as a descriptor for Middle Eastern peoples who are imagined as being in constant conflict with Israel, deemed by many to be motivated by antisemitism.[40] By suggesting that the UN is denying the same support they provide Arabs to the Jews, this teacher is claiming that the UN is colluding with these 'antisemitic Arabs' and it is thereby a signifier of an international system which, in this imagining, keeps Jews on the outside. By locating this problem in the UN this teacher is suggesting that it is a worldwide problem, of Jews never being allowed to truly be part of modern governmental institutions. While I will return to this again in Chapter Three, it must be stressed here that I am not arguing that this is the total sum of Jewish life in non-Jewish countries, for, as mentioned above, Jews in many ways do successfully live in these countries. Rather, it is that the teacher expresses these as concerns: in her rendering, Jews are permanently ill-at-ease, permanently discriminated against and second-class, in non-Jewish systems.

Furthermore, this teacher speaks of an amorphous mass of Jews, as though the Jews who were persecuted in the Holocaust are the same as those living in Israel and using firearms – there are no national, political or temporal distinctions made. In this way, Jews are a racialized group, defined by a form of lineage. The final important part of this teacher's statement is her description of what Jews do militarily versus what Arabs do: 'Arabs use certain methods of terrorism', implying large-scale organization and destruction; 'Jews use firearms', she stated, which implies a much lesser degree of death and destruction. In the generalized Western imagination at this time of a globalized 'War on Terror' which fundamentally involves the idea of a war between the Arab Middle East and the U.S. government and its allies, terrorism is figured as much more severe than the use of a firearm. Thus, according to this teacher, not only are Jews the victims of a double standard which is nationalized – according to Jews and Arabs (as though it is impossible to be both) – but that double standard also applies to their relative actions.

This was repeated by another teacher in the same school, who explained that the 'number one' thing she wants her students to learn from studying the Holocaust:

> is that for students today, our Jewish children today, to understand that as much as America is a very democratic society, life in the dawning years of the Holocaust was just as democratic in the respective societies, and the calamity of the nature of the Holocaust was able to transpire. I think it is important for our kids to understand that complacency and that easiness with which they [have] begun to regard American society in the twenty-first century is actually quite a myth. And they need to understand the factors that enabled the Holocaust to take place, they need to understand the conditions, they need to understand the reactions or lack of reactions coming from the outside world. They also have to understand what the victims of the Holocaust lost.[41]

This teacher seems to be arguing that this loss was, at least partly, of naivety and faith in the Western world, or perhaps the Jews' place within it. The Holocaust here is figured as a radical break, despite the fact that even immediately prior to the Holocaust Jews were not allowed into the U.S. (or Australia) to escape Nazism: the Holocaust was not necessarily the complete rupture which this teacher imagines that it was. Yet, if we approach it another way, the break the teacher describes can be understood as a moment when Jews became radically Other, or Outsiders. This teacher is attempting to impart knowledge of the precariousness of the Jewish position in 'democratic America'; she is trying to convince the students that they too should feel anxious and uncertain about what will happen to them. As I will discuss below with reference to Australia, in histories of migration anxiety arises from the racializing of a national group, and the making visibly different of those who can be distinguished as different. 'The factors that enabled the Holocaust to take place' are, in this telling, the racializing of difference. As long as difference within U.S. society remains racialized, Jews will be figured as Other; this is what haunts this teacher, as she narrates her anxiety through Holocaust narratives to her students.

Similarly, another teacher in a school in Brooklyn explained that she wants the students to understand the Holocaust as a:

> loss. It's not just an abstract 'Oh, once upon a time there were Jews who resided here', but we want them to feel the loss. We want them to know what was lost. There was a rich and vibrant life in Eastern Europe and Western Europe. And it's hard to say, but the 'Never Again' idea, which is problematic but nevertheless we want the kids to understand that this is what was lost and *don't ever think that it can't happen again* because we're living in a very dangerous world and *the kids today feel that*. And the slogan 'Never Again', is that in fact a reality? And lots of the kids feel that today we're living in a dangerous world and that I think that you have to be ever-vigilant about antisemitism and be aware that there are current lessons from the Holocaust.[42]

For this teacher the idea of 'Never Again' is important because there is, she and her students believe, a current and continuing threat. It is a dangerous and uncertain world – she dwells on this idea of danger, repeating that it is 'a dangerous world' – and remaining vigilant and attentive to antisemitism is one way to guard against this danger. Learning about histories of antisemitism links the experiences of her students today to those of Jews in the past – she wants them to understand what happened in the Holocaust as a way of linking them with both the past and future. The past is where the dangerous antisemitism led to the Holocaust, the future is where the dangerous world has the *potential* to lead to another Holocaust. These students are being taught to view themselves as part of one moment in a long history of antisemitism and persecution (or potential persecution).

This was repeated by a teacher at an all-girls school in Brooklyn, who stated that when teaching her students she explains that 'when you see an accusation about something where there's blood libels, or might be from the Protocol of [the Elders of] Zion, and I keep trying to show that it may be history, but it's also current events. It's ancient history, it's history and it's probably the future, unfortunately.'[43] What continues for this teacher is the linking of Jewishness with antisemitism – the history is perceived to be one of antisemitic persecution in a world of identity built on blood and heritage.

To return again to the larger U.S. Jewish context, we can see that this looking backwards and forwards through the lens of antisemitism can also be seen in an email sent by Rabbi Marvin Hier, Dean and Founder of the Simon Wiesenthal Center (SWC), in California, on March 28, 2007. The email was sent to a Wiesenthal Center email list at Pesach in order to ask for donations, and explained that:

> If there is anything the Jewish people have contributed to history, it is the importance of memory. We have survived only because we remember. We begin Passover each year by singing with our families and friends from the Haggadah, 'for it was not one man alone who stood up against us but in every generation there are those who will attempt to destroy us'. We recall the Crusades, the Pogroms, and the Holocaust. And now in our own time, the new plague of terrorism and the rebirth of antisemitism.[44]

The email then explained the various countries in which the SWC worked at the time, and the actions they had recently undertaken. Countries which were shown to have prevalent antisemitism which required combating were Belgium, Canada, Germany, Korea, Austria, Ukraine, Israel (by a German Bishop) and Japan. The email concluded with the following 'thought':

> In 1995, the then Chief of Staff of the Israeli Defense Forces, Ehud Barak, participated in a commemoration of the 50th anniversary of the end of the Second World War by piloting a plane that flew over Auschwitz concentration camp. As he flew over the former death camp he said, 'we have arrived 50 years too late'. The essence of our work is to remember when we can still make a difference. We need your help – we are prepared to do the work, but we cannot do it alone. Your support enables us to stand up to these haters and to protect the safety of Jews and good people everywhere.

The first quotation taken from this email demonstrates how the SWC locates attitudes to Jews around the world today as being dominated by antisemitic feelings. While it is important to take into account that these statements are being written in order to encourage donations to the SWC, and therefore there is a need to explain the work the Center undertakes, the email provides the impression that these problems of antisemitism are historical and continuing in a way which needs to be taken seriously. By referring readers to the Biblical origins of antisemitism, as well as to its vast history, the SWC makes it clear that antisemitism is something which may reappear in new forms, but is also entrenched and needs to be constantly remembered in order to be combated. We can see a link here to the Brooklyn teacher quoted previously, who similarly brought together the Holocaust and terrorism. The second quotation points to the limited ways in which it is conceived that antisemitism can be arrested: through military means, donating money, remembering and watching others take action. Yet, most importantly, what this email highlights is the apparently never-ending, all-pervasive and ever-powerful antisemitism which continues to exist. There is a deep-seated anxiety at work here: the project of existing as Jews in the world requires constant attention and work, for there are and always will be forces which 'attempt to destroy us'.

As such, this email from the SWC exemplifies the concerns which permeate these examples of American Jewish communities today: I describe it at length here not because it is unique or the only example, but as one example from many.

Jewishness has its roots in American society in an interplay between being insiders and outsiders, and has resulted in an ongoing negotiation of this place, as we saw in the examples which opened this chapter. This is a result of Jewishness being conceived variously in racial, national and economic terms: largely in terms of perceived qualities (and quantities) of whiteness and its attendant signifiers of belonging. In the terms of this book, this has caused great anxiety in Holocaust educators and others – as will be shown in the following section – leading many to convey ideas and histories of uncertainty of the place of Jews in the U.S. and the world more generally.

Australian Considerations

Before we can consider the permeation of these anxieties into Jewish discourses in Australia it is important to understand the ways in which Jewishness has been conceived of and articulated in this nation-state. Jewishness has a long history as being racialized in Australia, as part of a broader racializing of all migrants and citizens. As the historiography makes clear, in Australia, whiteness has coalesced around race. In his history of Australian immigration policies, James Jupp explains that racialization has been a central consideration in immigration policies.[45] Australia, he writes, is a country predominantly made up of immigrants, yet is also largely homogeneous in its racial and ethnic makeup.[46] This has occurred because of the existence of policies and pieces of legislation – such as the Immigration Restriction Act of 1901 and the Migration Act of 1958 – which instrumentalized the White Australia Policy.[47] Through various formal and informal procedures these Acts have worked for the great majority of Australia's history to ensure that immigration was restricted to British peoples. Indeed, even in the late 1930s, when the Governor-General, Lord Gowrie, argued that Australia must 'populate or perish', the Australian government was concerned about an influx of Jewish refugees, as well as other ethnic groups deemed to be 'non-white', such as Italians and Greeks.[48]

In 1938, according to historian Klaus Neumann, the Australian government decided that there should be a limit of 5,100 Jewish immigrants each year and that to determine who was and was not Jewish, immigration application forms would now require applicants 'to state whether or not they belonged to the Jewish race'.[49] Moreover, at the Evian Conference, which was called by Franklin Roosevelt in March 1938 to establish a world response to the problem of German Jewish refugees, the Australian representative (Thomas Walter White, the Minister for Trade and Customs) infamously argued that:

> [u]nder the circumstances, Australia cannot do more, for it will be appreciated that in a young country manpower from the source from which most of its citizens has sprung is preferred, while undue privileges cannot be given to

one particular class of non-British subjects without injustice to others. It will no doubt be appreciated also that, as we have no real racial problem, we are not desirous of importing one by encouraging any scheme of large-scale foreign migration.[50]

And indeed this approach did not cease with the Holocaust: in postwar Australia, the migration of Jews from Europe was still restricted.[51] Jewishness was being figured in Australian immigration discourses as racial – Jews were excluded on the basis of their perceived racial foreignness from a society that was attempting to construct itself as racially white. Jewishness was thereby conceived of as an indicator of non-whiteness, and, more than that, as a pollutant whose mere presence would cause a 'problem'. This Jewishness, however, was of a particular form, as Jews had been present in Australia since the earliest days of British colonization. British Jews, as well as other Jews who had arrived previously, were seemingly not caught up in this same racialization (or their presence conveniently forgotten).

Jupp explains the racial elements of Australian immigration policy as follows:

How, then, did Australia become so similar in its culture and ethnic makeup to [England]? Certainly not by accident. The whole thing was carefully and deliberately planned within the context of the worldwide British Empire . . . using immigration as a method of controlling population change . . . Australia has long and strong xenophobic, racist and insular traditions and they have always influenced immigration policy. Policy has always been influenced by ideologies: imperialism, racism, utilitarianism, economic rationalism and humanitarianism.[52]

And, as such, potential immigrants were considered along these ideological axes, grouped according to their perceived identities – and it was through these processes that these racialized identities were created and reinforced.[53] It follows that since Australian Federation in 1901, peoples coming to Australia have been assessed within a system of whiteness and thereby figured as being either within or apart from the nation. Racial discourses have dominated immigration legislation and formal practices and have figured British peoples – or Anglo-Celts, as Jupp named them – as white and all others, to varying degrees, as non-white.[54] After the White Australia Policy came the era of assimilation, wherein 'as in many other countries, assimilation was seen as necessary to full acceptance into society. This society was, itself, always changing its character in response to new arrivals and it was not always clear what "assimilation" might mean.'[55] Yet, Jupp explains, assimilation did always involve the push for the outward removal of traces of one's previous identity – language, religion and customs.[56] This was, for many, understandably a site for the playing out of an anxious relationship with the racialized Australian nation.

This ambivalent, anxious and intertwined relationship between Jews and the Australian state – as exemplary of Western nation-states more generally – has been explored by Jon Stratton. In a discussion of the White Australia Policy, Stratton explains that '[i]n the case of Australia, a settler-state where the nation itself had to be brought into existence, the ambivalent situation of the Jews was precisely played out through the processes employed to define and form the Australian nation'.[57] The Australian nation was being formulated along racial lines, which, as stressed previously, required that Jews were racialized in such a way that meant that Jews have struggled to be properly a part of Australian society. Stratton writes that:

> [t]he persistence of a racial antisemitism was linked to the Australian nationalist desire for a homogeneous white nation. From this time on, the fear for Australia's assimilated Jewry, caught in the ambivalence of their white/nonwhite status, was that any increased visibility for the Jews, any signs of racial/cultural difference, would mark them as a threat to the homogeneity of the nation.[58]

Jewish people were always a minority in Australia – the accentuation of the difference of the Jews was therefore not about a numerical strength or category, but rather one of making difference visible. This has meant that to find a place for themselves Jews have defined themselves (and been defined by wider society) at least partially along racial lines.[59] Yet this has been a task which cannot be completed – as Stratton suggests, Jews have occupied an interstitial space, being both white and non-white. Stratton claims that this has posed a threat to the Australian nation, but it is important also to consider that it has posed a threat to Jewishnesses: it has meant a partial (re)definition of Jewishness as racial. This in turn has led to a striving for homogeneity with the broader Australian nation, to a Jewish search for ways to replicate these 'white' ways of defining a community; it has also led to the maintenance of difference, in order to preserve the specificities of Jewish identities and cultures. The question of whether this is possible, and the negotiation of this possibility, produces anxiety.

If we turn to Holocaust education in schools in Melbourne we can see, in a similar manner to that which is expressed in New York, examples of an overwhelming fear and anxiety in the face of what is considered to be an ancient and continuing history of Jew-hatred. This hatred of Jews relies on Jews being positioned as essentially, or in some ways racially, Other. Two Melbourne curricula – from different points on the religious spectrum – explain at the beginning that:

> [i]n the pagan world, the Jews' God and laws were clearly the causes of Jew-hatred. Pagans generally tolerated different peoples and different gods, but the Jews and 'their' God did not merely differ, they threatened. The Jews' God alone was God, and He was the God everywhere – which meant, of course, that all gods of the pagans were false. Understandably, this infuriated the Jews' neighbours. The Jews of

the pre-Christian world were hated because they were Jews, not because they were rich, or successful, or for any other reason not directly related to their Judaism.[60]

They outline Christian antisemitism – which, it is asserted, is predicated on the idea that Jews killed Jesus Christ.[61] Islamic antisemitism, it is explained, 'is deeply rooted. Islam, too, was born from the womb of Judaism; it, too, was rejected by the Jews whose validation was sought'. The curricula explain that there was no antagonism between Judaism and Islam, or Jews and the Prophet Muhammad more directly, until:

> Jews rejected Muhammad's prophetic claims and refused to become Muslims. This alone infuriated Muhammad. But even more angering, the Jews publicly noted the errors in Muhammad's biblical teachings and may have even ridiculed his claims to prophecy. As a result, Muhammad turned against the Jews and their religion and he never forgave them.[62]

The explanation then links Christian antisemitism and Nazi antisemitism, exploring the ways in which Christian antisemitism informed Nazi ideology. This works to create a sense in which antisemitism – or the hatred and persecution of Jews – is eternal and ubiquitous, both natural and historical, and depends on Jewish assertions of difference. In short, it is inescapable, as long as Jews retain that difference. As evidenced by the fact that the two schools who use this document are based on different approaches to Judaism, this understanding is more pervasive than one interpretation of Judaism. Altogether, this provides the material ground for the anxiety – if antisemitism is constant and everywhere, where can Jews go to be safe as Jews? It ensures that an anxiety about Jewish difference follows.

Sexualizing and Gendering Anxious Jewishness in Melbourne

These anxieties over the place of Jews can also be seen in other more informal Holocaust education settings, such as in the March of the Living (MOTL) education sessions. The March of the Living programme is run throughout the Jewish world and involves Jewish students aged approximately 15–16 learning about the Holocaust, Israel and Zionism, and then travelling to Poland for Yom Hashoah (Holocaust Memorial Day) and to Israel for Yom Hazikaron (Day of Remembrance for Israel's dead soldiers) and Yom Ha'atzmaut (Israeli Independence Day), all three of which take place within the space of ten days in May each year.[63] In February and March 2007 I observed the education sessions in Melbourne, which were run by Holocaust educators from Jewish schools, Zionist youth group *madrichim* (leaders), and Holocaust survivors from Melbourne and Sydney.

At one of the sessions the students were divided into three groups and were taught about Israeli society and ideas of Zionism. One of the *madrichim*, Ilana, read the poem 'The City of Slaughter' by Chaim Nachman Bialik with the students.[64] The poem describes the Kishinev Pogrom, which took place on 6–7 April 1903 in Kishinev, a town in the Russian Empire. Ilana focused the students on one passage in particular, as follows:

> Descend then, to the cellars of the town,
> There where the virginal daughters of thy folk were fouled,
> Where seven heathen flung a woman down,
> [...]
> Note also, do not fail to note,
> In that dark corner, and behind that cask
> Crouched husbands, bridegrooms, brothers, peering from the cracks,
> Watching the sacred bodies struggling underneath
> The bestial breath,
> Stifled in filth, and swallowing their blood!
> Such silence will take hold of thee, thy heart will fail
> With pain and shame, yet I
> Will let no tear fall from thine eye.
> [...] Your deaths are without reason; your lives are without cause.[65]

Ilana used these passages to emphasize the difference between the 'Old Jew' – the Diaspora Jew – and the 'New Jew' – the strong, Zionist Jew living in the State of Israel. She explained that she specifically focused on this as it presents contrasting ideas of what it is to be a Jewish man – the Diaspora man was someone who would cower as his wife or daughter was being raped; he was the type of man who would not work for his own self-determination but would wait for others to grant it. Importantly, in Ilana's analysis of the poem the women were absent – the students were encouraged to read the poem from the perspective of the figure she identified as the weak man. Non-European Jews were also made invisible or absent as she spoke explicitly of the conflict over Jewish identity as coalescing in this Old (European) Jew and New (Israeli) Jew. Ilana directed her students away from the centre of the room (in the poem) and into the corner; away from the women, and towards the men.

In the teaching of this poem we can see an anxiety over the gendering and sexualizing of Jewishness. Ilana was comfortable, and indeed quite forceful, in her description and analysis of the men cowering in the corner. Her description involved them hiding and peering out *because* they lacked a hyper-masculine strength. The women, in their absence from her discussion, are also constructed in terms of lack – they lack the ability to be discussed, to be represented. They cannot speak. By not talking about them Ilana was excising them from the discussion, and therefore from their place in discussions of acceptable Jewishness. Their position as Jewish women being raped – the central image in this section of Bialik's poem – is pushed to the corner, and the men are dragged into the centre. Sex is pushed to the corner, and lack dragged into the centre. The anxiety here rests in the idea that Jewish women in the Diaspora are constituted by this raping – for Ilana, like the students to whom she speaks, lives outside Israel, in this Diaspora that she describes. She is, after all, also unconsciously narrating herself, her own femininity. Her anxious response can be detected in her inability (for it is more than mere reluctance) to speak of the women being raped. Indeed, it is perhaps unspeakable or unrepresentable for Ilana as part of the Jewishnesses which she seeks to convey. Rape is, for many, unspeakable.

When, in a later interview, I asked Ilana whether this lesson had been purposely gendered – that is, whether she had intentionally chosen a poem about the emasculation of Diaspora Jewish men – she said that she had not intended it to be a gendered lesson at all.[66] Rather, in her eyes, it was to be a lesson about self-determination, devoid of any gendered implications. Yet the gendered lessons continued as, in the session with the students, Ilana also demonstrated the difference between Old and New by showing the students posters from both the First and Second *Aliyah* (waves of Jewish migration to Israel), which were predominantly of strong, physical men – it was these men that she drew attention to, asking the students to describe the men. She also told the students, seemingly without any sense of irony, that these men look almost (but not quite) like Nazi posters of typical Aryan men.

Another source of anxiety that permeates the use of this poem in this context is that the audience was made up of young Jews of predominantly Eastern European heritage, who live in Melbourne and were about to travel to Poland and Israel. They were hesitant and uncertain about how they would feel about being in Poland, but seemed almost universally certain that Israel would be a site of happiness and empowerment.[67] This poem then functions as a reminder of the idea that Poland, and by extension potentially any Diaspora location, are not places of empowerment – that, instead, they are sites of sadness and pogroms, disempowerment and emasculation (or the potential for these things).[68] This is quite a forceful lesson to be teaching teenagers as they embark on this trip. The anxiety then, it seems, comes in the force of the lesson: that Ilana would choose to teach this lesson of Israeli strength by teaching about Diaspora death and destruction that brings shame, blood, dishonour, death with no reason and life 'with no cause'.

In using this poem it appears as though Ilana is seeking to convince the students that living in the Diaspora cannot be a choice – that one merely finds oneself there in a state of disempowered exile, but by choosing to leave, to make *aliyah*, one can make oneself an agent of history.[69] She is anxious that they could choose otherwise, and so aims to install her fears about emasculation in the minds of the students. And so, in this bringing together of the Holocaust and Zionism, she makes the decision to reinforce and perpetuate the narrative that Jews cannot be empowered in the Diaspora – that the only place where Jews can have self-determination is in

Israel, the 'Jewish nation-state'. The centrality of the nation-state to at once resolve and create further anxieties is underlined.

And thus we can see that in Australia there are a number of strands of anxieties over the ability of Jews to be a part of Australian society. From an examination of Australian immigration history more broadly we can understand that Jewishness has largely been racialized by the Australian state. This racial basis – and the exclusions wrought through its legislative effects – has been a source of consternation and anxiety in Melbourne, particularly since the Holocaust. As has been shown previously, this can be seen in various institutional practices and teachings within Melbourne Jewish communities. Alongside this racial basis has evolved other spheres of influence, such as nationality and gender. Altogether, we can appreciate that this is an anxiety which is founded on an apprehension that Jews as a group, however defined, have an ambivalent and uncertain place within Australia and America.

The teachers in this study therefore contain these anxieties in their teachings for a combination of reasons: the events of the Holocaust, the ways in which their identities are made different within Australian or American societies, and the predominance of Zionist discourses which play an important role in keeping these Jews anxious about their place in the Diaspora. The many discourses work together to create an anxious environment: an environment of distrust and fear that there is no place for Jews in a non-Jewish society. The ways in which teachers of the histories of the Holocaust manage this anxiety – the pedagogical negotiations which take place, of which we caught a glimpse in this chapter, and which can themselves be productive of anxious feelings – will now be discussed in the following chapters.

Notes

1. Michael Marrus explains that at the end of the war, in 1945, 'the Allies encountered no more than 100,000 Jews in Central Europe . . . We now know that about one million remained in Europe outside the Soviet Union. Some of these were liberated outside the Reich, others did not declare themselves as Jews to the liberating armies, and still others were not enumerated as such by the refugee workers in charge.' M.R. Marrus. 1985. *The Unwanted: European Refugees in the Twentieth Century*, New York: Oxford University Press, 331. For information on Jewish migration to Australia see S.D. Rutland. 2005. *The Jews in Australia*, Melbourne: Cambridge University Press, 10. Post-war Jewish immigration to Australia saw a significant increase in the Jewish population there. This was the largest mass increase, which contrasts with America, where larger Jewish immigrant populations had come from Russia at the end of the nineteenth and beginning of the twentieth centuries. See H.R. Diner. 2004. *The Jews of the United States*, Berkeley: University of California Press, 71–111, 259–65 and G. Sorin. 1997. *Tradition Transformed: The Jewish Experience in America*, Baltimore, MD: Johns Hopkins University Press, 54–6.

2. Stratton, *Jewish Identity in Western Pop Culture*, 118.
3. For an overview of the ways in which race, and gender, are fundamental to Australian and American national identities, see for example J. Hogan. 2009. *Gender, Race and National Identity: Nations of Flesh and Blood*, New York: Routledge, 17–33, 75–91; P. Wolfe. 2001. 'Land, Labor, and Difference: Elementary Structures of Race', *American Historical Review* 106(3), 866–905.
4. Hage, *White Nation*.
5. For information on Australia see, for example, J. Stratton. 1999. 'The Color of Jews: Jews, Race, and the White Australia Policy', in S.L. Gilman and M. Shain (eds), *Jewries at the Frontier: Accommodation, Identity, Conflict*, Urbana: University of Illinois Press, 309–34; Hage, *White Nation*. For America see K. Brodkin. 1998. *How Jews Became White Folks and What That Says About Race in America*, New Brunswick, NJ: Rutgers University Press, 1–24; M. D'Innocenzo and J.P. Sirefman (eds). 1992. *Immigration and Ethnicity: American Society – 'Melting Pot' or 'Salad Bowl'*, Westport, CT: Greenwood Press; B.O. Hing. 1997. *To Be an American: Cultural Pluralism and the Rhetoric of Assimilation*, New York: New York University Press; G.E. Pozzetta (ed.). 1991. *Assimilation, Acculturation, and Social Mobility*, New York: Garland Publishing. For an exploration of the way ideas of the American conception of the 'melting pot' are taught see T.R. Richardson and E.V. Johanningmeir. 2003. *Race, Ethnicity, and Education: What Is Taught in School*, Greenwich, CT: Information Age Publishing, in particular Chapter Six.
6. For a sample of works which explore the variousness of these identities see Kaye/Kantrowitz, *The Colors of Jews*; Stratton, 'The Color of Jews', 309–34; P.R. Bartrop. 1999. 'Living within the Frontier: Early Colonial Australia, Jews, and Aborigines', in S.L. Gilman and M. Shain (eds), *Jewries at the Frontier: Accommodation, Identity, Conflict*, Urbana, IL: University of Illinois Press, 91–110; E.L. Goldstein. 2006. *The Price of Whiteness: Jews, Race, and American Identity*, Princeton, NJ: Princeton University Press.
7. Reconstructionist Judaism is, according to the synagogue's website, centred around ideas of participation and continual development. The website states that 'Reconstructionists recognize the human authorship of all religious traditions and acknowledge that no tradition has a monopoly on religious truths. Our affirmation of Judaism as our own tradition implies no sense of exclusiveness or superiority with regard to others. On the contrary, we welcome dialogue with persons of good will in all traditions, both within and outside of Judaism.' Retrieved 23 February 2009 from http://www.westendsynagogue.org/reconstructionism.shtml. For a fuller description of the Reconstructionist movement see a book written by the founder of the movement, M.M. Kaplan. 1981. *Judaism as a Civilization: Toward a Reconstruction of American-Jewish Life*, Philadelphia: The Jewish Publication Society of America and the Reconstructionist Press.
8. Yet this information is available from http://icasualties.org/Iraq/index.aspx. Retrieved 21 September 2009. Some Jewish blogs have utilized this information, for example *Jewschool*. See Aryeh Cohen. 2009. 'Lest We Forget', 12 February. Retrieved 23 February 2009 from http://jewschool.com/2009/02/12/15184/lest-we-forget/.
9. For, of course, remembering is never devoid of politics. See Young, *The Texture of Memory*; Bal, Crewe and Spitzer (eds), *Acts of Memory: Cultural Recall in the Present*; Boyarin, *Storm from Paradise*.
10. B. Anderson. 1983. *Imagined Communities: Reflections on the Origin and Spread of Nationalism*, London: Verso, 132.
11. The USHMM focuses primarily on Jews as the victims of the Holocaust. While they do mention other groups, this is done sparingly. A similar focus on Jews in this way

will be explored in Chapters Three and Four. For other analyses of the USHMM see T. Cole. 1999. *Selling the Holocaust: From Auschwitz to Schindler, How History Is Bought, Packaged, and Sold*, New York: Routledge, 146–71; M. Berenbaum. 2006. *The World Must Know: The History of the Holocaust as Told in the United States Holocaust Memorial Museum*, Second Edition, Washington, DC: United States Holocaust Memorial Museum; and E.T. Linenthal. 1995. *Preserving Memory: The Struggle to Create America's Holocaust Museum*, New York: Viking Penguin. Philip Gourevitch presents a compelling and moving critique of the USHMM, questioning its purpose and politics. P. Gourevitch. July 1993. 'Behold Now Behemoth', *Harper's Magazine* 287(1718), 55–62.

12. Peter Novick makes this point as well. See P. Novick. 1999. *The Holocaust and Collective Memory: The American Experience*, London: Bloomsbury, 63–64.
13. She often does not make clear that this is a limiting approach. Rather, she makes some quite general conclusions about the 'whiteness' of Jews from this group.
14. Brodkin, *How Jews Became White Folks*, 9.
15. Ibid. Aileen Moreton-Robinson critiques Brodkin's work for its avoidance of discussion of Native Americans, arguing that Brodkin describes whiteness in relation to the blackness of slavery, and in doing so further represses the dispossession at the heart of the American nation-state. See A. Moreton-Robinson. 2008. 'Writing Off Treaties: White Possession in the United States Critical Whiteness Studies Literature,' in A. Moreton-Robinson, M. Casey and F. Nicoll (eds), *Transnational Whiteness Matters*, Lanham, MD: Lexington Books, 84–5.
16. Brodkin, *How Jews Became White Folks*, 9.
17. See Hage, *White Nation*.
18. This perhaps reflects the school of Whiteness Studies which was prevalent at the time Brodkin was writing. Led in America by David Roediger, who followed W.E.B. Dubois, focus was placed on whiteness as an effect of class and labour. This obviously laid the groundwork for Brodkin's work. See D.R. Roediger. 1999. *The Wages of Whiteness: Race and the Making of the American Working Class*, Revised ed., London: Verso. Roediger has also examined immigrant groups in the U.S. and the ways in which they have been made white and thereby accepted (albeit sometimes provisionally) within dominant American societies and power-structures. See D.R. Roediger. 2005. *Working Towards Whiteness: How America's Immigrants Became White. The Strange Journey from Ellis Island to the Suburbs*. New York: Basic Books. Similarly, David Theo Goldberg (whose work is part of a larger body of literature, which is too extensive to properly deal with here) juxtaposes Jewishness and African-Americanness, arguing that Jews in America, primarily by virtue of their class position, have been made white (where African-Americans have been made black). This, he says, also ensures that both groups are foundational to America. See for instance D.T. Goldberg. 1997. *Racial Subjects: Writing on Race in America*, New York: Routledge, 129–47. There has also been a focus on the racial qualities of whiteness. bell hooks was an early proponent of the importance of considering blackness as a racial category, with its own system of knowledge and control which arose through representations and cultural practices. See bell hooks. 1992. *Black Looks: Race and Representation*, Boston: South End Press. A more recent edited collection brought together various strands of conceptions of whiteness and blackness in terms of racial categories. See Ruth Frankenberg (ed.). 1997. *Displacing Whiteness: Essays in Social and Cultural Criticism*, Durham: Duke University Press. The work of Frankenberg generally has been foundational in this respect. See Ruth Frankenberg. 1993. *White Women, Race Matters: The Social Construction of Whiteness*, Minneapolis: University of Minnesota Press. Ann Pellegrini brings together ideas of blackness and Jewishness as racialized and embodied, alongside Jewishness as gendered. See Ann

Pellegrini. 1997. 'Whiteface Performances: "Race," Gender, and Jewish Bodies,' in J. Boyarin and D. Boyarin (eds), *Jews and Other Differences: The New Jewish Cultural Studies*, Minneapolis: University of Minnesota Press, 108–49.
19. One teacher, however, described her school as poor, and this seemed important to the way they approached their ideas about the Holocaust. Interview with Teacher A at School NYF.
20. Yet, class divisions do exist amongst Jews in New York, and in Melbourne. As demonstrated by a recent report, there is a vast, and often hidden, differential gap within New York Jewry. The UJA-Federation of New York Annual Report from 2007–08 shows this: in that year they raised a total of US$227.2 million, contributed by 65,000 donors. They also look after 244,000 Jews who are 'identified as poor' and 104,000 who are 'near poor'. See *UJA-Federation of New York Annual Report 2007-2008*, 'Part 2: Our Collective Impact'. Retrieved 18 December 2014 from http://d4ovttrzyow8g.cloudfront.net/259.pdf. This is similar to the situation in Australia. For the Australian context see Philip Mendes. 2006. 'Lifting the Lid on Poverty in the Jewish Community', in M. Fagenblat, M. Landau and N. Wolski (eds), *New under the Sun: Jewish Australians on Religion, Politics & Culture*, Melbourne: Black Inc., 357.
21. Jonathan Boyarin also discusses this, arguing that Jewish assimilation in America can only be understood as being part of a larger process of change which was occurring in America. See Boyarin, *Storm from Paradise*, 82–83.
22. Biale, 'The Melting Pot and Beyond', 27.
23. Ibid., 21–25. For a copy of the play accompanied by an introductory essay which draws out the main concerns of the play and provides a history of its creation and early performances see E. Nahshon (ed.). 2006. *From the Ghetto to the Melting Pot: Israel Zangwill's Jewish Plays. Three Playscripts by Israel Zangwill*, Detroit, MI: Wayne State University Press, 211–363. For a different discussion about Zangwill and *The Melting Pot*, which examines it in relationship to Jews, music and assimilation, see S.L. Gilman. 2006. *Multiculturalism and the Jews*, New York: Routledge, 73-84.
24. Biale, 'The Melting Pot and Beyond', 29.
25. Their novels include: J.S. Foer. 2002. *Everything Is Illuminated*, New York: Penguin Books; J.S. Foer. 2005. *Extremely Loud and Incredibly Close*, Boston: Houghton Mifflin; N. Krauss. 2005. *The History of Love*, New York: W.W. Norton & Company; N. Krauss. 2010. *Great House*, Camberwell: Viking Books; M. Chabon. 2007. *The Yiddish Policeman's Union*, London: Harper Perennial; N. Englander. 2000. *For the Relief of Unbearable Urges*, London: Faber and Faber; N. Englander. 2012. *What We Talk About When We Talk About Anne Frank: Stories*, New York: Alfred A. Knopf.
26. A recent article in the *Australian Financial Review* entitled 'Outsider No Longer' explores the literary history of Jews in New York, arguing that 'In its glory days [of the mid-twentieth century], Jewish-American writing was an indicator of a cultural shift ... that ushered in a final phase of assimilation for Jews at levels of American life previously unavailable to them.' This occurred, Vivian Gornick argues, due to the ways in which these Jewish-American authors played with language, creating new ways of writing and thinking. V. Gornick. 2009. 'Outsider No Longer', Review: *The Australian Financial Review*, 12 June, 1.
27. David Sax. 2009. 'Rise of the New Yiddishists', *Vanity Fair*, 8 April. Retrieved 16 April 2009 from http://www.vanityfair.com/culture/features/2009/04/yiddishists200904.
28. This can be seen, for instance, in the lyrics of the song 'Bublichki' from the 2006 album *Fresh Off Boat* by Golem, which plays with narrative time and language, moving between Yiddish and English, and seemingly between the past and the present. Golem, *Fresh Off Boat*, 2006, JDub Records. Retrieved 9 September 2009 from http://www.

golemrocks.com, or http://www.myspace.com/golemrocks. We can see this playing with time – creating 'a spatial, nonlinear ("diasporic") concept of time' in the poetry of Irena Klepfisz, as Jutta Schamp has noted. See Jutta Schamp. 1999. 'Beyond Assimilation: Difference and Reconfiguration in the Works of Irena Klepfisz, Jyl Lynn Felman, and Rebecca Goldstein', *ZAA* 47(3), 234. It should also be noted that in ultra-Orthodox communities in New York, Melbourne and Israel Yiddish is a vernacular language. But this is not the case in the more secular Jewish worlds which Sax writes of. Sax, 'Rise of the New Yiddishists'.
29. Peter Novick explores this anxiety and the way it has shaped American Jewish approaches to the Holocaust over the last twenty or so years. See Novick, *The Holocaust and Collective Memory*, 170–281.
30. Biale, 'The Melting Pot and Beyond', 27.
31. Gilman, *Multiculturalism and the Jews*, 147.
32. Biale, 'The Melting Pot and Beyond', 27–28. It is important to note here that Native Americans are not brought forward by these authors as an important group to consider in terms of the treatment of minority groups. See Chapter Four for a more in-depth discussion of this within a reflection upon settler colonial histories.
33. Ibid., 28.
34. Ibid.
35. S. Heschel. 1998. 'Jewish Studies as Counterhistory', in D. Biale, M. Galchinsky and S. Heschel (eds), *Insider/Outsider: American Jews and Multiculturalism*, Berkeley: University of California Press, 102–3.
36. John M. Efron. Summer 2004. 'From Mitteleuropa to the Middle East: Orientalism through a Jewish Lens', *The Jewish Quarterly Review* 94(3), 507.
37. Heschel, 'Jewish Studies as Counterhistory', 103.
38. Ibid., 112. For Todd M. Endelman this difference can be traced back to the beginning of the modern period, wherein 'from the viewpoint of the non-Jewish world, the problem with Jews was . . . their Jewishness, that is, their race, ethnicity, nationality. There was, then, a gaping discrepancy between the classic solution for the integration of the Jews – their conversion – and the problem – their essential Jewishness, which was seen as rooted in their flesh and blood and in the innermost recesses of their mind and was, thus, impervious to baptism.' T.M. Endelman. 1998. 'Memories of Jewishness: Jewish Converts and their Jewish Pasts', in E. Carlebach, J.M. Efron and D.N. Myers (eds), *Jewish History and Jewish Memory*, Waltham, MA: Brandeis University Press, 313.
39. Interview with Teacher A at School NYB. By juxtaposing Arabs and Jews in this way this teacher effaces the existence of Arab-Jews – Jews from Arab countries. Ella Shohat, amongst others, writes of this problem. See Shohat, 'Rupture and Return: Zionist Discourse and the Study of Arab-Jews,' in *Taboo Memories, Diasporic Voices*, 330–58. For a general exploration of the ways in which Mizrahi women face erasure in American Jewish communities today see the stories contained in L. Khazzoom (ed.). 2003. *The Flying Camel: Essays on Identity by Women of North African and Middle Eastern Jewish Heritage*, New York: Seal Press.
40. To pick but one example of this symbolic confluence, at the beginning of 2014 the Israeli 'Deputy Foreign Minister Zeev Elkin said Thursday that "the 1967 borders are Auschwitz borders" and therefore Likud has to reject any proposal to withdraw from the West Bank.' Barak Ravid. 2014. 'Deputy Foreign Minister: 1967 borders are Auschwitz borders', *Haaretz* 2 January. Retrieved 3 January 2014 from http://www.haaretz.com/news/diplomacy-defense/1.566644.
41. Interview with Teacher B at School NYB.
42. Interview with Teacher A at School NYD. Emphasis added.

43. Interview with Teacher A at School NYF.
44. Email received from Rabbi Marvin Hier, SWC Dean and Founder, (enewsletter@wiesenthal.net). 2007. 'Passover: A Time To Make A Difference', 28 March. Retrieved 18 December 2014 from http://www.wiesenthal.com/site/apps/nlnet/content2.aspx?c=ls KWLbPJLnF&b=4442245&ct=5852831#.VJJJj4uUekI.
45. J. Jupp. 2002. *From White Australia to Woomera: The Story of Australian Immigration*, Cambridge: Cambridge University Press. This point is made throughout, but for introductory ideas see 6–10.
46. Ibid., 5–6.
47. According to Klaus Neumann, '[i]n 1939, only 2 per cent of the non-indigenous population was not of Anglo-Celtic ancestry'. K. Neumann. 2004. *Refuge Australia: Australia's Humanitarian Record*, Sydney: UNSW Press, 16. Marilyn Lake and Henry Reynolds have explained that along with these two Acts, another important measure was the 'act of racial expulsion when the first parliament legislated to expel several thousand Pacific Islanders . . . who had been brought to labour in the sugar cane fields of north Queensland during the last decades of the nineteenth century'. Removing non-whites who were already inside Australia was as important as ensuring that none entered. M. Lake and H. Reynolds. 2008. *Drawing the Global Colour Line: White Men's Countries and the Question of Racial Equality*, Carlton: Melbourne University Publishing, 137.
48. Neumann, *Refuge Australia*, 16.
49. Ibid., 16–17.
50. Ibid., 17. This was of course incorrect – there were severe racial disparities and problems within Australia. A shortened version of this quote – which centres around the last sentence – has been used in a number of school curricula, and in Yad Vashem in Israel, as well as the Museum of Jewish Heritage: A Living Memorial to the Holocaust, in New York.
51. See, for example, M. Blakeney. 1987. 'The Australian Jewish Community and Postwar Mass Immigration from Europe', in W.D. Rubinstein (ed.), *Jews in the Sixth Continent*, Sydney: Allen & Unwin, 322–35.
52. Jupp, *From White Australia to Woomera*, 6.
53. Despite the changes introduced by the Whitlam government in 1972, 'wherein race, colour or creed would no longer be a basis for immigration control', racist policies of immigration continued, and continue today. See Ibid., 10, as well as the final chapters.
54. See also G. Tavan. 2005. *The Long, Slow Death of White Australia,* Melbourne: Scribe Publications, 4.
55. Jupp, *From White Australia to Woomera*, 21.
56. Ibid., 22.
57. Stratton, 'The Color of Jews', 311.
58. Ibid., 321.
59. For an exploration of this same process in an American context see Kaye/Kantrowitz, *The Colors of Jews*, esp. 1–30.
60. Curriculum of School MB, 4. Curriculum of School ME, 16. Both schools have the same document in their curricula, taken from D. Prager and J. Telushkin. 2003. *Why the Jews? The Reason for Antisemitism*, New York: Touchstone.
61. Curriculum of School MB, 5. Curriculum of School ME, 17.
62. Curriculum of School MB, 5. Curriculum of School ME, 17. This explanation is notably less severe than that of Pagan and Christian antisemitism. The latter explanations provide examples of the direct persecution of Jews; the explanation of Islamic antisemitism merely talks of Jews never being forgiven. The curricula continue on to

discuss modern antisemitism – which manifests in racial antisemitism and political antisemitism – as well. See Curriculum of School MB, 7–8; Curriculum of School ME, 18–21.
63. For information about March of the Living (MOTL) see http://www.motl.org/. Retrieved 8 August 2008. For information about the effects of trips to Poland on Israeli Jewish identity see A. Lazar et al. Fall 2004. 'Jewish Israeli Teenagers, National Identity, and the Lessons of the Holocaust', *Holocaust and Genocide Studies* 18(2), 188–204 and J. Feldman. Summer 2002. 'Marking the Boundaries of the Enclave: Defining the Israeli Collective through the Poland "Experience"', *Israel Studies* 7(2), 84–114.
64. Ilana, like all other names of teachers and educators in this book, is a pseudonym.
65. Chaim Nachman Bialik, *The City of Slaughter*, Retrieved 18 December 2014 from http://faculty.history.umd.edu/BCooperman/NewCity/Slaughter.html.
66. Personal communication with Ilana, 15 July 2007.
67. Or, at least, this was what they expressed in the space of the MOTL education sessions. It is always possible that that space did not allow for the full range of emotions and experiences to be explicitly shared, and that indeed, these education sessions were not just teaching the students about the past and the places to which they would travel, but were also teaching them the 'correct' emotions to express.
68. Significantly, the sessions run by the teachers and survivors for the students to learn about the Holocaust were held in the Melbourne Holocaust Museum, while the sessions run by the *madrichim* to talk about Israel were held around the corner in the house where *Habonim Dror* (a socialist Zionist youth movement) holds its meetings. The physical space needed to be changed in order to reinforce the fundamental differences between the Holocaust and Israel. For further discussion of the ways in which spaces and places are formulated see M. de Certeau. 1984. *The Practice of Everyday Life*, Berkeley: University of California Press.
69. Ella Shohat made a similar point, suggesting that within the Zionist viewpoint, the Diaspora Jew is 'someone "living outside of history"'. Shohat, *Taboo Memories, Diasporic Visions*, 217. We can see this also in writings by Jews who have moved to Israel. One of these, a man who moved from Melbourne to Israel, wrote on the tenth anniversary of his migration that 'I wanted to be able to take my destiny into my own hands, to make the news – and not simply read it. I wanted to be part of a Jewish majority, which wielded Jewish power, and created its own history – rather than have it dictated to it by those around it.' I. Bloch. 2013. 'Right Choice? Definitely. Right Reasons? It's Complicated', *Galus Australis*, 3 February. Retrieved 22 February 2013 from http://galusaustralis.com/2013/02/6767/right-choice-definitely-right-reasons-its-complicated/.

CHAPTER 2

'I Think It Makes It More Real That Way'
Chronology, Survivor Testimony and the Holocaust

> For it is *how* we represent the past that determines how we feel its nearness, that is to say, how we make its absence into a presence. The past is how we represent it.
>
> —Dan Stone, *Constructing the Holocaust*

> The kind of reading I have in mind would not assume a direct correspondence between words and things, nor confine itself to single meanings, nor aim for the resolution of contradiction. It would not render process as linear, nor rest explanation on simple correlations or single variables.
>
> —Joan Scott, 'The Evidence of Experience'

It is a difficulty – how, within the boundaries of the high-school classroom, to pass on to students ideas and knowledge about the Holocaust? How to translate that vast history into the parameters offered by the classroom? And then also, how to construct a history of the Holocaust which negotiates the anxiety which is brought up as teachers consider the place of Jews in non-Jewish, Western worlds in the aftermath of this terrible history? As we ponder these questions, we must note that complicating all of this are the problems not just of the constructedness of the school curriculum (and the limitations of any particular scenario, which in this case is the high-school classroom) and of the need to find age-appropriate ways of conveying such information to the students, but also the tremendous difficulties involved in understanding and transmitting histories of the Holocaust more generally.

In this chapter I examine the ways in which teachers attempt to teach their students the 'truth' of the Holocaust (and how they thereby construct that truth). For the teachers in this study this is, primarily, a truth which is accessed through chronological fact-based narrations of the Holocaust and survivor testimonies. This chapter discusses the ways in which these narrations and testimonies are deployed in the narrating of the history of the Holocaust – the use that is made of them – and complicates the teachers' ideas of what can be learnt from them. Explored in this chapter will be the presentation of the Holocaust as History. 'History' here refers to the idea of a verifiable and knowable, objective and scholarly history which, as will be shown, dominates the teaching of the Holocaust in these Jewish schools in Melbourne and New York today.[1]

This History or pedagogy is another arena in which the anxiety which I explored in the previous chapter is produced and played out. As has been explained, this book takes as a central thrust the argument that teachers of the Holocaust in Jewish schools in Melbourne and New York are faced with an anxiety about the place of Jews in both non-Jewish and Jewish worlds. Through the work of historians such as Yosef Yerushalmi – as will be discussed later – we can understand that the construction of histories following the models practised by surrounding societies has, for the last century, been a means of negotiating a place for Jews in the European non-Jewish societies in which they have lived. By adopting dominant historiographical practices, these historians have hoped that their histories would be considered acceptable, and that they would be able to be considered suitable citizens. This chapter will demonstrate the ways in which this practice continues in these examples of Holocaust education with the similar aim of attempting to find a place for Jews in the modern, Western world.

Two aspects in particular – the two most dominant aspects – of the historiography of the Holocaust as taught in Jewish schools are explored in this chapter. The first is the mode in which the Holocaust is narrated. I will explore the ways in which teachers construct a chronological narrative of the Holocaust in the mode of a modernist realist narrative. In this style of narrative the distinction between referent and signifier is elided.[2] This chapter will outline the chronological narratives which the teachers use when they teach about the Holocaust and then will seek to explain what appears to be a consistent choice to represent the history of the Holocaust in these chronological forms. An examination of the second aspect – the teachers' use of survivor testimonies – will then follow. By considering a number of examples of the ways that teachers express the value and utility of survivor testimony we can understand in greater detail the ways in which the concept of 'knowing' the Holocaust is relayed and transmitted to the students.

Before we can proceed to an analysis of the material which the teachers present, it is necessary to sketch the theoretical parameters of this inquiry. The modes of narration which the teachers use will be explored first, and the ideas of historians who have described and critiqued the role of narrative history will be explicated.

The work of Hayden White, who argued that historical narratives are based on culturally available modes of narration, is particularly useful here to complicate the concept and utility of narrative-based histories.[3] The use of survivor testimony will then be explored, along with the will to know the 'truth' of the Holocaust which inflects the teachers' understandings of the role and possibilities of testimony, through the application of Joan Scott's deconstruction of the category of experience. Scott complicates the truth value of 'experience', arguing that experience and discourse are not separable from each other; rather that experience is constituted within and through discourse.[4] This idea can move the possibilities offered by survivor testimonies in different directions, while still affirming the absolute importance of listening to survivor testimony. Finally, the search for understanding and knowledge through which these teachers approach Holocaust pedagogy will be explored. Through these various explorations, this chapter opens up for problematization the possibilities of 'knowing' what the Holocaust was.

Part I: Chronological Narratives

The idea that history should be narrated through chronological narratives is not unique to (these teachers of) the Holocaust. Indeed, the formulation of a historical narrative directed by progressively developing time is, Paul Ricoeur argues, necessary. While we will consider challenges to this idea, it is important to understand that, as Ricoeur has stated, the 'temporal character of human experience' is at stake in a narrative and the truth claims it makes.[5] Indeed, Ricoeur suggests, temporality – or time – directs and makes narratives meaningful.[6] Narrative and time, of some form, in this telling are inseparable. In this section I will explore a number of the ways in which this formulation is played out in chronological narratives – one particular incarnation of a temporal narrative – constructed by teachers in the schools under consideration. In particular, the following elements will be drawn out: that these chronologies are formulated as a series of stages which are made to appear as having naturally unfolded; that the chronologies which are taught in schools today are presented as occurring in the same manner as the Jewish people experienced them at the time; that chronologies are told as presentation of truth, rather than representation, not subjected to analysis; and that time is made always progressive and coherent. In short, the underlying premise is that chronological narratives are normalized and thereby their construction is made invisible.

While many theorists of trauma have considered the ways in which the Holocaust can be written, spoken, and thought about, for our purposes here the most pertinent analysis comes through the work of Eric Santner. Santner has complicated the usage of narratives to explicate and understand the Holocaust, suggesting that we can understand their use in terms of 'narrative fetishism'. By this, he explains, he 'mean[s] the construction and deployment of a narrative consciously or unconsciously designed to expunge the traces of the trauma or loss that called that narrative into being in the first place'. He contrasts the use of narrative as fetish with Freud's idea of 'the work of mourning', explaining that both 'are responses to loss, to a past that refuses to go away due to its traumatic impact'.[7] Whereas mourning work symbolizes the traumatic loss and thereby works through it, narrative fetishism, in Santner's formulation, works to remove the trauma and its associated uncertainties by holding the narrative as preeminent: in other words, by fetishizing the narrative as the definer of the Holocaust. In settling on a narrative which is continually reinscribed, that narrative is installed as the truth. The absences which are a part of the narrative are covered over and the history of the Holocaust comes to replace the Holocaust itself: to know the narrative, it is deemed, is to *know* the Holocaust. The Holocaust is thereby made coherent and knowable.[8] Coherence and knowability in the form of a chronological narrative serves to cover over the trauma and the gaps, silences and absences which constitute the traumatic subjects at the centre of the Holocaust. With this in mind, we can now turn to the work of the teachers to understand the ways in which they construct and utilize chronological narratives in this manner of narrative fetishism: as a means of managing a trauma through a focus on a particular narrative (style).

An approach which foregrounds a chronological narrative can be seen in the responses offered in interviews by most of the teachers, as well as in their curriculum documents. One teacher at a school in Melbourne explained that:

> we look at Jewish life in pre-war Europe; the rise of Nazism and the rise of Hitler; the ghettos; separate section on resistance. The Final Solution is a separate topic – we look at the camps, and the mobile killing units; a very little bit at the end of uplifting – we show a film at the end of 100 kids taken from Europe to Israel.[9]

This ordering of the events of the Holocaust serves implicitly to create a chronological narrative. Within this schema, moreover, there is a (modernist) progression, a building up of horror, wherein the Final Solution is segmented off from other Nazi means of dealing with Jews – the ghettos – by a discussion of resistance. And this modernist progression ends in a classic narrative style, with the 'uplifting' or 'positive' note. The Final Solution is presented as the pinnacle of the progression of Nazi acts of horror, segmented between Jewish resistance and the end of the Holocaust and creation of the State of Israel.

A teacher at a New York school described and expanded on one such chronological narrative. In her teaching she begins with stories of antisemitism in Europe prior to the Holocaust, then discusses:

> the rise of Nazi Germany and Hitler's agenda against the Jews, the platform of the Nazi party, the SA, the development of the youth movement . . . and how Hitler developed his concentration camps to the SS, the one-day boycott of Jewish shops and services, and the expulsion of Jews from universities, the

development of the Gestapo, the public book burning in Berlin, the Nuremberg Laws, and explaining how there was a steady development of Nazism within Germany and Jews were not necessarily prepared for how it would peak eventually, they thought that this was an isolated circumstance.[10]

She described the continued rise of Nazism, Kristallnacht, the Kindertransport, the political situation throughout Europe, the experiences of Jews in different parts of the Nazi Reich, the Einsatzgruppen, the massacre at Babi Yar, the Wannsee Conference, the death camps and concentration camps, before coming to the Allies invading Europe and liberating the camps. Jewish responses to the Holocaust are then explored through an examination of music, writings, sculpture and other forms of artistic response. This is a representative example of the chronological summary of the Holocaust which the vast majority of the history teachers interviewed present to their students.

At a Melbourne school, the curriculum divides the Holocaust into differentiated stages. There is a 'prehistory' to the Holocaust which covers the period 'From Biblical Times – 1933' and then there are four stages as follows: 'Stage 1: January 1933 – September 1939'; 'Stage 2: September 1939 – August 1944'; 'Stage 3: June 1941 – May 1945'; 'Stage 4: After the War – Post Holocaust issues.'[11] In labelling them as stages, a sense is created that each stage is discrete, each building on top of the previous one. A sense of time, and the events which occupy that time, as naturally and sequentially unfolding is created. Moreover, the effect is created whereby it can be understood that each stage comes together to create a whole: that the (first three) stages are smaller parts of one overall event (rather than, perhaps, a series of many events). This event is then known by the name of the Holocaust.

This idea of the Holocaust being composed of a series of 'stages' recurs in the curriculum of a school in New York. The curriculum states that:

> The Nazi campaign of discrimination, isolation, and mass murder of European Jews between 1933 and 1945 is without doubt the saddest and most difficult period of modern Jewish history. Both the Western and Eastern European Jewish communities were devastated by the deaths of six million Jews. A careful analysis of each stage of the Holocaust can help make some sense of how and why such a rich and diverse Jewish culture could be nearly annihilated within just a few years.[12]

In this example, a chronological narrative is deemed to be necessary. By explaining that 'a careful analysis of each stage of the Holocaust can help make some sense' attention is drawn to the idea that the Holocaust was a series of sequential stages, and that the main possible way to make sense of it is to view and understand it as such. By sequentially moving through the stages – the chronology – the whole can be understood. The stages, and the histories they bring, are thereby naturalized as a way to make understandable meaning out of the Holocaust.

The curriculum of a Melbourne school begins with a chronology, taken from *Yesterdays and Then Tomorrows*, published in 2002 by Yad Vashem.[13] This six-page chronology is placed before the page numberings begin, hence functioning as a sort of prehistory, or a way of setting a (discursive) scene. It takes the students from 1933 and the appointment of Adolf Hitler as Chancellor of Germany, to 1946 and the end of the Nuremberg Trials. A chronology such as this one works to establish the Holocaust as chronologically unfolding: the passage of time and the events which accompany it seem to flow on naturally. The vital information to be conveyed to the students becomes names, dates and places, even when detached from their historical, social and political contexts. By placing this at the very front of the curriculum it works to set the framework for the rest of the curriculum and the understandings of the Holocaust which it brings.

Similarly, across twenty-two pages of the curriculum of a school in New York a chronological narrative of the events of the Holocaust is presented.[14] The descriptions unfold, conveying a sense that even if decisions were made about events as time progressed, there was still a clear, logical progression. Each event followed the previous, and led into the next. It appears to be suggesting that if we stand back, perhaps with the benefit of hindsight, we can appreciate that this was the way it was: that there could have been no other way. The chronological narrative is, in this way, totalizing. Before the narrative of the events of 1933 to 1945 there is information about Jews in Eastern Europe before the war, and immediately following the narrative there is information about Jewish resistance, and non-Jewish rescuers and bystanders. The events of the Holocaust are thereby neatly segmented off from the rest of history: chronological time is normalized, and the ongoing effects of the Holocaust, which oftentimes permeate the present and rupture discrete chronological time, are evaded.[15]

Another Melbourne teacher explained that the chronology he follows consists of:

> a look at the prelude to the Holocaust, from post-World War I – Treaty of Versailles and so forth – who were the Jews of Europe. We then look at the rise of Nazi Germany and Hitler, and the outbreak of the Holocaust, as well as World War II. I try to distinguish between the two, not just call them both the same thing. And then we move on and say what actually was the War Against the Jews – we use Yehuda Berkovitz's title [sic] – and look at the ghettos, everything from Nuremberg, from Kristallnacht, all the way to 1945, including the resistance.[16]

The importance of the chronological narrative in guiding the history of the Holocaust was reiterated in his locating of the Holocaust within an overall message of Jewish chronological history:

> I can't say that there's a theme to the Holocaust. It's part of Jewish history – it follows the Year 9 curriculum, which is the Middle Ages up to the Balfour

Declaration, which follows the Year 8 curriculum, which is the Destruction of the Temple through the expulsion from Spain. We don't sort of isolate it as we have to do the Holocaust – it's part of the Jewish Studies programme, it's chronological, it has its own impact, its own meaning and so forth, its own uniqueness. But it is part of the whole.[17]

That whole, for this teacher, is produced through a chronological narrative. As he stated, in the teaching of this history 'we are chronologically driven'.[18] Another teacher in Melbourne made a similar comment, explaining that 'we just do an historical overview – these are the facts. This is the chronology of events; *this is how Jews found themselves caught up in it*.'[19]

This depiction of the chronological narrative as naturally unfolding, even for the subjects of that history as they are themselves involved in it, is a widely practiced technique of historical narration which has been interrogated by Hayden White. In his essay 'The Historical Text as Literary Artifact', White argues that the basis for historical narrations can be found in literature, as historical narration is closer to literary narration than to scientific research. He claims that history involves the narration of a story rather than the objective rehearsing of a set of verifiable facts which merely need to be discovered by the historian. White writes that '[i]t is frequently forgotten or, when remembered, denied that no given set of events attested by the historical record comprises a *story* manifestly finished and complete . . . We do not *live* stories, even if we give our lives meaning by retrospectively casting them in the form of stories.'[20] That is, lives can only be narrated as complete and coherent stories *after* the event. This contrasts with the teacher's assertion above: the teacher stated that she narrates the events as 'how Jews found themselves caught up in it', thereby obscuring narration's retrospective work of making meaning. Importantly as well, we note that there is never one story: when talking of 'Jews finding themselves caught up in it' there is a risk of homogenizing both Jews and 'it', the Holocaust. We can therefore understand that while the teacher asserts the naturalness of the narrative, the past does not contain the inevitability which this teacher proposes. As is the case with any other chronological narrative, the chronology is her formulation, narrated after the fact.

Similarly, a teacher in New York, describing the main topics of the Holocaust which she teaches, stated that 'we do obviously the chronological events about what happened'.[21] It is the apparent obviousness of this approach which is worthy of note. For this teacher, as for others, the obvious, truthful (and invisible) way in which to teach the Holocaust is as a chronological listing of events, with the 'significance' of the events highlighted along the way. This making invisible of the constructedness of the chronology should be understood and interrogated as being part of a project of making particular narratives hegemonic.[22] The historian Dan Stone, when writing about the treatment of Holocaust histories, asserted that '[w]hen one treats historiographical texts as "primary sources" . . . it is precisely language constituting reality that permits the historical text to appear, for the past itself is absent'.[23] The past is absent in the sense that the text being deciphered is a product of the present, and while it refers to the past events it describes, it uses language which defines the reality it seeks to describe. In this process the present text comes to replace the past. As Stone wrote, '[t]he past is accessible only through our representations of it; that is a well-established point. It follows, then, that an understanding of the textual construction of those representations is essential.'[24] These histories of the Holocaust, formulated according to the hegemonic structures of chronological narrative, need to be understood as constructions; their claims for naturalness (and, following that, invisibility), deconstructed, and the meanings which the narrative attains through the particularities of its constructedness understood.

Complicating the usage of chronological narratives

It seems that it is widely understood by teachers that a chronological narrative of the Holocaust is useful for their teaching as it is able to convey the bare facts or information. This is an understanding that we can gain not from anything explicitly stated by the teachers, but rather through a close reading of their pedagogical approaches. That is, in the interviews conducted for this project, the teachers did not explicitly state that chronological narratives contain this explanatory power. Indeed, in the interviews I did not explicitly ask the teachers why they utilize chronological narratives. This was primarily because I was interested in treating the interviews through an unfolding process of discourse analysis, whereby meaning was made of the teachers' words after the fact, rather than seeking to gain their personal insights into all matters. This lack of an explicit discussion does not mean, I do not think, that this understanding of the ways that teachers use chronological narratives does not hold. As we know, this approach is common in Western historiography generally. Indeed, as I will show, this is the predominant way in which the historically based chronological narrative is understood: that the chronological narration of a set of facts provides an objective telling of history, or a history without analysis. While I do not doubt that teachers supplement the chronological narratives with additional information and insights, it is important that we understand that for these teachers (despite their lack of acknowledgement of such), the chronological narrative serves the pedagogical function of providing the students with what is seen as the basic, or fundamental, information about the Holocaust.

The chronological narrative functions to present a history of the Holocaust as the verifiable, known, and absolute story, or 'truth' of what occurred, locating it within, as Marita Sturken explicated it, 'the limited binary of truth and falsehood'.[25] It is understood as 'presentation' rather than 're-presentation'.[26] White explained this mode of thinking as such:

> [t]hus for traditional historical discourse there is presumed to be a crucial difference between an 'interpretation' of 'the facts' and a 'story' told about them... Whereas interpretations are typically thought of as commentaries on 'the facts,' the stories told in narrative histories are presumed to inhere either in the events themselves (whence the notion of a 'real story') or in the facts derived from the critical study of evidence bearing upon those events (which yields the notion of the 'true' story).[27]

White is arguing here that it is commonly understood that the narrative representation of historical facts are a part of the facts themselves – that the facts are indistinguishable from the narrative.[28] According to White, however, this is never the case, as by representing a set of facts in a particular way, a particular set of meanings is inscribed.[29] Yet this is regularly obscured in writings about the Holocaust, such as those under examination here, which present fact-based, chronological descriptions of events as if these were the truth of what happened. As will be returned to later, it is being argued here that teachers present the history of the Holocaust in this manner as they believe it to be the most truthful – there exists the illusion that they are doing nothing more than 'presenting the facts', where the facts stand for themselves. This is believed to be the most ethical and appropriate response to the Holocaust: to enable their students to simply 'know' what happened.[30] This question, of what the possibilities are of 'knowing the Holocaust', will be explored further at the end of this chapter.

Indeed, the thirst for knowledge of the Holocaust has been unquenched and unquenchable for many people. One teacher explained that she teaches about the Holocaust because she wants to know what happened – that since she was in college she has wanted to gain more and more information. Another teacher echoed this.[31] It seems that for the teachers and schools which participated in this project, their teaching is motivated by this drive to *know* the Holocaust.[32] What I would like to open for question, however, is whether by learning facts, dates, names and places, teachers and students can *know* the Holocaust, or, indeed, any moment of history. Thus we must ask, what is it about mastering a chronological history, coupled with the survivor testimonies which are discussed below, which is so compelling?

This is a question that can be raised of historiography, history education, and Jewish history generally – I do not wish to suggest that Holocaust pedagogy is unique in facing this question. What is potentially unique, however, is the resolution, or answer, to this question. An answer to this, I am arguing following Eric Santner's work, as sketched previously, can be found in the specific uncertainties and anxieties which are produced as part of the traumatic aftermath of the Holocaust. By formulating a coherent narrative based on the predominant forms of historical narration in the Western world – including the Western Jewish world – these teachers feel they are able to hold onto something solid. That 'something' is their history: history provides bedrock upon which to locate uncertain identities, an uncertainty about the world, and the losses of living in it after the Holocaust. A known history can – for all of us – provide something solid to grasp onto. The anxiety is relieved through the adoption – or mimicry – of Western historical narrative practices, which results in the consolidation of these Jewish histories.

This can be seen in other moments of Jewish history, as outlined by Yosef Yerushalmi in his discussion of the Wissenschaft des Judentums movement.[33] The purpose of the Wissenschaft movement – which was a part of the Haskalah, the European-based version of the Jewish Enlightenment, in the nineteenth century – was to mould Jewish history within the same parameters of historiography practised in the Christian and secular societies which surrounded these European Jews.[34] While non-Jews had written histories of Jews, the Wissenschaft movement involved the reclaiming of Jewish history.[35] Yerushalmi argues that with the beginning of the Wissenschaft movement in the 1820s:

> suddenly, there are no apologies [for writing histories of Jews]. History is no longer a handmaiden of dubious repute to be tolerated occasionally and with embarrassment. She confidently pushes her way to the very center and brazenly demands her due. For the first time it is not history that must prove its utility to Judaism, but Judaism that must prove its validity to history, by revealing and justifying itself historically.[36]

Yerushalmi here is pointing to a similar consideration as is being discussed in this book: that at these particular historical junctures Jewish communities were struggling to find their place in the larger societies. In order to find a place they adopted the historiographical methods of those dominant societies. This was confirmed when he wrote that the new approach to historiography – that of the Enlightenment idea of history as scientific, known and verifiable – did not come 'prior to Jewish historical writing or historical thought'.[37] Rather, Yerushalmi wrote:

> [m]odern Jewish historiography began precipitously out of that assimilation from without and collapse from within which characterized the sudden emergence of Jews out of the ghetto. It originated, not as scholarly curiosity, but as ideology, one of a gamut of responses to the crisis of Jewish emancipation and the struggle to attain it.[38]

This 'assimilation', he explained, was not negative, but rather was a response with a considerable history within the lifespan of the Jewish people.[39]

Moreover, Yerushalmi commented that Jewish historians of the late twentieth century shared the same features, problems and attributes as historians more generally – they contributed something unique (a Jewish history) but were closely bound up in the dominant disciplinary practices.[40] We can therefore understand that it has perhaps become a commonplace that Jews in modern Western societies adopt the historiographical practices of the dominant societies in which they live. While in the nineteenth century this was undertaken to attempt to resolve the problem of how to manage emancipation, so too today this negotiation is a product of the desire to manage concerns about where Jews can fit into the world, in the context of contemporary forms of antisemitism and pressures of assimilation. This occurred in the Wissenschaft movement, and this approach to history continues in Jewish schools today.[41]

Amos Funkenstein, who has critiqued Yerushalmi's ideas of Jewish history and memory, argued that it is not necessary to ask what is original (or autochthonous) in Jewishness and what is a result of assimilation, as such a question produces ahistorical answers.[42] Instead, we need to view assimilation as a dialectic, where Jewishness is continually changing, both with and against the non-Jewish societies in which Jews live: in short, there is no 'stable essence' to Jewishness or Jewish writing. This also informs the approach of this book, where the argument is not being made that there exists a 'pure' Jewish historical narratorial content and style, but rather that Jewish (Holocaust) historiography is constantly changing, influenced to a large degree by surrounding (non-Jewish) historiographies. We can thereby locate this movement to narrate the history of the Holocaust within a larger modern Jewish historiographical movement which involves adopting the most dominant, and seemingly 'natural', of the West's historiographical inventions as a means of utilizing history to manage a range of uncertain feelings.

And thus from this understanding of the history of Jews negotiating modern Western approaches to historiography we can now ask in more detail what these approaches entail. This book is not arguing that Western historiography is monolithic or easily defined. The work this book undertakes is not to explore Western historiography, but rather to understand the ways in which Holocaust pedagogies in Jewish schools in Melbourne and New York today are formulated in accord with the central defining features of this historiography. These central ideas, according to George G. Iggers and Q. Edward Wang, are that modern normative Western historiography includes a 'linear approach and the idea of progress . . . and the search for causal explanations'.[43] That is, modern, chronological narratives are shaped by ideas of progress and linearity: their authors strive for coherence. Moreover, the idea of history which predominates in the teaching under examination was formulated by Leopold von Ranke. He argued that the task of history was 'merely to show what essentially/actually happened'. His basic idea, as articulated by Iggers and Wang, was that 'the starting point of historical studies must in fact be the rigorous examination of original sources. But Ranke was fully aware that history does not stop with facts, but that it must present a story'.[44] As David Carr explicates it, '[t]raditional narrative histories claim to tell us what really happened'[45] by, as Mark Cousins explains, putting the event (which is to be excavated and understood) at the centre of the narrative.[46] This idea of history and historiography necessitates the understanding that there is something which actually happened, and that it is the job of the historian (or history-teacher) to explain it. What happened can be understood simply by reading and bringing together various historical sources: the subjectivity of the historian is thereby deemed irrelevant as the truth of the past lies in the historical evidence.[47] This is the idea of historiography which the teachers deploy.

Time

Fundamental to the chronological narrative, alongside the events, is the institution and normalization of particular constructions of time. The importance of the regulation of time – such as in its division into sequential 'stages', as undertaken by one of the teachers discussed previously – in order to regulate people and ideas in modern society was explored by E.P. Thompson. Thompson explicated that time was regimented through the increased use of clocks in the eighteenth and nineteenth centuries, and with the Industrial Revolution of the nineteenth century, regulating the use of time in the workplace became a central mode of regulating the workforce. Time, in this understanding, is controlled and manipulated within industrial capitalism in order to regulate and pacify workers, during both their work and leisure time. The imposition of time schedules (including the teaching of history according to chronological time) intentionally regulates workers' time: time becomes a commodity, something which can be bought, sold, spent and saved.[48] And thus the owner of the time (variously the employer and the worker) can manage how the time is used. The use and understanding of time is made rigid and controlled. In arguing this, Thompson pointed to the ways in which time has been constructed in order to undertake a social and political task – regulating the social sphere in order to maximize its productive potential.[49] Time in this formulation has a pacifying effect, creating social order and regulation. In a rather similar sense, chronological historical narratives work to pacify the narrative, to create order and coherency in the histories of the Holocaust.

This idea of time is complicated through an exploration of survivor testimonies, which are one discursive space in which the past and the present intrude upon each other, rupturing the coherence which the chronological narratives institute. Lawrence Langer, who has worked extensively with the testimonies in the Fortunoff Video Archive, draws our attention to the particular way in which survivors articulate their experiences in these narrow frameworks of recorded testimony. He writes that:

> virtually all videotaped interviews begin in the same way, innocently conspiring to establish an atmosphere of familiarity: [interviewers ask the survivor to] tell us something about your childhood, family, school, community, friends – that is, about the normal world preceding the disaster. And most of them end in the same way too, implying a severance between the camp experience and what followed: tell us about your liberation (and your life afterwards).[50]

In this way, according to Langer, the interviewers often push the survivor into identifying an end to the Holocaust which provides, and produces, a sense of closure. However '[t]he narrators' imaginations remain chained to memories that have little to do with sequence or chronology . . . Oral testimony violates our own need for conclusions, thereby imposing on us an angle of vision wrenching us from familiar assumptions that govern our response to normal narrative.'[51] These testimonies can show us that time does not always follow a progressive, linear development, but rather can be disruptive and disjunctive. Time need not always be coherent and regulatory. Yet, in order to gain control in a world imbued with anxiety it is usefully constructed as such. Richard Terdiman describes this in relation to memory more generally.

In his book *Present Past* Terdiman writes that '[m]emory . . . complicates the rationalist segmentation of chronology into "then" and "now." In memory, the time line becomes tangled and folds back on itself.'[52] History, as shown above, is made to arise in the form of chronology: the teachers seek to present the history of the Holocaust as a sort of disconnected, unfolding and objective narrative. And the testimonies – or memories – of the survivors are brought in by these Holocaust educators and made to work in the service of that history. Memories in this sense are subjugated to History. Yet memories, Terdiman tells us, have the capacity to confuse the imposed rationality of chronology. Where the histories under examination delineate and literally segment the Holocaust into time-based capsules, memories transgress those borders, moving between past and present. As I will now show, through a discussion of survivor testimony, memories at times do not follow the chronology established in these histories of the Holocaust.

Part II: Utilizing Survivor Testimonies

For the teachers the presence of survivors in front of the students testifying to their experiences, or the ability to read their written words, provides a particularly important mode of Holocaust narration and understanding. It's important then for us to consider why this is so. In this section of the chapter I will explore the ways in which survivor testimonies are brought into the histories of the Holocaust, and the kinds of truths which they are seen to carry. Indeed, the use of survivor testimonies as a means of conveying the truth of the Holocaust is a further way in which these histories are made solid.[53] I will argue therefore that testimonies function, in part, to manage the teachers' anxieties. By providing a solid and known base, these histories can be regulated and contained, thus providing some control amongst the various unknowns which the Holocaust brings with it. The anxieties produced by not knowing can thereby be somewhat attenuated.

A number of teachers regularly invite survivors into their schools to talk to the students. Why do they do so? A Melbourne teacher explained that they have survivors speak at the school every year. In an interview she said that 'just about every survivor we've had every year – the kids going through the school are hearing this every year and not just a one off – they've all been different. Some have been in camps, some were hidden, one was on the death march, we've people who were kids in the camps. A real mix of stories and where they came from'.[54] For a different Melbourne teacher, survivors are brought in to speak as 'they're the best resources'.[55] She later commented that she encourages those students whose grandparents are survivors to talk to their grandparents:

> the most important thing for me is to bring in their grandparents, if their grandparents went through the Holocaust, and to find out their stories. It's a good thing for them to go home and start asking. Because a lot of them say, 'I think my grandmother was here', 'I think my grandfather was here', so I encourage them to go home and ask. So definitely stories – *I think it makes it more real that way*.[56]

This is echoed in the curriculum of this school, which explains, amongst a detailed description of the many different ways in which Jews rebelled against the Nazis, that '[i]n every ghetto Jews recorded the details of their nightmare in letters and diaries, so the *truth* would not be lost'.[57]

Survivor testimonies have also been captured in various books. One which is quoted in some of the curricula is *Hasidic Tales of the Holocaust* by Yaffa Eliach.[58] Two very different stories were drawn out by teachers: the first in the curriculum of a New York school, the second in the curriculum of an unrelated school in Melbourne. The first story is entitled 'Good Morning, Herr Müller' and it tells the story of a Hasidic rabbi, Herr Rabbiner, who would walk through his town in Poland every morning, greeting 'every man, woman, and child whom he met on his way with a warm smile and a cordial "Good morning". Over the years the rabbi became acquainted with many of his fellow townspeople this way and would always greet them by their proper title and name.' One person he would greet on the outskirts of town was Herr Müller, a Polish Volksdeutsche (ethnic German). When the war started the rabbi was deported, eventually to Auschwitz. Herr Müller joined the SS. One day at a selection in Auschwitz, the rabbi, who 'looked like a walking skeleton',

> had a great urge to see the face of the man with the snow-white gloves, small baton, and steely voice who played God and decided who should live and who should die. He lifted his eyes and heard his own voice speaking: 'Good morning, Herr Müller!' 'Good morning, Herr Rabbiner!' responded a human voice beneath the S.S. cap adorned with skull and bones. 'What are you doing here?' A faint smile appeared on the rabbi's lips. The baton moved to the right – to life. The following day, the rabbi was transferred to a safer camp. The rabbi, now in

his eighties, told me in his gentle voice, 'This is the power of a good-morning greeting. A man must always greet his fellow man.'[59]

What message does this pass on to the students, what 'truth' of the Holocaust? Without delving into the specifics of the lesson – which are perhaps not as important as the overall message – the centrality of the testimony of the survivor is highlighted here. The story uses survivor testimony to enforce a particular moral message. The morality tale works only – I would suggest – because it is a survivor telling it.[60]

The second story, 'Two Capsules of Cyanide', is based in the Janowska Road Camp, where, when the Jews would return to the camp at the end of the day, the SS would call out 'Who is the most respected race on the face of the earth?' to which the prisoners would have to respond 'The Third Reich'. They would then ask 'And who is the most accursed race on earth?' to which the prisoners would have to call 'The Jewish people!' Rabbi Israel Spira, the rabbi of Bluzhov, worked in the camp, along with a lawyer from Borislav named Hurowitz. One day the lawyer informed the rabbi that he had saved 'two thousand dollars' and with that money had purchased two cyanide capsules so that they could kill themselves and not be forced to participate in the degradation of the call-and-response. The rabbi refused to take the capsule, explaining that he would 'not be able to enter the World of Truth and face my illustrious ancestors as a murderer, as one who has taken a life – even his own life. Thank you, my friend, for your friendship.' That night, as they returned, the SS called out 'Who is the most respected race on earth?' In response, 'one voice that overpowered all the others' called out 'The Jews!' The question was repeated, and:

> 'The Jewish people are the most respected race on the face of earth!' proclaimed the same single powerful voice, and the echoes from what seemed like thousands of voices resounded from the surrounding hills: 'The Jews, the Jews, the Jews.' The S.S. men rushed in the direction of the dissident voice. On the ground lay stretched out the body of Hurowitz, the Borislav lawyer. On his lifeless face was frozen a smile of victory, and his gaping mouth continued silently to proclaim the eternity and greatness of the Jewish people.[61]

This story touches on something of the complexity of Jewish life in the Holocaust in a way in which a teacher perhaps never could: that there are no simple ways to live and die in the camps and that both were fraught. More significantly, once again the testimony of the survivor is brought to the centre, to convey a truth about the Holocaust.

A further example of the way in which teachers position the survivors as articulating the truth of the Holocaust, in a reified manner, was presented by a teacher at a school in New York, who explained that she has had 'actual' survivors come to speak to the students. She claimed that 'they had an *actual* survivor who fled to Shanghai come and speak, an *actual* survivor. And they have had both kinds of events; where you have an educator giving a lecture describing the topic of the Holocaust in detail and then a survivor who emerged from that experience.'[62] Survivor testimony is used here, in the similar manner to other teachers, as a truth-telling device: the truth arises from the powers and capacities of the juxtaposition of historical and personal stories, and from the perceived literal embodiment of the Holocaust, through the survivor being in the classroom. Similarly, a teacher at another New York school explained that she tells the students her 'father's story, which is very interesting to them, how he survived as a baby in the Krakow ghetto. And the kids *feel* it.'[63] We can see here examples of the collapsing of the gap between referent and signifier: the words of the survivor embody that event which has been given the name of the Holocaust. The survivor, in these invocations, *is* the Holocaust: they do not merely represent one aspect of it (and represent in a manner which is always deferred).

This approach to testimony and experience – which Joan Scott's work, as I will show, can help us to understand – is evidenced again in the words of a teacher at a Melbourne school. For this teacher, visiting the Holocaust Museum was a way of providing students with additional learning opportunities, 'to make it more real, more alive, and not just out of the book'.[64] Another teacher commented that visiting that museum is necessary as:

> it's important, first of all, to hear survivors speak. . . . So, I like for them to hear from survivors. I just think the whole museum is so well done. And it's good for them to see primary evidence. I mean, we do look at a bit of primary evidence, but being there, and having survivors talk to you is so important.[65]

When asked about the narrative of Kristallnacht that he teaches, the first teacher replied that he uses a reader, in which 'there are a number of first person accounts that we read. We also see it on the video . . . someone speaks who was there – both a German and a Jew . . . But that's true of all, of any key events – we read first person accounts of either witnesses, or participants or bystanders, survivors.'[66] The 'first person accounts' here are utilized for their truth-telling capacities: there is the inference that they possess and contain the truth of the event, and that by reading and listening to them, the students can know what happened. The silences and gaps which psychoanalytic theorist Shoshana Felman argues are inherent to these testimonies are elided in this usage of testimony.

Felman explains that her original approach to testimony involved an understanding 'that the essence of testimony is historical, and that its function is to record events and to report the facts of a historical occurrence.'[67] This historicity of testimony was challenged by her later readings and incorporations of Freudian and Lacanian psychoanalytic understandings of the subject and its testimonial capacities. In this later formulation, it was understood that 'the speaking subject constantly bears witness to a truth that nonetheless continues to escape him [*sic*], a truth that is, essentially, *not available* to its own speaker'.[68] This split subject – split off from a truth which constantly evades – which forms the subject of the testimonial does not appear to figure in the teachers' considerations of survivors and their testimonies. Survivors, on the contrary, are seen to *possess* the truth: to be able to describe the events which occurred in a fully truthful manner, encapsulating and containing the events within their testimony.[69]

The work of Joan Scott, and her analysis of the ways in which experience is used as the basis for writing histories, is important here. In her article 'The Evidence of Experience' Scott explains that it is problematic to write history in a manner which foregrounds individuals' experiences, as it takes 'the existence of individuals for granted', rather than questioning the very basis of the construction and production of subjective selves. This, she argues, 'operates within an ideological construction that . . . makes individuals the starting point of knowledge' and endows those individuals with certain specific characteristics – such as those of being a 'man, woman, black, white, heterosexual, and homosexual' – thereby naturalizing these categories.[70] Scott suggests here that the writing of history through a focus on the individual and their experience works to naturalize both experience and the existence of a coherent individual who has those experiences. Instead, Scott posits that we should understand both experience and the individual who has experiences as subjective, discursive and historical productions. It is a circular and productive movement, rather than one which has a clear starting point. Scott implores us to understand the 'productive quality of discourse', reminding us that 'subjects are constituted discursively and experience is a linguistic event (it doesn't happen outside established meanings), but neither is it confined to a fixed order of meaning'.[71] Indeed, this idea that discourse is productive is central to understanding the reading of the pedagogy which I am undertaking in this book.

This can help us to explain the motivations which the teachers maintain for teaching about the Holocaust: specifically, working to affect the students as individuals and as members of a Jewish group. A teacher in New York explained that she:

> go[es] through everything chronologically and any time I can make it personally meaningful to them, I try to do that. I explain to them from the beginning that it's not a dry piece of history like other pieces of history might be taught – it's not just names, and dates, and places and facts. There's more to it than that. So I have them do a lot of writing, journaling.[72]

This teacher is thereby able to bring something more to the chronology: it is the incorporation of the story into the students' personal narratives which gives it greater meaning. It is the chronology coupled with the impact on the individual students which gives the teaching of the Holocaust its impetus for this teacher. For her, the aim of the teaching of the Holocaust is to make it personally meaningful – certainly an important aspect of anyone's learning about such an event. Yet if Scott's argument is extended, it can be understood that when the teacher asks the students to write individually to express their responses and connections with the material they are learning, she is cementing the idea that the first response to these events should be for each of them as individuals. The individuality of their experience learning about the Holocaust is brought to the forefront. This is not to suggest necessarily that there is a more appropriate, collective, way of teaching these histories, but rather to open up a discussion about the work which these pedagogical methods are undertaking.

Holocaust-era diaries are used elsewhere in curricula to point to the truth of the Holocaust.[73] There are extracts from diaries written in three ghettos, written by Chaim A. Kaplan (in the Warsaw Ghetto), Dawid Sierakowiak and Oskar Singer (both in the Lodz Ghetto). It is explained that:

> These diaries draw us into a landscape of savage oppression. They help us gain a vivid sense of the fate and impending doom of a community. The resentment, anger, dismay, sporadic hope and seemingly indescribable conditions of ghetto life are captured in the moving words of their writers. It is from these diaries that we gain access to those who were trapped, whether they knew it as yet or not, in a scheme which would destroy nearly all the Jews of Europe. They help us imagine what we can never know.[74]

The writing here suggests that the diaries are able to convey something of the truth of what happened: 'they help us gain a vivid sense' of what happened. At the same time, knowledge is limited: we can 'imagine', but we cannot 'know'. What it is that can be gathered from these diaries is ambivalent. But emotions and feelings are 'captured' in the writings; the signifiers do the work of encapsulating the signified, so that the readers, sixty years on, can 'gain access' to the people themselves. Moreover, the suggestion is that we can know today that they were trapped, even if they did not know it as they were writing, and can therefore read something of this situation into their writings. How, it could be asked, is it possible to 'gain access' to something that was not known to exist at the time of writing? Can students retrospectively read this trapped-ness into the writings in the diaries?

This raises interesting questions regarding the use of chronological time. We can return here to the comment from a teacher, cited previously, that the students learn about the events of the Holocaust in the same way that the 'Jews found themselves caught up in it'. If time and causality is being posited as naturally and progressively flowing – moving forward, that is – does it disrupt this chronology to jump in at the middle and suggest that the reader can see in the diaries something of which, it is claimed, the diarists may not have known? On the contrary: it works to reinforce the supposed naturalness of chronological time. If time and events are naturally unfolding, even if the diarists *did not know* what was to happen, their writing will still foreshadow the events to come, because these were always going to be the subsequent events. In looking back at the diaries, the readers (the students) will be able to see the precursors to the genocide that was to follow. The diaries thereby are made to do the work of narrating that which the diarists most probably did not know, and could not have foreshadowed.

We can understand here that the teachers' narratives often work to collapse the distinction between the signifier and referent, as referred to earlier, in a way that the survivors themselves perhaps do not authorize. The narrative of the Holocaust – or the survivor testifying to their experiences of the Holocaust – is made to stand in for the Holocaust itself: language comes to *be* that which it is signifying.[75] That is, as is shown, when they speak about the ways in which survivor testimonies are used, the teachers appear to be asserting that the testimony contains the events within it: that the testimonies speak the truth of the Holocaust, and make the experience of learning about it more real for the students.[76] The narrating of the events contains something actual of the events.[77] James E. Young draws our attention to this problem with his explanation that 'things happen *and* they get told: two ontologically distinct categories which narrative only *seems* to collapse into a voraciously all-encompassing discourse'.[78] We can see this in the ways in which teachers talk about the Holocaust being made 'more real' or 'more alive' when a survivor speaks about it.[79] Narration, in this formulation, makes the past alive. The time and space (and language) gap between the happening and its narration is obscured.[80]

This approach has been critiqued by Joan Scott, who writes that 'historians' rhetorical treatment of evidence . . . depends on a referential notion of evidence which denies that it is anything but a reflection of the real'.[81] The real here we can understand, at its most basic, as conveying a sense of truth or reality: as an idea of the world or experience which is prior to, and unaffected by, discourse. She asserts that instead experience needs to be seen as 'a subject's history. Language is the site of history's enactment. Historical explanation cannot, therefore, separate the two'.[82] History, Scott argues, puts language to events or experiences. The effects of the contingency of language work upon that which the language is describing. Yet, more often, the use of evidence is performed in such a way that disguises the fact that it is historical: it is taken to be real in a way in which it never can be. Moreover, Scott writes, '[w]hen the evidence offered is the evidence of "experience," the claim for referentiality is further buttressed – what could be truer, after all, than a subject's own account of what he or she has lived through?'[83] It is this usage of evidence in Holocaust education which disguises the role of the teacher or historian in constructing the histories being composed, which naturalizes the types and contents of the narratives which are presented to students.

However we must also critique the usage of the individual who has these experiences. In the social history movements of the 1960s the aim of incorporating individuals' stories was to challenge the normative histories which had been based upon archival documentation: by incorporating stories of people hitherto unheard, histories can be made complex and deepened, and the very project of what it is to make history can be reassessed. This is, partially, the work which will be undertaken in the final chapter of this book: to argue for the necessity of including complex stories of the experiences of Jewish women as real people in narratives of the Jewish experience of the Holocaust. But opening up histories to the stories of individual people also works, according to Scott, to rest 'its claim to legitimacy on the authority of experience, the direct experience of others, as well as of the historian who learns to see and illuminate the lives of those others in his or her texts'.[84] As Scott explains, this idea of 'experience' and the authority which it carries must be critiqued. The final chapter of this book therefore, in a sense, replicates this problematic, but it also points to the ways in which the writing of these histories can be an (always attenuated) emancipatory project. By bringing out the ways in which teachers rest their claims for Jewish womanhood on individual stories of Jewish women we can understand the ways in which the authority of experience is reinforced. Therefore, while Chapter Five will discuss the ways in which women's experiences are described by teachers as though existing prior to discourse, the chapter will work to illuminate the discursive formulations of these understandings. What we must therefore note, of course, is that when I open for discussion the work that the use of survivor testimonies does in the high-school classroom, my intention is not to suggest that testimonies cannot – or should not – be used. They must be used, as the teachers recognize. But the work they undertake, and the versions of history they authorize, needs to be deconstructed and understood; and the complexity of the task facing the teachers needs to be reckoned with.

The Holocaust as unspeakable?

The articulation, as demonstrated above, of survivor testimony as capable of speaking the truth of the Holocaust works in part to erase the ways in which testimonies will always contain an aporia. Yet in the interviews it also became apparent that some teachers were aware that the horrors of the Holocaust are unspeakable for the survivors. A teacher at an all-girls' school in Melbourne explained that she uses the writings of:

> one of the eyewitnesses, a survivor, who gives a story of how kids were treated in daily life . . . how she talks about as a mother when she came to Auschwitz after being told by someone who was already there, some guy strode up to her and said, 'Let go of her child's hand'. And she screamed and she didn't. And he screamed at her and he physically tore, separated them and as a result obviously she survived and the child didn't. And now, as a mother, that it's impossible to talk about, that she has memories of herself, that she let go. And she understands rationally that if she hadn't of let go, she wouldn't be here, but that wouldn't have . . . And we, you know, I came across that, as I was looking at the material we have, that was obviously very powerful, she was a mother and a woman.[85]

This raises the problematic of unspeakability in a particular way. The teacher links a traumatic unspeakability to gender and to the feminized Holocaust victim: it is the woman who is unable to protect her child who is the subject of the unspeakable occurrence. The idea of a mother being separated from her daughter is, as the 'maternal metaphor' teaches us, a particularly horrific and unspeakable image, particularly when taught to girls.[86]

One New York teacher at an all-girls' school touched on the idea of the unspeakability of the horrors of the Holocaust in her interview in a similar manner. She explained that she will:

> bring in stories from interviews. There was one woman who was raped twice in the war and she never married. And she was the only woman that I interviewed – I interviewed over 60 people – and she was the only one who had not gotten married. Marriage was very, very important to survivors. They had to start a family and do something. And because of her experience of rape she didn't want to be part of it. She saw men, she went out with them, but she would never get married. She never told her story to anyone else. We were the only people who heard it.[87] But she wanted it recorded. And she died a couple of years after the interview. And that recording eventually wound up with her brother, who never knew her story, that she had never told. So, I always tell the girls that story, because, it puts, even though they never saw her, it puts a story that they can sort of relate to. And how you were just profiting and about how you have no value. So she was raped first by the Germans for stealing a piece of bread, and then after liberation, it was a very common thing by the Russians. Russians were notorious for raping. That, I think the girls could relate to, coming from the former Soviet Union.[88]

The point of this story then, for this teacher, was not just to convey to the students the particular example of the survivor's inability to speak of the horrors she faced. This story was also utilized to, in a sense, domesticate the Holocaust: to make it comprehensible for the students, and to give them a story which they could relate to and identify with. The strangeness – carried perhaps in the silence of the woman herself – and heterogeneity of this story, of the Holocaust, is thereby somewhat removed.

This gendered unspeakability arose also during an interview with a teacher at another New York school. When asked if she discusses sexual assault and rape perpetrated by the Nazis, she replied that they 'talked about that one year because we actually had a class on that . . . and one of the very horrible questions was about how a Jewish woman was used as a prostitute by one of the high-ranking Nazi officers. And it was a terrible discussion, but it was too, too difficult and you know, no, we don't, we don't . . . not really'.[89] The teacher's hesitancy comes across clearly in this statement. Her sentence, her explanation, is unfinished, dropping away at the end. It is quite clearly 'too difficult'.

Another teacher in New York explained that at her school a survivor came to speak at the Yom Hashoah commemoration. He 'was also very interesting. He also lived on the West Side and he didn't speak about his camp experience so much. He mostly spoke about his time in the ghetto. And a lot about the action when they moved everyone out, which we were surprised about because he was in quite a number of camps, but he didn't speak about that so much.'[90] That he did not speak of his time in the camps was worthy of mention, the possible traumatic reasons as to why left aside.

At times it seems as though the curricula – quite understandably – cannot manage the task of speaking about the Holocaust. The writing can, on occasion, be seen to be abstracted from the complexities of people. This abstraction can be seen, for instance, in the descriptions of what happened to children, and in the use of euphemism. The curriculum from a Melbourne school explains that, due to vast shortages inside the ghettos, there was a great deal of smuggling of food into the ghetto. It states that 'much of this smuggling was done by small children, who were forced to forgo their childhood and not infrequently to forgo life itself'.[91] To describe death as 'forgoing life' seems an obfuscation. The problems of speaking about the Holocaust – of the shifting definitions of life – jump out of this sentence.

Similarly, two pages in the curriculum of a school in Melbourne, taken from the historian Michael Berenbaum's book *The World Must Know: The History of the Holocaust as Told in the United States Holocaust Memorial Museum*, look at the massacre of Jews, Roma and Soviet Prisoners of War at Babi Yar.[92] There are quotes from a non-Jewish truck driver who was present at the scene, a member of the Einsatzgruppen group who carried out the massacre named Kurt Werner, and a survivor, Dina Pronicheva, who crawled out of the ravine after the Einsatzgruppen left. The three testimonies are of quite different qualities. Firstly, the truck driver and Werner's testimonies are in the first person, while Pronicheva's is narrated by Anatoli Kuznetsov, to whom she told her story. The truck driver's narrative is used to describe the overall scene. He tells of Jewish people arriving, undressing and leaving their clothes in specific piles. They were then led to a ravine, and forced to lie down on top of those who had come before them. A policeman who was standing on top of them then shot them in the back of their heads with a submachine gun. From here the story of what happened is taken up by Werner, whose work, Berenbaum informs the students, 'was unpleasant, and most difficult'. Werner explains that '[i]t's almost impossible to imagine what nerves of steel it took to carry out that dirty work down there. It was horrible ... That evening we were given schnapps again.' Finally comes the voice of Pronicheva, narrated through Kuznetsov: 'Her whole body was buried under the sand but she did not move until it began to cover her mouth ... She started to choke and then, scarcely realizing what she was doing, she started to struggle in a state of uncontrolled panic, quite prepared now to be shot rather than to be buried alive.' She was able to crawl out from under the sand, where she met a small boy who had also survived and crawled out. This description of what happened at Babi Yar ends by explaining the importance of naming the victims as Jewish. Yet we can see perhaps a different story emerging from the usage of survivor testimony here. The story begins and is directed most fully by the words of perpetrators and bystanders. The words of the bystander and perpetrator come to us 'unfiltered', but the words of the survivor are narrated through someone else: this is a significant difference. Perhaps this can be understood as evidence of the problems which teachers and historians have in the face of narrating the experiences of Holocaust survivors into history?

These very problems of language were not explicitly discussed by the teachers, yet many survivors have written about the inability of language to encapsulate their experiences. In his autobiographical book *Survival in Auschwitz* Primo Levi wrote of the need for another language to articulate the feelings of cold and starvation that people in the camps felt:

> Just as our hunger is not that feeling of missing a meal, so our way of being cold has need of a new word. We say 'hunger', we say 'tiredness', 'fear', 'pain', we say 'winter' and they are different things. They are free words, created and used by free men who lived in comfort and suffering in their homes. If the Lagers had lasted longer a new, harsh language would have been born; and only this language could express what it means to toil the whole day in the wind, with the temperature below freezing, wearing only a shirt, underpants, cloth jacket and trousers, and in one's body nothing but weakness, hunger and knowledge of the end drawing nearer.[93]

This problematic of language in the face of dehumanization is not fully grappled with by the teachers: it is taken that the language which is comprehensible to the students is enough to encapsulate the Holocaust and make it intelligible for them. Indeed, this problem – of what language can possibly be used to convey appropriate meanings – is one we all must grapple with.

Similarly, for Giorgio Agamben, 'Auschwitz is the radical refutation of every principle of obligatory communication.'[94] He explains that:

> [t]his is so not only because, according to testimonies, any attempt to induce a Kapo or an SS to communicate often ended in a beating; nor is it the case simply because . . . in certain camps the place of communication was taken by the rubber whip, ironically named *der Dolmetscher*, 'the interpreter'. Nor because 'not being talked to' was the normal condition in the camp, where 'your tongue dries up in a few days, and your thought with it'.[95]

Instead, the 'decisive objection is different. It is . . . the *Muselmann*', that radical figure which is a creation of the death-camp, of Auschwitz, which is between inhuman and human – the living dead, who did not speak.[96] It is the frightening effects which Agamben here points to which are covered over by the teachers. This is quite understandable: what Agamben is describing is truly terrifying.[97] But in effacing this something important of the Holocaust is lost. Perhaps though, this raises the very problems of representation which this chapter has attempted to describe: how to represent that which is not known to the survivors themselves? In the context of a system of historiography which is trying to negotiate anxieties about fitting in and which seeks solid ground, how to create new languages which undertake these tasks? The former question is approached by Saul Friedländer and others in their analysis of deep memory.

Charlotte Delbo, in her work *Auschwitz and After*, formulated the concept of deep memory, which was later taken up first by Lawrence Langer and then by Saul Friedländer.[98] Friedländer posits the notion of deep memory in contradistinction to common memory, arguing that they 'are ultimately irreducible to each other'.[99] Common memory, he explains, is deployed with the aim of providing closure for the individual undertaking the remembering. Deep memory prevents closure as '[a]ny attempt at building a coherent self founders on the intractable return of the repressed and recurring deep memory'.[100] Deep memory can be understood as the unreachable memories of the traumatic event which return in a displaced form to haunt the survivor. It is through the repetition of substitute signifiers that deep memories are expressed. James E. Young later took up Friedländer's questioning of the possibilities for the incorporation of deep memory. 'Is it possible', Young asks, 'to write a history that includes some oblique reference to such deep memory, but which leaves it essentially intact, untouched and thereby deep?'[101] This, precisely, is the problem which I am drawing attention to with regard to the work of the teachers of the Holocaust under examination. That teachers present the chronology that they do and use Holocaust testimonies in the manner sketched previously is, therefore, not simply a matter of their wanting to sculpt their historical representations in the dominant manner of the histories which surround them. Rather, the problem of repression and inaccessible, deep, memory also shapes the narratives being presented.

Deep memory, in this iteration, is opaque; this opens up the question of what will become of deep memory when there are no more survivors left. For, according to both Young and Friedländer, this memory is inaccessible to historians and the work they undertake in constructing histories of the Holocaust, and yet somehow needs to be registered as inaccessible. While various historians, filmmakers, authors and, indeed, the official Holocaust histories of Israel, have attempted to bring closure and narratives of redemption to representations of the Holocaust, because of deep memory they have failed.[102] This, Friedländer suggests, is part of a new historical awareness, a new historical condition.[103] He explains that 'Jewish historians ... seem to be at a loss to produce an overall history of the extermination of the Jews in Europe that is not a mere textbook presentation, an analysis of the internal cogs and wheels of the destruction machinery or a compendium of separate monographs. The "Final Solution" in its epoch has not yet found its historian; and the problem cannot be reduced to a mere technical issue.'[104] Indeed, these problematics of deep memory are such that they confound all manner of historians.

Yet we can see something approximating a reckoning with this form of memory in the exploration of liberation presented in some of the curricula. In the curriculum of a school in New York there is an article from *The Jerusalem Post* from

24 December 2003 entitled 'Siblings Reunited Six Decades after Holocaust'. It describes the story of two siblings reunited in Israel: each had thought the other was dead, but they were alive and living near each other for most of their post-war lives. The article concludes with the words of the brother, who states that "'It's hard to explain that feeling we have . . . It's hard to measure in terms of gain. It's all inside," Shilon [the brother] said. "You cannot explain it."'[105]

In another curriculum, from a school in Melbourne, similar quotes from three survivors are presented to demonstrate the difficulties which liberation brought. The quotes are from Hadassah Bimko, Primo Levi and Viktor Frankl, and the section in the curriculum begins with the words 'For the survivors, the moment of liberation was hopeful yet fearful'.[106] Bimko is quoted as writing that 'For the great part of the liberated Jews of Bergen-Belsen, there was no ecstasy, no joy at our liberation. We had lost our families, our homes. We had no place to go, nobody to hug, nobody who was waiting for us, anywhere. We had been liberated from death and from the fear of death, but we were not free from the fear of life'. Levi explains that 'The breach in the barbed wire gave us a concrete image of it. To anyone who stopped to think, it signified no more Germans, no more selections, no work, no blows, no roll calls, and, perhaps, later, the return. But we had to make an effort to convince ourselves of it, and no one had time to enjoy the thought. All around lay destruction and death'. And finally Frankl is quoted, stating that 'Timidly, we looked around and glanced at each other questioningly. Then we ventured a few steps out of the camp. This time no orders were shouted at us, nor was there any need to duck quickly to avoid a blow or a kick. 'Freedom' – we repeated to ourselves, and yet we could not grasp it'. Altogether, these quotes paint a picture of ambivalence, of a lack of sureness about what liberation meant, and what it would bring. Echoing this, the curriculum page ends with the words that 'Some survivors felt empty, even guilty that they had survived while so many others had not. Others felt nothing'. Here we can catch a glimpse of the complexity of feeling, meaning, time and place which lies within survivor testimonies.

This is repeated in another curriculum document from a different school in Melbourne. There are brief quotes from five survivors who were liberated which are introduced with the following words: 'For every survivor the day of liberation was engraved in his or her memory. The sight of those liberators affected every survivor. The overwhelming relief felt by them was accompanied by pain – so many loved ones had been killed, homes and possessions had been lost and Jewish life itself had been destroyed over much of Europe'. The final quote is from Maria Rebhun who was liberated from Lauenburg camp, in Pomerania. She said that 'We were in a daze. Barely moving, supporting the ones who were not able to make a step . . . we went to face new reality. Our minds were like a vacuum, our hearts empty of any desires. On the streets, ecstatic Russian soldiers offered us sweets and cigarettes amidst laughter and songs, but we were mute. Who are we? Where are we to go? Whom to turn to?'[107] These excerpts from these three different curricula raise the problems of time which were discussed previously: that when survivor testimonies are explored in depth, it becomes clear that the chronological ending of the Holocaust did not bring about its end in the memories of survivors. That, perhaps, there was no chronological end to the Holocaust, and that ambivalence is central to any account of the Holocaust. Indeed, these moments in the curricula point to the ways in which oblique complexities can be, and are being, pointed to without an attempt being made to resolve them.

The 'lack of closure', or unredemptory narrative, which Friedländer talked of is important. He elsewhere explains that '[e]ach individual [survivor] testimony remains a story unresolved'.[108] This understanding of testimony as unresolved and unresolvable is in part a product of deep memory. It is deep memory, and those signifiers which come up in the place of the memories, which ensure that Holocaust testimony can never have complete closure. When the testimony of the survivor is made to do the work of supplementing the historian – to provide complete, closed off narratives which describe a series of particular events and circumstances – then the lack of closure of the testimony can be covered over. Yet, as will be discussed in Chapter Three, there is a move by all the teachers to bring the narrative to a closure – to ensure that the Holocaust is finished, and the Jewish people reborn. This chronological narrative contradicts the ways in which, in survivor testimonies, the Holocaust continues to resonate.[109] At the moments outlined here, however, we can see something of the lack of closure. But these moments are few.

In the teachings which are being described in this research, the teachers often elide the gap between testimony and experience, between experience and representation. Indeed, by repeating histories in the ways in which they do, they work to cover over that gap in order to make the Holocaust comprehensible. In making the Holocaust comprehensible they are working to negotiate their anxious feelings: when the world can be understood, it is easier to find one's place within it. These historiographical responses are, we must understand, central to a negotiation of the anxiety over the place of Jews in the world which these teachers display.

Seeking to Know

Thus we can ask: where does all this lead? It leads, in short, to an appreciation of one of the dominating purposes of these examples of Holocaust education: to cope with the anxiety over the place of Jews in the modern Western world. The purpose of the construction of these particular histories has been, I have argued, to determine identity formulations in a situation which requires the negotiation of feelings of displacement and the accompanying anxieties. As I explored in the Introduction, through the narration of group histories one can (re)establish a group's identity. By formulating histories of the Holocaust according to the historical paradigms which exist for these teachers – in the Western world and in the Zionist communities in which they live – the teachers are, I am arguing, striving to make the Holocaust understandable and knowable. This is important in the face of the anxiety which these teachers struggle with, and it is not an uncommon response to such uncertainty. By fitting the stories of the Holocaust into the paradigms offered – the usage of chronological histories and survivor testimonies – the story of the Holocaust becomes comprehensible. Indeed, as Hayden White explains, it is perhaps inevitable and necessary that when narratives are being constructed the narrator reaches for culturally appropriate ways of narrating, which will make the narrative comprehensible to those who are to receive it.[110] And thus, as has been shown above, these teachers reach for the chronological narrative which predominates in Western Historical discourses. In turn, this helps to negotiate and work towards a resolution of the anxiety which these teachers exhibit.

Importantly for our purposes, this mode of narration works to foreground ideas of truth and comprehension. The exploration of the deployment of survivor testimony outlined the ways in which truth has been established: that the words of one who was there seemingly provide access to the event itself. The truth of the event, it is understood, is explained through the words of the people who were in the event. But yet, the teachers maintain a complex relationship to understanding the Holocaust – there are some aspects which, it seems, they feel can be completely understood (hence the move to use normative historical narratives, which present knowing as possible), and they seek to present their students with this full knowledge. It is the experience of the victims which they present as knowable. The same is not true of the perpetrators, about whom a similar search for knowledge does not occur. The teachers want to understand, and at times it seems as though they believe one can understand, but at other times they do not. This is a paradox of the representational mode which they embrace, which allows one to be easily convinced that they can, and do, understand. But there are also moments when the inability to know seeps through.

For one New York teacher, the important lesson for the students to learn is that 'there is no why'. When asked to explicate the main themes of her pedagogy she explained that she:

> think[s] what ended up being the main question that we looked at a lot, was what Primo Levi said "Why, why?", and the German guard turns back and says "There is no why in the concentration camps". That sort of ended up being the overarching interest of the students. You know, in school we are taught to ask why. To ask why these things happen. It's not so important to know the How or the What. You have to figure out why. And when they learn about the Holocaust, it is one of those things where the why just doesn't make sense. It's very easy to retreat back to the "this is what happened, these are the facts, these are the numbers". Not that those things aren't important but a lot of it is trying to figure what is almost impossible to figure out from a rational point of view. How do we

deal with that in a way that makes sense to them? And how to get them to move on from there.¹¹¹

This teacher opens up the possibility of a lack of knowing of 'why'. But she also, in a sense then, presents the idea that understanding and knowing the Holocaust can come about through learning that there is no way in which it can be understood. This is, potentially, a paradox at the heart of all Holocaust representation (including that which I am presenting in this book).

Regardless of the way in which the knowledge is presented, it is recognizable that the certainty of knowledge is placed at the centre of these histories of the Holocaust. This, we can understand, is a product of the playing out of a response to the anxiety which the teachers feel about the place of Jews. In foregrounding a stable idea of what the Holocaust entailed these teachers are working to manage the Holocaust's effects, one of which is instability in the world. This can be seen, for instance, in the words of a teacher in New York. For this teacher, learning about the Holocaust – the gaining of knowledge – is a way to remedy the effects of the Holocaust. In an interview she explained that 'a lot of my reading is on the Holocaust . . . it's a fascination. It's so unbelievable. You feel that there is so much loss that *you have to know something to get it back a bit*. To make it less anonymous.'¹¹² Making 'it less anonymous' involves making the Holocaust, in some way, known. And so, something can be recuperated; feelings of uncertainty can be lessened, through the very act of attempting to recover these histories.

For another New York teacher the focus of her teaching is not on a chronology of events, but rather on providing the students with the words and testimonies of survivors. She explained that she tries 'to personalize it because otherwise it's someone else's history. I want them to feel that it's their history.'¹¹³ It can become known – can become something that is a part of them – by listening to the words of survivors. Another New York teacher explained that her interest in the Holocaust does not stem from a personal connection – none of her grandparents were involved in the Holocaust – but rather that 'the tragedy itself spoke to [her] from a young age'. As a result, she 'wanted to understand and know about it.'¹¹⁴ This, it seemed, could be achieved by studying the history of the Holocaust, and learning about it in order to teach the next generation. What brings these disparate ideas from these teachers together is that they all encapsulate a desire to know.¹¹⁵ This desire exists, I am suggesting, because of the uncertainties which these teachers carry.

Similarly, much of the work of March of the Living focuses around instructing students in ways of knowing the Holocaust. This can be seen for instance in the students' information book for the Melbourne contingent in 2007. One of the activities the students were instructed to undertake before leaving for Poland was to eat and drink the types of foods which the Jewish prisoners would have eaten in the concentration and death camps. By sampling the amount of bread which they would have been given, or drinking the flavoured water which passed for coffee, the students are supposed to 'experience' and hence know what it was like for the survivors to experience these same foods and liquids in the camps: experience becomes equivalent to knowledge.[116] But, of course, eating and drinking something in isolation from the other material and emotional circumstances which accompanied this food, and the long duration through which such things were experienced, is to abstract the practices. This is recognized by The Shoah Teaching Alternatives in Jewish Education (STAJE)'s 'Guiding Principles for Teaching the Shoah in Jewish Schools' which states that teachers should:

> avoid simulation activities. We cannot possibly understand the extremity of circumstances endured during the Shoah. None of our students could ever imagine the hunger that Jews felt in the ghetto or the shock of confronting murder on a daily basis. Since we cannot even imagine it, we certainly cannot recreate it through activities that encourage students to put themselves in the place of victims, perpetrators or other people who lived during this period. Students can best understand the reality of this history through interaction with documents, artefacts, and testimonies, which serve as primary sources for learning and understanding the Shoah.[117]

The function of the 'simulation activity', however, is important for us to comprehend: it indicates that within Holocaust pedagogy, and Holocaust memorial practices more generally, the disjuncture between signifier and signified is often erased or covered over in order for teachers to manage their desire to know. Yet the STAJE still accepts that the aim of Holocaust pedagogy is to encourage students to 'understand the reality': the impulse to know remains (unexamined).

What then can we do with such information? How can the desire to know be more fruitfully deployed? According to James E. Young, '[t]he question becomes: can a historical narrative simultaneously assert itself as an authoritative version of events and point to its own provisionality? Conversely, we might also ask: at what point might the adequacy of narrative be judged partly on its revealed provisionality?'[118] This is a pertinent question for the teachers, most of whom seem to strive to avoid provisionality.[119] Indeed, could the very provisionality of knowledge about the Holocaust become the basis for knowing the Holocaust? Perhaps not, if we remember – as I have been arguing – that these histories are formulated in response to an anxiety about the place of Jews in the world. For, as has been suggested earlier, one way in which this anxiety is played out is through the construction of histories of the Holocaust in the mould of Western chronological narratives. To incorporate – much less point to – the provisionality of the narratives in a sustained way would further unsettle the anxious feelings. Instead, there is an evasion of the interpretative nature, and potential for rupture, of the historiographical practices, which is but one step in the normalization of the particular stories of the Holocaust that are taught in the Jewish schools under consideration. There is a logic being sustained here: that if these histories can follow the dominant Western modes, then it can be shown that Jews belong in History. And thus the anxieties can be lessened.

Notes

1. In the words of Gabrielle Spiegel, '"History" being understood in the traditional sense of "objective," formalized, and institutionalized modes of understanding and interpretation associated with the "modern" (nineteenth-century, positivist and cognitive modernism).' G.M. Spiegel. May 2002. 'Memory and History: Liturgical Time and Historical Time', *History and Theory* 41(2), 150.
2. See C. Caruth. 1996. *Unclaimed Experience: Trauma, Narrative, and History*, Baltimore, MD: Johns Hopkins University Press, 1–9.
3. His most significant work in this regard is *Metahistory*. H. White. 1973. *Metahistory: The Historical Imagination in Nineteenth Century Europe*, Baltimore, MD: Johns Hopkins University Press.
4. See J. W. Scott. Summer 1991. 'The Evidence of Experience', *Critical Inquiry* 17, 777, where Scott argues that experience and history are both articulated through discourse: the particular relationship which Scott writes of is one of inextricable and interdependent intertwining between discourse, experience and history.
5. P. Ricoeur. 1984. *Time and Narrative*, trans. Kathleen McLaughlin and David Pellauer, Vol. I, Chicago, IL: University of Chicago Press, 3.
6. Ibid.
7. E.L. Santner. 1992. 'History Beyond the Pleasure Principle: Some Thoughts on the Representation of Trauma,' in S. Friedländer (ed.), *Probing the Limits of Representation: Nazism and the 'Final Solution'*, Cambridge, MA: Harvard University Press, 144.
8. Dan Stone critiques this 'impulse towards coherence'. See Stone, *Constructing the Holocaust*, 212.
9. Interview with Teacher A at School MC.
10. Interview with Teacher A at School NYB.
11. Curriculum of School ME, 1. The dates in Stages Two and Three cross over because Stage Two begins with the 'Invasion of Poland', and then explores the ghettos, primarily within Poland, whereas Stage Three begins with the 'Invasion of Russia' and then explains Einsatzgruppen, deportations, camps and resistance. There is therefore some duplication in terms of dates, but the sense of the Holocaust being composed of chronologically defined stages remains.
12. Curriculum of School NYC, 24.
13. Yad Vashem. 2002. *Yesterdays and Then Tomorrows: Holocaust Anthology of Testimonies and Readings*, Jerusalem: The International School for Holocaust Studies, in Curriculum of School MB, no page number.
14. Curriculum of School NYC, 23–45.
15. The rupturing of time which comes with Holocaust survivor testimonies is explored in detail by Marianne Hirsch and Leo Spitzer, and Michael Nutkiewicz. See M. Hirsch and L. Spitzer. Summer 2006. 'Testimonial Objects: Memory, Gender, and Transmission', *Poetics Today* 27(2), 353–83 and M. Nutkiewicz. Winter-Spring 2003. 'Shame, Guilt, and Anguish in Holocaust Survivor Testimony', *Oral History Review* 30(1), 1–22. In both these articles, in different ways, the past is brought to bear on the present through testimonial and memorial products. This will be explored below in a discussion of deep memory, and can be seen particularly in *Maus*, by Art Spiegelman. A.

Spiegelman. 1996. *The Complete Maus: A Survivor's Tale*, New York: Pantheon Books. Richard Terdiman has argued that time is predominantly read as progressive – or chronological – in modern capitalist societies because of the necessities of production: temporality is inscribed as continually directed forwards in order to aid and control the impulse for production. Representation, or – as is the case in this chapter – history, is shaped by a progressive narrative because of the progressive demands of the social world. See R. Terdiman. *Present Past: Modernity and the Memory Crisis*, Ithaca, NY: Cornell University Press, 54. This will be explored further.
16. Interview with Teacher B at School MA. (Note that the *War Against the Jews* was written by Lucy Dawidowicz in 1975). This is reiterated in the curriculum document, which follows the following trajectory: The Aftermath of World War I – 1919–1939, the world's treatment of Germany following WWI, and the effect on its political and military goals; Jews of Europe Between the Wars 1919–1939: The cultural, social, and religious life of Jewish communities in Europe; Anti-Semitism and its Impact on the Jews of Europe; The Nazi Party and its rise to power; The War Against the Jews Begins: 1935–1939; Ghettos; Mass Murder of Jews throughout Nazi Europe; Concentration Camps; Resistance; Other Victims of the Holocaust; Rescue and liberation; Achieving a State; Holocaust literature. Curriculum of School MA, 3–10.
17. Interview with Teacher B at School MA.
18. Ibid. Here we see the impact of the confines of the school system: this teacher lays out how each of the units fits into a different year of study to create a larger Jewish Studies curriculum.
19. Interview with Teacher A at School MB. Emphasis added.
20. H. White. 1998. 'The Historical Text as Literary Artifact', in B. Fay, P. Pomper and R.T. Vann (eds), *History and Theory: Contemporary Readings*, Malden, MA: Blackwell Publishers, 23–4. Emphases in original.
21. Interview with Teacher A at School NYD.
22. Richard Terdiman writes of the exclusivity which hegemonic discourses bring, and the dominance involved in the making and reinforcing of hegemony: 'The privilege of any dominant discourse is to "go without saying". Dominant discourses claim to totalize the world of possible utterances – or would, if from within the confidence of hegemony, they felt the need to make claims at all. But of course by their privilege that is what they are exempted from doing to begin with'. Terdiman, *Present Past*, 19.
23. Stone, *Constructing the Holocaust*, 18.
24. Ibid.
25. M. Sturken. Winter 1998. 'The Remembering of Forgetting: Recovered Memory and the Question of Experience', *Social Text* 57, 117.
26. Geoffrey Roberts accorded with this approach, explaining that 'it is doubtful that narrative history "represents" the past at all; rather narratives *present* aspects of the past, albeit summarily and partially. The purpose of that presentation is not narrative mimicry of historical actuality but the *demonstration* and *display* of the answer to questions of the what, why, how and who of past events'. G. Roberts. 2001. 'Introduction: The History and Narrative Debate, 1960-2000', in G. Roberts (ed.), *The History and Narrative Reader*, London: Routledge, 9. Emphasis in original.
27. H. White. 1992. 'Historical Emplotment and the Problem of Truth,' in S. Friedländer (ed.), *Probing the Limits of Representation: Nazism and the 'Final Solution'*, Cambridge, MA: Harvard University Press, 39.
28. There are various theorists and historians who have argued against White's approaches to narrative and history. Some of these are brought together in Saul Friedländer's edited collection *Probing the Limits of Representation*, particularly responding to White's

chapter in this collection, 'Historical Emplotment and the Problem of Truth'. For instance, Amos Funkenstein argues for a conception of reality which, in a sense, pre-exists narrative. Carlo Ginzburg locates White's theorizations within an Italian school of historiography which, he argues, can assist the reader to understand the political implications of White's ideas of truth in history. Martin Jay extends White's argument about the linguistic nature of all events, arguing that when White argued that events can be emplotted in numerous ways, he is asserting that the events have a pre-linguistic life. Jay disagrees with this, asserting that events are always linguistic constructions. See A. Funkenstein, 'History, Counterhistory, and Narrative', 66–81, C. Ginzburg, 'Just One Witness', 82–96, M. Jay, 'Of Plots, Witnesses, and Judgements', 97–107, all in S. Friedländer (ed.), *Probing the Limits of Representation: Nazism and the 'Final Solution'*, Cambridge, MA: Harvard University Press, 1992.
29. White, 'Historical Emplotment and the Problem of Truth', 37. Eric Hobsbawm echoes this point. See E. Hobsbawm, 'The Revival of Narrative: Some Comments,' in G. Roberts (ed.), *The History and Narrative Reader*, London: Routledge, 299.
30. As will be shown in Chapter Three, the Zionist influence on these narratives means that they typically end with the creation of the State of Israel. This whole approach – of a chronological, progressive narrative which ends in redemption – goes against the approach to historiography articulated by Gabrielle Spiegel: 'the Holocaust put to rest, finally and forever, at least in the minds of many, a Western modernist, progressive, and ultimately optimistic view of history'. Spiegel, 'Memory and History', 150.
31. The first one was Teacher A at School NYE, the second was Teacher A at School NYA.
32. Dan Stone has identified this as a fundamental part of the movement in the 1960s and beyond to write fact-based histories of the Holocaust. See Stone, *Constructing the Holocaust*, 25.
33. Hereafter referred to as Wissenschaft.
34. Meyer, 'The Emergence of Modern Jewish Historiography', 167–68.
35. Ibid., 170.
36. Yerushalmi, *Zakhor*, 84. For a critique of Yerushalmi's understanding of Jewish memory and history see Funkenstein, *Perceptions of Jewish History*, 10–21.
37. For a discussion of Enlightenment history as scientific see A. Curthoys and J. Docker. 2006. *Is History Fiction?*, Sydney: UNSW Press, 69–89.
38. Yerushalmi, *Zakhor*, 85.
39. Ibid.
40. Ibid., 87–88.
41. Gershom Scholem critiqued the Wissenschaft movement for its emphasis on a Jewish history shaped in secular, scientific terms, rather than as fundamentally resting on Jewish religious aspects. For an exploration of this in terms of his personal narrative, which saw Judaism as fundamental to Jewishness and Zionism, see his interview in G. Scholem. 1976. *On Jews and Judaism in Crises: Selected Essays*, trans. and ed. W.J. Dannhauser, New York: Schocken Books, 17–20.
42. A. Funkenstein. Winter 1995. 'The Dialectics of Assimilation', *Jewish Social Studies* 1(2), 1–14.
43. G.G. Iggers and Q.E. Wang. 2008. *A Global History of Modern Historiography*, Harlow: Pearson Education Limited, 22.
44. Ibid., 122.
45. D. Carr. 1998. 'Narrative and the Real World: An Argument for Continuity', in B. Fay, P. Pomper and R.T. Vann (eds), *History and Theory: Contemporary Readings*, Malden, MA: Blackwell Publishers, 137. This is, of course, quite a limiting idea of what constitutes history. As shall be discussed further with reference to survivor testimony, the

presentation of a chronological narrative which articulates its history in terms of truth and falsehood closes off a broader consideration of what constitutes history. Moreover, of course, this is not the only version of modern Western historiography that exists. There are numerous historians, in Australia, the U.S. and elsewhere, who write history in ways which avoid linearity or normative narrative strategies.

46. M. Cousins. 1982. 'The Practice of Historical Investigation,' in D. Attridge, G. Bennington and R. Young (eds), *Post-Structuralism and the Question of History*, Cambridge: Cambridge University Press, 133. Cousins also argued that '[h]istorical scholarship bears more than a fleeting resemblance to this jurisprudential complex. It is not just that historically the emergence of historical scholarship and techniques of, especially, common law arguments have gone together. Nor is it just that the historian's skills might be described as forensic. It is that there is a parallel between the way in which the question of truth and evidence privilege the category of event'. Cousins, 'The Practice of Historical Investigation', 132. M.C. Lemon discussed the narration of a series of discrete events as fundamental to the chronological narrative. See M.C. Lemon, 'The Structure of Narrative,' in G. Roberts (ed.), *The History and Narrative Reader*, London: Routledge, 108, 112-13. He also suggested that, as such, a chronological narrative differs from a chronicle which presents the events, dates and facts without the story which binds them together. Lemon, 'The Structure of Narrative', 108. See also Stone, *Constructing the Holocaust*, 214; J.E. Young. December 1997. 'Toward a Received History of the Holocaust', *History and Theory* 46(4), 34. For a further, in-depth exploration of time, temporality and the circularity of narrative in historiography, see Ricoeur, *Time and Narrative*.
47. Iggers and Wang, *A Global History of Modern Historiography*, 123-24.
48. E.P. Thompson. December 1967. 'Time, Work-Discipline, and Industrial Capitalism', *Past & Present*, 38, 56-97.
49. Joyce Dalsheim made a similar point with regard to the 'busyness' of the classroom, highlighting the ways in which time is compressed in the classroom in order to convey particular ideas of history. This will be explored in greater depth in Chapter Three. See Dalsheim, 'Settler Nationalism, Collective Memories of Violence and the "Uncanny Other"', 151-70.
50. L.L. Langer. 1991. *Holocaust Testimonies: The Ruins of Memory*, New Haven, CT: Yale University Press, 67.
51. Ibid., 57.
52. Terdiman, *Present Past*, 8.
53. Tony Kushner provided a history of the development of various projects of writing down Holocaust survivor testimonies, which began in response to the Nuremberg Trials and as Yizkor Books, and have evolved into larger-scale collections developed through the Yale University Fortunoff Institute Video Archive, Steven Spielberg's Visual History Foundation, the United States Holocaust Memorial Museum, Yad Vashem and, on a smaller and more localizsed scale, the Melbourne Holocaust Museum. T. Kushner. Summer 2006. 'Holocaust Testimony, Ethics, and the Problem of Representation', *Poetics Today* 27(2), 276--78. In the early 1980s, Jack Kugelmass and Jonathan Boyarin assembled excerpts from sixty of these *yizkor bikuren* (yizkor books) into one collection to give a sense of life in the Polish *shtetl*. See J. Kugelmass and J. Boyarin. 1983. *From a Ruined Garden: The Memorial Books of Polish Jewry*, New York: Schocken Books. For a discussion of the *yizker bikuren* in the context of postmemory see Hirsch, *Family Frames*, 247. Diane L. Wolf explored the meanings made in Holocaust testimonies in the Spielberg Foundations archive, bringing a sociological perspective to her understanding. D.L. Wolf. 'Holocaust Testimony: Producing Post-Memories, Producing Identities,' in J.M. Gerson and D.L. Wolfd (eds), *Sociology Confronts the Holocaust:*

Memories and Identities in Jewish Diasporas, Durham, NC: Duke University Press, 154–75.
54. Interview with Teacher A at School ME.
55. Interview with Teacher A at School MB.
56. Ibid. Emphasis added.
57. Curriculum of School MB, 139. Emphasis added.
58. Y. Eliach. 1982. *Hasidic Tales of the Holocaust*, New York: Oxford University Press.
59. Curriculum of School NYC, 86.
60. One is led to wonder how such a story could possibly be told by a non-survivor. Could a morality tale of the Holocaust possibly be told by a non-survivor which suggests that the way to survive a selection at Auschwitz was by knowing the SS officer conducting the selection, and that the way to know someone is through polite and impersonal conversation?
61. Curriculum of School MB, 133.
62. Interview with Teacher A at School NYB. Emphasis added.
63. Interview with Teacher A at School NYD. Emphasis added.
64. Interview with Teacher B at School MA.
65. Interview with Teacher A at School MC.
66. Ibid.
67. S. Felman. 1992. 'Education and Crisis, or the Vicissitudes of Teaching', in S. Felman and D. Laub, *Testimony: Crises of Witnessing in Literature, Psychoanalysis, and History*, New York: Routledge, 8.
68. Ibid., 15. Emphasis in original. Michael André Bernstein similarly explored the impossibilities for the survivor of speaking about the Holocaust, as well as critiqued 'one of the most pervasive myths of our era ... [which] is the absolute authority given to first-person testimony'. See M.A. Bernstein. 1994. *Foregone Conclusions: Against Apocalyptic History*, Berkeley: University of California Press, 46–47.
69. I hope that the important distinctions between the deconstruction of ideas of truth which I am presenting, and the erasure of truth that Holocaust deniers present, are clear. There is no doubt that Holocaust survivors speak to many truths (and that their testimonies are essential): what these truths are, and how they are understood within the school classroom, is what is under exploration here.
70. Scott, 'The Evidence of Experience', 782.
71. Ibid., 793.
72. Interview with Teacher A at School NYC.
73. Curriculum of School MB, 88–89.
74. Ibid., 88.
75. Indeed, it must be remembered that, as Richard Terdiman notes, '[t]he "real" historical referents of our discussion will never fit between our pages. In representation, reduction is inevitable. "Reductionism" has had bad press, but we cannot avoid it.' Terdiman, *Present Past*, 22. The problems drawn out by survivor testimony and witnessing are also explored by Caroline Wake. See C. Wake. Spring/Summer 2013. 'Regarding the Recording: The Viewer of Video Testimony, the Complexity of Copresence and the Possibility of Tertiary Witnessing', *History and Memory* 25(1), 111–44.
76. Charlotte Delbo's poetry poignantly draws out the incomprehensibility of the Holocaust for those caught up in it. She wrote of people arriving at Auschwitz, that 'they expect the worst – not the unthinkable'. C. Delbo. 1995. *Auschwitz and After*, trans. R.C. Lamont, New Haven, CT: Yale University Press, 4. Elsewhere she wrote that 'Today I am not sure that what I wrote is true. I am certain it is truthful.' Ibid., 1. *Auschwitz and After* explores this in great depth.

96 | *Anxious Histories*

77. Gabrielle Spiegel complicates the idea of testimonies being utilized to tell histories through an exploration of chronological time. Spiegel, 'Memory and History', 159.
78. Young, 'Toward a Received History of the Holocaust', 34. Emphasis in original.
79. This will be elaborated on further. For a further discussion of this and other aspects of Holocaust survivor testimony, see Z. Waxman. 2004. 'Testimony and Representation', in D. Stone (ed.), *The Historiography of the Holocaust*, Hampshire: Palgrave Macmillan, 487–507.
80. Marianne Hirsch and Leo Spitzer discuss the temporal disjunctions embodied in Holocaust memorial objects – such as notebooks and recipe books – and their passing down through the generations. These 'testimonial objects' bring the past into the present in complicated and disjunctive ways. The past and the present, they argue, are not as separate as some might suggest (and as the use of chronology and survivor testimonies by the teachers under consideration suggests). Hirsch and Spitzer, 'Testimonial Objects', 353–83.
81. Scott, 'The Evidence of Experience', 776.
82. Ibid., 793.
83. Ibid., 777.
84. Ibid., 776.
85. Interview with Teacher A at School MC. We can also see here the problems of speaking for the teacher: her sentence at one point trails off, it is difficult for her to speak of this Holocaust trauma. Further exploration of this instance of unspeakability – of the teacher being unable to speak – is outside the scope of this book.
86. For a discussion of the maternal metaphor see C. Kahane. 2001. 'Dark Mirrors: A Feminist Reflection on Holocaust Narrative and the Maternal Metaphor', in E. Bronfen and M. Kavka (eds), *Feminist Consequences: Theory for the New Century*, New York: Columbia University Press, 161–88. I will return to this point in Chapter Five.
87. Michael Nutkiewicz explored the ways in which survivors often do not speak of private pains and sufferings, such as rapes. He explained, in part, that 'some experiences are so demoralizing that they can only be described as a state of being outside the human. Not even the communal or didactic aspect of the oral testimony project will matter to the survivor. The story remains "my secret."' Nutkiewicz, 'Shame, Guilt, and Anguish in Holocaust Survivor Testimony', 21. He argued throughout the article that 'survivors live with countervailing pressures: the struggle to forget and remain silent and the need to tell and to memorialize.' Ibid., 1.
88. Interview with Teacher A at School NYF. This teacher explained that many of the students in the school had migrated to the U.S. from the former Soviet Union.
89. Interview with Teacher A at School NYD.
90. The moving of 'everyone out' refers to the *Aktia*, the actions which occurred in the ghettos when large numbers of Jews were taken to the train station in the ghetto and deported to concentration and death camps. These were often scenes of chaos. Interview with Teacher A at School NYE.
91. Curriculum of School MB, 77.
92. Ibid., 95–96.
93. P. Levi. 1996. *Survival in Auschwitz: The Nazi Assault on Humanity*, trans. S. Woolf, New York: Touchstone, 123.
94. Agamben, *Remnants of Auschwitz*, 65. Jean-François Lyotard has also presented a compelling discussion of the problems of articulating the Holocaust. In his work *The Differend* he engaged with, amongst other things, the problems of there (in some ways) having been no survivors, and no means of assessing and understanding the

Holocaust. See J-F. Lyotard. 1988. *The Differend: Phrases in Dispute*, Minneapolis: University of Minnesota Press.
95. Agamben, *Remnants of Auschwitz*, 65. He is quoting Primo Levi, *The Drowned and The Saved*, 1989, 93.
96. Ibid.
97. This is expanded in Agamben's description, following Levi, of the death-camp world, where 'death cannot be called death'. Ibid., 70.
98. I will not explore his work on deep memory here, but Lawrence Langer discussed the role of deep memory and the distinction between common and deep memory in survivor testimony. See Delbo, *Auschwitz and After*, and Langer, *Holocaust Testimonies*, 4–6.
99. S. Friedländer. 1993. *Memory, History, and the Extermination of the Jews of Europe*, Bloomington: Indiana University Press, 119.
100. Ibid.
101. Young, 'Toward a Received History of the Holocaust', 23.
102. Friedländer, *Memory, History, and the Extermination of the Jews of Europe*, 121.
103. Ibid., 123.
104. Ibid., 129.
105. Curriculum of School NYC, 71–72.
106. Curriculum of School ME, 131. All quotes in this paragraph are from this page.
107. Curriculum of School MB, 123–24.
108. Friedländer, *Memory, History, and the Extermination of the Jews of Europe*, 121–22. Friedländer also asserted that 'in no recent work of art is this lack of closure as obvious as in Claude Lanzmann's film *Shoah*'. Ibid., 121. Esther Faye has similarly discussed the ways in which these historical forms can possibly work to overcome that which it is 'fundamentally impossible to remember', and suggested that instead the responsibility should be given to testimony. E. Faye. 2001. 'Missing the 'Real' Trace of Trauma: How the Second Generation Remember the Holocaust', *American Imago* 58(2), 527.
109. For a discussion of closure of the narrative of the Holocaust see, for instance, Friedländer, *Memory, History, and the Extermination of the Jews of Europe*, 131, 133.
110. White, 'The Historical Text as Literary Artifact', 20.
111. Interview with Teacher A at School NYA.
112. Interview with Teacher A at School NYE. Emphasis added.
113. Interview with Teacher A at School NYF.
114. Interview with Teacher A at School NYB.
115. Hans Kellner wrote of this desire as follows: 'The pressing need to represent the Holocaust in poetry, novels, films, drama, music, and history must come from a desire to repeat in the imagination happenings and events that horrify and fascinate. We only represent what we desire. The desire to represent the Holocaust, however, is not the desire to repeat it as an event, nor necessarily the desire to repeat the form-giving pleasure of representation itself; rather, it is a desire to repeat the Holocaust in a suitably altered form to meet complex, often contradictory, sets of present needs'. Kellner, '"Never Again" Is Now', 226.
116. Central Agency for Jewish Education. 2007. *March of the Living International (Australia) Study Guide*, 102–3. For a discussion of similar practices and the issues surrounding them see G. Weissman. 2004. *Fantasies of Witnessing: Postwar Efforts to Experience the Holocaust*, Ithaca, NY: Cornell University Press.
117. Education Department at the Museum of Jewish Heritage: A Living Memorial to the Holocaust. 2005. 'Shoah Teaching Alternatives in Jewish Education Presents: Guiding Principles for Teaching the Shoah in Jewish Schools', New York, 3.

118. Young, 'Toward a Received History of the Holocaust', 30–31.
119. Dan Diner also discussed the problems of writing a narrative history of the Holocaust, and integrating it into a broader history, which the teachers do not seem to deal with. D. Diner. 2003. 'The Destruction of Narrativity: The Holocaust in Historical Discourse', in M. Postone and E. Santner (eds), *Catastrophe and Meaning: The Holocaust and the Twentieth Century*, Chicago, IL: University of Chicago Press, 67–80.

CHAPTER 3

'From the Utter Depth of Degradation to the Apogee of Bliss'
Uncanny and Mimicking Diasporic Zionism

> In another's country that is also your own, your person divides, and in following the forked path you encounter yourself in a double movement... once as a stranger, and then as friend.
> —Homi Bhabha, *The Location of Culture*

> What can, for want of a better term, be called Zionist discourse (with its hybrid Enlightenment, romantic, revolutionary, and colonialist legacy, as well as its attendant assumptions regarding Jewish history and the diaspora), has permeated every aspect of modern Jewish culture.
> —Ammiel Alcalay, 'Exploding Identities'

And so we can now take the next step, moving from schematic appraisals of the ways in which anxieties of displacement produce particular formulations of Holocaust pedagogy, to inquiries into the political, cultural and social ways it is played out. These next three chapters will take different aspects of the curricula – the influence of Zionism, the haunting of settler colonialism (as the specific, relevant incarnation of nation-building), and the circumscribing of women's stories – as their particular focus. These elements each play a significant role in influencing the pedagogy's articulation of the place of Jews in modern, post-Holocaust Western non-Jewish and Jewish worlds. We will thus be able to end this book with a clearer picture of some of the ways in which the anxiety about the place of the Jews in these incarnations of the diasporic world is manifested in Holocaust education, and the ways in which Holocaust education can negotiate these anxieties.

To turn now to the influence of Zionism. Zionism is a governing ideology of the Jewish world in which the teachers are located: as will be shown, they all identify themselves as Zionists and teach about the Holocaust within the frameworks offered by diasporic Zionist thought. There are a number of ways in which different conceptions of Zionism influence the narratives of the Holocaust taught in the Jewish schools involved in this project. These include the looking towards Israel as the space of redemption, or the positive ending to the trauma of the Holocaust; the focus on Jews as the main group in the Holocaust; an endorsing of historical and continued Jewish uniqueness; the emphasis on particular kinds of resistance; and the use of legislation as a means of bringing the end of the Holocaust. Not all schools engage with Zionism in all of these ways, but all of the teachers interviewed for this project articulated a strong, if ambivalent, relationship with Zionism, and all of them deploy some of these modes for articulating the history and memory of the Holocaust. The ambivalence of this Zionism – as evidenced at an elementary level by the very fact that the people professing this Zionism live outside of Israel – is expressed in the different, occasionally contradictory ways in which the teachers adopt Zionist conceptions of the Holocaust and its historiography. In this chapter I will explore the ways in which these influences are being expressed in the Holocaust education under consideration and will describe in detail the relationship these examples of Holocaust education have to Zionism and Israel.

This is an explanation of one aspect of the mimicry which was discussed in the Introduction and which will be explored further – here we shall see the teachers mimicking Zionism as a means of negotiating their place, or their home, within the Jewish world and thereby within the broader societies in which they live. By almost (but not quite) replicating Zionist ways of teaching about the Holocaust these teachers (unconsciously) seek to manage their anxiety over where they, as Jews living outside Israel, can be located in relationship to Israel and to Zionism. For, as will be shown, Zionism carries with it a disavowal of the Diaspora. An anxiety then necessarily arises: how to be a part of something which is disavowed? The anxiety over this precarious status is played out through a limited utilization of Zionist lessons of the Holocaust: the mimicry is not complete or total. And thus, quite understandably, Holocaust education comes to exhibit an ambivalent relationship to Israel, Zionism and the Diaspora.[1]

This replication of Zionist modes of narration is gendered: the adoption of Zionist ideas of the Holocaust and modes of narrating it is a means of articulating a masculinist relationship to this aspect of Jewish history. Below will follow an exploration of the ways in which Zionism posits itself as the masculine Jewish identity to the Diaspora's feminine, and considers the Holocaust as a fundamental part of the play between the ideas of masculinity encompassed in conceptions of Zionist masculine strength and Diaspora feminine weakness.

A central tension being worked through in this chapter sits on the question of the place of Jews in relationship to other nations or peoples.² In a manner thoroughly structured by the Zionist narrative and spirit, these teachers predominantly present the Holocaust as an event which happened to and involved only Jews. Some teachers also engaged with another approach, seeking to suggest to their students that assimilating to the dominant Western societies is the best way to ensure safety for the Jewish people. This tension arises and is managed in a number of different ways by these teachers. The most useful way in which we can understand the negotiation of this tension, I will suggest, is through the lenses of Freud's idea of the uncanny and that of Bhabha's idea of mimicry. In the Introduction I explained the ways in which this mimicry operates; in this chapter we will trace Freud's conception of the uncanny and the ways in which these theorizations of societies are useful for our understanding of Jewish Holocaust educators' approaches to Zionism and the Holocaust.

Diasporic Zionism?

There are, of course, many different ways in which Zionism is currently, and has been historically, expressed.³ These range across the political and ideological spectrum. When in this chapter 'Zionism' is referred to as though it were a singular entity it refers to the generic ways in which teachers seem to understand and deploy ideas of Zionism. When asked, in their interviews, 'how do you characterize the school's approach to Zionism and relationship to Israel?', no teacher distinguished what form or politics of Zionism they were referring to when they said that they and their school was strongly Zionist. Indeed, it almost seems as though amongst the teachers in both Melbourne and New York there is a particular diasporic Zionism which has developed – a largely underarticulated one, where Zionism equates to a support and belief in the existence of a Jewish State of Israel and little explicitly more. This chapter will demonstrate how this particular version of Zionism simultaneously negotiates and heightens anxieties over the place of these Jews in relationship to Israel. Alongside this idea of Zionism sits a set of ideas about the West. What is being pointed to in these discussions of the West is a series of hegemonic ideas about nations, states and genders which developed out of the Enlightenment and have come to dominate what are commonly understood to be Western states. The U.S., Australia and Israel generally both self-identify and are identified more broadly as Western states, placing them within this Enlightenment tradition, as I outlined in the Introduction and Chapter One.

Almost every teacher interviewed explained that the school at which they taught is Zionist to its core. When asked whether the school was Zionist, answers included 'Oh very Zionist. Yes, very'[4]; 'Very Zionistic. So, we have, we march in the allegiance to Israel parade. We celebrate Yom Ha'atzmaut, commemorate Yom

Hazikaron. We have the Israel Action Committee which is actually probably in its tenth year so far'⁵; and, 'The school is heavily supportive of the State of Israel and we collect funds for the State of Israel and for the various causes within Israel. We study the history of the land.'⁶ Zionism here equates to support, both material and discursive, from afar. It is a mimicry of the forms of Zionism that require that Jews live in Israel, making Israel their home.

This is echoed by Danny Ben-Moshe who explains that 'Australian Jews proudly give themselves a slap on the back by declaring that Australia is the most Zionist diaspora Jewish community. Their claim is accurate. By all measures, Australian Jewry outdoes all other diasporas in their commitment to Israel.' For him, Australia Zionism is defined as including 'love and support for Israel, identification with Israel, commitment to the State of Israel, a belief in the need for a Jewish state and the right of Jews to have a homeland'. Ben-Moshe's evidence for this commitment is that Melbourne Jews visit Israel on holidays and make *aliyah* at far higher rates than anywhere else in the Western world; that 'per capita Australia is the highest contributor of philanthropic donations to Israel'; and that 'Jews lobby and campaign for Israel in a myriad of ways'.⁷ The importance of Zionism in American Jewishness historically has been explored by Mark Raider, who points to the specifically American characteristics of this Zionism: that American Jewish Zionism did not, and does not, preclude the continuation of Jewish life outside Israel, and, indeed, encourages it.⁸ As we can therefore see, in these incarnations of Zionism it is not necessary to live in Israel, but some sort of discursive and material connection is necessary. For example, of the fifteen teachers interviewed for this project, only three did not in some way directly link the end of the Holocaust with the beginning of the State of Israel. In this chapter we will see the many ways in which an ambivalent Zionism maintains an influence on narratives and discourses of the Holocaust as taught in these Jewish schools outside Israel, and the multitude of ways in which these narratives are shaped by mimicry and its attendant anxieties.

Legality as a Resolution of the Holocaust

There are two primary ways in which the Holocaust is, in these pedagogical examples, shown to have ended: through the reinstitution of the rule of law, and the creation of a Jewish nation-state. This section will take up the question of the rule of law, before, in the next, examining the importance placed on ideas of Jewish sovereignty. What connects these two elements is, as will be shown, that they are both part of an approach which places faith in modernity's institutions. This is part of a process of mimicry, a mimicry which seeks to manage anxieties about the place of (Diaspora) Jews in relation to these incarnations of modernity.

In these teachings, teachers deploy stories of legal systems coming into effect to penalize individual Nazis and the Nazi state, in particular through stories of the Nuremberg Trials. For one Melbourne teacher the trials are a narrative pitstop on the way to Israel. He explained that it is important to teach the students in a linear, chronological narrative progression, for once 'the Holocaust has happened, and the Nuremberg Trials are over . . . we're heading to a glorious future in Israel'.[9] The Trials are just a pause, but they are important in the narrative: Israel's 'glorious future' can only happen once the trials have taken place. For a number of teachers, the Nuremberg Trials are used to demonstrate the re-establishment of the rule of law; a re-establishment which, in this telling, ensures the safety of the Jewish people and, in some important ways, brings closure to the Holocaust. While most teachers begin their units on the Holocaust by teaching about antisemitism, and noting that it continues, this sits alongside an image of Jews as thriving in the West.[10] Jews in these imaginings could trust liberal democracies, and law-abiding nation-states, to look after them and their interests.[11]

This failed, in the words of two Melbourne curricula, when 'a criminal state was created'. The documents explain that:

> We are accustomed to due process of law, to a government which rules for the benefit of those who are being governed. When Hitler and his Brown Shirts came to power, they ignored all rules of law and justice. In order to maintain control, they changed the laws. In order to enforce their laws they changed the courts and filled them with their hirelings . . . A police state was established, conducted by criminals in terms of their own twisted values and carved out for their own benefit.[12]

It was this breakdown in due process and in the rule of law which signalled, according to this narrative, the beginning of the Holocaust. This breakdown was further evidenced by the Nuremberg Laws and Kristallnacht. Both of these events are taught about by every teacher interviewed for this project. They are used to signal to the students that Jews were now placed outside the State: that no longer were Jews to be protected by laws, but rather that legislation was being made which would deliberately harm them.

The importance of the rule of law in protecting Jews is returned to at the end of the curricula with discussions of the Nuremberg Trials. The emphasis on the Nuremberg Trials serves to teach the students that the rule of law can be reinstituted and that, when it is, Jewish interests can be served: that Jews should not fear Western ideas of government and law. It is the *breakdown* of these things which is to be feared. In an interview a teacher at a non-denominational school in New York explained that she discusses the Nuremberg Trials with her students as a 'form of closure'.[13] This strong belief in the rule of law comes not just from Western jurisprudence and history, but was also established in early Israeli statehood as the proper means of dealing with the remnants, the memories, of the Holocaust. As such, we can understand, the importance placed by these curricula on the law and Western jurisprudence mimics the importance which the Israeli state placed on these same institutions. Idith Zertal explains that 'Israel's legislature and courts, particularly in the first decade of statehood, were . . . the main stage on which society confronted the memory of the Holocaust and its gruesome specter'.[14] This was done, she argues, as part of the move to create a national history based on the State as the saviour: by introducing legislation to deal with the trauma of the Holocaust, the State was able to take control of the society's remembering.[15] The establishment of legislation took the responsibility for dealing with the Holocaust into the hands of the State, and out of the responsibility of the citizens. It placed the State in control of the Holocaust's legacy.

Zertal highlights how important collective remembering was to the new State, with its desire to establish a national identity.[16] Three key pieces of legislation were passed: the Nazis and Nazi Collaborators (Punishment) Law of 1950, which was aimed not at punishing Nazis, but rather at Jewish collaborators[17]; the Holocaust and Heroism Remembrance Law – Yad Vashem of 1953; and the State Education Law of 1953. The aim of these pieces of legislation was, according to Zertal, to 'delet[e] the shame of their mothers and fathers, the shame of Jews, the disgrace of the Jewish diaspora, [in order to] inaugurat[e] a new era, and reinvent themselves into a new world'.[18] They were to serve as vehicles for memory and pedagogy, whose introduction would resolve and thereby end the Holocaust.[19] Of course they could do no such thing, for the Holocaust, as a spectre haunting Israel and Zionism, has never ended.[20]

The final important legislative move by the Israeli government, and David Ben Gurion in particular, was the trial of Adolf Eichmann. Zertal explains that Ben Gurion's announcement to the Knesset (Israeli parliament) that Eichmann had been captured and was imprisoned in Israel was 'a consciousness-changing event. Finally the Holocaust could be faced, looked at, but from a very specific perspective – from a position of power, sovereignty and control'.[21] It was also an opportunity for a national pedagogical moment, wherein the nation could learn of Israel's supposed omnipotence as a direct counter to the perceived Jewish helplessness of the Holocaust.[22] Here we can identify the motivation behind Israel's use of legislation, and the narration of this legislation by Zionist teachers outside Israel. To be able to impose the rule of law indicates a certain incarnation of sovereign power which the Jews had not previously held as a nation. The teaching of legislation as a means of ending the Holocaust serves to (re-)establish Jewish power, as well as the safe place of Jews within the Western world. Yet there is a difference between the rule of law being established in Israeli history and in Holocaust teachings in Melbourne and New York today. In Israel the aim was to establish Jewish sovereignty; in these Holocaust teachings it is to establish the safety of Jews in Melbourne and New York. We can identify a slip in the Zionism of these Holocaust educators: they maintain a faith in Israel, but they do not teach about Israel's legislative turn. Instead, they teach about the Western world re-establishing control through the Nuremberg Trials. Faith here is being placed in the West, but through the legislative means (also) discursively offered by the Israeli state. Here we see the mimicry at work: the slippage between the mimic and the original is where the faith in law is being placed.

Giorgio Agamben points to this faith in Western legality as a problem. He writes that the trials of Nazis after the Holocaust have operated as a cover-up, a foil, or a screen. People have (mis)placed their trust in the law – in modern systems – as a way to deal with what happened. Agamben explains that:

> [d]espite the necessity of the trials and despite their evident insufficiency (they involved only a few hundred people), they helped to spread the idea that the problem of Auschwitz had been overcome. The judgments had been passed, the proofs of guilt definitively established. With the exception of occasional moments of lucidity, it has taken almost half a century to understand that law did not exhaust the problem, but rather that the very problem was so enormous as to call into question law itself, dragging it to its own ruin.[23]

Froma Zeitlin, writing about *The Reader*, a book which explores post-Holocaust Germanness, argues that the trial of a former SS officer in the book 'only emphasizes . . . the incommensurable gap between any legal procedure altogether, with its witnesses, evidence, and courtroom protocols, and the nature and extent of the horrific crimes committed'.[24] Similarly, Hannah Arendt, in a letter to Karl Jaspers, wrote that '[t]he Nazi crimes, it seems to me, explode the limits of the law, and that is precisely what constitutes their monstrousness. For these crimes, no punishment is severe enough. It may be essential to hang Goering, but it is totally inadequate. That is, the guilt, in contrast to all criminal guilt, oversteps and shatters any and all legal systems. That is the reason why the Nazis in Nuremberg are so smug'.[25] Yet, for the teachers under consideration here, the law – somewhat understandably – provides a source of comfort. In an anxious world, where there is a perception that the place of Jews is precarious, believing that the law is of assistance is a comfort.[26] This is all the more so when this is the lesson which both non-Jewish and Jewish Western ideologies carry with them.

Ending the Holocaust Story in Israel

Art Spiegelman, author of *Maus*, a comix which explores memory and the Holocaust, explained in an interview that:

> [t]he thing about *Maus* is that it's a diaspora novel, not a Zionist novel. It's about a destiny that exists in which Israel hardly figures, as opposed to most popular American culture about the Holocaust that posits Israel as some kind of happy ending, like *Schindler's List*, where the survivors get to end their story in Israel: the payback for the Holocaust is getting a homeland. To me, this is some kind of booby prize. When you've proved that nationalism is an absolutely virulent

disease, the solution isn't to give the people who got clobbered a nation, it's something else.[27]

Why, we may ask, is this not a perspective offered in Holocaust education in Jewish schools in Melbourne and New York today? Why do most teachers interviewed state that they follow this *Schindler's List* style of narrative: that the happy ending to the Holocaust is the State of Israel? What I am outlining throughout this book is an answer to this: that these teachers are articulating an (anxious) relationship to modernity and one of its most fundamental aspects – the nation-state, or group sovereignty. Sovereignty here can be understood as much more than simply the formation of a corollary between nation and state such that the dominant nation has control over the state. To explore this briefly, we can note that, through the work of Aileen Moreton-Robinson, we can understand sovereignty in a settler colonial state – such as Israel, the U.S. and Australia – as being constituted as 'patriarchal white sovereignty': as a form of racialised masculinist ownership of something akin to property. In this formulation the state carries a patriarchal and possessive logic whereby white citizen subjects possess the state and all the people within it, and are able to control and subjugate it and them. It is also that '[t]he possessive logic of patriarchal white sovereignty is predicated on exclusion': by excluding Indigenous and (producing as racialized through their exclusion) other racial others, group sovereignty is defined.[28] Exclusion, in this formulation, is therefore at the centre of this settler colonial incarnation of Western sovereignty.

We can understand that it follows then that with sovereignty comes an anxiety about the maintenance of that sovereignty. There is always the concern that the sovereign control be preserved. In order to manage their anxieties that they are not a part of the group which ensures the continuity of this control these teachers express faith in this system of modernity.[29] A primary way in which this is done is by adopting Western narratives of history, which so often end with a national declaration of independence. This then is the function of incorporating Zionist narratives of the Holocaust into the histories being narrated in these two locations. By this mimicking, in the manner outlined by Bhabha, of narratives of Jewish sovereignty – the creation of the State of Israel – as the happy ending to the Holocaust, as I am suggesting here that these teachers do, we can understand that these teachers are working to alleviate their anxieties that their place within a system of Jewish masculinist control and strength – or Jewish sovereignty – is in jeopardy.

A large number of teachers explained that after teaching about the Holocaust, they continue by teaching about the creation of the State of Israel. One teacher in Manhattan explained that she 'teach[es] the history of the development of the State of Israel after the Holocaust'.[30] Another teacher in Brooklyn explained that she brings together the Holocaust and Israel.[31] She 'teach[es] an elective course to seniors in High School. It's actually one semester on the history of the Holocaust and one semester on the history of Israel.'[32] A teacher in Melbourne described how after teaching about the Holocaust 'we move on to Nationhood and the State of Israel',[33] while a teacher in New York clarified that, at the time of the interview, they had no separate course on modern Israel. She explained that at the end of the course on the Holocaust they 'do a little bit of the trials and we'll do a little bit about the establishment of Israel'.[34] Another teacher deployed the same language, stating that '[a]fter the Holocaust, we do the State of Israel'.[35] Israel here is something one 'does', not just something one studies. In a sense, for these teachers, it is through their narration that 'the Nuremberg Trials' and 'Israel' come into being: they are being 'done'. These modernist enterprises – legal trials coordinated by the victors of World War II for Nazi actions, and the creation of a nation-state – are brought to the forefront and enacted by the teachers in their enunciation of their lessons.

Other teachers were more explicit in their deployment of the story of the creation of Israel as providing the redemption at the end of the story of the Holocaust. One Melbourne teacher explained that she discusses Israel so as to provide the students with an 'uplifting . . . , positive note'.[36] This teacher ends her course on the Holocaust by telling the story 'of 100 kids taken from Europe to Israel'.[37] It is a movement from Europe to Israel, not to Melbourne, which serves as the optimistic ending. This serves as a positive story not only because, as she suggested, it demonstrates that "we're still there, and Jewish life is still there".[38] For where is the 'there' in this story? The Holocaust occurred in Europe, not in Israel. The 'there', it seems, is Western modernity: it is a discursive 'there'-ness. Similarly, the curriculum at a school in Melbourne directly links the Holocaust, Israel and Europe. For 'Holocaust Memorial Day', it states, students should be 'able to a) Review the causes of the Holocaust; b) Understand the Holocaust and its relation to the State of Israel; and c) Analyse the impact of the Holocaust on European Jewry.'[39] For 'Israel Independence Day' students need to be 'able to: Understand the importance of Israel in light of the loss of the six million Jews in the Holocaust.'[40] In these two commemorations/celebrations, the creation of Israel as an effect of the Holocaust is reinforced.[41]

This idea of renewal and life continuing through the nation-state was echoed by another teacher who teaches about the Holocaust through a final-year subject called 'Religion and Society' at this same school. He explained that:

> [w]e look at the writings of [theologian] Irving Greenberg too. He wrote about the 'shattered covenant' and the way in which the Jews voluntarily renewed the covenant in the aftermath of the Holocaust – that notion that the Holocaust broke the covenant between God and the Jewish people, but the Jews chose voluntarily to renew it, and in that this is reflected in the establishment of the State of Israel in 1948, and the renewal of Jewish life in the aftermath of the Holocaust.[42]

This same teacher, when explaining his involvement in March of the Living said that he 'see[s] the March as reflecting the regeneration of Judaism and the Jewish people. It's just wonderful to see young Jewish people involved in the whole process, visiting the death camps and then ending the programme in Israel. *It's from destruction to rebirth*.'[43] The apparent simplicity of this statement reinforces its power.

When asked whether he teaches about medical experimentation, another teacher at this same school stated that he:

> like[s] to tell the kids it happened. I don't like dwelling on it in the classroom because I think it, you know you could just dwell on all the horror of the Holocaust and I don't like doing that. Again, I want the kids to see the Holocaust for what it was – very significant, if not the most significant event. But I just don't want to get into the ghoulish, macabre, disgusting side of it . . . I don't like to go overboard, not because I think the kids have to be protected. Nah, just, where do you draw the line? You'll never get to Israel. If you know what I mean. Not that I draw a direct link between the Holocaust and Israel, but there's more to learn about than just these terrible things.[44]

That he said those words – if you dwell on the horror you never get to Israel – even though he then, to an extent, backtracked, suggests that he believes that 'getting to Israel', through its narration into history, means that the Holocaust is over: that it is Israel which ends the horrors of the Holocaust. As I will show, in the Zionist imaginary these horrors are representative of what happens to the feminized Diaspora; and it is the masculinist Israeli nation-state which redeems the Jewish people.

This idea – that Israel ends the Holocaust – can be traced back to the earliest founders of the Israeli state, and in particular to the words of David Ben Gurion, the first prime minister. After being invited to a Holocaust memorial rally in 1952, Ben Gurion wrote that '[t]he one fitting tombstone in memory of European Jewry exterminated by the Nazi beasts is the State of Israel'.[45] At other times Ben Gurion had, according to historian Idith Zertal, written of Israel as the place for Jews' hopes and dreams: a place for the continuation of Jewish life.[46] However Ben Gurion viewed Israel – as either source of life or as tombstone (*matzeva* in Ben Gurion's Hebrew words) – the end point is the same, and it is that which is deployed by many of the teachers interviewed in this project: Israel ends the Holocaust. Israel fulfils this function only if its creation is in the name of an exclusivist Jewish sovereignty: only if the work it undertakes is on behalf of the Jews as such. And indeed, this is precisely the narrative that is told. This necessarily means that Palestinians are excluded from this nation-state, and the historical narrative. Israel, in this narrative, is, as Joseph Massad argues, declared as 'the state of Jews worldwide and not of its citizens'.[47]

Even when teachers are not explicitly teaching that Israel was the positive ending to the Holocaust, there is a narrative formula at play. This is the reason why they consistently look to a nation-state for rebirth, for stability and for continuity, rather than looking at migration to Australia or the U. S. (or anywhere else outside Israel), or discussing the continuity of Jewish life in Germany or Poland. There was only one teacher who followed up talking about the Holocaust with a unit on American Jewish history.[48] The teachers predominantly follow the modernist narrative of national life finding its expression in the advent of the nation-state.[49]

This narrative progression can be seen in the words and curriculum of a teacher in Melbourne. He made it clear throughout the interview that he believes that the emphasis in current conceptions of Jewishness for children should be on Israel and the future and not on the Holocaust. He stressed that he does not want to emphasize the horrors of the Holocaust to the students, as he does not aim to 'dwell on the bad things'. He asserted that 'I think we want to show them not just the suffering, but the bravery, the resistance, the survivors and the aftermath, and not just focus on the mourning.'[50] Moreover, as was explicated above, the Jewish Studies curriculum at this school explicitly links together the Holocaust and the foundation of the State of Israel. In the explanation of the 'Curriculum Focus' it states that '[f]inally the links between the war [Holocaust] experience and the creation of the State of Israel are made. The unit ends with the War of Independence and the establishment of Israel.'[51] A unit that began in Germany and moved through an examination of the Jewish experience of the Holocaust ends with the creation of the State of Israel. This creates a clear narrative progression of movement from death and destruction in Europe to life in Israel.

The centrality of Israel to Jewish identity was reiterated at a different point in the interview. This teacher explained that, with regard to March of the Living, he would 'rather kids went to Israel and skipped Auschwitz... Why does it take [going to Auschwitz] to feel Jewish? Can't you just feel Jewish because you're Jewish? Because of Israel, because of... whatever?'[52] Israel here is positioned as a more authentic Jewishness – it is equated with 'just' being Jewish – in a way which journeying to a scene of the Holocaust is not. A physical attachment to Israel, and a political attachment to Zionism, is figured here as more important for one's Jewishness than being physically close to Auschwitz (as the two are seemingly placed in competition).

The divergent Jewishnesses which Israel and the Holocaust have been made to signify was reiterated by an educator at the March of the Living education sessions in Melbourne.[53] This educator explained to the students that 'Poland for us, as we see it, is a place of ash', of people who died: Poland is, in short, a site of death.[54] He explained that for the students their journey would be one of movement from death (in Poland) to life (in Israel); from destruction to redemption.[55] Students were informed that Poland and Israel are two opposites for Jews: that Poland is 'all the bad things' and Israel is 'all the nice things'; Poland is death and destruction, while Israel is life. Poland was described as being an open wound for the Jewish people; it was described as representing not just a historical trauma, but one which continues. This educator then is acknowledging the continuation of the Holocaust: he is informing the students that the Holocaust continues in their very bodies. Yet there is an ambivalence here, for it is also Israel which, once again, concludes the Holocaust, in a manner which is both inscribed in the histories being taught and embodied in the memorial practices undertaken. This follows a typical Zionist narrative of Israel ending the Holocaust, albeit with this twist of ambivalent continuity.[56]

This narrative progression and its importance for Jewish identities was articulated most clearly and succinctly by a teacher at a school in Melbourne who explained that:

> What's of immense interest to me is the way in which the Shoah has come to be used as a process – which you've termed 'the construction of Jewish identity' – the process being, oh I don't know, from destruction to rebirth, to use metaphors, but there are other visual metaphors, namely, from the utter depth of degradation to the apogee of bliss three years later with the establishment of the State of Israel.[57]

At some of the more Orthodox, religious schools, an emphasis on the importance of Israel is taught from within a religious perspective. For instance, at an Orthodox school in New York, the teacher explained that she presents the story of the creation of Israel with 'an emphasis again on the relationship between God and the Jewish people and how miraculous the history of the State of Israel has been'.[58] Similarly, the curriculum of a modern Orthodox school in Melbourne, in discussing the treatment of Jews in Auschwitz on Rosh Hashanah (Jewish New Year) and Yom Kippur (Day of Atonement), ends by stating that:

> Only a few of those present at that Yom Kippur in Auschwitz in 1943 survived and lived to see the liberation. And every year at 'Yizkor' we remember with fright and shudder those exterminated. Yet their death was not meaningless, for they died for the Sanctification of the Name and thus helped to bring about the rise of the State of Israel – our deliverance.[59]

This narrative of a collective bliss or deliverance that eventuated from the creation of Israel is a mimicking of the Western narratives wherein national self-determination through the acquisition of patriarchal white sovereignty brings national relief and happiness.[60] And thus, whether teachers in interviews consciously described the creation of Israel after the Holocaust as the redemptive national end to the Holocaust, or in their teachings they followed a Zionist narratorial path of teaching about Israel's creation after the unit on the Holocaust, we can understand that the State of Israel is a constant, redemptive, masculinist presence in these teachings.

The Uncanny and Mimicry

It is useful to pause here and, utilizing the frameworks offered by Sigmund Freud and Homi Bhabha, come to a deeper understanding of the discursive practices at work in these teachings. There are many layers of ambivalences and anxieties which disrupt the teachers and their pedagogy. These can be understood with the assistance of Freud's theorization of *das Unheimliche* (the Uncanny), and Bhabha's conception of mimicry. Freud's idea of the uncanny is particularly useful to aid our understanding of the gendered distance created by Israel, or Zionism, away from the Jewish Diaspora.[61] Freud asserted that the 'quality of uncanniness can only come from the fact of the "double" being a creation dating back to a very early mental stage, long since surmounted – a stage, incidentally, at which it wore a more friendly aspect. The "double" has [since] become a thing of terror'.[62] The uncanny double is something which was once a part of the self, but has since become separated and thus frightening: it is 'in reality nothing new or alien, but something which is familiar and old – established in the mind and which has become alienated from it only through the process of repression'.[63] If we apply this to the Zionist discourse, we can understand that the Diaspora serves as (one of) Israel's uncanny others – the other being the Mizrahim, the Jewish Arabs.[64] The qualities of the Diaspora, figured as the feminine, are what Zionism represses – it is from the Diaspora that the Zionist has sprung, yet it is its diasporic qualities which Zionism disavows. In turn, it is the particular masculine nature of Zionism which needs to be continually reinforced so as to maintain the separation from Diaspora culture, which is positioned as feminized, incomplete and lacking.

The path that political Zionism has chosen – that of preferencing the Jewish people over all others and rebutting its inferior, uncanny, others – can be seen in the masculinity constructed and its accompanying violence. It could be argued that the violence that has characterized the nation-state results from a desire to assert the masculinity of the Israeli state in order to distinguish itself from the perceived passivity of the Diaspora.[65] Amos Oz makes this point in his essay 'The State as Reprisal', asking:

> Who, other than a *self-hater*, would feel the need to protest endlessly that we are strong and cruel and suntanned and we work on the land and love sports and we are bold and warlike? (In other words, *we are no longer* studious weaklings, full of pity, pale-faced and intellectual, hating bloodshed. In other words, shame on our ancestors, the gentiles must respect us now because we are not like our ancestors, we are like those who persecuted our ancestors.)[66]

Oz argues that Israel asserts itself in this way as 'an extended act of reprisal, not against the gentiles but against the gloomy past of the Jews in the diaspora'.[67] In other words, the nation-state of Israel asserts itself as violent and masculine in order to differentiate itself from Diaspora Jews as they perceive them to be (historically).[68] Notably, these Diaspora Jews are the ancestors of the hyper-masculine Israeli Jews: they are a former part of these Jews. What is uncanny and frightening about them is that it is literally from these Jews that Zionism has sprung, for modern political Zionism grew from the thinking of European Jews, with their perceived lack of strength.[69] The masculinization which occurs in response to this frightening uncanny figure is a mimicry of the dominant masculinity of Western modernity. This gendered element of Zionism is important, for Zionists (both in Israel and outside) are also seeking to mimic the embodied and discursive masculinities which are offered by the Western tradition. When the Diaspora-based teachers of the Holocaust mimic Zionist modes and methods of narration of the Holocaust they are also seeking to mimic and thus acquire the masculinity and masculinism that Zionism claims for itself.

How is this then dealt with by these teachers narrating and navigating Jewish histories and identities? Let us move through the steps. I am identifying here that for Zionism and for Zionists (whether inside or outside of Israel), the Holocaust is a haunting presence. It represents the possibility of extermination, or absolute destruction, or a radical and absolute disempowerment. If we view this through the lens of the uncanny we can understand that the Holocaust (being a representation of what Zionists believe could have happened only because Jews lived in the Diaspora and indeed is what necessarily happens to Jews in the Diaspora) remains as a spectral figure, escaping repression and frightening Zionists that it will happen again.[70] This uncanny then is a source of anxiety: Zionists can be seen to be scared and anxious that another Holocaust will occur. As Freud articulated it, it is a special kind of relationship between the uncanny double and the subject. Here the subject is Zionism and the uncanny double is the Diaspora: this is the most intimate relationship, which haunts and defines.

Zionists in the Diaspora (embodied here in the teachers whose words and work are under examination) search for ways to manage this haunting fear. They are unsure of how to deal with it: should there be an attempt at assimilation, whereby a homely place can potentially be found in the Western world? Should an attempt be made to establish themselves within dominant Zionist practices by making a home in Israel? Or should a diasporic Jewish distinctiveness from both Israel and the Western world be proposed? This is the central tension I am exploring in this chapter, and I believe that it can be understood with the assistance of Bhabha's concept of mimicry. It is a diasporist synthesis wherein, in the end, these teachers present all of these approaches to their students. They mimic modern Western ways of organizing identity and society *and* they mimic Zionism (which is in itself mimicking the masculinism and importance of national sovereignty which are fundamental to aspects of Western modernity). Home in this formulation is not within a spatial location, but within a discursive field, that of modernity.[71] This negotiation of modernity through mimicry then is a further source of anxiety, as the mimicry can never be complete – there is always slippage, gap or excess.

The mimicry is then a way of dealing with the anxiety caused by the frightening uncanny double. Yet it falters, because it cannot help but produce further anxiety: an anxiety that this diasporist Zionism is not enough. Moreover, as Bhabha explains, 'the menace of the mimicry is its double vision which in disclosing the ambivalence of colonial discourse also disrupts its authority'.[72] That is, the mimic does not just act upon itself, but also affects the authority of the subject of its mimicry. Thus we can see multiple layers of doubling in this teaching, each of which haunts and disrupts the dominant discourse. In this formulation, Zionism is haunted by the double of the Holocaust (the uncanny haunting) and the double of diasporist Holocaust education (the haunting of mimicry, which was a way of dealing with the prior haunting), both of which are figured as representations of the Diaspora. The diaspora – as a current material condition – disrupts the authority of Zionism by showing that Jews can live elsewhere.

Importantly, I am arguing that the steps being described here are not conscious decisions undertaken by these teachers. The teachers of the Holocaust do not, it would seem to me, actively choose to participate in the circulation of these discourses, nor are they conscious of the gendered elements of the discourses.[73] They are, instead, unconsciously seeking to negotiate their uncertainties about their place as Jews in the world, and the different resolutions presented by Zionism, the modern nation-state system of patriarchal, possessive sovereignty and their own personal experiences. These anxieties and ambivalences are hardly surprising; they are also incredibly productive. Negotiating the effects of different political claims is difficult, and is bound to induce a certain lack of surety as well as certain new ways of understanding one's place in the world. Thus, I am arguing, the teachers remain ambivalent and haunted, and this is expressed through their curricula and their articulations in interviews. Let us now return to an examination of the words of the teachers and their curricula to understand further the ways in which this mimicry is played out in order to manage their anxious feelings.

Zionist Types of Narratives: Focusing on Jews

Significantly, these narratives of the Holocaust focus primarily on Jews. In this section I will explore the ways in which these Jews are largely homogenized within these examples of Holocaust pedagogy. This occurs in order to formulate a national, European-esque, Jewish group. It is this group which, to a great extent, provides the foundation for Zionist ideas of Jewish nationalism. This is not to say that the formation of a coherent, homogeneous Jewish national group is exclusive to Zionist constructions of Jewishness, but to assert that the construction of such a homogeneous group is *fundamental* to Zionism. The Zionism which is being asserted in these teachings relies upon the existence of this homogeneous Jewish group and therefore the pedagogical construction of, and focus on, such a group is an important aspect to be explored. Moreover, the construction of this group explains one aspect of the mimicry which it is being argued occurs – that of the creation of a homogeneous national group which can be redeemed through national sovereignty.

Eurocentrism as homogenizing

The narrative of Jewish life moving from the Holocaust to Israel does important work in maintaining a Eurocentric story of the Jewish people. Melanie Kaye/Kantrowitz explains this, providing an outline of the narrative which such histories embrace. She writes that:

> [t]he Eurocentric story of the Jews begins with Abraham leaving his native Ur and settling in the promised land. Other milestones include the destruction of the Second Temple – and now we leave the Middle East, as though no Jews stayed; the Expulsion from Spain (usually the only recognition of non-Ashkenazi experience); and now it's Europe all the way: Blood Libels, Emancipation and Enlightenment, Pogroms, Immigration, the Holocaust; and escaping Europe, the crowning glory, the founding of the Jewish state of Israel, in which – almost like Columbus with America – the Zionists, having almost discovered Eretz Israel, defeat the savage indigenous people who aren't really there, and make the desert bloom.[74]

It is these last stages of the narrative which are being considered in this chapter: the Holocaust which is inevitably and necessarily followed by the creation of the State of Israel. Indeed, some of the teachers explicitly stated that they teach a Eurocentric story.

One teacher in Melbourne explained that at his school they are:

> very Europe, Eurocentric. We know that. I mean the curriculum is. I asked the kids yesterday – 'why do you think that is?' . . . We discuss the Jews of Germany, and Italy, and the Enlightenment – why don't we discuss the Jews of Baghdad? And the kids said, because more was happening in Europe, than there . . . in terms of the Enlightenment. I said it's probably correct. And most of us come from a European background. Most Jewish history books, curriculum, it seems. I mean, you read about Moses Mendelssohn, and I'm sure there is someone, some Jew in Baghdad equally important, but we don't read about him, so. We don't distinguish, because we're very Eurocentric, and perhaps if there was more time. I think we should see parallel . . .[75]

This is the most explicit statement by a teacher that his teachings are focused on European Jews. And there is also an uncertainty, or an ambivalence, about this move: the teacher is aware enough of the problems of such Eurocentrism that he poses it as a problem, or a question, for the students to resolve. But, in another sense, the ambivalence is resolved, or perhaps merely internally justified: it is answered that 'more was happening' in Europe, or that the students predominantly 'come from a European background'.

Similarly, a teacher at a school in Melbourne stated that she makes no distinction between Sephardi and Ashkenazi Jews, which is partly a result of only teaching about the experiences of Ashkenazi Jews.⁷⁶ A teacher at another school in Melbourne stated that they do not examine the involvement of Sephardi Jews as she 'hasn't looked at – because of time. Deportation from Salonika or somewhere else or North Africa, which we haven't done but that's something to think about also'.⁷⁷ A teacher in New York, when asked whether she teaches about Sephardi Jews replied '[n]ot so much. It only came up in the context of when we were looking at perhaps, Righteous Gentiles, which were the countries that favoured the Jews. How did they treat the Jews? There was a little bit of why the Jews couldn't go to Palestine – because of the British mandate. But there wasn't a lot about the Sephardi countries'.⁷⁸ Another teacher in New York explained that she was 'in the process of reading a few things that I want to put into the curriculum but it's not there yet'.⁷⁹ There was one teacher in New York who explained a differing mode of teaching, stating that, because the vast majority of her students are Sephardi she:

> look[s] at every country that the Holocaust affected. Obviously all Europe but we also spend time discussing the states of Sephardim during the Holocaust years because most of the Sephardi kids here think that it never happened to anyone Sephardic but of course that's not true. So we look at the experiences of the North African communities, we look at the Greek Jews, and the Sephardi communities in Western Europe, who suffered the same fate as the Ashkenazim did. That always surprises the students.⁸⁰

Encompassed in this teacher's words we can see both the problem and a solution. The vast majority of students and teachers think that the Holocaust was something which was done to Eastern European Jews. By teaching about other peoples and histories this knowledge can be altered. And, indeed, a number of the teachers expressed interest in teaching about Sephardic Jewish experiences, now that the possibility had been raised.

Jewish only: homogenizing through the erasure of other identities

It is through the focus being placed on a European history of the Holocaust and the Jewish people that a diverse set of histories are homogenized. This occurs because of the important role which coherent national histories play in constituting a national group. As Edward Said explicates, 'memory is not necessarily authentic, but rather useful . . . People now look to this refashioned memory, especially in its collective forms, to give themselves a coherent identity, a national narrative, a place in the world'. This can only occur by 'manipulating certain bits of the national past, suppressing others, elevating still others in an entirely functional way'.⁸¹ Histories of the Holocaust, taught within a Zionist framework, serve to narrate this nation's past. One Melbourne teacher articulated this quite precisely when she explained that:

> I think that when we teach the Shoah, we teach it because it's a Jewish school and part of being Jewish is having Israel, you know, as a land of the future . . . We see it very much in a Jewish experience and we do spend a very very small amount of time talking about other groups that have suffered and we talk about that we weren't the only ones to suffer, but there is no doubt that it was a Jewish experience.[82]

For a teacher at another Melbourne school it was important to differentiate linguistically between what was done to the Jews and what was done to other persecuted groups:

> If we take the entire Nazi period, we've had teachers here [in the same school] in the past who have addressed the Nazi persecution of gays, issues generally in relation to sexual preference, and have brought that under the general aegis of their Holocaust teaching. Which I always think is slightly different to teaching about the Holocaust per se, which would be more in relation to Jews.[83]

In the first part of this statement – that teachers in the past have brought up the treatment of other groups 'under the general aegis of their Holocaust teaching' – we can see the introduction of the histories of other groups. Yet these final words – that 'teaching about the Holocaust . . . would be more in relation to Jews' – work to constitute their removal from the field of Holocaust victims. This reinforces (a perhaps slightly ambivalent) Jewish specificity and uniqueness, and, in turn, the history of the Holocaust as centred on Jews (as homogenized).

Indeed, when the existence of different groups of Jews is established for students in both Melbourne and New York these are not based on identities but rather most predominantly on situation. This same teacher explained that 'every survivor we've had every year [to come speak to the students] . . . they've all been different. Some have been in camps, some were hidden, one was on the death march, we've people who were kids in the camps. A real mix of stories and where they came from.'[84] Another teacher in Melbourne explained that 'we've looked at different groups . . . we've talked about but we haven't studied . . . but we've talked about the Judenrat and the role of the resistance in the Warsaw Ghetto.'[85] A teacher in New York, when asked whether or not she breaks down the category of Jews in her teachings explained that:

> there is probably very little breakdown in terms of things like that. We talk about isolation, and how the Jews isolated themselves, which happened more in religious communities and, you know, how that impacted them. We talk about how in Berlin there was a high rate of hiding Jews and why that might be the case more than in Krakow. But those are the only times I can remember things like that coming up.[86]

Focus is placed on the Jews as one group, in terms of their identity categories. It is only Jews who are 'talked about' and thereby brought into the history.

Yet not all teachers incorporate the histories of different groups, or a recognition of difference within the experiences of Jewish peoples. Like the demonstrations of difference in experience it is most common that when Jewish people are broken into national groupings it is primarily to illustrate for students what happened to Jews in different places, rather than to articulate a difference in identities which are produced or enacted. While one is not necessarily preferable to another – and each could be critiqued for the histories which they draw on and the meanings they work to create – the distinction is notable. A teacher in New York explained that her:

> goal in teaching is to create a context and have them see the forest through the trees and understand each tree in and of itself. I first want them to see the chronological overall, the whole view of how the tragedy developed and the isolated experiences of Jews in each part of the tragedy. And that's exactly why we talk about the experience of German Jews versus Austrian Jews versus Polish Jews versus Jews under Nazi control and under Russian control, Jews in ghettos, Jews in concentration camps, Jews in slave labour camps, Jews working in ghettos [*sic*], the Jews in the Soviet Union.[87]

For another teacher in New York teaching about the experiences of Jews in different countries serves as a means of explaining the geography of Europe to her students. She explained that she looks at 'Poland extensively. Lithuania, France, we talk about Sweden and Norway and Denmark and the way Jews were treated there . . . compared to Poland. And Germany obviously. And I do a lot of map skills assignments, so they learn where these countries are, as Americans don't know where anything is.'[88]

For these teachers the Holocaust is a story of Jewish specificity and uniqueness. As follows a Zionist idea of Jewish identity Jews have unique experiences and these experiences must be labelled as such. While this is of course not a uniquely Zionist way of apprehending Jewish history (there are many forms of Jewish history-writing which would focus on the Jews in isolation), in this historical context it provides us with the clearest way of explaining this particular narration of Jewish and Holocaust history. The ways in which teachers achieve this differs: some homogenize all Jews; some do not mention other groups; others do mention different groups but with a focus on experience divorced from identity. We can see in this a particular response to the anxious feelings which the Holocaust necessarily generates: in light of this murderous history, are Jews as a coherent group safe? And can this be assured? One response, which was explored in Chapter Two, is some form of assimilation (but of course not a completely assimilatory process). In the previous chapter this assimilation was based on historiography: the adoption of dominant Western historical methodologies. This chapter will now turn to an examination of the ways in which histories of Jewish assimilation are brought into the teaching of the Holocaust. This, I am arguing, occurs as a means of negotiating the anxiety about the place of Jews in the world – one way of avoiding genocide could be some partial form of assimilation. This is particularly relevant when considered from a Zionist viewpoint, where the aim is the complete separation of Jews from other ethnic groups to guard against some (other) forms of assimilation.[89] It is therefore important to examine the ways in which teachers narrate a relationship to assimilation through the interviews and in their curricula.

A Zionist Jewish Distinctiveness

Teachers expressed a multitude of different attitudes towards assimilation – that is, at its most basic, towards the idea of Jews losing or retaining what is perceived to be their Jewish distinctiveness. For some teachers the most important lesson of the Holocaust is of a Zionistic Jewish particularity; for others, some partial form of melding with the dominant Western society is a valuable way of integrating into those societies and thus ensuring that another Holocaust does not occur. As I have shown, in the teachings it is the Jews, rather than any other victim group, who are at the centre of the narratives. The content of the Jewishness beyond this bodily presence or spirituality varies greatly, however. One teacher commented in an interview that 'we talk about the strength of the spirit of being Jewish and how people retained their Jewishness during and after and also about those who didn't. We talk about how we can't judge, having never been there, and we don't know what we would do, but how incredible to have gone through that and still believe in God.'[90] It is the religious aspects of Jewishness for this teacher that is most important. Yet there is also a relationship with assimilation being expressed here: it is the continuing relationship with a Jewish God after the Holocaust and into the new lives elsewhere that impresses the teacher. To be religious, to believe in a Jewish God, in the Christian society that is Melbourne indicates a certain resistance to assimilation.

The curriculum of another Melbourne school presents a similar hesitancy over assimilation. Included in the curriculum is an article written by Robert Weltsch, a Zionist author in Germany. It was written in 1933 and is entitled 'Wear it with Pride, the Yellow Badge'.[91] The author encouraged his readers to be proud of being Jewish and asserted that this can be demonstrated by wearing the yellow Star of David that the Nazis decreed must be worn by all Jews.[92] He suggested that the Jews take what was instituted as a badge of shame and dishonour – of being excluded from the dominant population – and turn it into a badge of honour. That is, Weltsch was not asserting that the literal meaning of the badge be changed – that it cease to represent Jewish difference – but that its symbolic reference be radically altered: that Jewish difference be seen as positive rather than negative. We can also understand that as Weltsch was Zionist, he therefore believed in the national difference of the Jewish people. The yellow badge then is a sign of national exclusivity, of a radical disinterest in assimilating. As I have shown, most of the teachers interviewed explained that they do not break down the category of Jews by nationality – it is a national Jewishness which is used to describe that category of victims called Jews. We can see here the reliance on a particular incarnation of Jewish nationalism – otherwise known as Zionism – and by extension Israel, as the provider of a home for Jews.

And here we can see an ambivalence rising, for there are also instances of assimilation into a non-Jewish state being taught as a means of avoiding another Holocaust, of ensuring that Jews can be at home and safe and thereby able to prosper. Indeed, the anxiety about the place of Jews and Jewishness is, in some curricula, managed through these stories of assimilation. The comparative stories of two Jews, one from an assimilated German family, the other from an unassimilated Polish family, are told in the curriculum documents of a Melbourne school.[93] The German Jew's name was Heinz Kissinger – by 1938, we are told, his parents had realized that Germany was not safe for Jews and so moved to the United States where the family all survived. There Kissinger further assimilated, changing his name to Henry, and eventually became the U.S. Secretary of State. The Polish Jew's name was Naftali Saleschutz and he and his family remained in Poland, where his whole family, except he and his brother, were killed during the Holocaust. After the war he married, moved to the U.S., changed his name to Norman Salsitz and had a daughter. This story appears to be teaching that assimilation has the ability to save. It was seemingly by moving to the U.S. and anglicizing their names that these two men were able to build their lives.

Similarly, the curriculum of a school in Melbourne has a brief discussion of German pre-war Jewish life, highlighting the ways in which German Jews were an integrated part of German society and had contributed greatly to the upper echelons of that society,[94] while the curriculum of a different school in Melbourne provides information about the ways in which Jews had lived in Germany for centuries, creating diverse Jewish cultures.[95] A page from this curriculum displays assimilation in Germany perfectly.[96] It teaches that Jews were involved in public life through recreation in public parks, shopping in public spaces, attending theatre and opera shows, and learning at both Jewish schools and state universities. Jews in this space had religious freedom and were full citizens. It was their assimilation into the German, non-Jewish state which was important to highlight as having been destroyed by the Holocaust.

Yet Zionism is based around the idea that Jews can never be at home in countries outside Israel, their mythical place of origin, and, moreover, that a national home is fundamental to national self-determination. How do the teachers negotiate this aspect of the pervasive anxiety that Zionist Jews outside Israel do not fit properly into Zionism? A solution is provided by David Biale, who notes that in the Zionist formulation, the creation of the State of Israel is a means of circumventing the impossibility of total assimilation in Europe:

> Just as the Zionists hoped that sovereignty would revolutionize the Jew internally, so they expected that a Jewish state would radically change how the nations treated the Jews ... Precisely because the Jews established a state like all the European states, they would be accepted as equals in the family of nations ... If they could not assimilate as individuals in Europe, their state could assimilate in a world of states.[97]

Israel therefore does the work on the national level which individual Jews are potentially incapable of: assimilating into European life through the making of a home. Israel also, potentially, makes Jews into just another national group, whose Diaspora fans out from a homely centre which necessarily asserts the national interests of the group. In the next section of this chapter I will bring forward this question of a national home by examining the problem of homelessness, of moments when it is taught that Jews had nowhere to go before, during and after the Holocaust. If the Jews had, and have, nowhere to go, a national sovereign space becomes, it would seem, all the more required.

A Certain Displacement

This Jewish distinctiveness and homogeneity is characterized, at times, through a narration of Jewish out-of-placeness. This displacement is narrated through histories which assert that the displacement of Jews which Nazi rule produced was a problem which stretched beyond Occupied Europe and to the rest of the world. This is presented firstly through descriptions of the Evian Conference. As two curricula described it, the resolution of the conference was such that 'it was clear that the [Nazi] policy of forced emigration would not work: no one wanted the Jews'.[98] These same two schools also highlight the voyage of the St Louis. The St Louis was a ship which departed from Germany in May 1939 with over 900 Jewish refugees, heading to Cuba, where the vast majority of passengers were denied entry. America and Canada also refused permission for the passengers to disembark, while England allowed only some to stay there. The majority, however, were taken to continental European countries, where they were eventually caught up in the war. These two stories, then – of the Evian Conference and the St Louis – are lessons about Jews not having a home anywhere in the world, lessons wherein students are being taught that the world is seemingly comfortable with Jewish exclusion.

This sentiment continues with descriptions of the reception of Jews after the War as students are told that there was nowhere for Jews to go, except to pre-state Israel (which was then named Palestine). One curriculum explains that some Jews were murdered when they went back to their homes in Poland, but that many others made 'their way to Western or Southern Europe, hoping to reach Eretz Israel'. It explains that 'Holocaust survivors played an important role in the struggle for the establishment of an independent Jewish State, which became the home for many of them. There they successfully rebuilt their homes and families. There they reconfirmed the ancient adage: "Am Yisrael Hay" (The People of Israel Live).'[99] This presents the idea of Israel – or the Jewish nation-state – as being the only space capable of providing a home for the Jews, and the only place which could enable Jewish life to be renewed.[100] There is a complex relationship with assimilation within this idea. These teachers are arguing for Jews to find themselves at home not within a non-Jewish state, but rather to create their own state which they can possess and manage. In that sense, they are arguing against assimilation into a non-Jewish state. But they are also adopting Western ideas of what it means to be at home: home is a masculinist space that can be controlled and dominated, rather than being wherever one is, wherever that may be.

As we look across these various examples of Holocaust pedagogy, we can see that the teachers are presenting different approaches to understanding the ways in which Jews can find their place within the non-Jewish worlds they inhabit: some are promoting assimilation, as in the stories of Kissinger and Saleschutz; others want a space which involves a partial assimilation; others desire a homely space, one which is outside the non-Jewish world altogether and where Jews instead are able to exert influence over non-Jews. In this sense, some of the teachers are also diasporists, interested in a worldwide community of Jews rather than simply all Jews being in the one homely location. There is a complicated and ambivalent relationship between emplacement and assimilation in the stories of the Holocaust being presented by these teachers in their schools in Melbourne and New York, as these are teachers and students who reside in non-Jewish countries.

Gendered Diasporas

If we return to the question of the relationship between Zionism and the Jewish Diaspora, and in particular the ways in which this relationship has been produced through its gendering, we can consider further the motivations which guide these Zionist impulses contained in the pedagogy. Importantly, the Diaspora necessarily occupies a prominent place in Jewish collective memories. For centuries, Jewish communities have flourished outside of Israel, although there has certainly been the maintenance of a connection with Israel. That is, a connection with a people Israel,[101] and with a particular space of origin, where many memories of the Jewish people are located. With the advent of the Israeli nation-state in 1948 this changed. No longer was a connection with a concept the aim of Jewish people; rather, in the Zionist framework, it was a connection with the nation-state which was required. No longer was the focus simply a community or a people; rather, it was turned onto the maintenance of borders. With this change in the path of the people of Israel came a new focus for Israelis – a central tenet of political Zionism became that the Jewish people could only be at home within the borders of the nation-state. As such, the Diaspora became reinforced as second-class, with those who inhabited it positioned as inferior, or femininized.[102]

This positioning of Diaspora Jews as the feminine to the Israeli nation-state's masculine can be seen occasionally in memorial projects outside Israel. For instance, at the 2006 Melbourne Yom Ha'atzmaut celebration concert, according to the *Australian Jewish News*, the 'ongoing love story between Australian traveler Roni . . . and Shai', an Israeli, was played out.[103] This pairing of feminine representation of Diaspora and masculine representation of Israel was not a coincidence – it exemplifies the masculine/feminine dialectic. Indeed, in the following week's *Australian Jewish News*, the front-page headline read: 'Celebrating the marriage between Australia and Israel'.[104] This was the aspect of the celebrations of Yom Ha'atzmaut which was foregrounded – that of a gendered and dependent relationship between Australia and Israel.

This works as part of a gendered system which posits the Holocaust as resulting from a characterization of Diaspora Jewishness as constituted by a feminization, which is also one shaped by shame. This can be seen in the curriculum of a school in Melbourne, wherein some types of resistance to the Holocaust are shown to be futile. The curriculum states that:

> every individual attempt to stand up to the Germans ended in death. The Jew who refused to budge when ordered, who spat at the German, who cursed him, who slapped his face, threw stones, or reached for a stick was slain on the spot. Thousands of such individual acts of resistance became nothing more than induced suicide. They left scarcely a record, except in the German statistics – more than 5,000 shot to death – and a few poignant memories.[105]

This paragraph is not clearly associated with the Jews of a particular town or village, despite the fact that it mentions 5,000 Jews being shot, which was obviously not describing the whole of the Holocaust. The message is instead a more general one: that individual Jews were defenceless in the face of Nazi brutality and that acts of supposed resistance were, in the end, unsuccessful. Notably, these are individual acts, *not* group acts. Within the Zionist ethos, the national group which resists militarily can be successful. When asserted in the context of the Zionist overtones of the school's teaching, this works as part of what Idith Zertal identifies as being central to understandings of the Holocaust: that it sets a tone. She writes that 'the Holocaust, along with its victims, was not to be remembered for itself but rather as a metaphor, a terrible, sublime, lesson to Israeli youth and the world that Jewish blood would never be abandoned or defenseless again'.[106] The message Zionist Israel, and its Diaspora counterparts, strove to take from the Holocaust was that the Jews would never again be 'lambs to the slaughter' but instead would resist and fight.[107] In this way, the defence of the Israeli nation-state's borders has become a protracted playing out of resistance to the Holocaust; the language of the Holocaust is used to encourage and to support displays of Israel's military strength.[108]

Gendered nationalisms, or, Zionism as a form of assimilation?

The differing ways in which Zionism and life in the Diaspora are gendered is fundamental to the anxieties which the teachers maintain and the mimicry which they undertake in the effort to relieve these anxieties. The teachers fear the emasculation and feminization which Zionism posits as constitutive of Diasporic Jewishness.[109] Yet they maintain lives outside Israel. This disjuncture is not resolved. Thus in this section I will now return to a discussion of the different ways in which historians and theorists have described the gendered aspects of Zionism and Diaspora Jewishness in order for us to understand the impetus for the teachers to mimic Zionist narratives of the Holocaust: to vouch for the potential masculine strength of the Diaspora in the face of allegations that the Holocaust represents a moment of Diasporic Jewish lack. In this formulation, differences which are embodied in individuals, or in national groupings, are mapped onto physical spaces: the lack which individual Jews living in the Diaspora are seen to embody can be reformed through the changing of national and territorial spaces.

As was explained in the Introduction, Melanie Kaye/Kantrowitz articulates this gendering as a female absence which arises from a perceived 'attenuated identity' that is possessed by those Jews living outside Israel.[110] Jon Stratton writes of this when, utilizing Freudian ideas of the femininity of the Jews, he argues that '[t]he modern, structural organisation of power was gendered. Its determining site was the phallic, male-dominated, Western State. Feminization was associated with a lack of social power.'[111] The teachers under examination in this book are anxious about whether or not they are masculine or feminine, in the terms described by Kaye/Kantrowitz and Stratton, as they are without national state power, and thus dependent on other states. And thus they (unconsciously) borrow an image of masculinity from Israel: they further an idea that a way to deal with the precariousness of the question of these Jews' perceived homelessness is to borrow ideas of home and its accompanying strength from both the West and Israel. In this imagining, Israel vouches for the strength and potential homeliness of all Jews. This idea of home has been articulated by Nikos Papastergiadis as 'more of a symbolic space than a physical place'.[112] Zionism, as practised by the teachers, works to fulfil this requirement for a symbolic space. Yet, of course, Zionist ideology is founded on the preference that Jews inhabit the physical space of Israel. This then brings us back to the understanding that, if the Diaspora and the Holocaust are feminized within Zionist discourse then to enable a masculine understanding of the Holocaust the history of the Holocaust needs to be taught from a Zionist perspective. What then constitutes this perspective, this particularly Jewish incarnation of nationalism which is seen to vouch for the strength of Diaspora Jews?

In designing a Jewish nationalism, Theodor Herzl – who is commonly considered to be the father of modern state-based Zionism – was profoundly influenced by the ways in which nineteenth-century German nationalism was being shaped. According to Tamar Mayer, Herzl admired the way in which Germans had been mobilized around the nationalist cause and believed that 'a similar future for the Jewish nation' was possible. He thought that this could be the cure for the 'problems caused by 2,000 years of living in exile'.[113] These problems materialized, Herzl believed, in the lacking masculinity of Jewish men in Europe.[114] As such, the reform of the Jews needed to take place primarily at the level of the physical; there needed to be a changing of the body.[115] Mayer writes that '[t]he *New Jew's* characteristics were to mimic those of the gentiles: tall, virile, close to nature and physically productive'.[116] This was, in short, an ironically assimilationist move in the face of an anxiety that Jews were not a robust national group. In this formulation, the problems (and resolutions) of individual bodies were being mapped onto a national group identity.

In order to reform these bodies which were (and are) perceived as lacking, training an army was central to Herzl's formulations. In the 1890s he wrote in his diary 'I must train the youth to be soldiers. But only a professional army ... However I must educate one and all to be *free and strong men*, ready to serve as volunteers if necessary. Education by means of patriotic songs, the Maccabean tradition, religion, heroic stage-plays, honor, etc.'[117] In this way he was not only drawing on the Germanic formulations current while he was writing, but also on a very specific tradition from Jewish history – that of a masculinity which it was believed was present during the times when the area which would comprise the modern State of Israel was dominated by Jews, but which, it was perceived, had slipped in the intervening years.[118] Thus, with the aim of the reclamation of that territory came the desire to reassert a (newly modernized and nationalistic) version of that masculinity. This disciplining of the body and thereby the nation through group activity is expressed – in a somewhat attenuated form – by Zionists outside Israel in many spaces, including through Zionist youth movements.

Zionist youth movements

The role of diasporic Zionist youth movements in the formation of Diaspora-based Zionist identities as a mimicry of Israeli Zionism is of great significance. As Tamar Meyer explains, 'Zionist youth movements, the new Hebrew education and paramilitary activities ... have been instrumental in the construction of the *New Jew*, the mythological symbol of Jewish nationalism.'[119] Their importance in histories of the Holocaust and as a way of understanding the linking of the Holocaust and Zionism arose in numerous interviews with the teachers of the Holocaust. Jewish Zionist youth movements are organizations spread across the Jewish world with connections with movements in Israel. In Melbourne and New York there are six different movements, ranging across the political spectrum.[120] Their only commonality is that they each identify as Zionist – the meaning of this Zionism differs greatly. The aim of these movements is to encourage Jewish people living outside Israel to move there (to make *aliyah*), or if they do not take this step, to maintain strong identities and practices as Zionists outside Israel. The importance of these groups in fomenting Zionism can be seen in the words of one Melbourne teacher who explained that he believes that 'the Holocaust serves to inform the Jewish identity of our students – either consciously or unconsciously – to a greater degree than any other factor, except ['possibly for those involved in Zionist youth organizations'] the establishment of the State of Israel and the subsequent history of the State'.[121] The link between Zionist youth movements and Zionist ideologies is, generally speaking, quite direct.[122] The ways in which Zionist youth movements are deployed in the teaching of the Holocaust, and within Zionist movements more generally, is therefore of great importance.

When asked if he teaches about the ways that under the Nazi regime gender roles stereotypically carried out by Jewish men and women changed, a teacher at this same school stated that he teaches his students about 'the importance of youth groups'. He describes to the students a situation wherein peer support for children in the camps and ghettos was vitally important as 'parents were effectively neutered as parents'. He teaches them that in the Warsaw Ghetto – where the most famous Jewish uprising took place – members of youth groups 'left their parents in favour of staying with their youth, with their fellow youth group members'.[123]

His focus therefore is on the failing of parents in the face of the Nazi regime – significantly, not just of one parent to be able to uphold their traditional role, but rather the failing of the whole family unit. When taken with his emphasis on Israel, this provides an interesting perspective. It can be considered that the youth groups served as a way of cementing relationships between peers, and of disrupting relations within families. It was through them that children were encouraged to seek support – and thus physical and emotional empowerment – rather than staying with their parents. By passing this on to his students, this teacher can be considered to be reinforcing the idea that when Jewish parents are placed under pressure, and are not capable of fulfilling their parental roles, the children should look to their peers – who represent here the national group – for support, rather than inevitably persisting with the family unit.

For a teacher at a school in New York, youth groups are linked in with other Jewish organizations that existed in the ghettos. Altogether these organizations represent Jewish movements of resistance. This teacher explained that:

> we talk a little about Zionism and how Zionist youth movements impacted the way people reacted and responded to being in the ghetto. And what their options were . . . particularly in the Warsaw Ghetto . . . we talked about school being resistance also, about publishing newspapers being resistance too. So we

talked about that. And that concept of wanting to build and having a goal outside and trying to connect to outside. And the people that weren't actually in Warsaw but that would come to Warsaw in order to help organize people.[124]

These people who came to the ghettos to help organize the Jews are fundamental also to the story of Lohamei Hagatteot, the Ghetto Fighters Museum near Haifa in Israel.[125] A *madrich* from Hanoar Haoved – an Israeli youth movement, which is connected with the worldwide movement of Habonim Dror – explained as he led me through the museum that this is a central message he teaches his students when he brings them through the museum: that youth movement leaders and members have a responsibility for their fellow Jews, and that this at its base involves resistance to oppression and repression. This resistance was itself centrally inspired by a desire to establish a 'productive kibbutz in Israel', and to inspire a movement of people to create a socialist world in Israel.[126]

The museum itself very clearly linked these ghetto fighters – who were highlighted as having been members of Zionist youth groups – to the soldiers of Israel.[127] At the main entrance and exit there is a sign which reads 'In respectful memory of the Ghetto Fighters, whose spirit lives on in the fighters of the Israel Defense Forces. May the legacy of their bravery be a blessing upon the thousands of generations to come.' In this way, through both the museum and the words of the teacher in New York, a direct link is made between the Holocaust and the importance of Zionist youth movements in the Diaspora. The Zionist youth movements provide the connection to the Israeli army which, as was explicated previously, offers the space for redemption of the (supposed) emasculated Diaspora Jews, and the continuation of Jewish life.

The emphasis on the role of youth groups is strongly evident within Zionist ideology. Herzl, when he was creating his Zionism, looked to German youth groups and gymnastics clubs as inspiration and moulded Jewish youth movements so that they would, according to Tamar Mayer, 'reject family traditions, revolt against bourgeois values, and emphasize instead a return to nature, simplicity and male comradeship'.[128] Mayer explains that the ideal New Jew was specifically a creation of the youth group: 'the youth movement graduate turned pioneer settler (*chalutz*), colonizer and defender – became the emblem of Zionism'.[129] As such, youth movements both within and outside Israel have served as a focus for Zionist energies, as a way of creating the ideal Zionist – the New Jew, with primarily masculine qualities.

By reinforcing the centrality of Zionist youth movements these teachers highlight the importance of Zionist communal organizations to the governing of Diaspora Jewish communities. As has been stated, this occurs as a means of negotiating the anxious feelings which permeate the teachings. By affirming the importance of Zionist organizations, which take as part of their primary occupation the reform of the Diaspora body and psyche, these teachers are working against what they perceive to be the emasculation of the Jewish people. In reinforcing the idea that Jews should find solidarity amongst each other and depend on other members of the nation to provide strength, the teachings display their Zionist influences. The Diasporic mimicry of Zionist teachings about the Holocaust – seen in this section through the importance given to youth movements, a type of Diaspora Jewish army – functions as a means of negotiating and managing these dominant anxious feelings about the place of Jews in the modern Jewish world. In this we can see echoes of the earlier anxieties which influenced the founders of Zionist thought.

A gendered Zionist Jewishness

To return to the question of what constitutes this Jewish nationalism, or Zionism, which vouches for the strength of the Diaspora, we can understand that, as well as an army, a re-formed nation requires a new language, history and national identity.[130] For Israel this was a further part of the project of masculinization.[131] Ronit Lentin argues that Jews in Israel have created themselves to be specifically Israeli rather than Jewish, demonstrated through their move towards a particularly embodied masculinity as defining of their character.[132] Yael Zerubavel explains that Israel in its formation looked to national myths of heroism as a way of creating 'a new type of Jew, tough, strong, and resourceful, who stands up to his enemies, a Jew who assumes charge of his own history and fate'.[133] Lentin accords with this view, arguing that 'conceptually, Zionist ideology resulted from Jews internalising the stigmatized position of the Jews as nomadic, homeless, and weak stranger and consciously or unconsciously wishing to reinvent themselves as its very opposite'.[134] The uncanny double of the Diaspora returns to frighten, pushing Zionism towards a mode of masculinity which is compelled to reject the supposed Diaspora femininity. Where the Diaspora (male) Jew is considered to be highly effeminate, the Sabra – the Israeli-born Jew – would be highly masculine, renowned for their bravery, physical strength and control of history.[135]

It is important to recognise that this movement to reform the masculinity of the Jewish body has a longer history than simply within Zionist discourse, and can also be seen to be part of non-Jewish European ideas of masculinity. This was explained by Tamar Meyer, who writes that:

> the impulse to feminize the Other was not new in the late nineteenth century: it had enabled modern society to build cohesiveness and influenced much of the anti-Semitic rhetoric of the time. The Jewish man's passivity was often caricatured and ridiculed on the streets of Europe and in European newspapers. Even more, the Jewish man's body was seen as 'aged, weak or effeminate', calling up yet another countertype to modern masculinity: homosexuality.[136]

Here we can see a debate occurring over what constitutes a proper European man in which the flaccid Jew (or homosexual) is positioned as lacking and Other.[137]

Christopher Forth sketched a similar battle in his description of masculinity in nineteenth-century France. Forth, in an examination of the Dreyfus Affair, argued that it was in part the differing masculinity embodied in Alfred Dreyfus that the French wanted to expel from their army and thus their society. The army sought to exemplify the spirit of adventure and this created and reflected a particular idea of masculinity. As such, the intellectual's masculinity was open to question – if they did not participate in this physicality of adventure their masculinity was found to be lacking. Thus Jews in nineteenth-century France – who were disproportionately not part of the army – were identified as not possessing the 'correct' type of masculinity.[138] While France is not Germany, of course, these ideas travelled across Europe. These Jews therefore, if we return to the ideas of Herzl's Zionism, required reformation, so that they could embody the masculinity of a European army. This was indeed part of Herzl's desire for Jews to embrace a type of masculinity which accorded with the dominant masculinities in the Western countries in which Jews were living: it was part of the move to 'normalize' the Jewish people.

We can understand the teachers' approaches to understandings of the Holocaust in this gendered context: they are unsure, or anxious, of their place in the Jewish world, and so they hold onto the masculinism of Zionist discourse to relieve their anxiety. It is a different form of Zionism which they seek to teach their students, and this is precisely where the slippage occurs in the mimicry which takes place. For they are not passing on an exact replication of this Zionism, as masculinity, but taking pieces of it for their students.

And thus we can come to understand that Zionist formulations of the Holocaust are deployed by teachers outside Israel as a means of negotiating the perceived lack of power that arises from living outside Israel.[139] The gendered discourses of Jewish identity which are articulated within Zionist histories come to exert influence upon Zionists in the Diaspora because these Diaspora Zionists – in this project, teachers of the Holocaust in Jewish schools – want to reaffirm their Zionism. Yet the concept of a Diaspora Zionist is seemingly antithetical, and, moreover, the Diaspora itself is counter to Zionist thought. Hence, completely understandably, there is an anxiety amongst these teachers that they do not appropriately fit into the Jewish world which Zionism constructs. An anxiety arises from the feelings of displacement that follow. If Zionists state that Jews are emasculated by living outside a Jewish national home, how can these Jews find a place for themselves? This question is not resolved. And as such, the anxiety and ambivalence comes through in the teachings. Zionism as a response to an anxiety about the place of Jews in the European world in the nineteenth century thus comes to represent a source of anxiety in New York and Melbourne in the twenty-first century. As I have shown, the Diaspora figures as an uncanny other, frightening Zionists not just in Israel but also in the Diaspora. Its uncanniness is profoundly gendered, representing the emasculation of the Jewish people.

The separation of Diaspora from nation-state in Zionist discourse arises from a particular construction exemplified through Herzl's ideas of what would make a successful Jewish state. It is important that it is understood in this way – as a construction – for it allows space for differing ideas of what forms the Jewish nation could take, as well as an understanding of the forms it has taken. One author to have identified the nation-state of Israel as not necessarily having to be seen as the culmination of the Jewish people is Sander Gilman, who, whilst at the Bet-Ha-Tefutzot (Museum of the Diaspora) in Israel, appreciated that:

> the overarching model for Jewish history has been that of the centre or core and the periphery. This model has been reinforced by the role that Israel and Zionist historians have had in reshaping the narrative of Jewish history. It was (and remains) the model of 'you' and 'us'. It is the imagined centre which defines me as being on the periphery.[140]

This idea of centre and periphery is a particularly Western way of conceiving of the Jewish people, and one which, in the tradition of Western colonialism, positions the periphery as inferior to the centre.[141] As such, in Gilman's reading of Israel's relationship to the Jewish Diaspora, Israel conceives of its periphery as its inferior inverse. In doing so, this dominant form of Zionism works within an assimilationist paradigm, striving to be like other Western nations, with the State as the most important and defining constituent of the nation. That is, by asserting that the Jewish nation is nothing – or, at the very least, is substantially inferior – without a patriarchal, possessive state, Zionism follows Western ideas about the importance of a state that is separate yet modelled on other states.[142] For the Jewish nation has existed without a state, and without physical borders to defend for centuries, yet in the modern Western world the bringing together of nation and state is posited as fundamental to sustaining an appropriately masculine nation.

If we return to the question of historiography – for it is the histories of the Holocaust as taught in Jewish schools which are under examination here – the implications of Gilman's ideas for the writing of history are particularly pertinent. Ephraim Nimni described this model of history-writing, writing that 'for the last 35 years, Jewish diasporas lived under the firm hegemony of the narrative of Zionism. This narrative continuously reaffirms the centrality of the State of Israel for Jewish diasporic life and politically subordinates the interests and security of Jewish communities to those of the State of Israel.'[143] That is, the imagining of Jewish nationalism is shaped by the discursive construction produced through historiography.

A Persistent Ambivalence

We can identify here the coming together of multiple Zionist discourses about the Holocaust and Diaspora Jewry in the teachings of the Holocaust which occur in Melbourne and New York. There is a persistent ambivalence: the teachers quoted herein are unsure about their place in the world as Zionist Jews living in the Diaspora. They have incorporated many Zionist ideas about the Holocaust into their teachings, yet various slippages occur. An anxiety persists because of this, but the adoption of Zionist narratives is undertaken as a means of dealing with the anxieties firstly that Jews do not have a space in the non-Jewish world, and secondly that they are not proper Zionists. These teachers mimic Zionism as a means of attaching themselves to a masculine, sovereign and dominant discourse of Jewish history.

Ronit Lentin, who migrated from Israel to Ireland, beautifully articulates the problem of simultaneously being at home and being displaced, being masculine and being feminine, and of being uncertain, or anxious, about how to negotiate those disjunctures to formulate a positive identity. She explains that to be a Jew is to be uncertain of one's place in the world. She

> was a member of 'the (Israeli) first generation to redemption', coached to despise those 'dia-spora Jews', for having allegedly gone passively to their death during the Shoah, 'like lambs to the slaughter'. Israel was the place where Jews would be proud again, would take up arms to fight their 'enemies', would never again 'go to their death like lambs to the slaughter'.[144]

But, she asserts, now she knows '[n]ot only that in constructing itself as a "new Jewish entity"; did Israel construct itself as masculine thereby "feminising" diaspora Jewry and the Shoah. But also that hero and non-hero, Israel and Jew – we are all the same. All (wo)men together. In re-enacting the dia-sporic experience, in re-exiling myself from my mother-land, I am Jew again. The epitome of strangerhood, homeless in my adopted Irish home.'[145] We can see here a poetic imagining of the ongoing homelessness of Jews – a homelessness which Lentin figures as a traumatic feminization, reliant on a traumatic imagining of the Holocaust, but just as importantly a powerful way to participate in the ongoing collective memories of the Jewish people.

Usefully, John Murray Cuddihy describes a comparison between the experiences of Jews and the Irish with regard to their place in relation to 'the modern West', and in particular to their moves from their previous homelands (Poland and Russia in the case of the Jews and Ireland in the case of the Irish) to New York. He explains that:

> [o]nce in the world of the modern West, the Irish and the Jews set about constructing social organizations and engineering conceptual apologia that would shelter themselves, their *Yiddishkeit* and '*Irishkeit*,' from the subversive lure of the massive American Thing. The Irish defined their enemy as a religious heresy and called it the Americanist heresy. The Jews, using their own word for apostasy, called it assimilation.[146]

To 'maintain their cultural belief and value system' for the Irish, and avoid 'assimilation' for the Jews, was to create their own range of cultural and social institutions, where they could remain as separate wholes, but simultaneously be part of the larger society.[147] Through these moves to avoid assimilation the internal anxieties about their place in these new sites of displacement and home are negotiated.

It is this disjuncture between being similarly displaced and at home, coupled with the ambivalence towards Diasporic homes, that has been explored in this chapter. By posing the Diaspora (and Diasporic Zionism) as the uncanny mimic of Israel and its nationalistic Zionism, I have outlined the ways in which teachers of the Holocaust in Jewish schools in Melbourne and New York are negotiating their anxieties over the place of the Jews in both the Western world and the Jewish world. These teachers represent an uncanny feminine other, or spectral haunting, for Zionism, and they are (unconsciously) aware of this. To counter their haunting place they mimic Zionist ways of narrating histories of the Holocaust. This mimicry can be seen in terms of the narrative progression, the two 'events' which are used to end the Holocaust – the creation of the State of Israel and the (re)institution of law as a means of dealing with the problems of the Holocaust – and the negotiation of different ideas of assimilation as a means of preventing the persecution of Jews. Throughout these histories these teachers negotiate the problematics of the place of the Jews in the Jewish and non-Jewish Western worlds.

Notes

1. I would remind readers here that when I refer to 'Diaspora' I am discussing the imagined space constructed in Zionist thought, which requires a centre and a periphery. There is also a world of diaspora that we can understand to include Israel (as just one more space in which Jews live, rather than a privileged space). It is the imagined space inaugurated in this latter thinking (with all its multitudes) that I refer to as diasporic. To revisit the prior discussion, see my Introduction.
2. David Biale points to the ambivalent relationship between Jewish and non-Jewish peoples at the core of current incarnations of Zionism. Sovereignty, according to Biale, has not relieved Jewish anxieties, but has brought its own set of insecurities and fears. Biale, *Power and Powerlessness in Jewish History*, 146.
3. For various histories and critiques of Zionism see, for instance: M. Brenner. 2003. *Zionism: A Brief History*, trans. Shelley Frisch, Princeton: Markus Wiener Publishers; Rose, *The Question of Zion*; J. Boyarin. 1996. *Palestine and Jewish History: Criticism at the Borders of Ethnography*, Minneapolis, MN: University of Minnesota Press. This chapter will be focused upon the relationship between Zionism and European Jewish histories (in particular through the focus on Holocaust education). Ella Shohat provides an excellent exploration of the relationship between Zionism and Sephardi and Mizrahi Jews. See Shohat, 'Sephardim in Israel', 1–35. For the ways in which this relationship is played out in one field – that of academia – see Lavie, 'Academic Apartheid in Israel and the Lillywhite Feminism of the Upper Middle Class'.
4. Interview with Teacher A at School ME.
5. Interview with Teacher A at School NYD.
6. Interview with Teacher A at School NYB.
7. D. Ben-Moshe. 2006. 'The End of Unconditional Love: The Future of Zionism in Australian Jewish Life', in M. Fagenblat, M. Landau and N. Wolski (eds), *New under the*

Sun: Jewish Australians on Religion, Politics and Culture, Melbourne: Black Inc., 108, 112. For a further exploration of Australian Jewish ideas of Zionism, see B. Bloch. 2005. 'Unsettling Zionism: Diasporic Consciousness & Australian Jewish Identities', PhD Thesis, University of Western Sydney. For a more personal critique of Australian Zionism, see A. Lowenstein. 2007. *My Israel Question*, Melbourne: Melbourne University Press.

8. For a discussion of American Jewish Zionism see M.A. Raider. 1998. *The Emergence of American Zionism*, New York: New York University Press, 2, and the whole book generally. J.J. Goldberg also explores American Zionism, describing it as a 'one-way love affair'. See J.J. Goldberg. 1996. *Jewish Power: Inside the American Jewish Establishment*, Reading, MA: Addison-Wesley Publishing Company, Inc., 366–67 specifically and the final chapter (337–67) more generally. Indeed, the whole book contains discussions of the relationship between American Jews, Zionism and the Israeli government. Jacob Neusner's edited collection also presents a series of examinations of different aspects of the relationship between American Jews/Jewishnesses and Zionism and Israel. See J. Neusner (ed.). 1993. *Israel and Zion in American Judaism: The Zionist Fulfillment*, New York: Garland Publishing, Inc.
9. Interview with Teacher C at School MA.
10. The curriculum of a school in New York begins with a page which compares a series of Canonical (Church) Law and Nazi Measures, lining them up against each other to show that the Church laws were repeated (in an updated form) by the Nazis. Curriculum of School NYG, 1. This same chart is also in the curricula of School ME, 19, and School MB, 6. The curriculum of one of these schools in Melbourne explores antisemitism in the 'Ancient World', 'Christian Antisemitism', 'Islamic Antisemitism', 'Antisemitism during the Middle Ages', 'Protestant Antisemitism', 'Christian Roots of the Holocaust', 'Racial Antisemitism'. Curriculum of School ME, 15--21. The curriculum of the other school in Melbourne contains the same information about antisemitism in the ancient world, the Christian world, the Muslim world, during the Middle Ages, the relationship between Christian and Nazi antisemitism, racial antisemitism, as well as political antisemitism and modern antisemitism. Curriculum of School ME, 4–8.
11. For a survey of what life was like for Jews in Europe prior to the Holocaust see Efron et al., *The Jews: A History*, Chapters 12–13. For an explanation shaped around experiences of antisemitism see H.L. Rubinstein et al. 2002. *The Jews in the Modern World: A History since 1750*, London: Arnold, 136–71.
12. Curriculum of School MB, 21; Curriculum of School ME, 41. Both schools use the same document.
13. Interview with Teacher A of School NYA.
14. I. Zertal. 2005. *Israel's Holocaust and the Politics of Nationhood*, trans. Chaya Galai, Cambridge: Cambridge University Press, 58.
15. See Ibid., 59.
16. Ibid. Idit Gil also provides a good summation of the various shifts in remembering of the Holocaust which have occurred in Israeli society. See I. Gil. 2012. 'The Shoah in Israeli Collective Memory: Changes in Meanings and Protagonists', *Modern Judaism* 32(1), 76-101.
17. Zertal, *Israel's Holocaust and the Politics of Nationhood*, 65.
18. Ibid., 60.
19. We can understand this through a Foucauldian reading of the purpose of legislation and education, which is to install and proscribe knowledge about an event. These power-imbued technologies of knowledge are productive of ideas of Israeliness and meanings of the Holocaust and its aftermath. See Foucault, *Power/Knowledge*.

20. See, for example, R. Lentin. 2004. 'Introduction: Postmemory, Unsayability and the Return of the Auschwitz Code', in R. Lentin (ed.), *Re-Presenting the Shoah for the Twenty-First Century*, New York: Berghahn Books, 12–13.
21. Zertal, *Israel's Holocaust and the Politics of Nationhood*, 95.
22. Ibid.
23. Agamben, *Remnants of Auschwitz*, 19–20.
24. F. Zeitlin. 2003. 'New Soundings in Holocaust Literature: A Surplus of Memory', in M. Postone and E. Santner (eds), *Catastrophe and Meaning: The Holocaust and the Twentieth Century*, Chicago, IL: University of Chicago Press, 198.
25. Arendt cited in Kellner, '"Never Again" Is Now', 228. For a critique of war crimes trials more generally, see G. Simpson. 2007. *Law, War and Crime: War Crimes Trials and the Reinvention of International Law*, Cambridge: Polity Press.
26. That the law can offer this comfort is not unique to Jews after the Holocaust. This, it could be argued, is a key function of the law. We should note though, that Zygmunt Bauman has made clear that we can also understand the Holocaust as not being an aberration that can be resolved by the reinstitution of the rule of law. He writes: 'The unspoken terror permeating our collective memory of the Holocaust (and more than contingently related to the overwhelming desire not to look the memory in its face) is the gnawing suspicion that the Holocaust could be more than an aberration, more than a deviation from an otherwise straight path of progress, more than a cancerous growth on the otherwise healthy body of the civilized society; that, in short, the Holocaust was not the antithesis of modern civilization and everything (or so we like to think) it stands for. We suspect (even if we refuse to admit it) that the Holocaust could merely have uncovered another face of the same modern society whose other, more familiar, face we so admire. And that the two faces are perfectly comfortably attached to the same body. What we perhaps fear most, is that each of the two faces can no more exist without the other than can the two sides of a coin.' This is the anxiety which I am charting in this book: that the Holocaust is not an aberration, but that it makes complete sense within the existing frameworks of the modern world in which this pedagogy takes place. Z. Bauman. 1989. *Modernity and the Holocaust*, Cambridge, Polity Press, 7.
27. N. Schmidt. 2007. 'Art Spiegelman: Walking Gingerly, Remaining Close to Our Caves', in J. Witek (ed.), *Art Spiegelman: Conversations*, Jackson: University Press of Mississippi, 222.
28. A. Moreton-Robinson. 2004. 'The Possessive Logic of Patriarchal White Sovereignty: The High Court and the Yorta Yorta Decision', *borderlands* 3(2). Retrieved 12 January 2008 from http://www.borderlands.net.au/vol3no2_2004/moreton_possessive.htm. See also Moreton-Robinson, 'Writing Off Treaties', 81–96. Charles Taylor traced the ways in which modernity has shaped the modern nation-state, and the types of modern nationalism which arise from this. C. Taylor. 1997. 'Nationalism and Modernity', in R. McKim and J. McMahan (eds), *The Morality of Nationalism*, New York: Oxford University Press, 31–55.
29. Ghassan Hage has explored some of the ways these feelings of anxiety and ambivalence are manifested within the constructs of the Australian nation-state. See G. Hage. 2003. *Against Paranoid Nationalism: Searching for Hope in a Shrinking Society*, Annandale, NSW: Pluto Press.
30. Interview with Teacher A at School NYB.
31. We can see here the practice of the fast-paced modern Western classroom in action – students are taught many things in quick succession, which leaves them with no time in between different units to distinguish the different histories they are learning. Joyce

Dalsheim argues that the 'busyness' of the modern, Western (and in her study, Israeli) classroom functions to keep students from thinking about and critiquing the narratives of their history, or collective memory, which they are hearing: that 'a sense of busyness is a powerful technique of hegemony'. Dalsheim, 'Settler Nationalism, Collective Memories of Violence and the "Uncanny Other"', 158–59. We can see another example of this 'busyness' in the 2007 Australian March of the Living trip. The itinerary for the Poland part of the trip (which was given to me by an educator) involved landing in Warsaw after the long flight from Australia at 11am on Thursday 12 April. Directly from the airport the participants drove to Gensia Cemetery and from there to see the 'sights of Warsaw', all of which are key sites in the Warsaw Ghetto: the Umschlagplatz, Mila 18, the Rapoport Monument, the Korczak Orphanage and Ghetto Wall. Not until 8pm that night did the participants check into their hotel. Particularly after a long flight, this is rather a long and one would imagine emotionally draining day for the first day in Poland. The rest of the stay in Poland is similarly cramped and busy.

32. Interview with Teacher A at School NYE.
33. Interview with Teacher A at School MD.
34. Interview with Teacher A at School NYA.
35. Interview with Teacher A at School NYD.
36. Interview with Teacher A at School MC.
37. Ibid.
38. Ibid.
39. Curriculum of School MA, 6.
40. Ibid.
41. Countering this linkage, Michael Fagenblat, in a 2009 talk to an audience gathered to watch the play *Seven Jewish Children*, to listen to a discussion about the play and to commemorate the *Nakba* (which is the Palestinian name for catastrophe, and designates the creation of the State of Israel and its attendant and continuing violence), argued that '[t]his play begins its so-called history of Israel with the Holocaust. This must be rejected by all sides. Historically speaking, this is absolutely unsupportable... Zionists should... dissociate the Holocaust from the state of Israel, because associating them leads to a completely distorted view of Israel's actual political strength and current reality.' Retrieved 21 May 2009 from http://sensiblejew.wordpress.com/2009/05/19/michael-fagenblats-presentation-at-the-seven-jewish-children-reading/. Avrum Burg, a former speaker of the Knesset who resigned and has since become an outspoken critic of Israel, also argues against the linkage between the Holocaust and the creation of Israel. For example, see an interview with him in *Time Magazine*. T. Karon. 2009. 'Can the Jewish People Survive without an Enemy?' *Time* 1 January. Retrieved 1 June 2009 from http://www.time.com/time/printout/0,8816,1869325,00.html.
42. Interview with Teacher A at School MA.
43. Ibid. Emphasis added.
44. Interview with Teacher B at School MA.
45. *Davar*, 22 April 1952, quoted in Zertal, *Israel's Holocaust and the Politics of Nationhood*, 84.
46. Ibid.
47. J. Massad. 2000. 'The "Post-Colonial" Colony: Time, Space, and Bodies in Palestine/Israel', in F. Afzal-Khan and K. Seshadri-Crooks (eds), *The Pre-Occupation of Postcolonial Studies*, Durham, NC: Duke University Press, 318.
48. Interview with Teacher A at School NYC. This teacher teaches a unit on Israeli history before teaching about the Holocaust, thus moving away from a strictly chronological narration of twentieth-century Jewish history.

49. Partha Chatterjee writes of this in relation to the Indian nation, and the prominent and important role that the construction of the modern state was given, as influenced by the English colonizers. See P. Chatterjee. 1993. *The Nation and Its Fragments: Colonial and Postcolonial Histories*, Princeton, NJ: Princeton University Press. Dipesh Chakrabarty explores this linkage between modernity and the nation-state with regards to India and governmentality. See 'Governmental Roots of Modern Ethnicity', 80–97 in Chakrabarty, *Habitations of Modernity*. For a more general exploration of nationalism and the way that it has coalesced in the nation-state, see Anderson, *Imagined Communities*. There are many other visions of sovereignty which exist alongside Western formations. Some recent publications present various ideas of Indigenous sovereignty. See H.-K. Trask. 1999. *From a Native Daughter: Colonialism and Sovereignty in Hawai'i*, Revised ed., Honolulu: University of Hawai'i Press; J. Barker (ed.). 2005. *Sovereignty Matters: Locations of Contestation and Possibility in Indigenous Struggles for Self-Determination*, Lincoln: University of Nebraska Press; A. Moreton-Robinson (ed.). 2007. *Sovereign Subjects: Indigenous Sovereignty Matters*, Crows Nest, NSW: Allen & Unwin. All of these publications present different, compelling visions for ways in which different sovereignties can (co-)exist with modern Western ideas of the necessity of the nation-state for group redemption. Unfortunately a full exploration of this is outside the scope of this book.
50. Interview with Teacher B at School MA.
51. Curriculum of School MA.
52. Interview with Teacher B at School MA.
53. Caryn Aviv and David Shneer have examined the narratives which MOTL presents, in the context of other traveling programmes to Israel and Eastern Europe which are offered in American Jewish communities. See C. Aviv and D. Shneer. 2007. 'Traveling Jews, Creating Memory: Eastern Europe, Israel, and the Diaspora Business', in J.M. Gerson and D.L. Wolf (eds), *Sociology Confronts the Holocaust: Memories and Identities in Jewish Diasporas*, Durham, NC: Duke University Press, 67–83.
54. David, March of the Living Education Session, 'Jewish Life in Pre-War Poland', 18 February, 2007.
55. Importantly, Melbourne is not figured as a step on this journey – the movement is from Poland to Israel, rather than from Australia to Poland to Israel and back to Australia. It is as though Jewish life in Australia is being effaced in the journey.
56. A typical Zionist narrative follows the story of Jewish destruction in the Diaspora and regeneration in Israel – a narrative of progress which involves a return to a 'golden age' of Jewish life that had occurred in Israel in antiquity, before the expulsion that occurred after the destruction of the Second Temple. Barbara Bloch explains this with reference to the work of Yael Zerubavel and the *Declaration of the Establishment of the State of Israel* (14 May 1948). See Bloch, 'Unsettling Zionism: Diasporic Consciousness and Australian Jewish Identities', 19. This approach serves to marginalize all Jewish narratives which are not part of this story of destruction and redemption, and to characterize Diaspora as inherently equating to destruction, a claim which does not seem accurate.
57. Interview with Teacher C at School MA. This contrasts sharply with the central theme of the history of the Holocaust articulated by the USHMM, which Michael Berenbaum explained as being 'not regeneration and rebirth, goodness or resistance, liberation or justice, but death and destruction, dehumanization and devastation, and above all, loss'. The USHMM, however, is deliberately an American institution 'charged to be a living memorial to the victims of the Holocaust by telling the story of their deaths – and their lives – to the American people', and its mission therefore is to tell a differently

nationalist story of the Holocaust, one wherein America provides the end to the Holocaust. This, of course, does not evade the focus on these modernist institutions as providing an end. Berenbaum, *The World Must Know*, 223, xix.
58. Interview with Teacher A at School NYB.
59. Curriculum of School MB, 116. It is notable that this is an Orthodox, religious narrative: here the nation-state is provided by God, seemingly in return for the sacrifice of Jewish lives in Auschwitz, rather than the sacrifice having inaugurated the nation as historical actors.
60. It also, as David G. Roskies has made clear, has existed in other aspects of Jewish historiography, wherein 'loss [has been] . . . the *precondition* of renewal'. D.G. Roskies. 1999. *The Jewish Search for a Usable Past*, Bloomington: Indiana University Press, 14, and see this book generally for more explorations of the narrative of loss and redemption in Jewish history-making. For discussions of this trope in Hebrew literature see A. Mintz. 1984. *Hurban: Responses to Catastrophe in Hebrew Literature*, New York: Columbia University Press.
61. On this the work of Daniel Boyarin – and his analysis of the negotiation of homophobia and masculinity within Freud's work and, in particular, his description of the uncanny – is helpful. See, for instance, D. Boyarin. 2003. 'Homophobia and the Postcoloniality of the "Jewish Science"', in D. Boyarin, D. Itzkovitz and A. Pellegrini (eds), *Queer Theory and the Jewish Question*, New York: Columbia University Press, 166–98.
62. S. Freud. 1955. 'The Uncanny', in J. Strachey (ed.), *The Standard Edition of the Complete Psychological Works of Sigmund Freud Volume XVII*, London: The Hogarth Press, 236.
63. Ibid., 241.
64. Another analysis of Israel's Zionist uncanny and its relationship with modernism can be found in an article by Barbara Mann. See B. Mann. Winter 2000. 'Modernism and the Zionist Uncanny: Reading the Old Cemetery in Tel Aviv', *Representations*, 69, 63–95.
65. Alisa Solomon explores this through the challenges presented by Dana International, the Israeli transsexual who won the Eurovision song contest in 1998. A. Solomon. 2003. 'Viva la Diva Citizenship: Post-Zionism and Gay Rights', in D. Boyarin, D. Itzkovitz and A. Pellegrini (eds), *Queer Theory and the Jewish Question*, New York: Columbia University Press, 149–65.
66. Amos Oz. 1995. 'The State as Reprisal', in *Under This Blazing Light*, Cambridge: Cambridge University Press, 67. Emphasis added.
67. Ibid., 69.
68. For an exploration of historical Diasporic male identities, wherein an examination is carried out of the ways in which the traditional Talmudic male Ashkenazi Jew is (what is understood in the Western world to be) a sissy, see Boyarin, *Unheroic Conduct*, xiii–xviii.
69. This fact – that modern Zionism came as a response to the perceived lack of strength of European Jews – is well documented. References to this are scattered throughout this book, but see, for example, Boyarin, *Unheroic Conduct*; Solomon, 'Viva la Diva Citizenship'; D. Boyarin, D. Itzkovitz and A. Pellegrini. 2003. 'Strange Bedfellows: An Introduction', in D. Boyarin, D. Itzkovitz, and A. Pellegrini (eds), *Queer Theory and the Jewish Question*, New York: Columbia University Press, 1–6; Gilman, *The Jew's Body*: S. Gilman. 1986. *Jewish Self-Hatred: Anti-Semitism and the Hidden Language of the Jews*, Baltimore: Johns Hopkins University Press.
70. Jacques Derrida explores the haunting nature of spectres, reading Hamlet and Marx against each other. See J. Derrida. 1994. *Specters of Marx: The State of the Debt, the Work of Mourning, and the New International*, trans. Peggy Kamuf, New York: Routledge.

71. A similar idea – wherein we are all 'passengers in a project called modernity' – has been articulated by Nikos Papastergiadis. See Papastergiadis, *Dialogues in the Diasporas*, 1.
72. Bhabha, *The Location of Culture*, 88.
73. This is reinforced by almost every interview conducted, when the teacher being interviewed would explain that they do not think of gender when considering what to teach. Similarly, when I interviewed a madricha, Ilana, who led March of the Living in 2007 and questioned her about the gendered implications of her teaching of Chaim Nachman Bialik's poem *The City of Slaughter* (see Chapter One for a discussion of this teaching) she asserted that she did not consider this at all in her teachings. Personal communication with Ilana, 15 July 2007.
74. Kaye/Kantrowitz, *The Colors of Jews*, 73. See also Alcalay, *After Jews and Arabs*, 3.
75. Interview with Teacher B at School MA.
76. Interview with Teacher A at School MC.
77. Interview with Teacher A at School MD.
78. Interview with Teacher A at School NYA.
79. Interview with Teacher A at School NYE.
80. Interview with Teacher A at School NYD.
81. E.W. Said. Winter 2000. 'Invention, Memory, and Place', *Critical Inquiry* 26(2), 179. Benedict Anderson concludes his discussion of the ways in which modern nations are formed and formulated with an exploration of the important role that history (and language) plays in naming places and maintaining group connections. See Anderson, *Imagined Communities*, 187–206.
82. Interview with Teacher A at School MC.
83. Interview with Teacher C at School MA.
84. Interview with Teacher A at School ME.
85. Interview with Teacher A at School MD.
86. Interview with Teacher A at School NYE.
87. Interview with Teacher A at School NYB.
88. Interview with Teacher A at School NYC. The different ways in which the Holocaust was enforced in different countries constitutes one page of the curriculum of a Reform school in Melbourne. There is a brief explanation of what occurred in different countries of Western Europe to the Jews. Each country (France, Belgium, Norway, Luxembourg, the Netherlands) is treated in one to two paragraphs, and the explanations are based on dates, numbers of people and measures instituted. These descriptions are therefore quite sparing, locating the explanations in empirical histories, rather than an in-depth exploration of what the victims experienced. Curriculum of School ME, 98–99.
89. Although, anecdotally, it seems that secular Jews in Israel often stop practising particular Jewish religious or cultural practices, and their Jewishness becomes expressed solely through their national identity. In a sense then, this is a form of radical national assimilation, wherein, like in other Western nation-states, national identity becomes inextricably bound up in the nation-state. This idea of Zionism as a form of assimilation will be explored in the next section.
90. Interview with Teacher A at School MC.
91. R. Weltsch. 'Wear it With Pride, the Yellow Badge', *Juedische Rundschau* (4 April 1933), 27.
92. Curriculum of School ME, 48–49.
93. Curriculum of School ME, 67.

138 | Anxious Histories

94. Curriculum of School MB, 25.
95. Curriculum of School ME, 9–12.
96. Ibid., 9.
97. Biale, *Power and Powerlessness in Jewish History*, 149.
98. Curriculum of School MB, 40. Curriculum of School ME, 51.
99. Curriculum of School ME, 129.
100. This potential which a homely nation-state carries was discussed by Ghassan Hage, as explicated in my Introduction.
101. The concept of a people Israel (symbolized, for instance, in the phrase *Am Yisrael Chai*, 'The People of Israel Live') has historical and biblical potency. It refers to the Jewish nation in its totality, rather than a group of people connected to a particular place or state.
102. The marginal place of women, as bodily and discursive representatives of the feminine, has been discussed with reference to the different treatment given to mothers who give birth to daughters and to sons by Omi Morgenstern-Leissner. See O. Morgenstern-Leissner. October 2006. 'Hospital Birth, Military Service and the Ties That Bind Them: The Case of Israel', *Nashim: A Journal of Jewish Women's Studies and Gender Issues*, 12, 203–41. For a gendered discussion of the ways in which places and spaces – towns, homes, hills, streets – in Israel are named after men, thus erasing the presence of women therein, see S. Reinharz. 2003. 'Women's Names and Place(s): Exploring the Map of Israel', in J. Tydor Baumel and T. Cohen (eds), *Gender, Place and Memory in the Modern Jewish Experience: Re-Placing Ourselves*, London: Vallentine Mitchell, 240–51. Importantly though, when I discuss this feminization, it is not necessarily attached to women, but is a force acting upon men too.
103. Staff Reporter. 2006. 'Stage Set for Yom Ha'atzmaut', *Australian Jewish News*, 28 April, 7.
104. D. Levin. 2006. 'Celebrating the Marriage between Australia and Israel', *Australian Jewish News*, 5 May, 1.
105. Curriculum of School ME, 87.
106. Zertal, *Israel's Holocaust and the Politics of Nationhood*, 96.
107. The idea that Jews went like 'lambs to the slaughter' serves to reinforce the idea that Diaspora Jews were, and are, weak and incapable of defending themselves in the face of Nazi destruction. This can be seen in the quote from Ronit Lentin which is at the conclusion of this chapter. Indeed, the phrase suggests that these Jews were willing participants in their own destruction. This functions to reinforce the power of Zionism, where Zionism is an ideology which requires Jews to militarily defend themselves. Biale, *Power and Powerlessness in Jewish History*, 158. Yael Zerubavel explored this with reference to the way that the Yishuv (the pre-state Jewish leadership in Palestine) from as early as 1942 utilized the history and metaphor of Masada (a moment in Jewish history when the Jews, on top of the mountain of Masada, killed themselves rather than surrender to the Romans in AD 73) to oppose the perceived passivity of the Jews in Europe. See Zerubavel, *Recovered Roots*, 70–76. Idit Gil explained that this was the lens through which the Holocaust was taught about in Israel, particularly in the first three decades of Israel's existence. Gil, 'Teaching the Shoah in History Classes in Israeli High Schools', 5–6.
108. Examples of this can be found in Lentin, 'Introduction: Postmemory, Unsayability and the Return of the Auschwitz Code', 12–13.
109. And in particular of Holocaust victims/survivors. Ronit Lentin explored this feminization and stigmatization. See R. Lentin. January–April 1996. 'A *Yiddishe Mame* Desperately Seeking a *Mame Loshn*: Toward a Theory of the Feminisation of Stigma in

the Relations between Israelis and Holocaust Survivors', *Women's Studies International Forum* 19(1/2), 88.
110. Kaye/Kantrowitz, *The Colors of Jews*, 195. Daniel Boyarin and Jonathan Boyarin write against this Zionist model, and through an examination of a Jewish culture of care both within Israel and the Diaspora have come to the conclusion that the State of Israel must rely more firmly on the diaspora, rather than dismissing it as an ideological aberration. Boyarin and Boyarin, 'Diaspora', 713.
111. Stratton, *Coming out Jewish*, 55.
112. Papastergiadis, *Dialogues in the Diasporas*, 3. He described Theodor Adorno's writing on exile, explaining that '"After Auschwitz" exile is, paradoxically, a permanent condition, even as redemption is not foreclosed but deferred to an indefinite future'. Ibid., 5. Zionism, as it is being argued here, refuses to accept that redemption is deferred and instead argues, in the fashion of Western modernity, that it was brought with the advent of the State of Israel. 'Exile' is thus refused as a permanent condition.
113. Mayer, 'From Zero to Hero', 285.
114. See Boyarin, *Unheroic Conduct* for an exploration of Jewish masculinity embodied in 'men'. An article in *Haaretz* problematizes the experiences of Israeli men in this field of masculinity, drawing attention to the ambivalent ways in which some men – in the case of the article, homosexual men – disrupt and are disrupted by these masculinities. See S. Lev-Ari. 2007. 'The Gay Man's Guide to Zionist Literature', *Haaretz*, 7 June. Retrieved 4 June 2009 from http://www.haaretz.com/hasen/spages/865688.html.
115. This has been explored through an examination of the 'Muscle Jew', the Jew with the strong masculine body, in two recent texts. See T.S. Presner. 2007. *Muscular Judaism: The Jewish Body and the Politics of Regeneration*, London: Routledge; M. Brenner and G. Reuveni (eds). 2006. *Emancipation through Muscles: Jews and Sports in Europe*, Lincoln: University of Nebraska Press.
116. Mayer, 'From Zero to Hero', 287.
117. Quote from T. Herzl. 1956. *Diaries*, edited by M. Lowenthal. New York: Dial Press, 37, cited in Ibid., 285. Emphasis in Mayer. It is notable that he is referring only to men here – that it was not seen as necessary for women to be a part of this army. Nira Yuval-Davis traces the involvement of women in the Israeli army, from the pre-state Yishuv to the 1980s. She argues that '[w]omen . . . can participate as "honorary" men in the army, until they start (and some strata of women are encouraged, by being excluded from the army, to start even earlier) to be mothers'. N. Yuval-Davis. Autumn 1985. 'Front and Rear: The Sexual Division of Labor in the Israeli Army', *Feminist Studies* 11(3), 670.
118. Mayer, 'From Zero to Hero', 285–86.
119. Ibid., 284.
120. See their websites for more information: *Bnei Akiva*: http://www.bneiakiva.org/; *Betar*: http://www.betar.org.au/ and http://www.betar.org/; *Habonim Dror*: http://www.habonimdror.org/ and http://www.hdoz.com/; *Hashomer Hatzair*: http://www.hashy.org.au; *Hineni*: http://www.hineni.org.au/; *Netzer*: http://www.netzer.org.au/. All retrieved 8 July 2009.
121. Interview with Teacher A at School MA. The ways in which postmemories of the Holocaust inform Jewish identities in young Jewish American adults is explored in the work of Debra Renee Kaufman. See D.R. Kaufman. 2003. 'Post-Holocaust Memory: Some Gendered Reflections', in J.T. Baumel and T. Cohen (eds), *Gender, Place and Memory in the Modern Jewish Experience: Re-Placing Ourselves*, London: Vallentine Mitchell, 187–96; D.R. Kaufman. 2007. 'Post-Memory and Post-Holocaust Jewish Identity Narratives', in J.M. Gerson and D.L. Wolf, 2007. *Sociology Confronts the*

Holocaust: Memories and Identities in Jewish Diasporas, Durham, NC: Duke University Press, 39–54.
122. There are, of course, students who attend these youth movements for the social aspects, rather than for political reasons, although this does not mean that they are not susceptible to the political messages which they are learning.
123. Interview with Teacher B at School MA.
124. Interview with Teacher A at School NYE.
125. For an explanation of its foundations and the meanings made in the museum see Young, *The Texture of Memory*, 237–40.
126. Personal communication with Avi, *madrich* with Hanoah Haoved. 29 August 2007.
127. The masculinism of the story of the Warsaw Ghetto Uprising can be seen in the descriptions of both the Nazis and the Jews in one curriculum. It states that 'On April 19, 1943, a German force, equipped with tanks and artillery, *penetrated* into the ghetto in order to resume the deportations. The Nazis met with *stiff resistance* from the Jewish fighters'. Curriculum of School NYG, 8 (Emphasis added). The gendered language here is striking.
128. Mayer, 'From Zero to Hero', 289.
129. Ibid.
130. Y. Zerubavel. 1994. 'The Historic, the Legendary, and the Incredible: Invented Tradition and Collective Memory in Israel', in J.R. Gillis (ed.), *Commemorations: The Politics of National Identity*, Princeton, NJ: Princeton University Press, 105–6.
131. For an exploration of the masculinization of Israeli space see, for instance, O. Ben-David. 1997. '*Tiyul* (Hike) as an Act of Consecration of Space', in E. Ben-Ari and Y. Bilu (eds), *Grasping Land: Space and Place in Contemporary Israeli Discourse and Experience*, Albany: State University of New York Press, 129–45; Reinharz, 'Women's Names and Place(s)', 240–51. For an exploration of the masculinisation of Israeli collective memory and history see for instance D. Boyarin. 1997. 'Masada or Yavneh? Gender and the Arts of Jewish Resistance', in J. Boyarin and D. Boyarin (eds), *Jews and Other Differences: The New Jewish Cultural Studies*, Minneapolis: University of Minnesota Press, 306–29; M. Katsav. 2006. 'Address by the President of the State of Israel at the Opening Ceremony for Holocaust Martyrs' and Heroes' Remembrance Day', Israel Ministry of Foreign Affairs, 24 April. Retrieved 18 December 2014 from http://www.mfa.gov.il/mfa/aboutisrael/history/holocaust/pages/address%20by%20president%20katsav%20on%20holocaust%20remembrance%20day%2024-apr-2006.aspx; Mayer, 'From Zero to Hero', 282–303; S. Roy. 2003. 'Living with the Holocaust: The Journey of a Child of Holocaust Survivors', in T. Kushner and A. Solomon (eds), *Wrestling with Zion: Progressive Jewish-American Responses to the Israeli Palestinian Conflict*, New York: Grove Press, 170–7; R. Shabi. 2006. 'The Fight to Not Fight', *The Guardian*, 17 April; Zerubavel, 'The Historic, the Legendary, and the Incredible', 105–23. For language see Y.S. Feldman. Winter/Spring 2000. 'Hebrew Gender and Zionist Ideology: The Palmach Trilogy of Netiva Ben Yehuda', *Prooftexts* 20(1 & 2), 139–57; R. Lentin. 1999. 'Re-Occupying the Territories of Silence: Israeli Daughters of Shoah Survivors between Language and Silence', in E. Fuchs (ed.), *Women and the Holocaust: Narrative and Representation*, Lanham, MD: University Press of America, Inc., 47–62; N. Seidman. 1997. 'Lawless Attachments, One-Night Stands: The Sexual Politics of the Hebrew-Yiddish Language War', in J. Boyarin and D. Boyarin (eds), *Jews and Other Differences: The New Jewish Cultural Studies*, Minneapolis: University of Minnesota Press, 279–305.
132. Lentin, 'A *Yiddishe Mame* Desperately Seeking a *Mame Loshn*', 92.
133. Zerubavel, 'The Historic, the Legendary, and the Incredible', 108.
134. Lentin, 'A *Yiddishe Mame* Desperately Seeking a *Mame Loshn*', 90.

135. Boyarin, *Unheroic Conduct*, xiii–xiv.
136. Mayer, 'From Zero to Hero', 286. This follows from what Mayer described as the movement of 'masculinity in Jewish Israel [as being] constructed vis-à-vis the effeminate Diaspora Jew and women, rather than the Arab'. T. Mayer. 2008. 'Nation and Gender in Jewish Israel', in D. Cowen and E. Gilbert (eds), *War, Citizenship, Territory*, New York: Routledge, 329. This gendering of men in France at this time is echoed in the work of George L. Mosse, who argued that Jews were discursively associated by the mainstream with homosexuals and, as such, were figured as effeminate. He equated 'the countertype' of masculinity with a lacking masculinity, otherwise called effeminacy. G.L. Mosse. 1996. *The Image of Man: The Creation of Modern Masculinity*, New York: Oxford University Press, 69. See also Shohat, 'Taboo Memories, Diasporic Visions', 217; Boyarin, 'The Colonial Drag', 237.
137. Daniel Boyarin, Daniel Itzkovitz and Ann Pellegrini also make this connection between the emergence of concerns about the European Jews' gender and sexuality – as being lacking and inadequate – and the emergence of the modern figure of the homosexual, in the late nineteenth century. Their definition is created together, with many of the sexologists who described the homosexual (and heterosexual, and other sexual categories of the time) being themselves Jewish. Boyarin, Itzkovitz and Pellegrini, 'Strange Bedfellows', 2–4.
138. C.E. Forth. 2004. *The Dreyfus Affair and the Crisis of French Manhood*, Baltimore, MD: Johns Hopkins University Press, 12.
139. Daniel Boyarin and Jonathan Boyarin view this as an assimilatory move, writing that '[t]he solution of Zionism – that is, Jewish state hegemony, except insofar as it represented an emergency and temporary rescue operation – seems to us the subversion of Jewish culture and not its culmination. It represents the substitution of a European, Western cultural-political formation for a traditional Jewish one that has been based on a sharing, at best, of political power with others and that takes on entirely other meanings when combined with political hegemony'. Boyarin and Boyarin, 'Diaspora', 712.
140. S.L. Gilman. 1999. 'Introduction: The Frontier as a Model for Jewish History', in S.L. Gilman and M. Shain (eds), *Jewries at the Frontier: Accommodation, Identity, Conflict*, Urbana: University of Illinois Press, 1.
141. For an exploration and critique of the relationships between centre and periphery, particularly with regard to history and historicism, see Chakrabarty, *Provincializing Europe*.
142. Hage, *Against Paranoid Nationalism*, 31. See S. Hall. 1987. 'The State in Question', in G. McLennan, D. Held and S. Hall (eds), *The Idea of the Modern State*, Milton Keynes: Open University Press, 1–28 for a discussion of the origins and contents of the modern nation-state.
143. E. Nimni. 2003. 'From *Galut* to *T'futsoth*: Post-Zionism and the Dis><Location of Jewish Diasporas', in E. Nimni (ed.), *The Challenge of Post-Zionism: Alternatives to Israeli Fundamentalist Politics*, London: Zed Books, 117.
144. R. Lentin. 2000. *Israel and the Daughters of the Shoah: Reoccupying the Territories of Silence*, New York: Berghahn Books, xiii.
145. Ibid., xiii–xiv.
146. J.M. Cuddihy. 1974. *The Ordeal of Civility: Freud, Marx, Lévi-Strauss, and the Jewish Struggle with Modernity*, New York: Basic Books, Inc., 166.
147. Ibid.

CHAPTER 4

'There Is No Doubt That It Was a Jewish Experience'
The Forgetfulness of a Haunting Settler Colonialism

> The 'Jew' stands for that experience of a lethal modernity, shared by the histories of slavery and colonialism, where the racist desire for supremacy and domination turns the ideas of progress and sovereignty into demonic partners in a *danse macabre*. In the half century since the Shoah, we have had to stand too often with, or in the place of, 'the Jew', taking a stance against the spread of xenophobic nationalism. To stand today beside the Palestinians, the Bosnian Muslims, the black South Africans or the Indian Dalits is to occupy a position from which the very discourse of modernity is eviscerated and needs to be rewritten from a place other than its enlightened or civilizational 'origins'.
> —Homi Bhabha, 'Joking Aside: The Idea of a Self-Critical Community'

As Ernest Renan has noted, group forgetting is central to the constitution of the nation. This, he suggests, is true of any nation. Indeed, in his essay 'What is a nation?', Renan argued that 'forgetting, I would even go so far as to say historical error, is a crucial factor in the creation of a nation', and as a result that a 'nation is therefore a large-scale solidarity'.[1] This point is important: all nations are brought together and constituted in some way through forgetting. Importantly, however, through a historical approach we can understand that this forgetting has particular qualities in different national formations. The forgetting that occurs, for instance, in France is different to that in New Zealand. The forces that shape the sense of belonging to a particular nation come with different histories and different memories, and produce different futures. The forgetting that occurs in a settler colony, I therefore want to argue in this chapter, is of a particular formation. And that formation, as I will show, impacts in particular ways on the memories and stories created by all members of the settler colony.

The memory-making which occurs in settler colonies is determined through a multitude of conscious and unconscious political and cultural processes, fashioned in a dialectical relationship wherein remembering and forgetting are reliant upon each other. The absence of particular memories results not simply from an inability to remember everything, but rather from attempts being made to formulate coherent cultural and national identities. In order to do so, some histories need to be highlighted and remembered; others are papered over, screened out, disremembered and forgotten. This, I want to suggest, affects *all* history-making processes which take place within the settler colony. If we focus on the historiographical questions being addressed within this book, a question which thus arises for us is, how do settler colonial techniques of memory impact upon the Holocaust memorialization which takes place within the settler colony? And, then we must ask, which histories and memories of the Holocaust are highlighted, and which are forgotten in the examples of Holocaust pedagogy under consideration here? And, following this, what historical narratives are thereby inscribed?

As I have demonstrated thus far, the teachings being explored in this book carry within them and are directed by an anxiety that these teachers feel over the dislocation of Jews in non-Jewish Western worlds, and in particular in the settler colonial countries in which they live. They are unsure that there is a place for Jews in these Western worlds, and in order to manage their anxieties they adopt, or mimic, Western ways of narrating History. That is, the teachers seek to place themselves and their narratives *in* History, to create a particularly Jewish History. There is thus an ongoing negotiation of difference, wherein some differences are to be embraced and others removed.[2] The history being taught is, largely, one of victimization, and it is a victimization which is peculiarly of the Jews.[3] In the construction of this narrative, the persecutions of other groups are often left aside, and sometimes forgotten. If we follow the ideas of scholars of memory such as Pierre Nora and James E. Young, we can understand that when histories are transformed into narratives, memories can ossify: what should be remembered is made more clearly defined, while anything outside the narrative is more easily forgotten.[4]

It is significant that the communities under consideration in this book are located in settler colonial nation-states: Australia and the United States.[5] In a settler colonial state the colonists have travelled from a homeland to what becomes the colony with the intention of staying there and then violently dispossessing and replacing the Indigenous peoples on the land.[6] This motive then serves to structure every aspect of society in a manner which continues indefinitely: in a somewhat haphazard process, colonial governments are formed, histories are written, and a particular form of colonial 'nativeness', sovereignty and belonging is claimed by the colonizers.[7] Indigenous peoples are physically removed, their cultures assaulted, and their histories actively forgotten by the colonizers and therefore within dominant national histories.[8] Even more importantly in the context of this chapter, the founding and continuing violence is forgotten in order to construct the national identity, in a manner described by Tony Birch as constituting 'the nation's twin genealogies of dispossession and forgetfulness'.[9] This importantly is not a one-off occurrence: the forgetting of the founding (genocidal) violence must be continually reinforced in order to combat the colonizers' anxiety that *they do not belong* on the colonized land.[10] Invasion, as Patrick Wolfe has explained it, is a 'structure, not an event,' for it continues to be played out within the settler colony after the initial moment.[11]

Scott Lauria Morgensen, in writing about settler colonial biopolitical structures in the U.S., exhorts us to include an account of settler colonialism in any discussion of goings-on within settler colonies: to recognize that all modes of sociality are formed from within, or produced by, settler colonial imperatives. Every group within a settler colony has a different relationship to the colonial structures at play, but it is important that we note that each group does have such a relationship.[12] It is this idea that, in part, propels this chapter: that, as Morgensen writes, 'we are caught up in one another, we who live in settler societies, and our interrelationships inform all that these societies touch,' and thus we need to reckon with this interrelationship in the writing of the histories that take place within any settler colony.[13] This is one part – other parts will be explored later – of what makes these histories of the Holocaust also histories informed by settler colonialism.

A question thus arises: how does this structure affect the histories of groups of migrants to these settler colonies? That is, how does the settler colonial mindset infiltrate the histories created by these later settlers/colonizers? A primary connection between the two processes of forgetting can be identified as arising from these similar anxieties about belonging: the Jewish pedagogy under consideration concerns itself, as I have shown, with the anxiety that Jews do not belong in these non-Jewish states, and that they must therefore continually (re)assert the validity of their presence. They do so, in part, through the formation of particular types and narratives of histories. Similarly, the colonizers are anxious that their claimed 'native' – or sovereign – position with regard to the settler colonial state will be undone, and so they must continually (re)assert their status and control over the state. Accompanying these anxieties is the desire to demonstrate that the belonging is not complete: colonizers do not wish to be seen as truly native or Indigenous (there is a claim of whiteness and of difference and dominance which persists), and these Jewish communities want to retain some Jewishness, and assert their enduring difference. There is thus a repudiation, or ambivalence, in the anxiety. Both sides of this anxiety, however, – its force and its repudiation – are negotiated through collective memories. And both of these forms of assertions – those from colonizers and those from these Jews – come, I will show, through the forgetting of violence. The claim for uniqueness which is embroiled in all aspects of the anxiety is aided by this forgetting. What precisely is forgotten, however, is different: this difference we can understand as arising from the mimicry which is at the centre of the relationship between this migrant group and the earlier colonizers. It is this mimicry which makes these histories of the Holocaust specifically settler colonial.

In this chapter I will explore the ways in which this can be seen in Jewish histories of the Holocaust: whereas in previous chapters the influence of a more generalized Western idea of historiography has been examined, in this chapter the focus will be placed specifically on settler colonial formulations of history. It will be understood that the settler colonial influence comes in a manner which can be understood as a haunting.[14] The teachers are not consciously influenced by settler colonialism, but rather it infiltrates their teachings in various different ways. Yet, in this haunting, these histories work – and this point is crucial – to position Jewish communities and individuals on the side of the settler colonial state, rather than as their violated subjects: in the teachings under consideration we can see that there is a desire to demonstrate that Jews fit in Australia and the U.S. (these countries which, as I have shown, are founded on inscribing and rejecting difference), and so the teachers demonstrate their adoption of national modes of remembrance.[15] It is by narrating Jewish history in accordance with the dominant historiographical practices of the nation-state in which these Jews live that the anxieties of a dangerous out-of-placeness are negotiated and the move is made for them to be lessened.[16]

But, importantly, as I have suggested, the forgettings which occur in Holocaust histories in these settler colonies are not of the same quality as those which exist in the colonists' settler colonial histories. Here is a key part of the haunting and mimicry which occurs: it is always and necessarily incomplete and imperfect. A similar foregrounding of the subject nation occurs, but what is being forgotten is substantively different. Whereas in settler colonial histories the founding violence perpetrated against the Indigenous peoples, as well as the continuing presence of these peoples, is forgotten in order for the colonizers to claim, and continually reassert, homeliness and belonging, in Jewish Holocaust histories other groups who were victims of the Nazis are forgotten in order for these teachers to claim a specific victim status. In both cases others – who are deemed to challenge their position within the specific histories – are being forgotten in order for the remembering group to locate themselves at the centre of the histories and thereby to constitute themselves as a group legitimately, and differently, in place. The forgetting which occurs is very specifically a covering over or screening out: it is a result of (and yet perpetuates) the anxiety that the teachers, and other producers of historical narratives, feel about the histories they forget. The memories which produce anxious feelings of displacement are screened out. Yet from behind the screen these genocides haunt and constantly disrupt the history-tellers. What is being remembered and forgotten may be different, but the effects and affects resonate.

This chapter begins with an exploration of the ways in which New York, the U.S., Melbourne and Australia were specifically included in the curricula and interviews, comparing these examples with the ideas of Holocaust nativization which have been explicated within different expressions of Holocaust historiography. The discussion will then proceed to an examination of different ideas of memory-work, with a particular emphasis on the ideas of screen memory articulated by Sigmund Freud. And finally the importance of the settler colonial contexts will be discussed through an explanation of the ways in which these forms of remembering haunt the histories of the Holocaust under consideration.

Nativization of Holocaust Memories

The making of common, normative, hegemonic national memories is a project requiring continual work. In *The Texture of Memory*, James E. Young analysed some of these memories through an examination of different memorials in America, Germany and Israel, thereby unravelling the ways in which Holocaust memorials are differently 'nativized' as part of the creation of national identities. He demonstrated that a nation is brought together through nationalized memories: shared memorializing 'fosters the sense of a common present and future, even a sense of shared national destiny'.[17] Moreover, it is in the act of participating in national memorial events and cultures that the group identity can be formed, as the 'remembering together becomes an event in itself that is to be shared and remembered'.[18] In his formulation, memorials to the Holocaust are formed to represent historical events so as, in part, to shore up the national ideals and identities of the country in which they are located, and which the memorial designers wish to accentuate.

It is important here to turn to the teachings under consideration. In what ways do these teachings specifically mention the cities or countries in which they exist? As we will see, the teachers rarely explicitly locate the histories of the Holocaust being remembered and taught within their national locations. In this next section then, I will explore the specific mentions of New York and Melbourne in turn, relating each to the histories of the nativization of Holocaust memories. From these examples we can understand that the nativization occurs not specifically in American or Australian ways, but in *settler colonial* ways which permeate the teachings in both cities: the remembering (and forgetting) is transnational, rather than simply national. This adds to our understanding of both the diasporic and anxious qualities of the teachings.

New York

In the teachings about the Holocaust in schools in New York there are very few explicit mentions of New York or the U.S. In only three interviews and one curriculum was either explicitly referred to. One teacher brought the U.S. into the conversation in her explanation of her description of pre-war Jewish life. She explained that they 'discuss Jewish immigration to America because that really precedes the Holocaust. So we discuss how there were waves of immigration over the course of time.'[19] The U.S. is therefore located as a place of pre-war safety for those Jews who migrated there.

Yet this same teacher explained that the Holocaust is used to narrate the potential perils of living in the U.S. In the interview, when asked what she is trying to teach her students when teaching them about the Holocaust, she replied:

> Okay, so I would say, number one, is that for students today, our Jewish children today, to understand that as much as America is a very democratic society, life in the dawning years of the Holocaust was just as democratic in the respective societies, and the calamity of the nature of the Holocaust was able to transpire. I think it is important for our kids to understand that complacency and that easiness with which they [have] begun to regard American society in the twenty-first century is actually quite a myth. And they need to understand the factors that enabled the Holocaust to take place, they need to understand the conditions, they need to understand the reactions or lack of reactions coming from the outside world.[20]

This comment reminds us of the anxiety which persists for these teachers about the place of Jews in the non-Jewish world. The aspect of the students' place in U.S. society which this teacher prioritizes teaching them is that they should be wary of their place within it. This teacher is not encouraging them to be a part of broader life in the U.S., but rather to feel that it is a *myth* that they could be comfortable there. Their Jewishness thereby overshadows their status as Americans; it is held up as a sign of their radical difference. For this teacher, it seems, there is little possibility of a syncretic American/Jewish identity, and this continued difference always has the possibility of tipping over into danger. When juxtaposed with her first comment, we can understand that this teacher carries a deep ambivalence and uncertainty over the possible relationships between Jews and the U.S.

We can identify here a disjuncture between language and practice. While the teacher stresses that these Jewish students cannot live safe lives in the U.S., she continues to live in New York. Discursively the U.S. represents a space where Jews are always potentially not at home, but materially the teacher has made New York her home. Moreover, the Americanization of the Holocaust story here becomes both located in history and ahistorical: what happened to the Jews in a particular historical time and place – Europe in the 1930s and 1940s – can be repeated anywhere else. It is a general and permanent Jewish experience. Jews are thereby homogenized as a group indefinitely defined through exclusion. The Holocaust here, and throughout this teacher's interview, functions as a story of being out of place, and as a specifically Jewish event. The claimed uniqueness of the Jewish Holocaust is an important part of the nativization of Holocaust memories in both the U.S. and Australia: it is, as will be shown, a part of the forgetting which occurs in the formation of national histories.

The words of this teacher contrast quite sharply with the response of a teacher at a school in Brooklyn. When asked whether she feels that her students have a particularly U.S.-based identity, she replied 'Yeah. Sure. [The school is] very Americanized. The kids are very into American culture. Music, movies, dress, everything. It's not a closed school. It's very open to American culture.'[21] For the students of this teacher then, living in the U.S. and participating in its cultures is not something to be constantly fearful and wary of. Rather, it is to be, and is being, embraced.

This U.S./Jewish identity is echoed in the curriculum of another school, although in a somewhat less precise manner. The curriculum contains a section which asks 'Are American Jews obsessed by the Holocaust?'[22] It explains that 'since the late 1970s, American Jews have paid an extraordinary amount of attention to the fate of the Jews in Nazi Germany' and then lists the various ways in which American Jews have 'paid attention' to the Holocaust: through producing literature and films, giving money to memorials, and learning about the Holocaust in Jewish schools. The problem is then raised that, according to 'some scholars and Jewish community leaders', perhaps young Jews in the U.S. are learning *too much* about the Holocaust:

> While the study of the Holocaust is important, they say, a focus on Jewish victimhood is no substitute for a solid Jewish identity in America... Many of these critics would like to see more balance in the American Jewish view of Jewish history, with more study of the whole range of the Jewish past. They would also argue for an American Jewish identity based more on Jewish values and traditions and less on a sense of victimhood or a determination 'not to give Hitler a posthumous victory'.[23]

What remains unclear, however, is the content of the 'American' in this 'American Jewish identity'. 'American Jewish identity' seems to be predicated upon a deeper engagement with Jewish history, rather than either a general American history, or the history of American Jewry. The writers of this curriculum seem to be suggesting that an American Jewish identity be situated primarily within a positive Jewish history. Perhaps then we can understand that the 'Americanness' arises from the positivity of the approach: that, now that Jews are in the U.S., they should focus on the positive elements of Jewishness. We can therefore see, in these four explicit mentions of the U.S., that there are a range of different approaches to the relationship between Jews, the U.S. and Holocaust memories. If each of these approaches echoes many others who share these views, we can appreciate that there is no one way in which these relationships are constructed. Rather, there is a series of somewhat ambivalent and uncertain attitudes.

Americanization of Holocaust Memory

The discussion in the previous section concentrated on the ways in which these Jews in the U.S. are remembering and representing the Holocaust within Jewish communities. But what of the remembrances which occur for non-Jewish audiences? This has been the focus of studies of the Americanization of Holocaust memories since James E. Young published his work *The Texture of Memory* in 1993.[24] The studies which have followed Young's intervention therefore engage with quite different issues to those examined in this book. However, the arguments presented are still important for us to consider as they provide us with a sense of the larger body of historiographical work into which we must locate the teachings under consideration here. They can provide us with a deeper sense of what constitutes the relationship between the Holocaust and American national identities within this historiography.

Young introduced the idea of the nativization of Holocaust memorials through a study of the U.S.'s foremost memorial to the Holocaust – the USHMM, located on the National Mall in Washington, D.C. – which was created to appeal to and engage all. This is demonstrated through the words of Michael Berenbaum, the director of the USHMM, who explained that the museum's Holocaust story would have to be:

> told in such a way that it would resonate not only with the survivor in New York and his children in Houston or San Francisco, but with a black leader from Atlanta, a midwestern farmer, or a northeastern industrialist. Millions of Americans make pilgrimages to Washington; the Holocaust Museum must take them back in time, transport them to another continent, and inform their current reality.[25]

The purpose of the USHMM, then, is to formulate a narrative of the Holocaust in order that it is not just comprehensible for an American audience, but is widely relatable. As such, the USHMM works to incorporate the Holocaust into a U.S. national narrative.

Tim Cole elucidates the process by which the museum works to do this by taking his readers on a walk through the USHMM, explaining the complicated way in which the museum asks its visitors to inhabit the identities of both a victim of the Holocaust and a U.S. soldier-liberator of the camps and thereby a rescuer of the

Jewish people.²⁶ He explains that '[r]ather than creating a museum of American pluralism, tolerance, democracy and human rights on the Mall, an anti-museum has been created of Nazi racism, intolerance, dictatorship and persecution. . . . At this anti-museum we are self-consciously told what it means to be "American" by being given a taste of what it means to not be "American".'²⁷ Americanness is identified in opposition to Nazism. This then becomes part of the settler colonial narrative, which will be outlined later. Cole does not himself make this connection, but he explicates that the USHMM tells this story of Jewish persecution as being un-American as '[i]t is so much easier to look at someone else's racism, intolerance, dictatorship and persecution in either our own past or our own present. Rather than learning from the past, we can leave comforting ourselves in the present that we are not like that. It carries the danger of inducing in us a feeling of self-righteousness.'²⁸ This is a self-righteousness which can only come with a forgetting of the settler colonial foundations of the U.S.: genocide is positioned as un-American, yet given the history of U.S. relations with Native Americans, it in fact lies at the foundations of the U.S. nation-state.²⁹ Moreover, the Holocaust is Americanized in the USHMM and elsewhere as a moment which is outside the American national character, yet it stands on the National Mall, alongside monuments to former presidents and memorials to other wars.³⁰ At the same time as it is being declared as outside the American story, it is being brought to the very centre of the national narrative. Its supposed unAmericanness is thereby being used as a central definer of American national identity.

Similar sentiments are echoed in the Holocaust museum in New York, the Museum of Jewish Heritage: A Living Memorial to the Holocaust.³¹ This museum is located in Battery Park, at the southern tip of Manhattan. Through its windows one can see the Statue of Liberty and Ellis Island. The Holocaust story is thereby positioned here within an American migrant narrative. Indeed, the very aim of the museum is to locate the Holocaust as a moment in the past, with the continuing U.S. Jewish communities as the 'Living Memorial.'³² As such, throughout the museum, visitors are reminded of the vibrancy of U.S., and in particular New York, Jewish life, yet the violence of colonization which enabled this migrant experience is not present.

Finally, the work of historian Peter Novick has proved useful in defining the constitution of this Americanization of the Holocaust, as well as the ways in which it has become part of the national American story.³³ Novick asserts, like Young and Cole, that the aim of incorporating the Holocaust into the American national identity has been to present a series of lessons.³⁴ The Holocaust is represented as a universal lesson; where Jewish educators, as will be shown, argue for the uniqueness of the Holocaust as a Jewish event, official American representations involve the claiming of the story as a universal human story.³⁵ Novick argues that the centrality of the remembrance of the Holocaust also works to obscure the history of slavery in the U.S. This, Novick writes, 'promotes *evasion* of moral and historical responsibility . . . And whereas a serious and sustained encounter with the history of hundreds of years of enslavement and oppression of blacks might imply costly demands on Americans to redress the wrongs of the past, contemplating the Holocaust is virtually cost-free: a few cheap tears.'[36] We can see an agreement between Novick, Young and Cole: the Holocaust is Americanized in a way which allows American audiences to both remember and disremember the Holocaust, while screening out American injustices. The U.S. is thereby allowed to remain a 'good' state, with persecution pushed outside it. This repeated centrality of forgetting will be taken up again further, when we consider the ways in which these examples of Holocaust pedagogy are shaped by settler colonial impulses to remember and forget.[37]

Melbourne

As is the case with teachings in New York, so it is in Melbourne: there were very few moments when either teachers in the interviews or the curricula refer explicitly to Melbourne. Only in three interviews and one curriculum was Melbourne explicitly mentioned. In one interview, a teacher explained that she uses the students' location in Australia to help them to locate themselves within the events. This teacher stated that she 'looked at various articles in the media as well as historical events that might be seen as antisemitic as well as obvious blatant prejudice and discrimination. As I said, we use examples [of discrimination and intolerance] of general Australian society as well.'[38] Here we see a linking of Jewish history with the histories of other peoples in Australian society. The specificity of the Jewish experience of antisemitism is reduced in order to draw productive comparisons. Jewish experiences of antisemitism are thereby drawn into a more general Australian story. This can be contrasted with the other comments on Australian Jewishness from different teachers.

Throughout his interview a teacher from another school in Melbourne vacillated between a focus on the specificity of being in Melbourne and a more general Zionist linkage of the Holocaust and the students' identities to Israel. He explained that it is the depth of the connection to the Holocaust which is unique in the Melbourne Jewish community:

> I believe that the Holocaust serves to inform the Jewish identity of our students – either consciously or unconsciously – to a greater degree than any other factor . . . The Holocaust bulks large in the thinking of the [school] community generally, and the Melbourne Jewish community at large. I think it's a significant factor in the formation of Jewish identity, in the maintenance of Jewish identity, and the perpetuation of Jewish identification.[39]

This, it can be understood, perhaps follows from the specificity of the Melbourne Jewish community: the majority of the community are descended from survivors of the Holocaust, having arrived in Melbourne after the Holocaust.[40] What makes this understanding of the role of the Holocaust Australian therefore is not something particular in the histories of the Holocaust but rather lies in the Holocaust's centrality to these Melbourne Jewish identities. The particularity of the Melbourne Jewish identity in this understanding is therefore not a result of a nativization towards Australian themes, but rather a product of the specifically Australian history of Jewish movement and migration.

We can see this contrasted in an interview with a teacher at another school, where it was explained that:

> Judaism is a very rich culture and religion and there is just so much there, of which the Holocaust is a part and may be a bigger part at this time because we're still only sixty years from the Holocaust, but certainly it's only a small part of being Jewish today – there's so much more. I think Israel probably gets a much bigger emphasis here and also being an Australian Jew, we do a lot of interfaith stuff with non-Jewish schools; with Christian schools and with Islamic schools. We sort of like the kids to be involved in Australian life as Jews. That's a fairly strong emphasis throughout the school as well.[41]

In this teacher's understanding of Jewish identities in Melbourne, the Holocaust is not as significant as other aspects of Jewish history, religion or culture. The particularly Australian feature of Jewish identity for her students is the interfaith perspective that comes from living in what is popularly understood as a multicultural society.[42] For the second teacher the Australian particularity comes from the centralization of the Holocaust in Jewish identity; for the third teacher the particularity was in the decentring of both the Holocaust and Israel. What unites these teachers, however, is that they prioritize the students' Jewishness over their Australianness. As the third teacher explained, 'we sort of like the kids to be involved in Australian life as Jews'. The Jewishness comes *prior* to the Australianness. They are deemed separate identities, and the Jewish difference is important to evoke. Of course, for the second teacher, Australianness barely garners a mention. He highlights instead the unique centrality of the Holocaust: it is the remembering of the particularity of that experience which shapes the Melbourne Jewish community. We will return to this idea when discussing the forgetting which occurs in the formation of nations. This forgetting in the Australian (and U.S.) national narrative requires the centralizing of a dominant group's experiences and the making peripheral of other narratives. Similarly, for this second teacher, the particularity of the Melbourne Jewish community lies in its remembering of this Jewish event (coupled with the ongoing story of the Jewish nation-state). For the third teacher, it is Melbourne Jewry's Jewishness, which its members carry with them even when involving themselves in the wider Melbourne society, which makes this community particular. Indeed, the wider involvement which this teacher highlighted is one based on faith or religion, where the Jewishness of the students is necessarily brought to the forefront.

The one curriculum which mentions Australia does so on three occasions. The first is a discussion of the 'War Crime Trials in Australia'; the second mentions the Melbourne Child Survivors of the Holocaust group which was formed in 1990 and has published a book with the stories of some members of the group. Included in the curriculum are two of the stories, both of which tell the stories of the subjects' lives in Europe during the war, not their post-war Australian lives.[43] The third mention of Australia is in information about the Second Generation, talking specifically about the Melbourne organization 'Descendants of the Shoah, Inc.'[44] This type of information being transmitted accords more closely with the words of the first teacher discussed above – it is the centralizing of the Holocaust, and the particularity of this centralizing which occurs in Melbourne, that is highlighted. These three linkages between memories of the Holocaust and Melbourne-based identities are united by their primary reliance on Jewish identities. It is the Jewishness which is placed first; then the fact of their existence in Melbourne. A certain degree of difference is to be accentuated.

Australianization of Holocaust Memory

Very little has been written about the 'Australianization' of the Holocaust. Indeed, thus far not much has been written at all about Holocaust commemoration in Australia. Whereas in the U.S. historians have written about the memorialization of the Holocaust for non-Jewish audiences, in Australia the reverse is true. There are two main historians of the Australianization of the Holocaust for Jewish audiences, but neither has looked at its Australianization for non-Jewish audiences.

In her 2001 publication Judith Berman presented the first sustained examination of Holocaust commemoration in Jewish communities in Australia. She argued that there has been little Australian influence on the memories being expressed in Holocaust museums, at Yom Hashoah ceremonies, and in school curricula, as these commemorative acts are most predominantly directed inward, to the Jewish community. In her book, Berman writes of a seemingly 'pure' Jewish memory of the Holocaust, untainted by the social, cultural and political conditions in which it is created.[45]

In 2005 historian Avril Alba wrote about the Holocaust memorializing which occurs in the Sydney Jewish Museum (SJM).[46] Like Berman, Alba locates the specificity of the Australian Jewish Holocaust commemorative project in the fact that it has been primarily survivors who have built the memorial institutions, thereby asserting that Australian Jewish memory in this context takes its principles predominantly from the Jewish tradition, rather than the Australian historical tradition.[47] Alba concludes that:

> [t]hus, unlike the American or Israeli Holocaust museums, the SJM exhibition does not attempt to recast the Holocaust experience into either a humanist or nationalist mould. In the words of the SJM's first curator, Sylvia Rosenbaum, 'One cannot use the Holocaust to tell other stories.' Rather the display aimed to 'Tell the story of the Holocaust simply, truthfully and honestly so that it would never happen again.' The survivor experience in Australia and not an Australian Jewish experience as such has therefore determined the SJM's shape of memory.[48]

We see here once again the idea that there exists an 'honest' Holocaust memory, untainted, in a sense, by history or politics. Yet, as has been shown, memories do not exist prior to the discourses within which they become possible. They are always created by their social conditions. In the words of James E. Young, 'the motives of memory are never "pure"'.[49] I want here, therefore, to make a contribution to the opening up of discussions about the contexts and motives of these memories.

Collective Remembering and Forgetting

In constructing a particular memory of the past an attempt is made to control the future identity of a community. This memory construction occurs through the processes of remembering, and also through strategic, and often unconscious, forgetting.[50] For instance, in Yom Hashoah commemorations in Australia, some experiences, such as those of Jewish collaborators or the 'lack of assertive response from some Jewish communities world-wide to the plight of European Jewry under Nazism' are, according to Berman, 'strategically forgotten'.[51] These memories are deliberately not talked about, and thus pushed to be forgotten, as they have the potential to shame living Jewish communities. Similarly, John R. Gillis discusses the importance of deliberate forgetting in constructing a national collective memory,[52] while Julia Epstein employs the term 'disremembering' – taken from Toni Morrison's *Beloved* – to discuss the ways in which memories are often not deliberately forgotten but are repressed, and thus not remembered.[53] These constructions of memories and histories become all the more important in light of the anxious histories which are under consideration here and which serve to determine the content of the remembering and forgetting which occurs.

Screen memory

Sigmund Freud's concept of screen memory can be usefully deployed to help us understand the ways memory works in the type of settler colonial national remembering which can be seen in the Holocaust education under examination.[54] Screen memory, as Freud described it, takes place in the psychic battling between different forces of memory which then work to obscure and replace the event being remembered. Freud explained that:

> one of these forces takes the importance of the experience as a motive for seeking to remember it, while the other – a resistance – tries to prevent any such preference from being shown. These two opposing forces do not cancel each other out, nor does one of them (whether with or without loss to itself) overpower the other. Instead, a compromise is brought about.[55]

As a result, the original experience is not recorded, but rather is replaced with a 'mnemic image' which screens out the aspects of the original experience which were objectionable.[56] The psychic process which Freud described takes place in infancy, as a way of dealing with early traumatic experiences. Similarly, the colonizer's memories – of violent colonization – which we are to explore here took place originally, albeit they still continue, in the infancy of the settler colonial states. What is important for our purposes is the understanding that screen memories arise from a division between impressions which the psyche wishes to remember and those that demand to be forgotten.

In the case of Holocaust education this division arises from the battle between remembering the Holocaust as a violent and deep trauma for the Jewish people, and remembering that there were other victims of this same violence. The original experience – that of masses of different people with varying experiences and identities, all involved in the Holocaust – is screened out, while memories of other genocides which have occurred and continue to occur are downplayed. Instead, an idea of the Holocaust as a peculiarly and uniquely Jewish event is remembered.[57] This follows the screen memory process of settler colonialism, wherein the violent colonization perpetrated by the colonizers is forgotten and replaced with a memory of peaceful nation-state building.[58] The work of screen memory is thus fundamental to our understanding of this aspect of the Holocaust education under consideration.

While Freud was, of course, discussing the state of individual psyches, this does not preclude his work from being applied to the collective, as I am doing here. Numerous historians have demonstrated that the conditions which initially described the individual can be successfully mapped onto a group.[59]

Remembering and Forgetting Other Genocides and Histories

I want to argue here that teachers often do not teach their students about different histories – that, as in Australian and U.S. national histories, in the teaching of the Holocaust in the Jewish schools under consideration there is predominantly an obscuring or forgetting of other histories of genocide.[60] The motivations behind the forgetting may be – and certainly are – substantially different, but the patterns of forgetting recur. Yet there are also times when teachers do bring in these other histories. This is the imprecision of the haunting which is in place, or part of the ambivalence of the remembering and its accompanying anxieties. This section will begin by exploring the times when teachers, both in Melbourne and New York, ask their students to locate the Holocaust in broader histories, and will then discuss the moments when they evade these histories. Then, with reference to the work of theorists such as Patrick Wolfe, Chris Healy and David Stannard, this section of the chapter will work to explain why these forgettings take place. Through this we will come to understand that these Australianizations and Americanizations are neither always consistent nor coherent, which is indicative of the anxieties and insecurities in the teachers and the communities in which they live. This is also the imprecision of settler colonialism.

Remembering other genocides

A teacher at a school in Melbourne explained that a focus on the persecution of groups other than Jews is part of the teachings of the school.[61] She stated that they:

> did a lot on prejudice and discrimination and though most of the examples are antisemitic ones, but we . . . talk more generally than that. That's actually quite a focus of the whole school, tolerance and understanding and so on. So, I could say I put a lot of emphasis on that pre-history from that point of view and looked at various articles in the media as well as historical events that might be seen as antisemitic as well as obvious blatant prejudice and discrimination. As I said, we use examples of general Australian society as well.[62]

This focus on groups other than Jews was echoed by a number of teachers. One New York teacher explained that this was part of dealing with the question of 'how do these students live and work with this memory and what are they supposed to do about it?'[63] One answer proposed by this teacher is for the students to involve themselves in protesting other genocidal acts: almost all of her students had attended a 'Save Darfur' rally which had taken place in New York in September 2006.[64] This linking of different genocides is echoed in the curriculum of another New York school, which includes an article from the *New York Times*, entitled 'Survivors Describe the Evils of Genocide'. It discusses the fruitful interactions of two survivors of genocide – David Gewirtzman and Jacqueline Murekatete, who survived the Holocaust and the Rwandan Genocide respectively – and their educational activities in high schools in Long Island, New York, as they go together to discuss genocide with the students.[65]

In other examples, two Melbourne educators claimed that the lessons of the Holocaust are about creating respect for others. For one teacher, this can also serve as a lesson on the particular historical status of Jewish people. She explained that:

we just sort of say, that because these people were Jewish this is what happened to them, but we hope that, well my hope – and why I teach it, and at university, and take March of the Living over and over – is that the kids will learn that there shouldn't be a distinction between classes and races and religions and whatever, but that we should be more tolerant of everybody. And that's one of the things I say to them – not to be – because we talk about the victims, and we talk about the perpetrators, and we talk about the bystanders – and so I say to the kids it's very important not to be one of the bystanders. As Jewish people we have a real social responsibility to be like this. Really to learn, so we don't let it happen again.[66]

Here we see forgetting and remembering intertwined. The teacher stated that she asks her students not to be bystanders in the world today – an important demand – but does not mention the possibility that they could become perpetrators. Why not? Perhaps, we can surmise, it is seen as too obvious: of course she would not want them to be perpetrators. But this then involves a forgetting that, as people living in Australia, a settler colonial state, they have benefited from, and continued, the dispossession of the Indigenous peoples there.[67] This distancing of responsibility for genocide in her statement is coupled with a desire for a tolerance which comes with the belief that 'there shouldn't be a distinction' between peoples, rather than an embracing of difference.[68] Somewhat similarly, a sign at the entrance to the USHMM presents an analogous distancing. It reads, 'The next time you see injustice, The next time you witness hatred, The next time you hear about genocide: Think About What You Saw.' In this way, injustice, hatred and genocide are things which readers of this sign could only see, witness or hear about. The idea that the person reading this sign could *undertake* these actions is seemingly unthinkable.[69]

An educator for the March of the Living in Melbourne in 2007 stressed to the students that '[o]ne of the lessons of the Holocaust is that you don't treat people as objects, as symbols'.[70] Students were encouraged to see the Polish people with whom they would interact as people, rather than as a mass of perpetrators. Ironically, he also told the students that they, by going to Poland, 'are resurrecting the past, embodying the dead . . . [Y]ou represent not only yourselves today but also the past Jews who lived there'. As such, the students were being asked to homogenize the Jewish experience and to arrive in Poland as symbolic of Jewish victimhood, of what characterizes the Jewish national story. This educator was simultaneously asking the students to be symbols and rejecting the very idea that people can be symbols. Here the understandable uncertainty about what it means to be a descendant of a victim of genocide, and how to remember that genocide, comes to the fore.

For another New York teacher, it is the students' position as American Jews which uniquely places them in a position to protest ongoing conflicts such as the genocide in Darfur. In order to encourage them to take collective action she described to them the U.S.'s inaction during the Holocaust. It was important to her that the students understood that the problems which the Holocaust raises are ongoing:

> I want them to understand that it is very recent and it is very important to understand what happened. And I teach a lesson on [the] American response because that is really important and given who we are as a school – that we go to rallies for Darfur, we go to these things to understand that Americans have always done this and here is a point where we didn't. And where Jewish Americans didn't and should have, should have done more. And didn't do more. And so we talk about that.[71]

While this teacher draws on the students' identities as Jewish Americans to encourage them to take action, she also stresses to them that their Jewishness is more central to their identities than their Americanness. When asked whether she utilizes stories and ideas of the Holocaust to teach her students what it is to be Jewish, she replied that she 'think[s] it goes along with all the other things that they've learned and that we're trying to convey to them. And the importance of Never Again. And the importance of this as being a part of our heritage, more so than Thomas Jefferson or the founding fathers of the United States.'[72] It is the particular Jewish experience which is used to remind the students that they might live in the U.S., and therefore should adopt American 'values', but they are primarily to identify themselves as Jewish: they should retain their difference. This is reinforced through the teaching of the Holocaust as a Jewish event. For underlying these important and commendable remembrances of other genocides is the sometimes unspoken, but always alluded to, knowledge of Jewish specificity and the accompanying belief that Jews are always victims, never the perpetrators.[73] We see here, again, this tension in different ideas of what Jewish difference can mean.

Forgetting other genocides

We can turn now to the problem of the different types of forgetting which occur and thereby foreground Jewish Holocaust experiences. At the beginning of the curriculum of a Melbourne school there are extracts from a speech by Professor Yehuda Bauer to the Bundestag on 27 January 1998. He stated that '[y]ou see, for the first time in the whole of history, people that were descended from three or four of a particular kind of grandparents – in this case Jewish – were condemned to death just for being born. This, the mere fact of having been born, was by itself their deadly crime, which had to be avenged by execution. This has never happened before, anywhere.'[74] The emphasis of Bauer's speech here is that this fact – that Jews were killed for merely being born – makes the Holocaust worse than any other genocide. The inference seems to be that in other genocides people are killed for better, more justifiable, or more understandable reasons.

Bauer is also quoted as saying that:

> [i]n the book of which I have spoken before, are the Ten Commandments. Maybe we should add three additional ones: 'You, your children and your children's children shall never become perpetrators'; 'You, your children and your children's children shall never never allow yourselves to become victims'; and 'You, your children and your children's children shall never, but never, be passive onlookers to mass murder, genocide, or (let us hope it may never be repeated) to a Holocaust-like tragedy.'[75]

If we move beyond his problematic statement that some people 'allow' themselves to be victims of genocide, we can focus on the gradations of destruction implicit in the final 'commandment'. Bauer spoke of 'mass murder, genocide, or . . . a Holocaust-like tragedy'. While there can certainly be considered to be a legal and motivational difference between mass murder and genocide – at least according to the United Nations' definition of Genocide[76] – to make this distinction between genocide and a 'Holocaust-like tragedy' is to claim that the Holocaust is, in some way, *beyond* other genocides. Bauer – and the teacher who utilizes this speech – is making the claim that the Holocaust must be seen as separate to, and worse than, other genocides. A hierarchy of destruction is asserted, with the Holocaust at the pinnacle.

This constituting of Jews as the paradigmatic victims, in light of the Holocaust's uniqueness – for it was unique and singular, as all genocides are, but as particularly this genocide is for a Jewish audience – is somewhat common and can be seen in a number of the curricula in both cities.[77] One Melbourne curriculum explains that:

> Although there have been many instances of mass murder in human history, the Holocaust was unique. The Holocaust was intentional and premeditated. Unlike other state policies in modern history that resulted in the death of entire populations – such as the Australian treatment of the Aborigines and the British treatment of Irish peasants, which led to mass death from famine – the murder of the Jews was the goal of Nazi policy from at least 1941 onward.[78]

However, these differences do not hold up under closer examination: it was not accidental, as the quote seems to imply, that either Australian Aboriginal people or Irish peasants were killed in large numbers. These were intentional policies and practices. Indeed, there have been many other instances of 'intentional and premeditated' genocide. By asserting that the Jews are the sole group to have endured premeditated genocide this curriculum has the potential to reinforce a history of Jewish particularity which is based on the disremembering – or active forgetting – of other atrocities. The important uniqueness of the Holocaust, one imagines, could be highlighted in many ways for a Jewish audience without the assertion that other genocides were somehow lesser, or a denial that they were indeed genocide (which can thus, in the case of settler colonial genocides, result in a continuation of that genocide). Scholars such as Dan Stone, Ward Churchill, David Stannard and Michael Rothberg point us to the ways in which knowledge of particular moments and effects of violence and atrocity can be enhanced by considering multiple atrocities together, and usefully and importantly argue against the zero-sum forms of remembrance that produce a forgetting of other people's experiences.[79] Indeed, Stannard argues that by approaching the Holocaust as an event situated in history we can understand the connections between the perpetration of this genocide and others, such as the genocides by settler colonists against indigenous peoples.[80] To fail to see these connections – to think of the Holocaust as a completely unique, and hence ahistorical, event – is, these authors suggest, to deny these histories. We can thus understand the importance of learning about Jewish experiences of the Holocaust alongside other peoples' experiences of genocide.

And yet, Jews are repeatedly singled out as having a special role due to having been victimized in a particular and homogeneous way.[81] To return to a statement made by a teacher which was discussed in Chapter One, we can note that a teacher in New York referred to the 'treatment' of Israel by the United Nations to emphasize this point. She explained that she:

> discuss[es] the attitude of non-Jews towards Jews and how it's unpredictable at times and how Jews are normally subjected to a double standard whereas – you know, let's say for example, in Middle Eastern conflicts, the Arabs can use certain methods of terrorism and afflict others in various ways, but when the Jews use firearms, the UN enacts a resolution against their use of firearms and so on. So there's a double standard, and the double standard has always been prevalent in Jewish history and in the Holocaust, talking about the build-up or rise of Nazi Germany and how the Jews were subjected to double standards in the Nuremberg Laws and how the propaganda led the Germans to believe they were actually true.[82]

Here this teacher focuses on Jewish specificity, moving between and equating the historical circumstances of the Holocaust and present-day politics, thereby reinforcing the idea that the homogenized Jewish nation is characterized by victimhood.[83] We can see in this statement an overwhelming anxiety that this victimhood will be ever-present, whatever the time and place. And yet, paradoxically, it is the very emphasis on victimhood that mobilizes and reinforces this particular incarnation of national consciousness. It is a particular analysis of the United Nation's responses to the interactions between Israelis and Palestinians – or in her description, Jews and Arabs – which enables this description of Jews as perennial victims to exist. And this approach can only exist when certain things are forgotten. In particular, the forgetting of the post-Holocaust settler colonial relationship between Israelis and Palestinians.[84] In this example, as recurs throughout settler colonial histories, we can see clearly the ways in which anxieties about the place of

Jews in the Western world are bound together with a historical forgetting, which in turn works to reinforce the anxiety.

Some of the teachers explained that they do make mention of the presence of other, non-Jewish victims of the Nazis, but this occurs in a cursory fashion. One teacher in Melbourne explicated that, contrary to what she had heard about another school where the Holocaust is taught as part of a general course on genocide, she teaches about the Holocaust as having been a particularly Jewish event.[85] She stated that:

> I think that when we teach the Shoah, we teach it because it's a Jewish school and part of being Jewish is having Israel, you know, as a land of the future . . . We see it very much as a Jewish experience and we do spend a very very small amount of time talking about other groups that have suffered and we talk about that we weren't the only ones to suffer, but there is no doubt that it was a Jewish experience.[86]

This is a multi-layered comment. The teacher begins by linking the teaching of the Holocaust as a Jewish event to Israel as a site of the future of the Jewish people, thereby teaching about the Holocaust very much as a Jewish national story wherein the Jewishness of the history and its subjects is reinforced. The suffering of others is mentioned, but as extraneous to the story: their place on the periphery is highlighted by the teacher's emphasis that they spend a '*very very* small amount of time talking about other groups'.[87] The Holocaust is identified as a Jewish event, or a 'Jewish experience'. While others are partially remembered as having suffered, their suffering is made explicitly less than that which Jews endured. The experiences of Jewish people are inscribed as unique, and the history of the suffering of others is shaped primarily by forgetting.[88] This is, of course, not to suggest that Jews were not targeted by the Nazis because they were Jewish – they certainly were – nor to downplay the history of antisemitism within which this genocide took place. But, importantly, others were victims of the Nazis for similar reasons and as part of the same, broader mindset of national racial purity. While Jews were a large victim group, they were not the only victims, nor was their victimization completely separated or separable from that perpetrated against others.

Another teacher explained that she makes an effort to teach about other victim groups, noting that 'in our school there has been a tradition that we have candles of different sizes and shapes to symbolize the different types of people – not just 6 million Jews but also the homosexuals and Gypsies [*sic*] and the political prisoners and the children. So we make quite a big thing of all different types of people who were killed, not just Jews.'[89] In this memorial activity, different groups are highlighted as different and simultaneously homogenized: each candle stands for a different persecuted group, but within each group no distinction is made. This reminds us, indeed, of the difficulties of memory: each memorial act comes with its push for remembrance, but also forgetfulness.

Similarly, the curriculum of a school in Melbourne contains a page with the heading 'A Mosaic of Victims: Jews but not only Jews'. It explains that 'though the destruction of the Jews was at the centre of Nazi ideology, Jews were not the only victims of the Nazis. Nazi racism was directed against a mosaic of victims.'[90] By calling them a 'mosaic of victims' there is a sense in which the parts do not exist without an understanding of the whole: a mosaic necessarily comprises many small pieces which come together to produce a more complex and complete picture. It is interesting then that these other groups are, in a similar manner to that undertaken by the teacher above, sidelined and thereby homogenized. They are differentiated to an extent certainly, but there is little information beyond a brief reference. Another teacher, in the U.S., echoed this approach, remarking '[o]h, by the way, if you're talking about in terms of just racism in general, although our focus is on Jewish history, I do mention that there is persecution of homosexuals, and the disabled, and the African-American, and Russian POWs. I do mention that but I don't discuss it at large because our focus is on Jewish history.'[91] It is notable that Roma and Sinti, and Slavs – the other groups of peoples who were racially defined and targeted by the Nazis – are not mentioned by this teacher. When different groups are mentioned, as they are in these two examples, they are defined as peripheral to the main story, which is one of Jews being persecuted. While it is perhaps inevitable, and to a degree necessary, that what was done to the Jews will be the focus of any specifically *Jewish* history of the Holocaust, it is important that we critique and understand the ideas of history which authorize this focus, as well as comprehend what it produces. What it produces, I am arguing here, is an understanding of the genocide as having occurred, in a sense, in isolation. Rather than the Holocaust as having resulted from a modernist, particularist Aryan nationalism which targeted *all* its Others, the problem is reduced to a Jewish one. Let us now explore this in relation to the settler colonial aspects of Holocaust history-writing.

Settler Colonial Forgetting

I am not arguing here that the centrality of forgetting in the construction of the national identities is unique to settler colonialism or to Holocaust memory, nor that the Jewish peoples inside these two nation-states – the U.S. and Australia – are inherently different to any other nation. What I am suggesting is that the most useful way to examine these two nation-states and the national forgetting (or ambivalent remembering) which occurs is through their theorization as settler colonies. The forgetting of the foundational, and continuing, colonial violence at the centre of the settler colonial state's history has an important function in ensuring the continuation of the settler colony. This function lies in the possibilities it creates for the constant assertion of the validity of the colonizers' claims to nativeness (although, again, not to actually being 'native'), and through this to control of the nation-state.[92] The creation of national narratives which crystallize around this particular screening out of the Indigenous peoples has, as a result, become central to the Jewish immigrants' project of making a place for themselves in the host settler colony. This is important in the context of this book, which is examining Jewish group anxiety about the place of Jews in these non-Jewish worlds. As stated earlier, the forgetting of the Indigenous peoples in the settler colony and the founding violence which produced these nation-states is mimicked by these Holocaust histories, which forget the genocidal violence perpetrated against others: both processes of forgetting exist in order to negotiate anxieties about out-of-placeness, and a relationship to difference. Both place the subjects of the histories at the centre of the national histories and thus work to justify the presence of these subjects in these (uncertain) spaces.[93]

This settler colonial anxiety about out-of-placeness is, in an important sense, a diasporic uncertainty. Colonial settlers are anxious about their place in the world as they are outside the metropole and thus fear being considered inferior. But they are also the imperial force in the periphery, where they believe themselves to be superior. Deborah Bird-Rose, in explaining Ann Curthoys' ideas, writes that the colonists' 'sense of belonging to this continent . . . is haunted by fears of "a symbolic loss of legitimacy and permanency of their sense of home. So keenly aware of being themselves displaced, many non-indigenous Australians have fiercely taken on their new country as Home."'[94] In this sense, their diasporic position – their location outside the metropole homeland – produces a haunting anxiety. There is also, as I have suggested, an anxiety that the settlers are not entitled to be in the place in which they are now located: hence they must construct histories which declare their right to be there.[95] And so they find ways to formulate histories which can make their nation-state, in Ghassan Hage's formulation, a 'homely' one.[96] Very similar anxieties can be detected in the teachings under examination. There is an ongoing negotiation of the place of these Jews, and this negotiation is haunted by an anxiety that, in the end, these Jews and their narratives have no right to be there. In this way we can see the haunting of the settler colonial anxiety in the teachings being considered.

It is important here to gain a more detailed understanding of settler colonialism. Patrick Wolfe explains that in the settler colonial project, invasion is a 'structure, not an event': invasion brings with it ongoing colonial ways of being, rather than acting as a one-off and discrete occurrence.[97] Wolfe argues that in the settler colony it is control of the land which is the 'primary object and governing motive': fundamental to this is the governing of cultures and histories.[98] In this settler colonial formulation, relationships between the colonizers and the Indigenous peoples are governed by a 'logic of elimination' wherein the colonizer seeks to control and eradicate the Indigenous peoples, whether by killing them or through techniques of cultural assimilation. All the technologies of empire are brought together to enable this and, as Wolfe states, the law is brought to the service of colonization, formulating legislation which controls and makes legitimate colonial relationships to land.[99] Within this viewpoint, the structure of invasion and the accompanying discourses of control and forgetting which it is argued characterize settler colonialism permeate and inform aspects of the colonial societies of Australia and America.[100] This is not to suggest that Indigenous peoples are always forever forgotten, for there are always ways of evading, and remembering outside of, these settler colonial formations.

Where Wolfe writes of the law, it is useful in the context being discussed here to think of the place of histories within the structures of settler colonization.[101] To enable the settler colonial nation-state to continue, the colonizer must write histories. It is in these histories that a great deal of forgetting occurs. Primarily this is the forgetting of what was, and continues to be, done to Indigenous peoples. The forgetting of the foundational and continuing violence occurs in order to justify the colonizers' presence and control. Again, this is not to suggest that national histories which take note of the presence of Indigenous peoples cannot be, and are not being, written. For they are. But they do not occupy the same position of dominance as these other histories. Why is this important when considering histories of the Holocaust as taught in Jewish schools? The importance, I am arguing, arises from the anxiety which permeates Holocaust education. The teachers are unsure of their place in the non-Jewish American and Australian nations in which they find themselves, and they fear a genocidal reprisal. How then to actively make sure that this does not happen, even if, as some also believe, it is inevitable?

I am arguing, just as I have argued in other chapters with regard to other aspects of Western history-making, that these teachers seek to mimic settler colonial modes of narration. In order to avoid persecution themselves, they seek to adopt the narrative ploys of the colonizer – to locate themselves in the space created by the colonizer. They remember along the lines of these settler colonial histories which foreground the subject nation and forget the violence wrought upon others. Whether or not this can be done – whether Jews can truly join the space of the colonizer – is another question: I am merely arguing here that this is what the teachers are seeking to do, albeit while retaining a certain difference. That is, to resolve their anxieties, these teachers are attempting to mimic and thus join those settler colonial histories which also retain a sense of difference, both from Indigenous peoples and the metropole.[102]

Chris Healy has delved into the dominant practice of settler colonial forgetting in an Australian context. For Healy, as for Wolfe, the making of colonial identities is not simply a one-off event. Rather, it is an ongoing and ever-evolving project: '[f]ar more than a moment of first contact or fatal impact, Aboriginality [– that is, the ongoing dialectic of Indigenous and non-Indigenous identity formation –] is a "contact zone" in an extended field that's both colonial and postcolonial'.[103] That is, the creation of the concept or category of 'Aboriginality' is part of an ongoing process of continuing colonization. For Healy, a central aspect of this is the narration of histories, or collective memories, of what constitutes Indigenous people. Central to *that* is the continual re-forgetting of Indigenous people. Healy is not writing here of real people, but rather of their representations, which take on the force of reality. He explains that:

> [a]t the broadest level, [he is] refer[ring] to remembering and forgetting the occupation of the continent by indigenous people and the British colonization of the same continent. 'Events' such as these are remembered through a variety of institutional and habitual practices, from property law to naming country, public rituals and language. In this sense, remembering and forgetting takes us directly to how historicity – a lived experience of being in history – is constitutive of everyday life.[104]

Everyday life and identity is constructed by understandings of how one fits into history. This is as true in the relationship between colonizer and colonized that Healy and Wolfe outline as it is for the Holocaust educators whose works are under examination.

Healy explains further that throughout the last 200 years of colonization of Australia, Aboriginal people have been continually forgotten, even when they are present. Indeed, it is their very presence which is continually forgotten. Colonial dissenters – caught up in narratives of invisibility – ask, 'Why weren't we told?', as though they never have been.[105] Yet, as Healy shows, there have always been these stories hovering in the background; it has taken a willingness to know for people to become aware.[106] Thus he concludes that the forgetting repeats itself: for the last two centuries people have asked themselves and others why they did not know, and have failed to recognize that they are actively forgetting. Similarly, as Anna Clark has shown, this forgetting is transported to the teaching of Australian history in Australian schools, wherein people at all levels of the country – public intellectuals, writers of 'history', and members of government, most notably the then-Prime Minister John Howard – derided the idea that Australia has a genocidal history.[107] Clark argues that this forgetting is a wilful blindness to the acts of the Australian state which thereby serves political ends. It works to reinforce a positive narrative of Australia's past, and thereby maintain the sovereignty of the Australian state.[108] By forgetting the violent, colonial past and its continuations in the present, the rightful presence of the colonizers can be asserted.

Here we can observe a distinction between these broader national narratives and those being expressed in the Holocaust education under examination. Where these official national histories continually forget the founding and continuing violence in order to legitimate the presence and control of the colonizers in the state, the Jewish Holocaust histories forget other people's victimizations as a means of presenting an exclusivist victim-based history of the Jewish nation.[109] There are thus, in some ways, quite different – both historically as well as politically or ethically – motivations at work. What each forgetting serves to do – and here is the affinity – is to place the nation's history at the centre of the narrative, thereby forgetting other nations and peoples, in order to negotiate anxieties of out-of-placeness. It is the creation of these histories which place the subjects of the history within history, and thus constitute them as legitimately in place. Moreover, if settler colonialism is a structure, then that structure involves the continual (re)creation and (re)assertion of settler colonial histories. To fit comfortably within the settler colonial state – that is, to avoid being placed on the side of the persecuted colonized – it is important to create narratives which mimic the being-in-history and legitimacy which the colonizers present as foundational. And so these teachers present simulacra of these narratives through their Holocaust education. This mimicry which I am identifying in this chapter presents slippages: whereas the settler colonial nation is forgetting the foundational violence which constituted the nation, the Jewish Holocaust histories are forgetting the violence done to others in order to constitute themselves as a legitimate part of the settler colonial nation. The similarity is that histories of both are constituted through a national forgetting; the difference is what is being forgotten. Moreover, whereas the colonizer possesses material power to enact their narrative upon others, the Jewish narrative can claim no such state-based power in Melbourne or New York. In short, these teachers seek to claim a space for themselves within the settler colonial state which has historically been denied to them because of their migrant, non-white, status. These teachers, through their mimicry, work to enter the colonizer's space.

Ambivalent Settler Colonial Holocaust Memories

I have argued here that what makes these histories of the Holocaust being taught in these Jewish schools particularly Australian and American is not, as previous scholars have suggested, their calls to American values of freedom and democracy, nor their presentation of a 'pure' Holocaust narrative, presented 'simply' to remember. Rather, it is their settler colonial quality, and the forgetting which is constitutive of this approach. What makes the forgetting at the centre of these histories specifically settler colonial is the shared anxiety about the place of the settlers in the nation. For the original colonizers the anxiety is that they are not native, and, as such, there is a constant need to (re)assert their dominant place in the settler colonial nation. It is a status which is never fixed and which is shaped by an anxiety that they do not belong, while also never truly wanting to be Indigenous. Similarly, as I have made clear throughout this book, there is an anxiety that Jews do not properly fit in these societies, and so they constantly need to (re)assert that they do belong. This is the similarity between settler colonial and these Jewish motivations to write histories and remember, or forget. These teachers mimic in the hope of joining the ranks of the settled, in order to attempt to ensure that they are not the victims of genocide again. But they also seek to retain and reinforce a Jewish difference, thus reminding us of the ambivalence at the heart of notions of belonging, and the limitation on the forms of belonging offered by the settler colonial state: only certain forms of difference are perceived as acceptable.

This mimicry helps us to understand the deeply ambivalent relationship between migrant Jewish populations and earlier colonizers. This ambivalence is perhaps best articulated by Albert Memmi, who wrote of Jews in a Tunisian context, but whose words ring true for the histories being discussed here. In his text *The Coloniser and the Colonised* Memmi wrote that:

> the situation of the Jewish population [is as] eternally hesitant candidates refusing assimilation. . . . Their constant and very justifiable ambition is to escape from their colonized condition [in Tunisia], an additional burden in an already oppressive status. To that end, they endeavour to resemble the colonizer in the frank hope that he may cease to consider them different from him. Hence their efforts to forget the past, to change collective habits, and their enthusiastic adoption of Western language, culture and customs. But if the colonizer does not always openly discourage these candidates to develop that resemblance, he never permits them to attain it either. Thus they live in painful and constant ambiguity. Rejected by the colonizer, they share in part the physical conditions of the colonized and have a communion of interests with him; on the other hand, they reject the values of the colonized as belonging to a decayed world from which they eventually hope to escape.[110]

Here we see articulated the uncertainty about the relationship Jews today maintain with both colonized and colonizer. It is this uncertainty, and the liminal – or productively in-between – place of Jews in the settler colonies under consideration, which permeates the Holocaust pedagogy under consideration here.

In this chapter I have demonstrated the various ways in which Australian and American national historical discourses have been mimicked by teachers of the Holocaust in the Jewish schools under consideration in this project. I have argued that, most importantly, these teachers have adopted the importance of forgetting in constructing historical narratives. This results in a set of narratives which, like settler colonial narratives, are often ambivalent. This is produced, in part, by the presence of settler colonialism not as a conscious operative force upon the histories of the Holocaust, but rather as a haunting influence upon the teachers and the histories they are creating. It hovers in the background, exerting influence in varied and uncertain ways. This in turn leads to further anxiety: that the histories of the Holocaust being created do not fulfil the requirements of national histories and do not adequately negotiate the anxieties about the place of Jews in the world which permeate the teachings. The mimicry occurs as the teachers work to ease their anxiety over the place, or lack of a place, of Jews in the non-Jewish Western world. What eventuates is a history of the Holocaust shaped by a focus on Jews to the almost complete exclusion of others. This we can identify as, in part, a settler colonial history.

Notes

1. E. Renan. 1993. 'What is a Nation?' in H.K. Bhabha (ed.), *Nation and Narration*, London: Routledge, 11, 19.
2. This returns us to the ideas of ambivalence which I have discussed at other points in this book.
3. This contrasts with the universalist analysis offered by, for example, Zygmunt Bauman, who locates the Holocaust as a problem of modernity. See Z. Bauman. 1989. *Modernity and the Holocaust*, Cambridge: Polity Press.
4. James E. Young writes that '[t]o the extent that we encourage monuments to do our memory-work for us, we become that much more forgetful. In effect, the initial impulse to memorialize events like the Holocaust may actually spring from an opposite and equal desire to forget them.' Young, *The Texture of Memory*, 5. We can see these ideas in Pierre Nora's discussion of lieux de memoire, as mentioned in my Introduction. There is a link here between Holocaust memorials and educational narratives, but it is not being suggested that they are the same thing. Yet the writings that exist on Holocaust memorials are usefully applied to educational narratives.
5. For a discussion of U.S. settler colonialism and the ways in which it has impacted on both colonized and colonizers over time see D. Janiewski. 1995. 'Gendering, Racializing and Classifying: Settler Colonization in the United States, 1590-1990', in D. Stasiulis and N. Yuval-Davis (eds), *Unsettling Settler Societies: Articulation of Gender, Race, Ethnicity and Class*, London: SAGE Publications, 132–60. See also, for instance, K. Ellinghaus. 2006. *Taking Assimilation to Heart: Marriages of White Women and Indigenous Men in the United States and Australia, 1887-1937*, Lincoln: University of Nebraska Press; A. Goldstein. Fall 2008. 'Where the Nation Takes Place: Proprietary Regimes, Antistatism, and U.S. Settler Colonialism', *South Atlantic Quarterly* 107(4), 833–61.
6. See, for instance, P. Wolfe. December 2006. 'Settler Colonialism and the Elimination of the Native', *Journal of Genocide Research* 8(4), 387–409.
7. This 'nativeness' is always claimed to a degree, and with limitations: the colonizers, of course, do not actually want to be treated as colonized Indigenous peoples. The nativeness which is claimed is a 'patriarchal white sovereignty', as outlined by Aileen Moreton-Robinson, which I explored in Chapter Three.
8. This is not to suggest that all Australian and U.S. national histories comply with this settler colonial narrative. As will be shown, there are some which write against it. But, importantly, this is the peculiarly settler colonial narrative which the teachers under consideration display.
9. T. Birch. 2002. '"History Is Never Bloodless": Getting It Wrong after One Hundred Years of Federation', *Australian Historical Studies* 33(118), 45. Tracey Banivanua-Mar explores this violence, bringing it into conversation with other discourses and acts of violence which formulated the indentured labour trade between Australia and the Pacific. See Banivanua-Mar, *Violence and Colonial Dialogue*, 7–14, 70–100. For a different, but equally interesting and important, study of colonial relationships of violence see M. Taussig. July 1984. 'Culture of Terror-Space of Death. Roger Casement's Putumayo Report and the Explanation of Torture', *Comparative Studies in Society and History* 26(3), 467–97. For a discussion of the importance of violence to the occurrence of

the Holocaust, and the ways in which this violence was not specific to the Holocaust, see Chapter Three, 'It Almost Needn't Have Been the Germans: The State, Colonial Violence, and the Holocaust', in Stratton, *Jewish Identity in Western Pop Culture*, 53–76.
10. For a brief exploration of the anxieties which these forgettings are in response to in settler colonial populations, see Banivanua-Mar, *Violence and Colonial Dialogue*, 80 and Goldstein, 'Where the Nation Takes Place', 833–34.
11. P. Wolfe. 1999. *Settler Colonialism and the Transformation of Anthropology: The Politics and Poetics of an Ethnographic Event*, London: Cassell.
12. S.L. Morgensen. 2010. 'Settler Homonationalism: Theorizing Settler Colonialism within Queer Modernities', *GL* 16, (1–2), 120.
13. S.L. Morgensen. 2011. *Spaces Between Us: Queer Settler Colonialism and Indigenous Decolonization*, Minneapolis: University of Minnesota Press, 1.
14. This idea of haunting arose for me in response to Alex Lubin's ideas of comparisons as spectral hauntings. Although this chapter does not use the ideas of haunting in the precise manner in which Lubin does – Lubin analyses the ways in which comparisons are made between the U.S. and Israel, whereas this chapter makes the comparison itself, between Holocaust and settler colonial histories – a similar understanding of haunting is useful. Haunting in Lubin's description is something which is not present but exists as a spectre, shadowing the histories such that meaning and knowledge is inscribed. See A. Lubin. Fall 2008. '"We Are All Israelis": The Politics of Colonial Comparisons', *South Atlantic Quarterly* 107(4), 671–90.
15. See P. Wolfe. 2008. 'Structure and Event: Settler Colonialism, Time, and the Question of Genocide', in A.D. Moses (ed.), *Empire, Colony, Genocide: Conquest, Occupation, and Subaltern Resistance in World History*, New York: Berghahn Books, 102–32.
16. What I am suggesting here is that there is an out-of-placeness which is important to assert: difference is not being removed entirely.
17. Young, *The Texture of Memory*, 6.
18. Ibid., 7.
19. Interview with Teacher A at School NYB.
20. Ibid.
21. Interview with Teacher A of School NYD.
22. Curriculum of School NYC, 43.
23. Ibid.
24. For instance, for a recent exploration into Holocaust education in U.S. schools generally, see T.D. Fallace. 2008. *The Emergence of Holocaust Education in American Schools*, New York: Palgrave Macmillan.
25. Michael Berenbaum, in Young, *The Texture of Memory*, 337. Notably, the museum is not required to 'resonate' with Native Americans. Michael Berenbaum has also discussed the Americanization of representations of the Holocaust. See M. Berenbaum. 1990. *After Tragedy and Triumph: Essays in Modern Jewish Thought and the American Experience*, Cambridge: Cambridge University Press. See also H. Flanzbaum (ed.). 1999. *The Americanization of the Holocaust*, Baltimore, MD: Johns Hopkins University Press.
26. Cole, *Selling the Holocaust*, 152–53.
27. Ibid., 157–58.
28. Ibid., 158.
29. In this chapter I use the terms Native American, Aboriginal and Indigenous to variously describe the peoples of Australia and the U.S. I am thoroughly aware that none of these words is entirely precise or uncontested in usage, and that there are a range of other namings which I could have used. I have used these words when I have felt they

best encapsulated the particular peoples whose histories I was discussing, or to point to the transnational relationships which exist.
30. For a further exploration of this see F. Davis Ruffins. 1997. 'Culture Wars Won and Lost: Ethnic Museums on the Mall, Part I: The National Holocaust Museum and the National Museum of the American Indian', *Radical History Review* 68, 79–100.
31. For an exploration of the educational lessons in the Museum of Jewish Heritage, see G. Short. Summer 2000. 'The Holocaust Museum as an Educational Resource: A View from New York City', *The Journal of Holocaust Education* 9(1), 1–18.
32. Personal communication with Paul Radensky, Museum Educator for High Schools at the Museum of Jewish Heritage: A Living Memorial to the Holocaust, 1 November 2006.
33. Novick, *The Holocaust and Collective Memory*, 6.
34. As Novick argues, '[t]he Holocaust, everyone agrees, is the bearer of urgently important lessons – not just for Jews but for all of us.' Ibid., 238.
35. Ibid., 239.
36. Ibid., 15. Emphasis in original. It is notable here that Novick did not mention the dispossession of Native Americans alongside the enslavement of blacks. It is clear that even for historians commenting on others' forgetting, it is sometimes too difficult to mention the founding and continuing violence of the American settler colonial state.
37. Patrick Wolfe points to this problem of the ways that Western nations discuss the Holocaust and displace discussions of the genocides which they have perpetrated when he notes that 'whereas the Holocaust exonerates anti-Semitic Western nations who were on the side opposing the Nazis, those same nations have nothing to gain from their liability for colonial genocides.' Wolfe, 'Settler Colonialism and the Elimination of the Native', 402.
38. Interview with Teacher A at School ME.
39. Interview with Teacher A at School MA.
40. This is a part of the generally accepted story of Australian Jewry. See W.D. Rubinstein. 1986. *The Jews in Australia*, Melbourne: AE Press; H.L. Rubinstein. 1987. *Chosen: The Jews in Australia*, Sydney: Allen & Unwin; S.D. Rutland. 1997. *Edge of the Diaspora: Two Centuries of Jewish Settlement in Australia*, 2nd revised ed., Sydney: Brandl & Schlesinger; Rutland, *The Jews in Australia*.
41. Interview with Teacher A at School ME.
42. Jon Stratton comments on the multiculturalism of Australia. See J. Stratton. 1998. *Race Daze: Australia in Identity Crisis*, London: Pluto Press. See also Hage, *White Nation*; Jupp, *From White Australia to Woomera*; Tavan, *The Long, Slow Death of White Australia*; L. Kramer (ed.). 2003. *The Multicultural Experiment: Immigrants, Refugees and National Identity*, Paddington, NSW: Macleay Press. For discussions of multiculturalism and Jews in an American context see Gilman, *Multiculturalism and the Jews*; D. Biale, M. Galchinsky and S. Heschel (eds). 1998. *Insider/Outsider: American Jews and Multiculturalism*, Berkeley: University of California Press.
43. Curriculum of School MB, 201–3.
44. Ibid., 186, 204. The section on War Crime Trials in Australia explains that numerous former Nazis migrated to Australia, that there was one trial of a suspected Nazi war criminal (that of Ivan Polyukhovich in 1993 – he was acquitted) and that others have been mooted but not occurred.
45. J.E. Berman. 2001. *Holocaust Remembrance in Australian Jewish Communities, 1945-2000*, Crawley, WA: University of Western Australia Press, 156.

46. See A. Alba. Winter/Spring 2005. 'Integrity and Relevance: Shaping Holocaust Memory at the Sydney Jewish Museum', *Judaism: A Quarterly Journal of Jewish Life and Thought* 54, 108–15.
47. Ibid: 108–9.
48. Ibid: 110. Quotes by Rosenbaum originally in Berman, *Holocaust Remembrance in Australian Jewish Communities*.
49. Young, *The Texture of Memory*, 2. Kerwin Lee Klein has critiqued the language with which Young described memory. See Klein, 'On the Emergence of Memory in Historical Discourse', 136.
50. Forgetting can come in numerous forms. Indeed, in one sense, Holocaust denial works as an ironic form of Holocaust disremembering, performing remembrance as denial: Holocaust denial does not involve the forgetting of the Holocaust, but rather a great deal of speech about it. In this way it is quite different to the colonial forgetting – which involves not speaking – which is being described in this chapter.
51. Berman, *Holocaust Remembrance in Australian Jewish Communities*, 54–55.
52. Gillis, 'Memory and Identity', 7.
53. J. Epstein. 2001. 'Remember to Forget: The Problem of Traumatic Cultural Memory', in J. Epstein and L.H. Lefkovitz (eds), *Shaping Losses: Cultural Memory and the Holocaust*, Urbana: University of Illinois Press, 192.
54. Michael Rothberg makes this same claim for the utility of the ideas of screen memory in helping us to understand the memory-processes at work in the division of memories being explored here, noting that 'the displacement that takes place in screen memory (indeed, in all memory) functions as much to open up lines of communication with the past as to close them off'. Rothberg follows this line of communication between seemingly conflicting memories – particularly with regard to the convergence of colonial, decolonizing and Holocaust memories – in his development of the idea of 'multidirectional memory'. Rothberg, *Multidirectional Memory*, 12.
55. S. Freud. 1986. 'Screen Memories', in J. Strachey (ed.), *The Standard Edition of the Complete Psychological Works of Sigmund Freud, Vol. III*, London: The Hogarth Press, 307.
56. Ibid.
57. Of course, this approach is not purely a product of Holocaust education. For instance, according to a posting on the American Jewish blog *Jewschool*, in June 2009 the New York City Parks Department decided to 'add prominent elements commemorating the persecution and murder of "homosexuals, Jehovah's Witnesses, the disabled, political prisoners and Roma and Sinti Gypsies [sic]" to the public Holocaust Memorial in Sheepshead Bay'. Rep. Dov Hikind, a Jewish member of the New York State Assembly, said in response that, 'To include these other groups diminishes their memory... These people are not in the same category as Jewish people with regards to the Holocaust... It is so vastly different. You cannot compare political prisoners with Jewish victims'. chillul Who?. 2009. 'Dov Hikind, Holocaust Denier', *Jewschool*, 8 June. Retrieved 9 June 2009 from http://jewschool.com/2009/06/08/16576/dov-hikind-holocaust-denier.
58. This is echoed by the editors of a recent collection entitled *Quicksands: Foundational Histories in Australia and Aotearoa New Zealand*, which explored different ways in which these foundational histories have been constructed. The editors state that 'settler histories have obstructed our perception of the past by disposing of it in particular ways. Settler narratives have produced the settler as an autonomous maker of settler progress and society; these narratives have been developmental and linear; they have suggested that "we" started with nothing and ended up with something, not least by

clearing the land.' K. Neumann, N. Thomas and H. Ericksen, 'Conclusion', in K. Neumann, N. Thomas and H. Ericksen (eds), *Quicksands: Foundational Histories in Australia and Aotearoa New Zealand*, Sydney: UNSW Press, 239.
59. See, for instance, M. Bratu Hansen. Winter 1996. '"Schindler's List" is Not "Shoah": The Second Commandment, Popular Modernism and Public Memory', *Critical Inquiry* 22(2), 292–312; N. Levi. Spring/Summer 2007. '"No Sensible Comparison"? The Place of the Holocaust in Australia's History Wars', *History and Memory* 19(1), 124–56. Indeed, as Neil Levi notes, the Holocaust has been described by theorists such as Miriam Hansen and Andreas Huyssen as a screen blocking out memories of other genocides.
60. This section, and indeed this chapter as a whole, is focused on the ways in which victims of genocides are remembered, rather than perpetrators. It is interesting to note that, in a general sense, perpetrators are most commonly discussed as being inhuman subjects whose motives and actions cannot be understood. As such, their actions are, in a sense, pushed beyond the realms of the human, making the possibility of the students, the teachers, or anyone whom the students may know being perpetrators, suspect. In a sense then, the teachers are arguing for the students and themselves to be thought of as in the position of the beneficiaries of settler colonialism, without the brutality of colonization. This is quite an understandable, if ambivalent, position. Some of this will be taken up again later, but, in general, further discussion of this is, unfortunately, outside the scope of this book.
61. Sophie Gelski and Jenny Wajsenberg encourage this approach. See S. Gelski and J. Wajsenberg. 2004. 'Teaching the Holocaust Today', in K. Kwiet and J. Matthaus (eds), *Contemporary Responses to the Holocaust*, Westport, CT: Praeger, 222.
62. Interview with Teacher A at School ME.
63. Interview with Teacher A at School NYA.
64. Ibid. This was also mentioned by Teacher A at School NYG. A 2007 article by Mahmood Mamdani provided an excellent exploration and critique of the ways in which diverse American groups, communities and individuals have come together in order to protest, in a depoliticized manner, the events in Darfur, particularly within the 'Save Darfur' movement. See M. Mamdani. 2007. 'The Politics of Naming: Genocide, Civil War, Insurgency', *London Review of Books,* 8 March. Retrieved 8 July 2009 from http://www.lrb.co.uk/v29/n05/print/mamd01_.html.
65. Curriculum of School NYC, 73–4.
66. Interview with Teacher A at School MB.
67. There are numerous texts which explore this in various different ways, for example Moreton-Robinson, ed., *Sovereign Subjects*; C. Healy. 2008. *Forgetting Aborigines*, Sydney: UNSW Press; Behrendt, 'Home: The Importance of Place to the Dispossessed', 71–85.
68. Wendy Brown provides an excellent critique of discourses of tolerance which are used by Holocaust educators and scholars. See W. Brown. 2006. *Regulating Aversion: Tolerance in the Age of Identity and Empire*, Princeton, NJ: Princeton University Press, in particular 107–48.
69. For an expansion of this idea see J. Silverstein. May 2010. '"We're Dealing with How Do We Live and Work with This Memory and What Are We Supposed To Do About It": Making Use of Jewish Liminality', *Borderlands* 9(1).
70. David, March of the Living Education Session, 'Jewish Life in Pre-War Poland', 18 February 2007.
71. Interview with Teacher A of School NYC.
72. Ibid.

73. As Ella Shohat argues, with reference in particular to Israel, '[t]he suggestion that a history of other victims might be told, that there might be victims of Jewish nationalism, leads to violent opposition, or, in the case of liberals, to epistemological vertigo.' E. Shohat, 'Antinomies of Exile: Said at the Frontiers of National Narrations', in M. Sprinkler (ed.), *Edward Said: A Critical Reader*, Oxford: Blackwell, 134. See also A. Ophir. 2000. 'The Identity of the Victims and the Victims of Identity: A Critique of Zionist Ideology for a Post-Zionist Age', in L.J. Silberstein (ed.), *Mapping Jewish Identities*, New York: New York University Press, 174–200.
74. Curriculum of School MB, 3.
75. Ibid.
76. The United Nations makes this clear, with a specific body of laws which relate to genocide. See the United Nations website, which provides the convention and other relevant information, in particular United Nations, *Convention on the Prevention and Punishment of the Crime of Genocide*. Retrieved 18 December 2014 from https://treaties.un.org/doc/Publication/UNTS/Volume%2078/volume-78-I-1021-English.pdf.
77. Amira Hass, an Israeli journalist, comments on the political implications of this in an Israeli context, arguing that the discourses about the Holocaust in Israel serve to distance the Holocaust from histories of other genocides perpetrated by Europeans, whether in Europe or as colonizers; and to 'minimise and blur' the dispossession of the Palestinian people. As such, within an Israeli context, the Holocaust screens out a great many histories and politics. A. Hass. 2007. 'The Holocaust as Political Asset', *Haaretz* 1 May. Retrieved 8 May 2007 from http://www.haaretz.com/hasen/spages/849669.html. With that said, there is something which is importantly unique about the Holocaust, especially for the Western world, and for Jews (just as any historical event or moment is unique in some way). For those of us who are the descendants of survivors, a certain recognition of the uniqueness can be affirming. The question we must all face, however, is what the effects for others are on the claims for uniqueness. It is important to note the particularity of the destruction and its special place in history, without creating a hierarchy of suffering; we must recognise both particularly and sameness across time and space. Indeed, this is why comparative genocide studies is a fruitful discipline, helping us to learn something new about everything under examination, while competitive genocide studies is not.
78. Curriculum of School ME, 93.
79. As David Stannard has written, '[a] secondary tragedy of all these genocides . . . is that partisan representatives among the survivors of particular afflicted groups not uncommonly hold up their peoples' experience as so fundamentally different from the others that not only is scholarly comparison rejected out of hand, but mere cross-referencing or discussion of other genocidal events within the context of their own flatly is prohibited'. In this work, Stannard criticises Holocaust historians who section off the history of the Holocaust from other events generally, or other genocides in particular, arguing that it is a form of denial. D.E. Stannard. 1992. *American Holocaust: Columbus and the Conquest of the New World*, New York: Oxford University Press, 151–52. See also W. Churchill. 1997. *A Little Matter of Genocide: Holocaust and Denial in the Americas 1492 to the Present*, San Francisco: City Lights Books; D. Stone. 2008. 'Biopower and Modern Genocide', in A.D. Moses (ed.), *Empire, Colony, Genocide: Conquest, Occupation, and Subaltern Resistance in World History*, New York: Berghahn Books, 171–72. Michael Rothberg argues that instead of seeing collective memory as a 'zero-sum struggle over scarce resources' for representing those memories, memory should be understood as 'multidirectional: as subject to ongoing negotiation, cross-referencing, and borrowing; as productive and not privative'. Rothberg in this book

makes particular reference to Holocaust memorializing within decolonizing and colonial contexts. Rothberg, *Multidirectional Memory*, 3.
80. Stannard, *American Holocaust*, 185. Michael Rothberg makes this same point. Rothberg, *Multidirectional Memory*, 310–11.
81. There is much debate around the question of the Holocaust's uniqueness. For more information see, for instance, H.L. Feingold. 1983. 'How Unique Is the Holocaust?', in A. Grobman and D. Landes (eds), *Genocide: Critical Issues of the Holocaust*, Los Angeles: The Simon Wiesenthal Center, 397–401; S.T. Katz. 1996. 'The Uniqueness of the Holocaust: The Historical Dimension', in A.S. Rosenbaum (ed.), *Is the Holocaust Unique? Perspectives on Comparative Genocide*, Boulder, CO: Westview Press, 19–38; D. LaCapra. 1998. *History and Memory after Auschwitz*, Ithaca, NY: Cornell University Press; N. Levi and M. Rothberg. 2003. 'General Introduction: Theory and the Holocaust', in N. Levi and M. Rothberg (eds), *The Holocaust: Theoretical Readings*, Edinburgh: Edinburgh University Press, 1–22; D.E. Stannard. 1996. 'Uniqueness as Denial: The Politics of Genocide Scholarship', in A.S. Rosenbaum (ed.), *Is the Holocaust Unique?: Perspectives on Comparative Genocide*, Colorado: Westview Press, 163–208; L.S. Dawidowicz. 1975. *The War against the Jews, 1933-1945*, New York: Seth Press; Y. Bauer. *Rethinking the Holocaust*, New Haven, CT: Yale University Press.
82. Interview with Teacher A at School NYB. See Chapter One, where this same quotation is placed in a broader context of racialized Jewishnesses.
83. For one example of this discourse, we can look to Avraham Burg's recent book, which explores this idea of Jewish victimhood as being a foundation for Israeli identity. See A. Burg. 2008. *The Holocaust Is Over; We Must Rise from Its Ashes*. New York: Palgrave Macmillan.
84. For discussions of Israel and settler colonialism see G. Piterberg. 2008. *The Returns of Zionism: Myths, Politics and Scholarship in Israel*, London: Verso; L. Veracini. 2006. *Israel and Settler Society*, London: Pluto Press; P. Wolfe. 2007. 'Palestine, Project Europe and the (Un-)Making of the New Jew: In Memory of Edward W. Said', in N. Curthoys and D. Ganguly (eds), *Edward Said: The Legacy of a Public Intellectual*, Melbourne: Melbourne University Press, 313–37; H. Obenzinger. Fall 2008. 'Naturalizing Cultural Pluralism, Americanizing Zionism: The Settler Colonial Basis to Early-Twentieth-Century Progressive Thought', *South Atlantic Quarterly* 107(4), 651–52; S.I. Troen. December 1999. 'Frontier Myths and Their Application in America and Israel: A Transnational Perspective', *The Journal of American History* 86(3), 1209–30; Stratton, *Jewish Identity in Western Pop Culture*, 87–92. For a contrary viewpoint, where Zionism is positioned as a form of colonialism, but not settler colonialism, see I. Pappé. Fall 2008. 'Zionism as Colonialism: A Comparative View of Diluted Colonialism in Asia and Africa', *South Atlantic Quarterly* 107(4), 614.
85. This statement about the other school is in fact incorrect. At this school, at the time this interview took place, at the same time as they teach about the Holocaust in Jewish Studies, they offer a separate elective entitled 'Comparative Genocide Studies'. Indeed, this works to perpetuate the very idea that this teacher was talking about – it separates the Holocaust off from all other genocides, and teaches the students that it was a particularly Jewish event.
86. Interview with Teacher A at School MC.
87. Emphasis added. Alternatively, perhaps her repeating of 'very' signified a snag in her thinking. Perhaps she caught herself as she was speaking and realized that she does not spend enough time 'talking about other groups'. It is difficult to know.
88. A. Dirk Moses writes of this in relationship to the discussion of other genocides in Australia, arguing that the Holocaust is held up as the benchmark of genocide. Other

genocides are thus denied as being genocide. See A.D. Moses. 2003. 'Genocide and Historical Consciousness in Australia', *History Compass* 1, 1-13.
89. Interview with Teacher A at School ME. 'Gypsies' here refers to Roma and Sinti, peoples who were victims of genocide as part of the project of the Holocaust. 'Gypsy' is a pejorative term, linked with the Romanian term 'Ţigani'. See S. Woodcock. 2007. 'Romania and Europe: Roma, Rroma and Ţigani as Sites for the Contestation of Ethno-National Identity', *Patterns of Prejudice* 41(5), 493–515, for a discussion of the construction of these identities. While, as she makes clear, Gypsy and Ţigani are not the same thing, Woodcock's discussion in this article is still highly relevant and useful.
90. Curriculum of School MB, 27.
91. Interview with Teacher A at School NYB.
92. Tony Birch explores this in a discussion of the Australian Centenary of Federation Celebrations, where he notes that 'an acceptance of *its own history* by non-Aboriginal Australia requires questioning, re-thinking, and a re-evaluation of the Australian psyche'. This is because, as Birch argues, '[t]here is a lot at stake, and much to be lost by those who believe that a pre-Mabo status quo should be maintained, where the past is remembered as a cultural *terra nullius* and the rights of Aboriginal people are forever denied.' Birch, '"History Is Never Bloodless"', 45. For an exploration of the linkage between the recognition of these histories and sovereignty claims see T. Birch. 2007. '"The Invisible Fire": Indigenous Sovereignty, History and Responsibility', in A. Moreton-Robinson (ed.), *Sovereign Subjects: Indigenous Sovereignty Matters*, Crows Nest, NSW: Allen & Unwin, esp. 110. For an explanation of the place of this founding violence in Australian (and Israeli) histories see L. Veracini. October 2003. 'The Evolution of Historical Redescription in Israel and Australia: The Question of the "Founding Violence"', *Australian Historical Studies* 34(122), 326–45.
93. The material effects of each is different: one secures control of the nation-state, the other secures a place within.
94. D. Bird Rose. 1999. 'Hard Times: An Australian Study', in K. Neumann, N. Thomas and H. Ericksen (eds), *Quicksands: Foundational Histories in Australia and Aotearoa New Zealand*, Sydney: UNSW Press, 14.
95. Allaine Cerwonka examines the ways in which 'settler Australians redefine and legitimate their claim to the land'. See A. Cerwonka. 2004. *Native to the Nation: Disciplining Bodies and Landscapes in Australia*, Minneapolis: University of Minnesota Press. Julie Evans discusses this settler colonial anxiety in the context of constructions of settler citizenship. See J. Evans. 2002. 'Safer as Subjects Than Citizens: Privilege and Exclusion in the Transition to Nationhood in Australia and Natal', in T. Banivanua Mar and J. Evans (eds), *Writing Colonial Histories: Comparative Perspectives*, Melbourne: History Department, University of Melbourne, 168–69.
96. Hage, *White Nation*, 20.
97. Wolfe, 'Structure and Event', 103.
98. Wolfe, "Logics of Elimination," 2.
99. This is particularly pertinent in light of the discussion in Chapter Three of the ways in which the rule of law is understood in the Holocaust education.
100. For an excellent comparison of the techniques of colonialism in Australia and America, as well as Brazil, see P. Wolfe. June 2001. 'Land, Labor, and Difference: Elementary Structures of Race', *American Historical Review* 106(3), 866–905. Gabriel Piterberg brought this understanding of settler colonialism to an analysis of Israel and Zionism. He argues that Zionism is a settler colonial ideology and that it is important to look at national literatures to understand the relationship between Zionist Israeli national identity and other settler colonial narratives. See Piterberg, *The Returns of Zionism*,

xii–xiii. Piterberg also discusses the dislike for universalism which is such an important part of Zionist ideology, reinforcing the idea that histories of Jewish people (and in particular the Holocaust) should be remembered as specifically Jewish (as has been highlighted). Ibid., 149–50.
101. For a broader discussion of the place of history-writing in constructing and negotiating colonial relationships see D. Chakrabarty. *Provincializing Europe.*
102. We saw this in Chapter Three as well, with the attempts to join Zionist histories, which themselves have attempted to write Jews into Western histories. These are projects of normalization, as was explored in Chapter Three. It must be noted that there are moments, outside of these Holocaust histories, when in Australia Jews have strongly identified with Aboriginal people. This is particularly so in a number of grassroots movements, as well as in the case of fights for land rights, where a number of the lawyers acting on behalf of Aboriginal land claimants were Jewish. For one account of this, see M. Castan. 2006. "Memory and Mabo: Advancing Aboriginal Justice", in M. Fagenblat, M. Landau and N. Wolski (eds), *New under the Sun: Jewish Australians on Religion, Politics and Culture*, Melbourne: Black Inc., 325–33.
103. Healy, *Forgetting Aborigines*, 7–8. Bain Attwood explains this 'as follows: the aboriginal people who lived in this continent for 40,000 years or more before the coming of Europeans in 1788 were not the homogeneous group implied by the name "Aborigines"; rather, they were named and have named themselves "Aborigines", "blacks", "Kooris" or "Murris" etc. only in the context of colonisation and of their ensuing relationship with Europeans – who, conversely, came to be called "Australians".' B. Attwood. 1989. *The Making of the Aborigines*, Sydney: Allen & Unwin, x.
104. Healy, *Forgetting Aborigines*, 9.
105. This is the title of a book by the Australian historian Henry Reynolds. H. Reynolds. 1999. *Why Weren't We Told? A Personal Search for the Truth About Our History*, Melbourne: Penguin.
106. Anna Haebich similarly argues that the ways in which 'assimilation' practices in the twentieth century in Australia were put to, and understood by, the white public was 'of an imagined, seamless, unproblematic and inevitable passage from a receding Aboriginal past to an assimilated present of modern suburban domestic life'. A. Haebich. 2002. 'Imagining Assimilation', *Australian Historical Studies* 33(118), 63. In other words, that these narratives pushed the violence of assimilation to the background, but did not completely erase this violence.
107. Clark, 'Teaching the Nation', 15–22. Henry Reynolds, amongst others, has written explaining that Australia does indeed have a genocidal history. See H. Reynolds. 2001. *An Indelible Stain? The Question of Genocide in Australia's History*, Ringwood: Viking Press. Ann Curthoys, through careful attention to the definitions of genocide offered by Raphael Lemkin (Lemkin was a Polish Jewish jurist who coined the term and defined the concept of genocide), has argued that the treatment of Indigenous peoples in Tasmania constituted genocide. See A. Curthoys. 2008. 'Genocide in Tasmania: The History of an Idea', in A.D. Moses (ed.), *Empire, Colony, Genocide*, New York: Berghahn Books, 229–52.
108. The work of Aileen Moreton-Robinson and Ghassan Hage, outlined in previous chapters, can usefully help us to understand this exclusivist sovereignty. See Moreton-Robinson, 'The Possessive Logic of Patriarchal White Sovereignty'; Hage, *White Nation.*
109. This is problematized when we consider that they are all Zionists and, as I demonstrated in the previous chapter, end their narratives of the Holocaust with the creation of the State of Israel. Yet the inconsistency of the histories should not make us wary of

coming to these conclusions – these histories are only beginning to be written, and, as has been shown, are manifestly ambivalent.
110. A. Memmi. 1990. *The Colonizer and the Colonized*, London: Earthscan Publications, 81–82. For an extended discussion of Memmi's articulation of the relationships between Europe, modernity, colonialism, and Jews, see Stratton, *Jewish Identity in Western Pop Culture*, 44–52.

CHAPTER 5

'Why the Role of Women Was Any More Special Than the Role of the Rest of Them'

Circumscribing Jewish Femininity in Holocaust Pedagogies

> Whatever is unnamed, undepicted in images, whatever is omitted from biography, censored in collections of letters, whatever is misnamed as something else, made difficult-to-come-by, whatever is buried in the memory by the collapse of meaning under an inadequate or lying language – this will become, not merely unspoken, but unspeakable.
> —Adrienne Rich, quoted in 'In the Name of Feminist Film Criticism'

> The future historian w[ill] have to dedicate a proper page to the Jewish woman during this war. She will capture an important part in this Jewish history for her courage and ability to survive. Because of her, many families were able to get over the terrors of these days.
> —Emmanuel Ringelblum, *Diary and Notes from the Warsaw Ghetto*

Jewish women in the concentration and death camps of the Holocaust ceased menstruating, one teacher in Melbourne explained, as a result of the 'physical impact of being in the camps, of malnutrition, malnourishment and so forth'. In order to aid his students in understanding this he compared 'it to elite women marathoners, and some swimmers, [who] stop having their period because of physical stress'. For this teacher, discussion of the cessation of menstruating is discussed 'incidental[ly], and not through plan'.[1] At first glance the comparison between elite athletes and malnourished concentration camp inmates seems perplexing. What is the correlation between Jewish women's suffering during the Holocaust and elite athletes excelling at their chosen pursuits? The comparison, it would seem, is not based on women's experiences. What we can learn from this comment is something quite different.

The teacher's explanation encapsulates a central problem in the writing of histories of Jewish women and the Holocaust that became evident through the interviews conducted and the curricula examined: it points to a lack of language or historical understanding through which the experiences of Jewish women can be adequately articulated.[2] The teacher makes a comparison that has a certain logic, one that seemingly lies in women's corporeal bodies. He is, we could say, making a statement about biology, rather than history. In this chapter I address this problem of historical narration by asking how these teachers of the Holocaust in the Jewish schools in Melbourne and New York under consideration in this book talk about Jewish women and their experiences. I will explore the ways in which sharp lines are drawn around the constitution of Jewish women in these histories of the Holocaust.[3] This chapter demonstrates the ways in which the teaching of histories of women in the Holocaust fits into the broader negotiations of Diaspora Jewishness in these two cities: by containing womanhood and femininity, Diaspora Jewish masculinity – and through it, it is seemingly thought, the position of Jews outside Israel – can be potentially recuperated and given a firm ground upon which to stand. It is through the production of particular histories of women and femininity that an acceptable masculinity can be produced. As such, the problems of representation are problems of anxiety: how to represent a femininity which, as I demonstrated in Chapter Three, is a source of anxiety? How to do so when discussing women in particular? While in Chapter Three we explored some of the ways in which feminization adheres to institutions, structures and depictions of men, in this chapter we will explore how it adheres to, and creates, categories of women.

Following Claire Kahane we can understand that it is important to consider that '[i]f gender is inseparable from symbolic form so that representation always bears the trace of the gendered subject, how is that trace manifested in representation?'[4] I will show here that it is evident that a concern about the feminization of Diaspora Jewish history propels the anxiety which these teachers carry. As such, the definitions and ideas of Jewish women which circulate – and in particular in Holocaust education – are of great importance to these teachers. Holocaust education, therefore, through specific teachings about the experiences of Jewish women, forms part of the process of negotiating the place of Jews in diasporic places such as New York and Melbourne.

Femininity and masculinity, women and men are all historically produced, separatable but interrelated categories.[5] Femininity and masculinity refer to a series of cultural, social, political and historical factors which have been associated at times with bodily incarnations, but also with institutions, practices and discourses. The terms women and men refer to discourses which centre on the conception that these factors inhere in embodied and biological forms. This chapter will show that femininity and masculinity impact upon the ways in which these histories of the Holocaust describe Jewish women, but also exist outside of the binary categories of women and men: we can therefore speak of Jewishness as gendered, of Jewish men as feminized, and of Jewish womanhood contained in order to circumscribe this feminization.

While women's identities cannot be subsumed into the sign 'woman' (for the very fact of signification means that not everything can be encompassed in language, that some things will remain unarticulated),[6] 'woman' is a powerful regulatory sign, and one of many, often competing, structures and forces in society which work together to produce subjects. This chapter takes as its central concern when and how teachers deploy the sign 'women' in their curricula, and what ideas of 'women' they are creating. For, as Elizabeth Cowie explains, representations of 'woman' (as object, subject, sign and signifier)[7] do not merely reflect back onto society already existing and fixed ideas and definitions, but rather they create these definitions – or signs – as they represent them.[8] The histories of the Holocaust under consideration in this chapter borrow ideas of Jewish women's experiences and histories from other sources while simultaneously taking part in the fixing of these ideas. It is a mutually existing condition which perpetuates the circulation of signifiers and their meanings. Historical representations, then, help maintain certain ideas of Jewish womanhood in the face of this aspect of the anxiety which shapes these examples of Holocaust pedagogy.

I begin this chapter by detailing the ways in which Jewish women in the Holocaust are written into the histories being presented in the Jewish schools under consideration.[9] Because of the fact that, as will be shown, women are rarely explicitly spoken of, it is important to understand the ways in which these moments are constructed, and the ideas they convey. The chapter will then discuss the ways in which different historians have written these women into the histories of the Holocaust, thus providing a basis for the question to be asked: how are women represented in these examples of Holocaust pedagogy? From there feminist ideas of history and historiography will be taken up in order to understand further the implications of the ways in which these histories formulate Jewish womanhood. The primary materials will then be returned to with an in-depth discussion and exploration of the ways schools talk about women when utilizing women's memoirs and testimonies in their teaching. From these materials we will be able to understand how boundaries are drawn around what constitutes Jewish womanhood in these teachings, thus enabling teachers to draw boundaries around the feminization of Diaspora Jewries and thereby relieving somewhat their specifically Zionist anxieties about the gendering of Jews.

Teaching about Jewish Women: An Overview

In the curriculum of a Melbourne school there are two pages dedicated exclusively to 'Women in the Shoah'. These pages begin by explaining that 'the study of the experiences of women during the Shoah is a relatively new field of research by scholars of the Shoah', noting that 'those involved in this area of study strongly claim that women's experiences, risks and fears were different to men's by virtue of them being women'.[10] These pages mention the differences in experience which came with the fact that women could pass as non-Jews more easily than men; the problems associated with being child-bearers and mothers; and stories, often untold, of sexual abuse, rape and involvement in the forest partisans. Ravensbrück, the concentration camp built for women only, is also discussed, one of the only times Ravensbrück is mentioned amongst the curricula examined for this book.[11]

A second important point which is made here, and is absent in other curricula, is that the Judenrat – which are mentioned in every curricula – consisted of men only and thus, in the words of the curriculum, 'women's voices were not heard amongst those making decisions and planning strategies for their communities'.[12] Thus knowledge about the marginal place of women in these community organizations and in formal positions of power within these Jewish ghetto communities is conveyed. The photograph that the teacher has placed with this section also holds symbolic import, bearing the description 'women and children arriving at Auschwitz-Birkenau', and picturing a group of women and children looking nervously into the camera.[13] The final impression one receives then, is of the innocence and victimization of women in the Holocaust, as well as of their linkage with children.

While many curricula provide passing references to women or integrate them within a larger narrative, this is the only curriculum to specifically include a section on Jewish women. Yet the inclusion can be problematized. One problem is shared with Western historiography more generally, which treats women as a subsection of the broader community through a lens of separation and difference. Indeed, this is a product of Holocaust historiography broadly: the curriculum highlights the fact that the study of Jewish women came as a separate and late field of inquiry to Holocaust studies and that it centres on the idea that women are essentially different (to men, or to real historical subjects). By placing a discussion of women in these two separate, discrete pages, the historiographical problem is repeated and the assumption that women as a group are not part of the larger dominant Jewish narrative of the Holocaust, but are separate and peripheral, is reinforced.

This sectioning off of women as a separate group occurs quite literally in this curriculum: two separate pages are presented which confine women to the periphery of the Holocaust narrative, while also neatly containing their stories. In a more general sense – and following the idea of the purpose of historical education that I outlined in the Introduction – we can understand that the teacher here is, in part, constructing histories which will tell the students what it is to be a Jewish woman. A Jewish woman, it is asserted, is this and nothing more. Unconsciously, we can understand them to be saying that Diasporic masculinity can thereby be (partially) redeemed. What 'this' is will be explored in greater depth later.

The representation of women as a coherent, definable group is repeated in numerous curricula. Many of the curricula contain descriptions of women involved in various aspects of the Holocaust – in resistance, as mother-figures, as victims, as particularly religious or as surviving – but they were all put forward as 'women'. The identity category of 'woman' is thereby somewhat homogenized, and there is little production of discursive differences between and amongst people. Often teachers explain that they explore the experiences of Jews in different countries, that they teach about children and women, and that one's approach to religion would have made one's life different when asked; yet all of these factors were presented as outside the main narrative, by implication leaving the main story for those who are referred to as men. In the presentation of women's identities as women without reference to other possible aspects of their identities, their 'womanness' is contained: their complex and interwoven subjective histories are forgotten. Yet, as Parveen Adams has shown, subjects are formed through the making of links in the symbolic chain – by placing together culturally relevant discourses, institutions and ideas in order to create and maintain identities.[14] These identities can only be created and represented through interactions with collectives. When Jewish women in the Holocaust are represented as outside of the world – when these links in the chain are not shown – it becomes difficult for them to be understood as full subjects. And thus they become symbolic of something else.

A female teacher at a school in New York stated in her interview that even though she presents the story of the Holocaust as made up of many competing narratives, she rarely speaks with her class about women and their experiences. The examination of women's and men's separate experiences, however, had been the subject of debate amongst the students. Indeed, Rochelle Saidel, the historian and author of *The Jewish Women of Ravensbrück*, had spoken to her class. Afterwards, the teacher explained, amongst the students 'half of them learnt some really new things and the other half were not so impressed about why the role of women was any more special than the role of the *rest of them*'.[15] Many of the students 'say that the situation was so extreme that you can't really measure who had it better and who had it worse'. She later informed me that she had told her students that she was being interviewed for this project, and that one student had said that '"the Nazi system is inherently patriarchal." That . . . in traditional history we are always looking at men, we are always looking at the powerful men. We don't look at the poor, we don't look at the women.'[16]

It is enlightening that a number of students regarded the teaching of women's experiences specifically as inappropriate because 'you can't really measure who had it better and who had it worse', and that they deemed women to be no more 'special' than other people. The first comment establishes comparative work as competitive, with the inclusion of women's narratives regarded as setting up a competition between, one would presume, women's and men's experiences in the Nazi world. The second comment assumes that a study of women's narratives detracts from the study of 'the rest of them', which we can understand to most likely mean men (as well as trans, intersex and genderqueer peoples). Through both these competitions, the boundaries of womanhood, and thus manhood, are reinforced.

The final comment from the teacher tells us something about a relationship between Holocaust and broader historiographies. The student (via the teacher) elides the gap between the 'Nazi system' and 'traditional history', pointing at the same time to the similarities between them, which lie in their participation in and reinforcement of patriarchal practices and systems of knowledge. This points to a similar problem involved in the writing of Holocaust histories through the frameworks offered by traditional Western historiography: is it possible to critique the Nazi patriarchal system from within a patriarchal system of knowledge? In a sense, these teachers face an impossible problem. And indeed, these problems of historiography are, it seems, a source of concern for these teachers, perhaps expressed best in this teacher's repeating her student's ideas. This final comment is key for another reason: it points to the existence of dominant modes of Western historiography, which prioritize the narratives of men over those of women. The teachers then – in the limited time they have available to them to teach about the Holocaust – are informed by historiographical practices more generally, many of which assert the importance of men's narratives. This then is a problem which historians generally must face and reckon with.[17]

Unsurprisingly perhaps, teachers at all-girls' schools generally teach about the experiences of women more often than do teachers at co-educational schools. Teachers at these girls' schools explained that they wanted to use examples that their students could relate to.[18] For instance, one teacher at such a school explained that it:

> makes it meaningful for them [to use examples of women]. And I think that as a woman, you can relate to that. . . . [T]here were a lot of testimonies I could have used, I thought that one [which gave 'a narrative from a diary about how she remembers their mother, how she saved all week and put away some of their rations so that on Friday nights there was always something for Shabbat, and on Pesach, how they coped and on all the *yontifs* that somehow always miraculously there was always something. And so talking about how all week she would put aside from her rations and things like that.'[19]] was very powerful for the girls . . . There are a few different articles, one about Pesach, one about Hanukkah, and one about Shabbat, and I think that there's a significance, that the girls will relate to them; because not all of them, but many of them, sing every Friday night, every Shabbat . . . And so we talk about how meaningful it must have been that it

continued on even if it was only ordinary soup with potato peel in it. And what that woman had done in order to get that.[20]

When asked whether she teaches the course in a particular way because she teaches in a girls' school, another female teacher replied that:

> because it is primarily a girls' setting, I am able to focus on the experience particularly on women, on mothers, young girls. I am also perhaps able to get into the more emotional reactions of women and girls . . . [P]erhaps if I was dealing with more of a male-dominated clientele . . . I don't think I would teach it any differently. Maybe I would spend more time focusing on the map, focusing on elements that stereotypically interest boys such as time, space, money, the building of machinery, the building of trains, transport. You know, they will come up wherever necessary amongst the female population, but perhaps I would spend a little bit more time on that, on those aspects.[21]

She continued that 'really I don't believe that I short-change the girls because, it's not an experience of girl versus boy. It's the same experience.' Here we can see an ambivalence surrounding the histories of women and men. It is claimed that the experiences of the Holocaust were the same for women as for men, and that teaching about women rather than men (or feminine experiences rather than masculine ones) does not establish a competitive framework. Teaching about women here becomes an important and useful pedagogical tool: a way of engaging a particular group of students. The teacher rejects the idea that she is 'short-changing' her students, but also offers this as a consideration. If it was a different experience – to be a woman or a man during the Holocaust – does that mean that to teach about women is to 'short-change' the students? Why is this framed in terms of deprivation rather than elucidation, in a manner similar to the teacher above who spoke in terms of competition? Perhaps though this sentiment is partly representative of the dominant ideas of Holocaust pedagogy today – that in the end it was the same experience for all Jews, and women's experiences are predominantly used to make the Holocaust more meaningful for women students today. In this incarnation of Holocaust pedagogy, the Holocaust, once more, remains primarily as the domain of men, and women are inscribed in it as peripheral.

This motivation for teaching about women is captured in a statement by one teacher who said that 'you want to make [the Holocaust] more specific than this great big lot of information that all Jews experienced the Holocaust in the same way'.[22] Women's stories thus serve at times to complicate and broaden students' ideas of what happened to the Jews in the Holocaust. They are also used to encourage the students to relate to the Jews in these stories. Women in these instances are pedagogical tools, and point to the ambivalence which they provoke: there is an anxiety about what to do with these women and how, in the context of a Zionist Jewish worldview, where the Diaspora is positioned as feminine, to locate in history these people and stories.²³ Yet, as will be shown, the content and ideas which are signified by the name 'woman' in Holocaust education are made to work to delineate the boundaries of Jewish womanhood and actively negotiate the anxieties about the Diaspora gendered Jew.

There is little noticeable difference between the ways in which women are constituted in these examples of Holocaust education in Melbourne and New York. Indeed, several transnational commonalities can be drawn out: women depicted as mothers and as victims, issues of sex, sexuality and bodily inscribed femininity, and discussions of women and resistance.

Did Jewish Women and Men in the Holocaust have Different Experiences?

Before we can consider the ways in which teachers bring Jewish women into the histories of the Holocaust which they teach, it is necessary to understand the variety of ways in which historians have narrated such women's experiences. The question of whether Jewish women as a victim group in the Holocaust had distinct experiences was first raised in an academic context at a conference in the U.S. in 1983.²⁴ Various historians, beginning with Joan Ringelheim, have argued that while Jewish women and men under the Nazis may have faced the same final destination, the journey was considerably different as '[t]he end – namely annihilation or death – does not always describe or explain the process'.²⁵ Ringelheim's project was 'to make graphic the complexity of these Jewish women's lives because of the connections between biology and sexism'.²⁶ Moreover, she claimed, it is not enough simply to say that women behaved differently to men, without either acknowledging the various subject categories within that broader category of 'woman', or referring to the very specific historical contexts within which these women were operating. This demonstrated for Ringelheim the existence of what she termed a 'split memory', between 'traditional versions of the Holocaust' and women's individual experiences which do not fit into those narratives.²⁷ She asserted that 'the split between genocide and gender-specific trauma exists not only in the memories of witnesses but also in the historical reconstruction by scholars'.²⁸ This can be seen, for instance, in the segmenting off in the teacher's curricula discussed previously. Ringelheim made clear the ways that these 'traditional' narratives of the Holocaust are constructed to avoid women's experiences, and as such she argued for a broadening of the narratives, or versions, of the Holocaust which are written.

Sybil Milton, writing in 1984, similarly argued that women faced particular circumstances precisely because they were women, and that these were worthy of study. She pointed to Kristallnacht, the German pogrom of 9–10 November 1938, when 30,000 German-Jewish men were sent to concentration camps, yet 'no women were arrested or deported to camps'.[29] She further argued that in the camps women were punished differently to men because 'the Nazis recognized the importance of camp friendships and bonding in women's resistance and survival'.[30] The SS also used a different language to describe male and female inmates: women in Ravensbrück were generally called '*Schmukstücke* (literally translated as pieces of jewellery)' while the male inmates were '*Muselmänner* (the emaciated walking corpses of Auschwitz and other camps).'[31] Through such examples, Milton called for an understanding of the different experiences that women would have had, as a result of their different treatment at the hands of the Nazis together with the social practices which had been created by Jewish women and men.

Over a decade later, Lenore J. Weitzman and Dalia Ofer wrote of the situation that faced Jews when they arrived at the selection ramp at the death camps. Pregnant women, alongside women with children, were instantly sent to their death, the Nazis 'thus link[ing] the destiny of women and children'.[32] This decision, they argued, demonstrates the Nazi linkage of women with traditional Western ideas of womanhood, particularly that of motherhood. They cited a number of specific cultural and biological differences in the ways in which Jewish women experienced the Holocaust, ranging from the effects of living in a patriarchal Jewish society prior to the Holocaust, to the situation thrust upon them by the Nazis.[33] They cautioned, however, that:

> it is essential that women's experiences not be discussed exclusively in terms of motherhood or sexuality. To do so marginalizes women and, ironically, reinforces the male experience as the 'master narrative'. Rather, it is important to pay attention to the particularity of gendered wounding that both sexes experienced.[34]

Weitzman and Ofer maintained that to fully appreciate the role gender played in the Holocaust, it must be imbued into every moment. Yet, as seen in this chapter, the contrary often occurs: the curricula under consideration describe women's experiences as gendered, while the rest of the history is left without this gendered inflection. Indeed, as I will argue, womanhood is reduced to femininity, and femininity cemented to womanhood.

A number of anthologies looking at Jewish women in the Holocaust have also been published.[35] The most significant for our purposes is one of the first, edited by Carol Rittner and John K. Roth in 1993. In their introduction they outlined their reasons for advancing the study of this area, namely that 'similar experiences are not identical . . . and in the Shoah differences between men and women made a significant difference'.[36] Jewish women, they explained, were targeted because they were Jewish and differences in experience during the Holocaust resulted from differences in biology and sexuality. They cited reproduction as an example, arguing that 'any consistent Nazi plan had to target Jewish women specifically as women, for [*halachically*] they were the only ones who would finally be able to ensure the continuity of Jewish life'.³⁷ The introduction focused primarily on the concentration camp of Ravensbrück as a means of delving into an examination of Jewish women in the Holocaust.

Most recently, and almost thirty years since this field of study was begun, Myrna Goldenberg and Amy H. Shapiro have co-edited a volume which examines issues of 'gender and the Holocaust'. They note the historiographical importance of continuing to conduct such studies, thereby demonstrating that the project of understanding the Holocaust through women's histories is not complete. In their introduction, Goldenberg and Shapiro write that:

> This collection of essays is meant to introduce new discourse, to upset traditional ways of knowing and telling, to stimulate the creation of new knowledges that reflect a diversity of experiences and ways of knowing, and to offer sophisticated interpretations of the relationships between men and women and the experiences of women in regard to the Holocaust. But . . . it is also meant to inspire scholars and theorists to rethink their understanding of the Holocaust in light of this gendered study and examination of what European Jewish and non-Jewish women did and had done to them between 1933 and 1945. We hope these chapters will disrupt or at least create some discomfort around traditionally accepted assumptions, interpretations, and perspectives on the Holocaust so that theorists will ask, 'How does the introduction of a gender analysis change or inform what I know?'³⁸

In these studies, biology, culture and social practices combine to identify and define Jewish womanhood in the Holocaust, opening up a broad series of historical and historiographical questions. Different scholars have identified varying processes of gendering which resulted both from the ways in which the women were produced as gendered by the Jewish cultures in which they lived before the Holocaust, or through their gendered treatment by the Nazis. The larger project within which these approaches are situated, however, is to imbue histories of the Holocaust with greater complexity and depth, a project which is taken up at times in the pedagogies under examination in this book. But alongside this, we see a grappling with what Jewish womanhood means. As I have demonstrated throughout this book, the anxiety which is evident in the teachings is in many ways a logical outcome of both the history and memory of the Holocaust, and the force of the project of creating historiographies. Therefore, it is not surprising that, when faced with an anxiety over gender, the way in which women will be discussed is informed (largely unconsciously) by this anxiety. I thus want to argue that women's Holocaust stories and experiences provide a means of negotiating the signification of emasculation: by clearly defining Jewish womanhood along a series of key ideas and tropes, anxieties about Diaspora Jewish emasculation can be somewhat relieved. That is, if Jewish femininity can be identified, segmented off and contained, then a masculinity can be constructed which is clearly in opposition to

188 | *Anxious Histories*

this known femininity. In order to better understand the dialectical relationship which produces the negotiation of these anxieties, this chapter now considers how some key theorists have historically and historiographically constituted the category 'woman'.

What Makes a 'Woman' (a Subject of Historical Inquiry)?

Within historiographical movements there has been a recent transition away from considering the category of women as naturally given and instead paying attention to the ways in which categories of gender are constructed in different times and places.[39] My argument in this chapter is shaped in particular by the way theorists Joan Scott and Judith Butler have considered women and gender as categories of inquiry. Through an examination of their work, and the application of their ideas to the pedagogy under consideration, we will be able to gain a sense of what is meant when we speak of Holocaust educators teaching about 'Jewish women'.

Joan Scott is one of the foundational historians who argued for a conception of gender as culturally constructed through language and discourse. Her work explored the difficult balancing act within Western historiography between a tendency to essentialize women to achieve political aims and 'an historicizing approach [which] stresses differences among women and even within the concept of "women"'.[40] Scott, like Butler and Denise Riley, questioned the very concept of a category called 'women', arguing that it needs to be understood historically rather than as essentialized and naturally occurring.[41]

Judith Butler continued this project of destabilizing categories by arguing that there is no woman or man prior to their articulation. That is, language – as articulation – does not just represent women, but constitutes them.[42] In her book *Bodies That Matter*, Butler asked:

> [w]hat are we to make of constructions without which we would not be able to think, to live, to make sense at all, those which have acquired for us a kind of necessity? Are certain constructions of the body constitutive in this sense: that we could not operate without them, that without them there would be no 'I,' no 'we'?[43]

This chapter examines the ways in which women in the Holocaust historiography and pedagogy are articulated and constructed, founded on this idea that the category women does not exist prior to its being articulated and that those articulations have gained the social, political and cultural currency to mean that without them, there is no subject.

While the ideas expounded by Scott and Butler are in no way uncontested, this chapter nevertheless insists that sex and gender are linked – that the importance of sex only becomes apparent and relevant when the culture (in this case the various Nazi and Jewish cultures) acts with assumed, constructed knowledge about what being a man or a woman means, and how people whose bodies appear to define them as either man or woman should act. This encapsulates the idea that difference is not neutral – that to identify someone as either man or woman has meaning beyond the word itself, and that the words 'man' and 'woman' are signs or symbols for a range of power relations and cultural constructions, that also have material effects, about what it means to be either a man or a woman. When people are labelled either man or woman they are thus constituted.

I am arguing here that in the Holocaust pedagogy taught in the schools under examination, a central determinant of how Jewish women are articulated are current ideas of Jewishness and the Holocaust. As I have explored throughout this book, Holocaust education is produced by the cultures and societies in which it is situated, rather than by the past itself. Yet in teaching about women in particular ways today they are constructed as having been that way in the past. Through the language employed to describe women, men, and that often invisibly gendered population called 'Jews', identity categories of women, men and Jews are created. As I have discussed, a number of historians have shown that women would have had different experiences to men because of the social, cultural and political conditions and relationships which were expressed in people through their bodies. More significantly for this project, however, is the role this teaching plays in the project of negotiating the gendering of contemporary Jewish discourses, rather than specific individual people and their bodies.

All teachers interviewed for this project were asked whether or not they talked about women in their teachings. Even allowing for the fact that teachers may have tailored their answers to impress their interviewer and hence could have overemphasized the degree to which they discuss women, most of the teachers answered that they rarely brought women up as a separate group.[44] Importantly, however, there was a general understanding of which group in society was being referred to by this question. It is to this group that we now turn – the group that is understood culturally to be identified as 'women', as problematic, complex and unstable as this term may be. Following Michel Foucault – to whom Scott and Butler are themselves indebted – it is argued that power does not just restrict what women can do, but rather constitutes what 'women' are.[45] In other words, representations of Jewish women in the Holocaust both reflect and constitute contemporary understandings of Jewish womanhood and femininity, by producing a set of key, known, and defined, categories.

Specific Representations of Women in Holocaust Pedagogy

Women as mothers

The discursive construction of (Western) women's predominant role being that of mothers is not new or particular to Holocaust narratives.[46] Some of these

Holocaust narratives demonstrate to students that women's particular role is as mothers, with the depiction of women as carers or as self-sacrificing for the benefit of their families. For instance, motherhood is foregrounded in the curriculum at one all-girls' school from the beginning. One of the first things students encounter in the curriculum book is the story of Sarah Schenirer, who is labelled the 'Mother of the Beth Jacob schools'. In a brief history, taken from writings by historian Lucy Dawidowicz, Schenirer – who shares a first name with the first of the Four Matriarchs in the Jewish tradition – is discussed as someone who worried about the future of the Jewish people because, in Vienna at the beginning of the twentieth century, Jewish girls were not particularly religious.[47] She formed a Beth Jacob school in order to re-instil Judaism within young women.[48] This story thus serves as a framing device.

Other teachers enmeshed women and motherhood in different ways. A teacher at a co-educational school explained that she talks about motherhood experiences in the Holocaust 'throughout' the subject:

> I'm talking about the dilemma of motherhood throughout the Kindertransport, the selection process in the concentration camps, the ghetto, the role of children smuggling and so on and how mothers were sacrificing themselves to enable them to do it or how mothers sacrificed their rations for their children or how they sacrificed in order for their children to receive an education in the ghettos. I talk about mothers and children.[49]

Another co-educational school presents a similar picture of mothers as self-sacrificing. The curriculum notes that in the ghettos the Jews 'sought to help one another, often showing an amazing degree of self-sacrifice. Thousands of mothers refused to save their own lives by handing over their children. Thousands of people went to their deaths rather than abandon their families.'[50] Thus one of the main forms in which students at these schools learn about Jewish women in the Holocaust is as sacrificing mothers. Because fathers are not discussed in the same way, parenthood is shown to be the domain of women.

The role of the 'maternal metaphor' in Holocaust literature has been explored by Claire Kahane. She argues that the trauma of the Holocaust is difficult to grasp, that signifiers are unable to represent the 'real event', and thus that authors 'seek tropes that can transmit the texture of traumatic memory' in order for their audiences to be able to personally engage with the horrors about which they are reading.[51] As such, she suggests, the forced separation of mother from child becomes a particularly powerful and emotional trope, 'effectively capturing the perversion of human bonds that was a primary consequence of the Holocaust'.[52] The sacrificial mother, then, is such a recurring image in Holocaust pedagogy partially because it is a signifier with cultural currency for both teachers and students. Its continued use in turn reiterates its centrality. Yet, as Kahane cautions, the maternal metaphor also domesticates the horrors of the Holocaust, making it seem comprehensible and articulatable.[53]

The curricula also contain more specific ideas of what constitutes appropriate Jewish motherhood. An example of this is mothers as made 'crazed' by their trauma. A co-educational school presents the writings of a man, Albert Hollender, discussing a train transport from Paris to Auschwitz in 1942. He described the situation as follows:

> We arrived worn out, dehydrated, with many ill. A newborn baby, snatched from its mother's arms, was thrown against a column. The mother, crazed with pain, began to scream. The SS man struck her violently with the butt of his weapon ... Her eyes haggard, with fearful screams, her beautiful hair became tinted with her own blood. She was struck down with a bullet in the head.[54]

This is perhaps the ultimate picture of virtuous womanhood the students are presented with: that of a beautiful mother, killed because of her desire to save her child. Does this make banal the Holocaust, as Kahane suggested is possible? Not necessarily. The story is designed to shock – as perhaps all stories of the Holocaust are capable of and should – and provoke an emotional response. And yet it is a story of beauty versus violence, of motherhood versus death. The woman is intrinsically good, and her suffering somewhat relatable.[55] In these teachings we can thus see Jewish womanhood being linked, perhaps inextricably, with motherhood.

Women as victims

As the Holocaust was a period when Jews were brutally victimized it is perhaps unsurprising, and indeed necessary, that Jewish women are often presented as victims in these narratives of the Holocaust. The particular ways in which this victim-status is presented, however, is important to explore. Sometimes this is within the context of particular practices of victimization, such as rape or the treatment of pregnant women, while at other times the teachers utilize women and children as symbolic of the innocence of the Jewish people and the brutality of the Nazis. In these presentations of Jewish victimization women are important for what they represent – Jewish innocence – rather than as discrete people, or even as a collective of real human beings. Women are made into an anonymous pedagogical tool intended to emphasize the innocence of Jews.

This construction is undertaken in a number of different ways. The curriculum of a co-educational school explains that '[a]t first, the DP [Displaced Person] camps [at the end of the war] consisted primarily of single men. Fewer women had survived.'[56] In reminding the students that so many more women died, a strong emotional response is most probably elicited from the students. By juxtaposing the brutality of the Nazis with the killings of the Jewish women, another curriculum, at a New York school, reminds students of Jewish innocence. The curriculum states that '[t]he brutal SS man with his truncheon stood alongside the commander with the Ph.D. in law, both of whom were directly involved in the mass shootings of naked women and children.'[57] It states this, despite the fact that it was not only the women who were stripped naked and shot; men were killed in this way as well. Moreover, it was not just the commanders who were educated but so too, potentially, were the women and children being shot. More importantly, perhaps, is the foregrounding of education as a site of difference: the Nazis were educated, while the women and children were their opposite, naked, lacking and mute, simply part of an amorphous mass. And yet this discourse takes place in the classroom, a site of education. The association of women with weakness and futility is further established when the same curriculum describes the murder process at the death camps, where '[t]he elderly, the sick, children, pregnant women, and those who could not walk were sent immediately to the gas chambers. Those who could work were sent to the labor camps, usually segregated by sex.'[58] Pregnant women, as well as other 'weaker' groups, are thereby inextricably linked to instant death, while men and capable women are linked to labour and postponed death.[59]

A teacher from another co-educational school described her school's Yom Hashoah ceremony, wherein traditionally the students organize the ceremony. She explained that in 2005:

> one of the rooms that they did was dehumanization. So they took clips from a very old movie and I don't remember the name any more but it was with Vanessa Redgrave. They show her coming to the concentration camp and getting her hair cut. Most people when you think about getting your hair cut, they don't think it's such a big deal. But what the Nazis did was in this scene where they cut the hair was so powerful, that you feel the degradation and you feel the impact of the cutting of the hair, that they used that scene and talked about it with the [younger] kids.[60]

We could read this Yom Hashoah activity as presenting Jewish women as passive victims, having their heads shaved. It demonstrates how the somewhat banal act of getting one's hair cut, something the teacher identified as being for most people not 'such a big deal', was transformed into a story of humiliation and victimization. The intention here, as the teacher explains, was to use the film to teach the students about 'dehumanization'. The woman in this story therefore comes to exist as symbolic – she tells the story of Jewish victimization, dehumanization and innocence. This dehumanization is central to the experience of Jews in the Holocaust. The 'Jewish woman having her head shaved' thereby becomes one sign of Jewish suffering.

We can see this sign of a lost femininity – which, in placing lack and absence (in the form of hair made absent) at the centre of identity, feminizes these people who suffer – repeated in the words of a female teacher at another school. She explained that she raises the 'particularly terrible' experience for women of having their heads and bodies shaved in order to 'talk about the depersonalization of the victim and dehumanizing of the victim . . . and I say, "Imagine the actual experience of a woman shorn of everything that makes her beautiful and she suddenly becomes this disgusting, abominable number."'[61] The story, once again, only functions with a woman, unnamed and imagined, as its subject.

The theme of sexual violence is also prominent in Holocaust education, amongst the images of Jewish womanhood. Sexuality is not presented as a positive element of womanhood but rather as a part of women's victimization. Jewish women's sexuality is used to teach students about the absolute victimhood of the Jews, while also teaching them that sexuality can be dangerous and shameful for women. For instance, in a co-educational school's curriculum it teaches that 'in Czestochowa, on a frosty night in January 1940 . . . [o]thers – especially young girls – were taken into the synagogue now transformed into police headquarters, forced to undress, sexually shamed, and tortured'.[62] While this may have been the experience of women who were raped or sexually assaulted – that they felt shame – it is significant that the shame in this statement is associated with sex, rather than the other forms of torture which occurred. Why is this euphemism – 'sexual shaming' – used? Perhaps it was because the students were deemed too young to know about sex. Yet this curriculum is for students aged 15–16 years old; an age where, certainly in Melbourne, they are already somewhat aware of sexualities. Perhaps it was because the teacher believed that the women who were sexually assaulted would have felt shame. Yet, as others have explained, in narrations of the Holocaust written after 1945 – as this was – much of the violence perpetrated by the Nazis against the Jews was a source of shame.[63] Why then is sexual assault particularly shameful?

The most significant answer to this question is that sexual assault and rape are deemed by Melbourne society generally to bring shame upon the victim, and that this was also the case in Polish Jewish society in the 1940s.[64] To describe sexual assault as 'sexual shame' is therefore perhaps somewhat historically accurate, although we can never know how the particular women in this story experienced their sexual assaults. But to present this euphemism to students is to continue this approach: to reinforce that the language of shame describes automatically and in totality the experience of being sexually assaulted. The students are thus taught that this was the way in which women experienced sexual assault: that by virtue of being victim to this particular type of Nazi violence, a violence perpetrated most predominantly against women, they were shamed.[65]

This totalizing language of shame associated with sexuality and the shaving of heads works to provide students with a series of symbols of Jewish innocence and victimhood, rather than elucidating individual people's stories or groups of peoples' stories. But there are also some teachers who, at least partially, explore individual women's stories of the Holocaust. This can be seen in the words of the teacher at an all-girls' school in New York, who brought up the subject of Jewish women being raped throughout her interview. As well as discussing it in broad conceptions, she singled out individual stories to illustrate her larger points. She explained that she encourages the students to read memoirs and testimonies of their own choice, and when they bring in what they are reading she will:

> bring in stories from interviews [she has conducted]. There was one woman who was raped twice in the war and she never married. And she was the only woman that I interviewed – I interviewed over 60 people – and she was the only one who had not gotten married. Marriage was very, very important to survivors. They had to start a family and do something. And because of her experience of rape she didn't want to be part of it. She saw men, she went out with them, but she would never get married. She never told her story to anyone else. We were the only people who heard it.[66]

In this way – because the teacher personalized the event – she was able to express the victimization that comes with being raped by the Nazis, as well as the lasting effects of such an experience, while not utilizing such an experience as evidence of the general victimization of Jews or of Jewish women. This teacher is describing an event which produced a feeling of shame, and the after-effects of a shameful experience, but is pointing to the limitations of this shame: to the silence that it produces.

While some teachers discuss rape perpetrated by Nazis, no teacher mentions the rapes perpetrated by Jewish prisoners in the ghettos and camps (and nor do they discuss men being raped). This is perhaps to be expected. But as a result, rape remains depicted as a mode of oppression perpetrated by the absolute evil in the Holocaust. This can serve to further reinforce the silences which exist both in the historical record and in current-day discourses. Discussions of rape become another means of reinforcing to the students that, in the Holocaust, Jews were absolutely innocent and Nazis were completely guilty – that, in a more general sense, a part of being Jewish entails being innocent: there is no 'grey zone'.[67]

Pregnancy, abortion and menstruation

Despite the elevated role of motherhood in teachings of the Holocaust, pregnancy, and the particular problems it brought women, is rarely discussed. Only one school in Melbourne teaches about pregnancy – and at this school it is part of the formal written curriculum – while almost all the teachers at the New York schools explained in interviews that it will be mentioned in passing only, either raised by the students or mentioned by the teachers.[68] When asked whether or not they taught about pregnancy in their classes, teachers offered comments such as 'a little bit',[69] 'it comes up occasionally. Usually not',[70] and that 'there's too much to discuss – I don't really have time to go into it'.[71]

One teacher at an all-girls' school explained that:

[i]f it comes up, then I will certainly address it. I will certainly address it, and only in a way that ... never at the expense of robbing the dignity of the survivors. Never in a way that we are passing judgement or you know, most concepts that really come up will be ... if pregnancy comes up, it will be that a woman wants to ensure the survival of her family line. And somehow that concept of pregnancy revitalizes and gives a woman hope. I don't look to bring these topics in.[72]

There are a number of seemingly contradictory responses to pregnancy contained in this statement: that discussing pregnancy has the capacity to 'rob the dignity of the survivors'; that discussing pregnancy seems to invite 'passing judgement' and a teacher needs to make a conscious decision not to do so; and that pregnancy can be discussed as a means of, in the context of the Holocaust, ensuring survival of families, providing hope and revitalizing individuals and communities. Here we can see a deep ambivalence about these sorts of discussions: they are seen as difficult topics for a high-school classroom to manage, but they are also difficult for the teacher to understand. Perhaps therefore we can understand that these topics are avoided because of a desire to avoid discussion of these ambivalences and contradictions. Teaching about the Holocaust, and focusing in on particular sources of trauma, is – perhaps inherently – incredibly difficult.

Another teacher, at a co-educational school, explained that she teaches her students that:

families are the women's domain, with the Nazis, that take care of the children. That if you were pregnant you automatically go to the gas chambers but then on the other hand, there were all these experiments being done on these newborns and when all these experiments were done ... they were still sent to the gas chambers. So, pregnancy wasn't the feature of what we were getting at, but it was more of the general processes of how the camps functioned and the rationale behind all these things that they did.[73]

In this example, women's experiences of pregnancy in the Nazi system are being used to illustrate the complex experience of living in the camps.

Another teacher talks about pregnancy 'a little bit' in the context of ghetto life, to discuss the different experiences that Jewish men and women would have had during the Holocaust. She commented in an interview that 'when I can show something, I do. When, if there's a tale about a woman, and she wants to have an abortion and she doesn't want to be pregnant in the ghetto because what's going to happen to this child. So we do look at that.'[74]

Linked to this mention of abortion is the final aspect of pregnancy taught in multiple schools: the actions of Dr Gisella Pearl. According to one teacher, Pearl is mentioned as 'a gynaecologist and physician before the war and her role in the camps' performing abortions which were requested by the women. She explained that she mentions 'in passing about how babies were killed, pregnant women were forced to abort and they were forced to live with their legs tied together'.[75] For both this teacher, and for the other teacher who mentioned Pearl in interviews, her story was kept brief – it constituted in one case a lesson or so of discussion, in another, one sentence in the curriculum.[76] It also constituted two sentences of the larger two-page examination of 'Women in the Shoah' mentioned previously. This mention of Pearl, however, describes the doctor as a 'he', thus altering the place of the story in the Holocaust narrative.[77] Thus many aspects of pregnancy were covered by teachers in New York; however it was never examined in any great depth, and was discussed predominantly in the context of the increased role that pregnancy would play in ensuring that Jewish women were victimized by the Nazis.

Another aspect of women's bodies that multiple teachers explained that they cover, albeit in quite different ways, is menstruation. Only three teachers – one from Melbourne and two from New York – said that they talk about menstruation, but for all of them it was a topic which may be brought up by the students, rather than one which they introduced. The teacher at a girls' school explained that she discusses it with her students 'because they do come across it. I don't know, I can't go out and say it, but I think it probably comes from what happened and what it would have been like. And basically in the camps it just didn't happen.'[78] This was the aspect of menstruation which this teacher highlighted – that it ceased in the camps but it has never been proven why this was the case. A similar motivation pushed another teacher to mention menstruation. She explained that she talks about menstruation in the following context:

> Because of starvation, many of the women stopped menstruating. That was part of the whole dehumanizing thing. That women were made to feel like a creature and not a [human] . . . and that one of the most fantastic things after the Holocaust, so many women expressed relief that once they were fed and healthy again, they started menstruating again and could have children. . . . So, we mention starvation and menstruation.[79]

For this teacher, menstruation was a means of discussing the way in which Jews were dehumanized by the Nazi project and to illustrate the joy that accompanied liberation. Menstruation is, of course, linked here to women's bodies and to the effects wrought on women's bodies in various different ways by the Holocaust. Starvation – which was experienced by everyone – is linked explicitly to women here. The weakness of the body is linked to women and thereby reinforced as feminized.[80]

Women as resisters

A concentration on Jews' resistance enhances the paramount position of Jewish innocence in the histories of the Holocaust which are taught in the schools under examination. Narratives of individual women serve predominantly to teach the students that women's resistance was different to that undertaken by men *because* of their femininity; this, once more, constructs Jewish women as different to men and cements the boundaries between women and men. By discussing the actions of women who resisted primarily, although not exclusively, outside the terms of physical, military-based resistance – women are described predominantly in terms of spiritual resistance or as couriers – physical uprisings are maintained as the domain of the masculine, allowing work to be done to recuperate Diaspora masculinity. My examination of resistance here will begin with an exploration of women's involvement as general members of the resistance, then examine acts of resistance specifically undertaken by women, and finally focus on individual women who are highlighted as having participated in the (physical) resistance. Only three curricula – two from Melbourne and one from New York – specifically included women as having been active members of the resistance, while three teachers – all from New York – in interviews said that they discuss women and their involvement in the resistance.

The only curriculum to talk about women as having been general members of the resistance – rather than as solely performing tasks specifically undertaken by women – was a co-educational school in Melbourne. This curriculum explains that women 'created centres of resistance and led underground organizations. They were involved in attempted ghetto uprisings and camp revolts.'[81] In another part of the curriculum, women are singled out where men are not: under the heading '[r]evolt was almost impossible, but many Jews fought back wherever and however they could', seven separate examples of resistance are mentioned. Six of these are left unnamed, while the seventh reads '[h]eroic women fought in the underground. Hannah Szenes parachuted into Europe to help escapees. Chaika Grossman led ghetto uprisings in Poland.' While this curriculum works at times to integrate women's participation in resistance into the main narrative of the Holocaust, by sexing only one example of resistance it is implied that all other acts were performed by men. In this way men remain the invisible standard, with some individual women the named exceptions.

The teacher at a girls' school explained that she teaches the students about 'the pride of resistance' and 'how people stand up to something that is not right'. She stated that she talks primarily about the partisans but encourages the students not to judge those who did not resist as 'you take the family away, you take the clothing away, you strip them of money, food, their homes, and the male leadership, and they broke up towns and they purposefully didn't put people together who could have had unity'.[82] She also uses the story of the woman being deported from Paris to Auschwitz, mentioned previously, to explain the resistance which occurred there.

Two curricula and one teacher discuss women's specific acts of resistance. A co-educational school included numerous mentions of women's resistance as an adjunct to the men's. The first description focuses on women as couriers between ghettos, and between the ghetto and the outside world, as 'young women ... could easily pass as non-Jews' and thus were more likely to undertake this type of work.[83] Further into the curriculum there is an outline of 'the dilemmas of resistance' which presents four different leaders of the resistance – one a woman – debating whether or not to resist and outlining their influences, which were often Israel and Zionism.[84] Women are shown to be most active in the background of the resistance, with men predominantly leading the uprisings.

Similarly, another co-educational school, as well as presenting women as generally involved in the resistance, highlighted that 'much is still unknown about the involvement of women in armed resistance. However, it is known that women acted as couriers' amongst other more general activities. This section also highlights the particular predicament facing women: '[t]he dilemma of remaining with family as caregivers or "abandoning" them in order to participate in armed resistance was excruciating'.[85] This sentence works in part to homogenize the experiences of women in the resistance – there is the underlying assumption that all women had families that they were primarily responsible for, that becoming involved in the resistance would have meant leaving their families, and that that would have been a dilemma for all of them. In this one sentence there are a series of assumptions about the role of women in Jewish life.

The final teacher to outline different resistance activities undertaken by women was from a co-educational school. This teacher commented that some acts of resistance, such as the Warsaw Ghetto Uprising and the work of the forest partisans, receive a lot of scholarly attention, and thus she was keen to introduce other forms of resistance to her students. In order to do so she chose the physical incarnation of acts of spiritual resistance, such as the continuation of the practice by women of going to the *mikvah*, even though it meant risking their lives.[86]

While the focus on women's participation in resistance was primarily on non-militaristic resistance – forms of resistance which are feminized through their emphasis on non-physically violent actions, rather than on strong, capable and violent bodies – there were times when teachers presented information about women's involvement in armed uprisings. This, however, was undertaken through the examination of the actions of one individual, as opposed to the broad unnamed groupings which were mentioned above. Interestingly, in the past, a common individual to be recognized in Holocaust education – particularly for her ability to maintain a positive innocence throughout her Holocaust oppression – was Anne Frank and her widely read diary.[87] The interviews conducted and curricula examined for this study demonstrate that Anne Frank has become less widely studied in Jewish schools. Indeed, she was only occasionally a focus for the schools, and her diary appeared on the occasional optional reading list. However when she is used it is to illustrate a certain naïve, feminine innocence.[88]

Another woman stands in Frank's place as a figure of resistance: Hannah Szenes. Szenes was a Jewish woman who was a member of the Hagana in Mandate Palestine, who parachuted into Yugoslavia and then made her way into Hungary. There she was caught by the Nazis and was tortured and murdered. Schools from both cities and from the Reform to the Modern Orthodox utilize the story of Hannah Szenes to exemplify the actions of women in the resistance.[89] Other popular figures in Melbourne curricula include Zivia Lubetkin, who participated in the Warsaw Ghetto Uprising, and Rosa Robota, who led the revolt at Auschwitz, both of whom were involved in Zionist organizations either before or after the war.[90] These three figures represent significantly different approaches to resistance as compared to Anne Frank. While Frank represents the innocence of the Jewish people, Szenes, in the words of one curriculum, 'contradicts the stereotype of the unresisting or fleeing victim as much as of the helpless woman'.[91] Lubetkin and Robota both assert Jewish physical and moral strength. Moreover, as one curriculum comments, Szenes was born in Budapest 'the birthplace of Theodore Herzl, the father of modern political Zionism'.[92] Thus Szenes's story functions to highlight the active role some Jews played in resisting the Nazis and, more importantly, that Zionism, and a strong connection to Israel, fuelled this defiance. Szenes is therefore important not for who she was, but for what she represents: the liberating potential of Zionism and the strong aggressive (masculine) Jewish body.

These individual women then do not rupture the boundaries of womanhood established in these teachings, but they point to the ambivalence contained within these historical renderings. They are exceptions to the rule, foregrounded perhaps because they are obviously linked to Zionism and the masculine power which Zionism claims to bring.

Ambivalent Representations of Women

In these teachings we can see that teachers do not have a specific and conscious strategy for depicting women as either symbolic of Jewishness or as individual people. As a result, representations of women fluctuate between the two. At times, women are presented as signs, designed to impart variously conceptions of Jewish innocence and Nazi guilt, the importance of Zionism and resistance in the life of Jews or the significance of particular ideas of Jewish motherhood. In these instances, women are therefore not present in the curricula to teach students about the experiences of women, but rather because the women serve to instruct students about the broader Jewish experience.

At other times, particularly at all-girls' schools, teachers utilize stories of women's experiences to personalize the horrors of the Holocaust for their students so that they can, on some level, relate to what they are learning about. As a pedagogical tool, women's experiences serve to make the Holocaust more comprehensible and thus more 'human'. Yet women continue to function as a sign, thus emphasizing that we do not yet have the language with which to understand the Holocaust and the experiences of Jewish women within it.

In describing the ways in which teachers present stories of women's experiences my intention has not been to assess the historical veracity of these claims. Most of these stories have a basis in the histories written, and even if they do not this is not what is most important. The truth claims of these histories are not being weighed here. Rather, in this chapter my interest has been located in the ideas of Jewish womanhood selected to be a part of these historical records. The teachers expressed a hesitation in focusing on Jewish women in their teachings; when they focused on these women and their experiences it was in passing. The question this chapter has engaged with is, why then are these certain moments chosen?

Above all, the teaching of the Holocaust, as has been explored in various different ways throughout this book, has come to play a role in the project of attempting to resolve the anxieties felt by many in Jewish communities over the place of the Jews in these two Western spaces. In order to achieve this resolution, teachers and their narratives adopt modern Western modes of writing history, and in this instance this involves marginalizing women's experiences and simultaneously centring and making invisible men's experiences *as* men's experiences. That is, men's experiences become the invisible standard – the explanation of what happens to the whole group, with women serving as marginal to the main narrative or as symbolic of certain qualities of the group. Women's histories are contained within what are made to be the acceptable parameters of femininity. As such, perhaps by these techniques, Diaspora masculinity can be recuperated. There is a dialectical relationship: a certain form of femininity is necessary to make the acceptable form of masculinity appear. We can understand that the same result entails from the negotiation of both of these anxieties: whether attempting to fit in with dominant Western historiography or with Zionist thought, women's stories are contained. In this containing, femininity as a discursive construction is controlled and restricted to women's bodies and actions, thereby helping to make a claim that Diaspora men do not share this femininity. It is thus in this chapter that we saw the coming together of the various manifestations of the anxieties which this book charted in different ways, with the eventual result that we can now understand the ways in which these anxieties aid in determining the histories being written.

Notes

1. Interview with Teacher B at School MA.
2. Elizabeth D. Heineman explored the problem of language and speakability with reference to Nazism and sexuality more generally. See E.D. Heineman. January/April 2002.

'Sexuality and Nazism: The Doubly Unspeakable?', *Journal of the History of Sexuality* 11(1/2), 22–66.
3. Histories of the Holocaust are, of course, not the only place where Jewish womanhood is defined. For examinations of other such histories see, for example, R.-E. Prell. 1999. *Fighting to Become Americans: Jews, Gender, and the Anxiety of Assimilation*, Boston: Beacon Press; P.E. Hyman. 1995. *Gender and Assimilation in Modern Jewish History: The Roles and Representation of Women*, Seattle: University of Washington Press; M.A. Kaplan. 1991. *The Making of the Jewish Middle Class: Women, Family, and Identity in Imperial Germany*, New York: Oxford University Press; A. Cantor. 1995. *Jewish Women/Jewish Men: The Legacy of Patriarchy in Jewish Life*, San Francisco: Harper San Francisco.
4. Kahane, 'Dark Mirrors', 162.
5. To write of femininity and masculinity, men and women, is, of course, to inadvertently reinforce the binary relationship between these categories. It is not the intention of this chapter to reinforce these divisions. Yet it is important that the pedagogy under examination fails to consider questions of sex, gender and sexuality and the binaries which constitute their formulation. Therefore, while not endorsing such namings and categorizations, for ease of description this chapter will refer to men and women, as though there is such a binary relationship, for, importantly, there is this relationship in the discourses under examination. The descriptions of masculinization and feminization break down these binaries somewhat, but not completely. It is outside the scope of this book to interrogate this in any more depth, but these ideas have their grounding in Queer theory. For an exploration of Queer theories of gender and sexuality see, for example, the first chapter ('Introducing Bisexuality') of S. Angelides. 2001. *A History of Bisexuality*, Chicago: University of Chicago Press. See also J. Butler. 1990. *Gender Trouble*; D. Fuss. 1989. *Essentially Speaking: Feminism, Nature & Difference*, New York: Routledge.
6. See P. Adams and J. Minson. 'The "Subject" of Feminism', in P. Adams and E. Cowie (eds), *The Woman in Question: M/F*, London: Verso, 81–101.
7. Cowie, 'Woman as Sign', 117–18.
8. Ibid., 133.
9. In this chapter Jewish women will sometimes, for the sake of brevity, be referred to simply as women. In doing so the intention is not to convey the idea that all women (or all women persecuted by the Nazis) are Jewish. However, within the world of the curricula it is only Jewish women who are talked about, and thus who are the subject of this chapter. It therefore becomes redundant to repeatedly describe them as Jewish.
10. Curriculum of School MB, 119.
11. Ibid., 120.
12. Curriculum of School MB, 119.
13. Ibid., 120.
14. P. Adams. 1990. 'Representation and Sexuality', in P. Adams and E. Cowie (eds), *The Woman in Question: M/F*, London: Verso, 233–52.
15. Interview with Teacher A of school NYA. Emphasis added.
16. It is perhaps interesting to note that when Nazi perpetrators are discussed, they are primarily figured as men, not women. Further exploration of this is outside the scope of this book.
17. Indeed, this problem is certainly not limited to Holocaust education, or to high-school education. Historians of all manners struggle with, and reinforce, this approach. While feminist historiography has created a great deal of change, there is still much work to be done at all levels of historiography.

18. For instance, in interviews with Teacher A of School NYB, Teacher B of School NYB, Teacher A of School NYF, and Teacher A of School MC. Similarly, a teacher at a co-educational school in New York commented that it is important to bring in women's experiences when she can 'because we have a lot of girls in our school. They need to know that women played a part.' Interview with Teacher A of School NYC.
19. *Yontif* is the Yiddish word for a Jewish festival or holiday. The quote in the brackets is from the same interview.
20. Interview with Teacher A at School MC.
21. Interview with Teacher B at School NYB.
22. Interview with Teacher A at School NYD.
23. Jacques Derrida pointed to a similar problem in a discussion of the association between 'the figure of the Jew and the woman': 'we should interrogate not only anti-Semitism of the kind that has emerged in European societies or nations, at the times when they have exalted the values of roots, the army, force, virile and fraternal qualities, and so on (we could find lots of examples of this, some old, some less old, some completely contemporary), but we should also ask the question of every nation and every state, including Israel (of the inside of that which, in the Jewish tradition, has been able to give rise to nation, state, army, fraternity, and so on). What becomes of the woman there? What becomes of the value of femininity?' J. Derrida. 2004. 'A Testimony Given ... ' in E. Weber (ed.), *Questioning Judaism*, Stanford, CA: Stanford University Press, 49.
24. E. Katz and J. Ringelheim (eds). 1983. *Proceedings of the Conference on Women Surviving the Holocaust*, New York: Institute for Research in History.
25. J. Ringelheim. 1998. 'The Split between Gender and the Holocaust', in D. Ofer and L.J. Weitzman (eds), *Women in the Holocaust*, New Haven, CT: Yale University Press, 350.
26. J. Ringelheim. 1993. 'Women and the Holocaust: A Reconsideration of Research', in C. Rittner and J.K. Roth (eds), *Different Voices: Women and the Holocaust*, New York: Paragon House, 378.
27. Ringelheim, 'The Split between Gender and the Holocaust', 344.
28. Ibid.
29. S. Milton. 1984. 'Women and the Holocaust: The Case of German and German-Jewish Women', in R. Bridenthal, A. Grossmann and M. Kaplan (eds), *When Biology Became Destiny: Women in Weimar and Nazi Germany*, New York: Monthly Review Press, 301.
30. Ibid., 306–7. Emphasis in original.
31. Ibid., 308.
32. L.J. Weitzman and D. Ofer. 1998. 'Introduction: The Role of Gender in the Holocaust', in D. Ofer and L.J. Weitzman (eds), *Women in the Holocaust*, New Haven, CT: Yale University Press, 10.
33. Ibid., 1. As a means of establishing their theoretical basis, they make the point that they will be viewing gender as the socially and culturally constructed roles of men and women in our societies, while utilizing sex as an indicator of biological differences.
34. Ibid., 16. As will be seen, many of the teachers represent Jewish women as having had different experiences because of such stereotypically gendered embodied experiences.
35. Other anthologies of women's Holocaust histories include: Katz and Ringelheim, *Proceedings of the Conference on Women Surviving the Holocaust*; E.R. Baer and M. Goldenberg (eds). 2003. *Experience and Expression: Women, the Nazis, and the Holocaust*, Detroit, MI: Wayne State University Press; E. Fuchs (ed.). 1999. *Women and the Holocaust*, Lanham, MD: University Press of America, Inc.; V. Laska (ed.). 1983. *Women in the Resistance and in the Holocaust: The Voices of Eyewitnesses*, Westport, CT: Greenwood Press; D. Ofer and L.J. Weitzman (eds). 1998. *Women in the Holocaust*, New

Haven, CT: Yale University Press. R.G. Saidel and S.M. Hedgepeth (eds). 2010. *Sexual Violence Against Women During the Holocaust*, Waltham, MA: Brandeis University Press, 2010. R. Bridenthal, A. Grossmann and M. Kaplan (eds). 1984. *When Biology Became Destiny: Women in Weimar and Nazi Germany*, New York: Monthly Review Press is an anthology which has, as one chapter, an examination of Jewish women's histories during this period. It contains histories of other women as well, thus locating Jewish women within broader histories.
36. C. Rittner and J.K. Roth. 1993. 'Prologue: Women and the Holocaust', in C. Rittner and J.K. Roth (eds), *Different Voices: Women and the Holocaust*, New York: Paragon House, 3.
37. Ibid., 2.
38. M. Goldenberg and A.H. Shapiro. 2013. 'Introduction', in M. Goldenberg and A.H. Shapiro (eds), *Different Horrors/Same Hell: Gender and the Holocaust*, Seattle: University of Washington Press, 6–7.
39. Kathleen Canning provided an excellent summary of the various moves in feminist theory over time. See K. Canning. 2006. *Gender History in Practice: Historical Perspectives on Bodies, Class & Citizenship*, Ithaca, NY: Cornell University Press, 3–62.
40. J.W. Scott. 1996. 'Introduction', in J.W. Scott (ed.), *Feminism and History*, Oxford: Oxford University Press, 1.
41. See J.W. Scott. 1999. *Gender and the Politics of History*, Revised ed., New York: Columbia University Press; D. Riley. 1988. *'Am I That Name?': Feminism and the Category of 'Women' in History*, London: Macmillan. Scott's approach has come under considerable debate amongst feminist historians. See for example the debate between Scott and Linda Gordon, wherein they review each other's works and respond to the reviews, in *Signs* 15(4), Summer 1990, 848–60. See also the recent forum on Scott's 1988 article 'Gender: A Useful Category of Historical Analysis' in *American Historical Review*, 113(5), December 2008, 1344–430.
42. Butler, 'Contingent Foundations: Feminism and the Question of "Postmodernism"', 16. In Butler's formulation sex emerges as part of the same masculinist discourse as gender; while it is commonly posited that sex is natural while gender is constructed, Butler argued that the language which articulates this difference brings this difference into being. Hence, one is no more natural – nor discursive – than the other. J. Butler. 1993. *Bodies That Matter: On the Discursive Limits of 'Sex'*, New York: Routledge, 5–7.
43. Butler, *Bodies That Matter*, xi.
44. Esther Faye explores the ways that interviewers and interviewees interact. E. Faye. Summer 1995. 'Psychoanalysis and the Barred Subject of Feminist History', *Australian Feminist Studies* 22, 77–97.
45. M. Foucault. 1978. *The History of Sexuality: Volume One: An Introduction*, London: Penguin.
46. The literature on motherhood is quite large. For examples, see A. Dally. 1982. *Inventing Motherhood: The Consequences of an Ideal*, London: Burnett Books Ltd; M. Benn. 1998. *Madonna and Child: Towards a New Politics of Motherhood*, London: Jonathan Cape. For critiques of Western constructions of motherhood, see H. Ragoné and F. Winddance Twine (eds). 2000. *Ideologies and Technologies of Motherhood: Race, Class, Sexuality, Nationalism*, New York: Routledge. For an exploration of Jewish mothers and motherhood, see J. Antler. 2007. *You Never Call! You Never Write! A History of the Jewish Mother*, New York: Oxford University Press.
47. The four Matriarchs are Sarah, Rebecca, Rachel and Leah. The three Patriarchs are Abraham, Isaac and Jacob.
48. Curriculum of school NYC, 3–4.

49. Interview with Teacher A at School NYB. Similar sentiments were expressed in an interview with Teacher A at School NYF.
50. Curriculum of School ME, 119.
51. Kahane, 'Dark Mirrors', 164.
52. Ibid.
53. This was discussed in greater detail in Chapter Two. With regard to the use of the maternal metaphor as a trope for articulating the trauma of the Holocaust, Kahane explained that 'If we understand the first trauma of infantile life to be the trauma of maternal loss, the use of a traumatic breach in the mother–child relation to figure an unrepresentable historical trauma has a logical inevitability as well as a universal affective power. Yet in looking at Holocaust narrative with feminist eyes, I am made uncomfortable by the ubiquitous presence of mother and child as figures of traumatic loss. Is it not perhaps too easy to use that dyadic ideal of intimacy to evoke the reader's emotional identification with the agony of separation?' Ibid.
54. Curriculum of School MB, 102.
55. A contrasting idea of motherhood can be found in the work of Katharina von Kellenbach, who writes of women's choices as mothers, and potential mothers (i.e. pregnant women) in terms of resistance. See K. von Kellenbach. 1999. 'Reproduction and Resistance During the Holocaust', in E. Fuchs (ed.), *Women and the Holocaust: Narrative and Representation*, Lanham: University Press of America, Inc., 19–32.
56. Curriculum of School ME, 131.
57. Curriculum of School NYC, 59.
58. Ibid.
59. I must repeat here that my point in this discussion is not to question the historical accuracy of the teachings, but rather to look at what they affirm, or achieve. This is the approach I have taken throughout this book. And thus – for instance – while it is certainly accurate to state that visibly pregnant women were generally sent straight to death in the death camps, we must look at what such teachings authorize, or at what ideas of the experience of Jewish womanhood they perpetuate.
60. Interview with Teacher A at School NYE. The movie with Vanessa Redgrave being referred to here is *Playing for Time* (1980).
61. Interview with Teacher A of School NYD.
62. Curriculum of School ME, 73. Taken from Lucy Davidowicz's *The War Against the Jews*.
63. See, for instance, E. Faye. 2003. 'Being Jewish after Auschwitz: Writing Modernity's Shame', *Australian Feminist Studies* 18(42), 245–59; T. Kaplan. Autumn 2002. 'Reversing the Shame and Gendering the Memory', *Signs* 28(1), 179–99; Nutkiewicz, 'Shame, Guilt, and Anguish in Holocaust Survivor Testimony', 1–22.
64. Anna Reading, for example, wrote of the shame and silence surrounding Jewish women's experiences of being raped in the camps. A. Reading. 2002. *The Social Inheritance of the Holocaust: Gender, Culture and Memory*, Hampshire: Palgrave, 57–59. Joanna Burke examined the silence and trauma of rape more generally. See J. Burke. 2007. *Rape: A History from 1860 to the Present Day*, London: Virago, 429. The diary of a woman living in Berlin as the war ended provided a very important exploration of rape (and the various emotional responses to it, including shame) in German post-war society. Although this book does not explore Jewish women's feelings or experiences at all, it provides an interesting narration of non-Jewish German women's experiences of living in a war-time rape culture. Anonymous. 2005. *A Woman in Berlin*, London: Virago.

65. Michael Nutkiewicz explored the ways in which one man spoke of his experience of being raped in the Holocaust. At the time it occurred, he explained, the man did not experience it as shameful. It occurred in a private space (as opposed to out in the open) and therefore was different, but not shameful. It was only much later, after the war, when no-one else spoke of similar experiences that the man decided not to tell anyone, and began to experience feelings of shame with memories of his experience (which he remembered constantly). Nutkiewicz, 'Shame, Guilt, and Anguish in Holocaust Survivor Testimony', 1–22.
66. Interview with Teacher A of School NYF. A common, inaccurate, thought in Holocaust scholarship is that, because of the Nazi racial purity laws, Nazis did not sexually assault or rape Jewish women. According to Weitzman and Ofer, while many have looked to the Holocaust as a site of extreme sexual assault, this has not necessarily been the case. While 'Jewish women were more likely than men to be subjected to sexual harassment and rape', the 'incidence of rape by the Nazis appears to have been rare . . . based on the diaries and testimonies we have read'. In making this assertion, they fail to take into account that because this was the dominant thought after the war, Jewish women may have felt unable to speak about their experiences and thus have often remained silent. Indeed, they may not have had the language to articulate it. The result of this is that stories of rape and sexual assault remained silenced. Weitzman and Ofer, 'Introduction: The Role of Gender in the Holocaust', 7–8. However, women's stories of being raped have been told: for many examples of Jewish women talking about their experiences of being raped, and their stories being sensitively told, see M. Goldenberg. November 1996. 'Lessons Learned from Gentle Heroism: Women's Holocaust Narratives', *Annals of the American Academy of Political and Social Science* 548, 78–93.
67. Ruth Linn discussed an example of the ways in which, in Israel, stories which complicate the idea of Jews as absolute victims are silenced. R. Linn. 2004. *Escaping Auschwitz: A Culture of Forgetting*, Ithaca, NY: Cornell University Press.
68. The school which mentioned it formally in the curriculum was the school mentioned above which had two pages on women's particular experiences. Curriculum of School MB, 119–20.
69. Interview with Teacher A of School NYC.
70. Interview with Teacher A of School NYE.
71. Interview with Teacher A of School NYB.
72. Interview with Teacher B of School NYB.
73. Interview with Teacher A at School NYA. A similar statement was made by two other teachers. Interview with Teacher A at School NYE and Interview with Teacher A at School NYB.
74. Interview with Teacher A at School NYC.
75. Interview with Teacher A at School NYF.
76. Interview with Teacher A at School NYD.
77. Curriculum of School MB, 120. It is possible, of course, that the 'he' is simply a typographical error.
78. Interview with Teacher A at School NYF.
79. Interview with Teacher A at School NYD.
80. Sander Gilman explored the ways in which the (predominantly male) European Jewish body has been constructed, often as corrupted, weak and lacking. See S. Gilman. 1991. *The Jew's Body*. For various different explorations of constructions of the Jewish body, see H. Eilberg-Schwartz (ed.). 1992. *People of the Body: Jews and Judaism from an Embodied Perspective*, Albany: State University of New York Press.

81. Curriculum of School MB, 161.
82. Interview with Teacher A at School NYF.
83. Curriculum of School ME, 111. This same sentiment is repeated on 119.
84. Ibid., 120. Significantly, socialism and communism, which were also important motivations for Jews' involvement in violent resistance, are not mentioned.
85. Curriculum of School MB, 161.
86. Interview with Teacher A at School NYD. A *mikvah* is a Jewish ritual bath.
87. Tim Cole and Lawrence Langer have both explored the meaning, cultural currency and influence which the story of Anne Frank, and her Diary, has had. Cole, *Selling the Holocaust*, 23–46 and L.L. Langer. 2006. *Using and Abusing the Holocaust*, Bloomington: Indiana University Press, 16–29.
88. For instance, in the curriculum of a co-educational school in Melbourne, an extract from Frank's diary is placed in a section on Spiritual Resistance – highlighting in particular her 'moral courage' – alongside information about a man performing religious practices and men standing up to the SS and dying on their own terms. These are very different gendered forms of resistance. Curriculum of School MB, 131.
89. Hannah Szenes is mentioned in the following curricula: School ME, 124; School MB, 178–9; School NYC, in a project that the students work on. For an exploration of Szenes's 'place of honour in the Israeli pantheon', see J. Tydor Baumel. July 1996. 'The Heroism of Hannah Senesz: An Exercise in Creating Collective National Memory in the State of Israel', *Journal of Contemporary History* 31(3), 521–46.
90. Schools who mention Zivia Lubetkin: School ME, 108; School MB, 147. Schools who mention Rosa Robota: Curriculum of School ME, 131; Curriculum of School MB, 151–153. Both of these women were mentioned as part of a tour of the museum of Lohamei Hagatteot that I went on. The curriculum of School MB also mentions the story of Anna Heilman, who was a member of the Zionist youth movement HaShomer HaTzair before the war, was a courier during the Warsaw Ghetto Uprising and was in Auschwitz, where she was involved in the blowing up of the crematorium, along with, it is noted, Rosa Robota. The page on Heilman concludes by noting, in writing that is in bold, that she survived. It then explains that 'She recalled, "I'm not sure how many people were involved because there was such great secrecy . . . The last order of the day in HaShomer HaTzair was that we were not going to let ourselves be taken alive. We were all going to die, but were not giving our lives for nothing."' There seems to be a hesitancy here on the part of the teacher who compiled this information: Heilman is celebrated for living, but the concluding quote from her seems to suggest that death was seen by her Zionist peers as the correct way to approach possible capture by the Nazis. The message being passed on by the juxtaposition of these two aspects of Heilman's life is uncertain, marked by an anxiety over whether life or death was, in this situation, preferable. Curriculum of School MB, 161.
91. Curriculum of School MB, 178.
92. Ibid.

CONCLUSION

'It's an Unusual Topic You've Chosen'
Negotiating Emplacement through History-Making

> Far from being a neutral exercise in facts and basic truths, the study of history . . . both in school and university, is to some considerable extent a nationalist effort premised on the need to construct a desirable loyalty to and insider's understanding of one's country, tradition and faith.
> —Edward Said, 'Invention, Memory, and Place'

> The 'Jew' is no more defined by Israel than by antisemitic diatribe. The 'Jew' exceeds both determinations, and is to be found, substantively, as this diasporic excess, a historically and culturally changing identity that takes no single form and has no single telos.
> —Judith Butler, *Precarious Life*

This book began its life as an exploration of the ways in which the experiences and lives of Jewish women who lived and died in the Holocaust are taught about in Jewish schools in Melbourne and New York. The questions I was exploring in those early days were focused on the idea that there were certain histories which were not being taught. And, more than that: that there were significant political, historical and emotional reasons for these omissions. In interviews with teachers in Melbourne this seemed to hold true. Some of the teachers expressed astonishment that the question was being asked: why would they talk specifically about women? It was 'an unusual topic', one seemingly outside the boundaries of Holocaust histories.[1] Other teachers were delighted that the question had been raised. It had never occurred to them to do so, but having heard the idea they were open to beginning to rethink the histories of the Holocaust and the peoples who constituted them. Some teachers asked me to send them suggestions of things to read on the subject. The teaching of Holocaust histories, indeed, is a challenging pursuit, and one which we all recognize requires ongoing conversation and change.

And it was in these interviews, as well as in interviews with teachers in New York, that it became apparent that the erasure of women from these histories could not be considered in isolation. If these histories of the Holocaust were to be historicized then they needed to be located within their national histories: both Jewish and Australian/U.S. and in the many spaces in which these overlap and construct each other. It was with this understanding that it became clearer that these teachers and the approaches they took in their teaching about the Holocaust could be understood to be fundamentally anxious and ambivalent, and that these anxieties and ambivalences often operate at the level of the unconscious. And, moreover, that the teachers carry with them an uncertainty about where, precisely, Jews and their Jewish histories can fit into the worlds and nations in which they live. The teachers want (sometimes desperately) to be a part of the worlds in which they live, but the very histories they are narrating tell them a different story, one which is dominated by violent and traumatic displacement. These stories, in many ways, produce impossibilities. As many of the teachers understand it, the history of Jews in the West – and in the Diaspora more generally – is a story of displacement which leads to persecution. There is a saying within some Jewish cultures today, that each Jewish festival consists of a narrative of 'they tried to kill us, they failed, let's eat'. It is said as a joke, but it rings true as a reminder of a seemingly precarious position. How to be in a world, how to write histories of a world, in which the recurring story is one of death and survival? How to be in a world where this is not ancient history, but the recent past and in the eyes of many the continuing future?

The histories which I have examined in this book are deeply troubled and troubling. At times it felt like the anxiety was overwhelming, or excessive. The teachers know that they need to convey something of the Holocaust – they want their students to *know* what happened – but they themselves are not certain of what can be known and what meanings can be made of this traumatic past. But, nevertheless, they narrate these histories of what happened, as they surely must. In their effort to negotiate their anxieties they often produce all-encompassing, totalizing histories. They create histories which have the potential to do the work of producing emplacement. These are histories which often do not historicize, which do not openly speak of their historical, political and national contexts. This is, in many ways, completely understandable. The teachers are working within the confines of the modernity in which we all live, and which restricts all of us (in different ways). I hope that within the text of this book I have pointed to the ways that the constructions of Holocaust pedagogies are – almost inevitably – messy, difficult, and contradictory. They are also, it must be repeated, guided by particular sets of politics and ideologies. Through an examination of the interactions between the structures in the general society, and those within Jewish communities, which produce these historiographies, I hope I have demonstrated some of the impossibilities at the heart of Holocaust education, and provided a sense of the politics which guides the teachings explored. We all must grapple with these impossibilities, and with these politics, and the histories they produce. Indeed, we must remember that these histories which are being written – and the languages and discourses being used – are incredibly productive.

And so the work of this book has therefore been to try to bring those historical contexts to bear upon the histories of the Holocaust which are being taught in Jewish schools in Melbourne and New York. By beginning with the question of what was not being talked about, I have raised a number of different histories and issues which are not being openly discussed. I have also worked to problematize that which *is* being talked about. I have moved through various facets of education about the Holocaust, exploring the structures of the histories as well as their contents. The settler colonial and Zionist influences upon these teachings have been considered, and the ways in which Jewish women's experiences are taught has been examined. This exploration has been located within the structures of anxiety which seem to dominate many incarnations of twenty-first century Jewishnesses in New York and Melbourne: anxieties about how to be comfortable with difference in the face of societies which are unsettled by one's very own difference. This book has also, hopefully, opened up for discussion the limitations of Western forms of belonging, nationalism, and history-making.

In the process of writing this book, in many ways I have avoided reading and writing about many of the horrors, traumas and violence of the Holocaust. In part, this was intentional: I am not dealing with what happened there, but rather the ways that its history is taught. But when I speak to my friends – those who also attended a Jewish dayschool – many of them comment that the overwhelming memories they have of this education are of being traumatized, and the violence that produces that trauma is perhaps not captured here. And thus, in not truly delving into the violence of the Holocaust in this book, I hope that readers do not feel like the Holocaust has been sanitized. Its horrors, as anyone who has studied it must know, are overwhelming and they are important. Learning how to transmit knowledge of them – to readers and to students – is an ongoing task for us all.

And thus we can ask: why do these teachers teach about the Holocaust? This was a question which I did not ask of them and whose answer we can only guess. But the centrality of the Holocaust to Jewish identities in Melbourne and New York today perhaps gives us a sense of why this heavy task is undertaken. Some of the teachers expressed ambivalence about the centrality of the Holocaust, making comments such as 'why can't you be Jewish because you're Jewish', rather than because of the Holocaust.[2] Other teachers, however, expressed no such qualms, and indeed appeared to dedicate much of themselves to these histories.[3] Regardless of their personal interests and antipathies, these teachers all have a great deal invested in the teaching of the Holocaust. Through their teaching they ensure that something of the Holocaust will be remembered by future generations. For all the anxieties and ambivalences which histories of the Holocaust raise, these teachers do not completely respond with silence. They respond instead with speech. There is much work being undertaken in these histories. Primarily, as we have seen, this is the work of negotiation. A negotiation of what it is to be Jewish and Zionist in these locations of Melbourne and New York, sixty years after the Holocaust. In short, this book explored some ideas of what it is to be, at the beginning of the twenty-first century, a troubled diasporic Zionist Jew with one eye turned towards the past, the other peering hesitantly into the future, and both feet planted in traumatic histories.

It has been the argument of this book that Holocaust education in Jewish schools in Melbourne and New York at the beginning of the twenty-first century is part of a long history of Jews negotiating their place within the modern, Western world. It is not that Jews are separate from that world – for they have always been integral to Western modernity – but rather that being identified, both by themselves and by others, as a separate nation to those in which they live, has required constant negotiation. This has led to anxious feelings: feelings of a desire to belong but also to retain a fundamental difference. I have therefore examined the many ways in which these anxieties are negotiated through the writing and teaching of histories of radical exclusion, exemplified in the overwhelming horrors of the Holocaust. It is through the narration of the histories of the Holocaust that we can identify the ways in which national histories work to constitute group identities. In narrating the groups' past, present and future identities are managed.

We have seen this throughout the book, in the ways in which the shape of the narratives are constructed; in the ways in which Zionist histories influence these understandings of the Holocaust and its aftermath; in the haunting impact which settler colonialism has on what can be remembered alongside the Holocaust; and on the ways in which women, some of the very people at the centre of the events, are allowed to enter into these histories. Through these examples we have been able to catch a glimpse of some of the ways in which a diasporic Jewishness is formulated: through mimicry, memory, ambivalence and anxiety.

It is this which makes the 'diasporic excess' of which Judith Butler writes. The histories and identities which have been discussed are not containable. These identities are movable and mutable; they slip and slide, and become part of a project of formulating responses to feelings and experiences of displacement and unwantedness. The carriers of these identities are constituted as simultaneously permanently out-of-place and living securely at home. There is mimicry and creation as the teachers formulate approaches to Jewishnesses which are both part of long histories and engaged in producing new responses. These are histories which are variously Jewish, non-Jewish, masculine, feminine, Zionist, settler colonial, diasporic, biblical, modern, anxious, certain and all of these categories mixed up together. Indeed, it is in the very struggle to negotiate a place of belonging as Jews in these modern, Western worlds that transformative gendered diasporic Jewish characters, histories, languages and collective memories can be, and are being, created. There is much to be learnt from these histories and struggles.

Notes

1. Interview with Teacher A at School MA.
2. Interview with Teacher B at School MA.
3. Various teachers explained that besides teaching histories of the Holocaust at their schools, they had lectured on it at universities, lead March of the Living trips and New York Heritage Tours, had academic works on Holocaust studies published, and are engaged in ongoing quests for knowledge of what happened. Interviews with Teacher A at School MB, Teachers A and B at School MA, Teacher C at School MA, Teacher A at School NYD, Teacher A at School NYE and Teacher B at School NYB.

Bibliography

Online Sources

Cohen, A. 'Lest We Forget' (12 February 2009). Retrieved 23 February 2009 from http://jewschool.com/2009/02/12/15184/lest-we-forget/.
Betar Australia. Retrieved 8 July 2009 from http://www.betar.org.au/.
Betar U.S.A: Zionist Youth Movement. Retrieved 8 July 2009 from http://www.betar.org/.
Bnei Akiva of the United States and Canada. Retrieved 8 July 2009 from http://www.bneiakiva.org/.
B'nei B'rith Anti-Defamation Commission Inc. 'Jews in Australia' (2009). Retrieved 21 June 2009 from http://www.antidef.org.au/www/309/1001127/displayarticle/1001458.html.
Habonim Dror America: The Labor Zionist Youth Movement. Retrieved 8 July 2009 from http://www.habonimdror.org/.
Habonim Dror Australia. Retrieved 8 July 2009 from http://www.hdoz.com/.
Hashomer Hatzair Australia. Retrieved 8 July 2009 from http://www.hashy.org.au/.
Hier, Rabbi Marvin (enewsletter@wiesenthal.net). 'Passover: A Time To Make A Difference' (28 March 2007). Retrieved 18 December 2014 from http://www.wiesenthal.com/site/apps/nlnet/content2.aspx?c=lsKWLbPJLnF&b=4442245&ct=5852831#.VJJJj4uUekI.
Hineni Youth Australia. Retrieved 8 July 2009 from http://www.hineni.org.au/.
'History: World Union for Progressive Judaism'. Retrieved 31 March 2014 from http://wupj.org/About/history.asp.
Iraq Coalition Casualty Count (2009). Retrieved 21 September 2009 from http://icasualties.org/Iraq/index.aspx.
Katsav, Moshe. 'Address by the President of the State of Israel at the Opening Ceremony for Holocaust Martyrs' and Heroes' Remembrance Day'. *Israel Ministry of Foreign Affairs* (24 April 2006). Retrieved 18 December 2014 from http://www.mfa.gov.il/mfa/aboutisrael/history/holocaust/pages/address%20by%20president%20katsav%20on%20holocaust%20remembrance%20day%2024-apr-2006.aspx.
Liss, "My Cousin Sammy (OR: The Single-Issue Voter: A Portrait)". Retrieved 24 June 2009 from http://sensiblejew.wordpress.com/2009/06/23/my-cousin-sammy-or-the-single-issue-voter-a-portrait/; Retrieved 2 January 2014 from http://galusaustralis.com/2009/06/261/my-cousin-sammy-or-the-single-issue-voter-a-portrait/.
March of the Living. Retrieved 8 August 2008 from http://www.motl.org/.
Netzer Australia. Retrieved 8 July 2009 from http://www.netzer.org.au.
North American Federation of Temple Youth. Retrieved 8 July 2009 from http://www.nfty.org/.
Sensible Jew. 'Michael Fagenblats' Presentation at the Seven Jewish Children Reading' (19 May 2009). Retrieved 21 May 2009 from http://sensiblejew.wordpress.com/2009/05/19/michael-fagenblats-presentation-at-the-seven-jewish-children-reading/.

UJA-Federation of New York. *Jewish Community Study of New York: 2002* (October 2004). Retrieved 21 June 2009 from http://www.ujafedny.org/atf/cf/%7BAD848866-09C4-482C-9277-51A5D9CD6246%7D/JCommStudyHouseholdandPopulation.pdf.
UJA-Federation of New York. 'Part 2: Our Collective Impact'. *Annual Report 2007-2008* (2009). Retrieved 18 December 2014 from http://d4ovttrzyow8g.cloudfront.net/259.pdf.
West End Synagogue: A Reconstructionist Congregation. Retrieved 23 February 2009 from http://www.westendsynagogue.org/reconstructionism.shtml.
Who?, chillul. 'Dov Hikind, Holocaust Denier' (8 June 2009). Retrieved 9 June 2009 from http://jewschool.com/2009/06/08/16576/dov-hikind-holocaust-denier.

Curricula

Education Department at the Museum of Jewish Heritage: A Living Memorial to the Holocaust (2005). 'Shoah Teaching Alternatives in Jewish Education Presents: Guiding Principles for Teaching the Shoah in Jewish Schools', New York.
Curriculum of School MA (2006).
Curriculum of School MB (2006).
Curriculum of School MD (2006).
Curriculum of School ME (2006).
Curriculum of School NYB (2006).
Curriculum of School NYC (2006).
Curriculum of School NYG (2006).
Itinerary for 2007 Australian March of the Living trip.
'David'. March of the Living Education Session. 'Jewish Life in Pre-War Poland' (18 February 2009).
Central Agency for Jewish Education. *March of the Living International (Australia) Study Guide* (2007).

Interviews

Interview with Teacher A at School MA (2 February 2006).
Interview with Teacher B at School MA (2 February 2006).
Interview with Teacher C at School MA (2 February 2006).
Interview with Teacher A at School MB (25 February 2006).
Interview with Teacher A at School MC (27 April 2006).
Interview with Teacher A at School MD (26 April 2006).
Interview with Teacher A at School ME (7 May 2006).
Interview with Teacher A at School NYA (16 November 2006).
Interview with Teacher A at School NYB (10 November 2006).
Interview with Teacher B at School NYB (28 November 2006).
Interview with Teacher A at School NYC (24 October 2006).
Interview with Teacher A at School NYD (26 October 2006).
Interview with Teacher A at School NYE (1 November 2006).
Interview with Teacher A at School NYF (2 November 2006).
Interview with Teacher A at School NYG (20 November 2006).

Newspaper Articles

Hass, A. 'The Holocaust as Political Asset', *Haaretz* (1 May 2007). Retrieved 8 May 2007 from http://www.haaretz.com/hasen/spages/849669.html.
Lev-Ari, S. 'The Gay Man's Guide to Zionist Literature', *Haaretz* (7 June 2007). Retrieved 4 June 2009 from http://www.haaretz.com/hasen/spages/865688.html.
Levin, D. 'Celebrating the Marriage between Australia and Israel', *Australian Jewish News* (5 May 2006), 1.
Ravid, B. 'Deputy Foreign Minister: 1967 borders are Auschwitz borders', *Haaretz* (2 January 2014). Retrieved 3 January 2014 from http://www.haaretz.com/news/diplomacy-defense/1.566644.
'Stage Set for Yom Ha'atzmaut'. *Australian Jewish News* (28 April 2006), 7.
Weltsch, R. 'Wear it With Pride, the Yellow Badge', *Juedische Rundschau* (4 April 1933), 27.
Zwartz, B. 'Holocaust Link Sours Jewish-Muslim Ties', *The Age* (6 February 2009), 1–2.

Personal Communication

Email from Principal A at School NYH (28 November 2006).
Personal communication with Ilana (*madricha* [leader] on March of the Living) (15 July 2007).
Personal communication with Paul Radensky, Museum Educator for High Schools at the Museum of Jewish Heritage: A Living Memorial to the Holocaust (1 November 2006).
Personal communication with Avi, *madrich* with Hanoah Haoved (29 August 2007).

Poems and Songs

Bialik, C.N. *The City of Slaughter*. Retrieved 18 December 2014 from http://faculty.history.umd.edu/BCooperman/NewCity/Slaughter.html.
Golem. *Fresh Off Boat* (JDub Records, 2006). Retrieved 9 September 2009 from http://www.golemrocks.com, or http://www.myspace.com/golemrocks.

Secondary Sources

Adams, P. 'Representation and Sexuality', in P. Adams and E. Cowie (eds), *The Woman in Question: M/F* (London: Verso, 1990), 233–52.
Adams, P. and J. Minson. 'The "Subject" of Feminism', in P. Adams and E. Cowie (eds), *The Woman in Question: M/F* (London: Verso, 1990), 81–101.
Adorno, T. W. *Can One Live after Auschwitz? A Philosophical Reader*, trans. R. Livingstone and Others. Edited by R. Tiedemann (Stanford, CA: Stanford University Press, 2003).
Agamben, G. *Remnants of Auschwitz: The Witness and the Archive* (New York: Zone Books, 1999).
Alba, A. 'Integrity and Relevance: Shaping Holocaust Memory at the Sydney Jewish Museum', *Judaism: A Quarterly Journal of Jewish Life and Thought*, 54 (Winter/Spring 2005), 108–15.

Alcalay, A. *After Jews and Arabs: Remaking Levantine Culture* (Minneapolis: University of Minnesota Press, 1993).
———. 'Exploding Identities: Notes on Ethnicity and Literary History', in J. Boyarin and D. Boyarin (eds), *Jews and Other Differences: The New Jewish Cultural Studies* (Minneapolis: University of Minnesota Press, 1997), 330–44.
Anderson, B. *Imagined Communities: Reflections on the Origin and Spread of Nationalism* (London: Verso, 1983).
Angelides, S. *A History of Bisexuality* (Chicago, IL: University of Chicago Press, 2001).
Anonymous. *A Woman in Berlin* (London: Virago, 2005).
Antler, J. *You Never Call! You Never Write! A History of the Jewish Mother* (New York: Oxford University Press, 2007).
Attwood, B. *The Making of the Aborigines* (Sydney: Allen & Unwin, 1989).
Auron, Y. *The Pain of Knowledge: Holocaust and Genocide Issues in Education*, trans. Ruth Ruzga (New Brunswick, NJ: Transaction Publishers, 2005).
Aviv, C. and D. Shneer. *New Jews: The End of the Jewish Diaspora* (New York: New York University Press, 2005).
———. 'Traveling Jews, Creating Memory: Eastern Europe, Israel, and the Diaspora Business', in J.M. Gerson and D.L. Wolf (eds), *Sociology Confronts the Holocaust: Memories and Identities in Jewish Diasporas* (Durham, NC: Duke University Press, 2007), 67–83.
Baer, E.R. and M. Goldenberg (eds). *Experience and Expression: Women, the Nazis, and the Holocaust* (Detroit, MI: Wayne State University Press, 2003).
Bal, M., J. Crewe and L. Spitzer (eds). *Acts of Memory: Cultural Recall in the Present* (Hanover, NH: University Press of New England, 1999).
Banivanua-Mar, T. *Violence and Colonial Dialogue: The Australian-Pacific Indentured Labor Trade* (Honolulu: University of Hawai'i Press, 2007).
Barker, J. (ed.). *Sovereignty Matters: Locations of Contestation and Possibility in Indigenous Struggles for Self-Determination* (Lincoln: University of Nebraska Press, 2005).
Bartrop, P.R. 'Living within the Frontier: Early Colonial Australia, Jews, and Aborigines', in S.L. Gilman and M. Shain (eds), *Jewries at the Frontier: Accommodation, Identity, Conflict* (Urbana: University of Illinois Press, 1999), 91–110.
Bauer, Y. *Rethinking the Holocaust* (New Haven, CT: Yale University Press, 2001).
Bauman, Z. 'Exit Visas and Entry Tickets: Paradoxes of Jewish Assimilation,' *Telos* 77 (Fall 1988), 45–78.
———. *Modernity and the Holocaust* (Cambridge: Polity Press, 1989).
———. *Modernity and Ambivalence* (Cambridge: Polity Press, 1991).
Baumel, J.T. 'The Heroism of Hannah Senesz: An Exercise in Creating Collective National Memory in the State of Israel,' *Journal of Contemporary History* 31(3) (July 1996), 521–46.
Behrendt, L. 'Home: The Importance of Place to the Dispossessed', *South Atlantic Quarterly* 108(1) (Winter 2009), 71–85.
Ben-David, O. '*Tiyul* (Hike) as an Act of Consecration of Space', in E. Ben-Ari and Y. Bilu (eds), *Grasping Land: Space and Place in Contemporary Israeli Discourse and Experience* (Albany: State University of New York Press, 1997), 129–45.
Ben-Moshe, D. 'The End of Unconditional Love: The Future of Zionism in Australian Jewish Life', in M. Fagenblat, M. Landau and N. Wolski (eds), *New under the Sun: Jewish Australians on Religion, Politics and Culture* (Melbourne: Black Inc., 2006), 108–25.
Benn, M. *Madonna and Child: Towards a New Politics of Motherhood* (London: Jonathan Cape, 1998).
Berenbaum, M. *After Tragedy and Triumph: Essays in Modern Jewish Thought and the American Experience* (Cambridge: Cambridge University Press, 1990).

———. *The World Must Know: The History of the Holocaust as Told in the United States Holocaust Memorial Museum*, 2nd edition (Washington, D.C.: United States Holocaust Memorial Museum, 2006).
Berman, J.E. *Holocaust Remembrance in Australian Jewish Communities, 1945-2000* (Crawley, WA: University of Western Australia Press, 2001).
Bernstein, M.A. *Foregone Conclusions: Against Apocalyptic History* (Berkeley: University of California Press, 1994).
Bhabha, H.K. *The Location of Culture* (London: Routledge, 1994).
———. 'Joking Aside: The Idea of a Self-Critical Community', in B. Cheyette and L. Marcus (eds), *Modernity, Culture and 'the Jew'* (Cambridge: Polity Press, 1998), xv–xx.
Biale, D. *Power and Powerlessness in Jewish History* (New York: Schocken Books, 1986).
———. 'The Melting Pot and Beyond: Jews and the Politics of American Identity', in D. Biale, M. Galchinsky and S. Heschel (eds), *Insider/Outsider: American Jews and Multiculturalism* (Berkeley: University of California Press, 1998), 17–33.
Biale, D. (ed.). *Cultures of the Jews: A New History* (New York: Schocken Books, 2002).
Biale, D., M. Galchinsky and S. Heschel (eds). *Insider/Outsider: American Jews and Multiculturalism* (Berkeley: University of California Press, 1998).
Biale, D., M. Galchinsky and S. Heschel. 'Introduction: The Dialectic of Jewish Enlightenment', in D. Biale, M. Galchinsky and S. Heschel (eds), *Insider/Outsider: American Jews and Multiculturalism* (Berkeley: University of California Press, 1998), 1–13.
Birch, T. '"History Is Never Bloodless": Getting It Wrong after One Hundred Years of Federation', *Australian Historical Studies* 33(118) (2002), 42–53.
———. '"The Invisible Fire": Indigenous Sovereignty, History and Responsibility', in A. Moreton-Robinson (ed.), *Sovereign Subjects: Indigenous Sovereignty Matters* (Crows Nest, NSW: Allen & Unwin, 2007), 105–17.
Blakeney, M. 'The Australian Jewish Community and Postwar Mass Immigration from Europe', in W.D. Rubinstein (ed.), *Jews in the Sixth Continent* (Sydney: Allen & Unwin, 1987), 322–35.
Bloch, B. 'Unsettling Zionism: Diasporic Consciousness and Australian Jewish Identities' (PhD thesis, University of Western Sydney, 2005).
Bloch, I. 'Right Choice? Definitely. Right Reasons? It's Complicated', *Galus Australis* (3 February 2013). Retrieved 22 February 2013 from http://galusaustralis.com/2013/02/6767/right-choice-definitely-right-reasons-its-complicated/.
Bold, C., R. Knowles and B. Leach. 'Feminist Memorializing and Cultural Countermemory: The Case of Marianne's Park', *Signs* 28(1) (Autumn 2002), 125–48.
Boyarin, D. 'Masada or Yavneh? Gender and the Arts of Jewish Resistance', in J. Boyarin and D. Boyarin (eds), *Jews and Other Differences: The New Jewish Cultural Studies* (Minneapolis: University of Minnesota Press, 1997), 306–29.
———. *Unheroic Conduct: The Rise of Heterosexuality and the Invention of the Jewish Man* (Berkeley: University of California Press, 1997).
———. 'The Colonial Drag: Zionism, Gender, and Mimicry', in F. Afzal-Khan and K. Seshadri-Crooks (eds), *The Pre-Occupation of Postcolonial Studies* (Durham, NC: Duke University Press, 2000), 234–65.
———. 'Homophobia and the Postcoloniality of the "Jewish Science"', in D. Boyarin, D. Itzkovitz and A. Pellegrini (eds), *Queer Theory and the Jewish Question* (New York: Columbia University Press, 2003), 166–98.
Boyarin, D. and J. Boyarin. 'Diaspora: Generation and the Ground of Jewish Identity', *Critical Inquiry* 19(4) (Summer 1993), 693–725.

Boyarin, D., D. Itzkovitz and A. Pellegrini. 'Strange Bedfellows: An Introduction', in D. Boyarin, D. Itzkovitz and A. Pellegrini (eds), *Queer Theory and the Jewish Question* (New York: Columbia University Press, 2003), 1-18.
Boyarin, J. 'Reading Exodus into History', *New Literary History* 23(3) (Summer 1992), 523-54.
———. *Storm from Paradise: The Politics of Jewish Memory* (Minneapolis: University of Minnesota Press, 1992).
———. *Palestine and Jewish History: Criticism at the Borders of Ethnography* (Minneapolis: University of Minnesota Press, 1996).
Boyarin, J. and D. Boyarin (eds). *Jews and Other Differences: The New Jewish Cultural Studies* (Minneapolis: University of Minnesota Press, 1997).
Brenner, M. *Zionism: A Brief History*, trans. Shelley Frisch (Princeton, NJ: Markus Wiener Publishers, 2003).
Brenner, M. and G. Reuveni (eds). *Emancipation through Muscles: Jews and Sports in Europe* (Lincoln: University of Nebraska Press, 2006).
Bridenthal, R., A. Grossmann and M. Kaplan (eds). *When Biology Became Destiny: Women in Weimar and Nazi Germany* (New York: Monthly Review Press, 1984).
Brodkin, K. *How Jews Became White Folks and What That Says About Race in America* (New Brunswick, NJ: Rutgers University Press, 1998).
Brown, W. *Regulating Aversion: Tolerance in the Age of Identity and Empire* (Princeton, NJ: Princeton University Press, 2006).
Browning, C.R. *Ordinary Men: Reserve Police Battalion 101 and the Final Solution in Poland* (New York: Harper Collins Publishers, 1992).
Bucur, M. 'An Archipelago of Stories: Gender History in Eastern Europe', *American Historical Review* 113(5) (December 2008), 1375-389.
Burg, A. *The Holocaust Is Over; We Must Rise from Its Ashes* (New York: Palgrave Macmillan, 2008).
Burke, J. *Rape: A History from 1860 to the Present Day* (London: Virago, 2007).
Butler, J. *Gender Trouble: Feminism and the Subversion of Identity* (New York: Routledge, 1990).
———. 'Contingent Foundations: Feminism and the Question of "Postmodernism"', in J. Butmer and J.W. Scott (eds), *Feminists Theorize the Political* (New York: Routledge, 1992), 3-21.
———. *Bodies That Matter: On the Discursive Limits of 'Sex'* (New York: Routledge, 1993).
———. 'Universality in Culture', in J. Cohen (ed.), *For Love of Country: Debating the Limits of Patriotism* (Boston, MA: Beacon Press, 1996), 45-52.
———. *Precarious Life: The Powers of Mourning and Violence* (London: Verso, 2004).
Canning, K. *Gender History in Practice: Historical Perspectives on Bodies, Class & Citizenship* (Ithaca, NY: Cornell University Press, 2006).
Cantor, A. *Jewish Women/Jewish Men: The Legacy of Patriarchy in Jewish Life* (San Francisco, CA: Harper San Francisco, 1995).
Carr, D. 'Narrative and the Real World: An Argument for Continuity', in B. Fay, P. Pomper and R.T. Vann (eds), *History and Theory: Contemporary Readings* (Malden, MA: Blackwell Publishers, 1998), 137-52.
Caruth, C. *Unclaimed Experience: Trauma, Narrative, and History* (Baltimore, MD: Johns Hopkins University Press, 1996).
Castan, M. 'Memory and Mabo: Advancing Aboriginal Justice', in M. Fagenblat, M. Landau and N. Wolski (eds), *New under the Sun: Jewish Australians on Religion, Politics and Culture* (Melbourne: Black Inc., 2006), 325-33.
de Certeau, M. *The Practice of Everyday Life* (Berkeley: University of California Press, 1984).

Cerwonka, A. *Native to the Nation: Disciplining Bodies and Landscapes in Australia* (Minneapolis: University of Minnesota Press, 2004).
Chabon, M. *The Yiddish Policeman's Union* (London: Harper Perennial, 2007).
Chakrabarty, D. *Habitations of Modernity: Essays in the Wake of Subaltern Studies* (Chicago, IL: University of Chicago Press, 2002).
———. *Provincializing Europe: Postcolonial Thought and Historical Difference* (Princeton, NJ: Princeton University Press, 2008).
Chatterjee, P. *The Nation and Its Fragments: Colonial and Postcolonial Histories* (Princeton, NJ: Princeton University Press, 1993).
———. *The Politics of the Governed: Reflections on Popular Politics in Most of the World* (Delhi: Permanent Black, 2004).
Cheyette, B. *Diasporas of the Mind: Jewish and Postcolonial Writing and the Nightmare of History* (New Haven, CT: Yale University Press, 2013).
Churchill, W. *A Little Matter of Genocide: Holocaust and Denial in the Americas 1492 to the Present* (San Francisco, CA: City Lights Books, 1997).
Clark, A. 'Teaching the Nation: Politics and Pedagogy in Australian History' (PhD thesis, University of Melbourne, 2004).
Clifford, J. *Routes: Travel and Translation in the Late Twentieth Century* (Cambridge, MA: Harvard University Press, 1997).
Cohen, R. *Global Diasporas: An Introduction* (London: UCL Press, 1997).
Cole, T. *Selling the Holocaust: From Auschwitz to Schindler, How History Is Bought, Packaged, and Sold* (New York: Routledge, 1999).
Cousins, M. 'The Practice of Historical Investigation', in D. Attridge, G. Bennington and R. Young (eds), *Post-Structuralism and the Question of History* (Cambridge: Cambridge University Press, 1982), 126–36.
Cowie, E. 'Woman as Sign', in P. Adams and E. Cowie (eds), *The Woman in Question: M/F* (London: Verso, 1990), 117–33.
Crewe, J. 'Recalling Adamastor: Literature as Cultural Memory in "White" South Africa', in M. Bal, J. Crewe and L. Spitzer (eds), *Acts of Memory: Cultural Recall in the Present* (Hanover, NH: University Press of New England, 1999), 75–86.
Crowe, D.M. *The Holocaust: Roots, History, and Aftermath* (Boulder, CO: Westview Press, 2008).
Cuddihy, J.M. *The Ordeal of Civility: Freud, Marx, Lévi-Strauss, and the Jewish Struggle with Modernity* (New York: Basic Books, 2008).
Curthoys, A. 'Genocide in Tasmania: The History of an Idea', in A. Dirk Moses (ed.), *Empire, Colony, Genocide* (New York: Berghahn Books, 2008), 229–52.
Curthoys, A. and J. Docker. *Is History Fiction?* (Sydney: UNSW Press, 2006).
Dally, A. *Inventing Motherhood: The Consequences of an Ideal* (London: Burnett Books, 1982).
Dalsheim, J. 'Settler Nationalism, Collective Memories of Violence and the "Uncanny Other"', *Social Identities* 10(2) (2004), 151–70.
Davis, N.Z. and R. Starn. 'Introduction', *Representations* 26 (Spring 1989), 1–6.
Dawidowicz, L.S. *The War Against the Jews, 1933-1945* (New York: Seth Press, 1975).
Delbo, C. *Auschwitz and After*, trans. Rosette C. Lamont (New Haven, CT: Yale University Press, 1995).
Derrida, J. *Specters of Marx: The State of the Debt, the Work of Mourning, and the New International*, trans. Peggy Kamuf (New York: Routledge, 1994).
———. 'A Testimony Given . . . ', in E. Weber (ed.), *Questioning Judaism* (Stanford, CA: Stanford University Press, 2004), 39–58.

Diner, D. 'The Destruction of Narrativity: The Holocaust in Historical Discourse', in M. Postone and E. Santner (eds), *Catastrophe and Meaning: The Holocaust and the Twentieth Century* (Chicago, IL: University of Chicago Press, 2003), 67–80.
Diner, H.R. *The Jews of the United States* (Berkeley: University of California Press, 2004).
D'Innocenzo, M. and J.P. Sirefman (eds). *Immigration and Ethnicity: American Society – 'Melting Pot' or 'Salad Bowl'* (Westport, CT: Greenwood Press, 1992).
Docker, J. *1492: The Poetics of Diaspora* (London: Continuum, 2001).
Edelman, L. *No Future: Queer Theory and the Death Drive* (Durham, NC: Duke University Press, 2004).
Efron, J.M. 'From Mitteleuropa to the Middle East: Orientalism through a Jewish Lens', *The Jewish Quarterly Review* 94(3) (Summer 2004), 490–520.
Efron, J., S. Weitzman, M. Lehmann and J. Holo. *The Jews: A History* (Upper Saddle River, NJ: Pearson Prentice Hall, 2009).
Eilberg-Schwartz, H. (ed.). *People of the Body: Jews and Judaism from an Embodied Perspective* (Albany: State University of New York Press, 1992).
Eisen, A.M. 'Rethinking Jewish Modernity', *Jewish Social Studies* 1(1) (Fall 1994), 1–21.
Eliach, Y. *Hasidic Tales of the Holocaust* (New York: Oxford University Press, 1982).
Ellinghaus, K. *Taking Assimilation to Heart: Marriages of White Women and Indigenous Men in the United States and Australia, 1887-1937* (Lincoln: University of Nebraska Press, 2006).
Elliott, D. 'The Three Ages of Joan Scott', *American Historical Review* 113(5) (December 2008), 1390–403.
Endelman, T.M. 'Memories of Jewishness: Jewish Converts and Their Jewish Pasts', in E. Carlebach, J.M. Efron and D.N. Myers (eds), *Jewish History and Jewish Memory* (Waltham, MA: Brandeis University Press, 1998), 311–29.
Englander, N. *For the Relief of Unbearable Urges* (London: Faber and Faber, 2000).
———. *What We Talk About When We Talk About Anne Frank: Stories* (New York: Alfred A. Knopf, 2012).
Epstein, J. 'Remember to Forget: The Problem of Traumatic Cultural Memory', in J. Epstein and L.H. Lefkovitz (eds), *Shaping Losses: Cultural Memory and the Holocaust* (Urbana: University of Illinois Press, 2001), 186–204.
Eschebach, I. 'Engendered Oblivion: Commemorating Jewish Inmates at the Ravensbruek Memorial 1945-95', in J. Tydor Baumel and T. Cohen (eds), *Gender, Place and Memory in the Modern Jewish Experience: Re-Placing Ourselves* (London: Vallentine Mitchell, 2003), 126–42.
Evans, J. 'Safer as Subjects Than Citizens: Privilege and Exclusion in the Transition to Nationhood in Australia and Natal', in T. Banivanua Mar and J. Evans (eds), *Writing Colonial Histories: Comparative Perspectives* (Melbourne: History Department, The University of Melbourne, 2002), 165–83.
Fallace, T.D. *The Emergence of Holocaust Education in American Schools* (New York: Palgrave Macmillan, 2008).
Faye, E. 'Psychoanalysis and the Barred Subject of Feminist History', *Australian Feminist Studies* 22 (1995), 77–97.
———. 'Missing the "Real" Trace of Trauma: How the Second Generation Remember the Holocaust', *American Imago* 58(2) (2001), 525–44.
———. 'Being Jewish after Auschwitz: Writing Modernity's Shame', *Australian Feminist Studies* 18(42) (November 2003), 245–59.
Feingold, H.L. 'How Unique Is the Holocaust?', in A. Grobman and D. Landes (eds), *Genocide: Critical Issues of the Holocaust* (Los Angeles: The Simon Wiesenthal Center, 1983), 397–401.

Feldman, J. 'Marking the Boundaries of the Enclave: Defining the Israeli Collective through the Poland "Experience"', *Israel Studies* 7(2) (Summer 2002), 84–114.
Feldman, Y.S. 'Hebrew Gender and Zionist Ideology: The Palmach Trilogy of Netiva Ben Yehuda', *Prooftexts* 20(1 & 2) (Winter/Spring 2000), 139–57.
Felman, S. and D. Laub. *Testimony: Crises of Witnessing in Literature, Psychoanalysis, and History* (New York: Routledge, 1992).
Flanzbaum, H. (ed.). *The Americanization of the Holocaust* (Baltimore, MD: Johns Hopkins University Press, 1999).
Foer, J.S. *Everything Is Illuminated* (New York: Penguin Books, 2002).
———. *Extremely Loud and Incredibly Close* (Boston, MA: Houghton Mifflin, 2005).
Forth, C.E. *The Dreyfus Affair and the Crisis of French Manhood* (Baltimore, MD: Johns Hopkins University Press, 2004).
Foucault, M. *The History of Sexuality: Volume One: An Introduction* (London: Penguin, 1978).
———. *Power/Knowledge: Selected Interviews and Other Writings 1972-1977*, edited by C. Gordon, trans. C. Gordon, L. Marshall, J. Mepham and K. Soper (Brighton: Harvester Press, 1980).
Francisco, J. *Far from Zion: Jews, Diaspora, Memory* (Stanford, CA: Stanford University Press, 2006).
Frankel, J. 'Assimilation and the Jews in Nineteenth-Century Europe: Towards a New Historiography?', in J. Frankel and S.J. Zipperstein (eds), *Assimilation and Community: The Jews in Nineteenth-Century Europe* (Cambridge: Cambridge University Press, 1992), 1–37.
Frankenberg, R. *White Women, Race Matters: The Social Construction of Whiteness* (Minneapolis: University of Minnesota Press, 1993).
Frankenberg, R. (ed.). *Displacing Whiteness: Essays in Social and Cultural Criticism* (Durham, NC: Duke University Press, 1997).
Freud, S. *The Problem of Anxiety*, trans. Henry Alden Bunker (New York: The Psychoanalytic Press and W.W. Norton & Company Inc., 1936).
———. 'The Uncanny', in J. Strachey (ed.), *The Standard Edition of the Complete Psychological Works of Sigmund Freud Vol. XVII* (London: Hogarth Press, 1955), 219–52.
———. 'Screen Memories', in J. Strachey (ed.), *The Standard Edition of the Complete Psychological Works of Sigmund Freud, Vol. III* (London: Hogarth Press, 1986), 303–22.
Friedländer, S. (ed.). *Probing the Limits of Representation: Nazism and the 'Final Solution'* (Cambridge, MA: Harvard University Press, 1992).
Friedländer, S. *Memory, History, and the Extermination of the Jews of Europe* (Bloomington: Indiana University Press, 1993).
———. *Nazi Germany and the Jews, Vol. I: The Years of Persecution, 1933-1939* (New York: Harper Perennial, 1997).
Fuchs, E. (ed.). *Women and the Holocaust* (Lanham, MD: University Press of America, Inc., 1999).
Funkenstein, A. 'History, Counterhistory, and Narrative', in S. Friedländer (ed.), *Probing the Limits of Representation: Nazism and the 'Final Solution'* (Cambridge, MA: Harvard University Press, 1992), 66–81.
———. *Perceptions of Jewish History* (Berkeley: University of California Press, 1993).
———. 'The Dialectics of Assimilation', *Jewish Social Studies* 1(2) (Winter 1995), 1–14.
Fuss, D. *Essentially Speaking: Feminism, Nature & Difference*, (New York: Routledge, 1989).
Galchinsky, M. 'Scattered Seeds: A Dialogue of Diasporas', in D. Biale, M. Galchinsky and S. Heschel (eds), *Insider/Outsider: American Jews and Multiculturalism* (Berkeley: University of California Press, 1998), 185–211.

Garber, Z. *Shoah: The Paradigmatic Genocide. Essays in Exegesis and Eisegesis* (Lanham, MD: University Press of America, 1994).
Gelski, S. and J. Wajsenberg. 'Teaching the Holocaust Today', in K. Kwiet and J. Matthaus (eds), *Contemporary Responses to the Holocaust* (Westport, CT: Praeger, 2004), 219–47.
Ghosh, A. *In an Antique Land* (New York: A.A. Knopf, 1993).
Gil, I. 'Teaching the Shoah in History Classes in Israeli High Schools', *Israel Studies* 14(2) (Summer 2009), 1–25.
———. 'The Shoah in Israeli Collective Memory: Changes in Meanings and Protagonists', *Modern Judaism* 32(1) (February 2012), 76-101.
Gillis, J.R. 'Memory and Identity: The History of a Relationship', in J.R. Gillis (ed.), *Commemorations: The Politics of National Identity* (Princeton, NJ: Princeton University Press, 1994), 3–24.
Gilman, S.L. *Jewish Self-Hatred: Anti-Semitism and the Hidden Language of the Jews* (Baltimore, MD: Johns Hopkins University Press, 1986).
———. *The Jew's Body* (New York: Routledge, 1991).
———. 'Introduction: The Frontier as a Model for Jewish History', in S.L. Gilman and M. Shain (eds), *Jewries at the Frontier: Accommodation, Identity, Conflict* (Urbana: University of Illinois Press, 1999), 1–25.
———. 'Is Life Beautiful? Can the Shoah Be Funny? Some Thoughts on Recent and Older Films', *Critical Inquiry* 26(2) (Winter 2000), 279–308.
———. *Multiculturalism and the Jews* (New York: Routledge, 2006).
Gilroy, P. *There Ain't No Black in the Union Jack: The Cultural Politics of Race and Nation* (London: Routledge Classics, 2002).
Ginzburg, C. 'Just One Witness', in S. Friedländer (ed.), *Probing the Limits of Representation: Nazism and the 'Final Solution'* (Cambridge, MA: Harvard University Press, 1992), 82–96.
Goldberg, D.T. *Racial Subjects: Writing on Race in America* (New York: Routledge, 1997).
Goldberg, J.J. *Jewish Power: Inside the American Jewish Establishment* (Reading, MA: Addison-Wesley Publishing Company, Inc., 1996).
Goldenberg, M. 'Lessons Learned from Gentle Heroism: Women's Holocaust Narratives', *Annals of the American Academy of Political and Social Science* 548 (November 1996), 78–93.
Goldenberg, M. and A.H. Shapiro. 'Introduction', in M. Goldenberg and A.H. Shapiro (eds), *Different Horrors/Same Hell: Gender and the Holocaust* (Seattle: University of Washington Press, 2013), 3–9.
Goldstein, A. 'Where the Nation Takes Place: Proprietary Regimes, Antistatism, and U.S. Settler Colonialism', *South Atlantic Quarterly* 107(4) (Fall 2008), 833–61.
Goldstein, E.L. *The Price of Whiteness: Jews, Race, and American Identity* (Princeton, NJ: Princeton University Press, 2006).
Gordon, L. 'Response to Scott', *Signs* 15(4) (Summer 1990), 852–53.
———. 'Review of *Gender and the Politics of History* by Joan Wallach Scott', *Signs* 15(4) (Summer 1990), 853–58.
Gornick, V. 'Outsider No Longer', *Review: The Australian Financial Review* (12 June 2009), 1–2, 10–11.
Gotzmann, A., and C. Wiese. 'Introduction', in A. Gotzmann and C. Wiese (eds), *Modern Judaism and Historical Consciousness: Identities, Encounters, Perspectives* (Boston, MA: Leiden, 2007), xiii–xxii.
Gourevitch, P. 'Behold Now Behemoth', *Harper's Magazine* 287(1718) (July 1993), 55–62.
Gramsci, A. *Selections from the Prison Notebooks of Antonio Gramsci*, trans. and ed. Q. Hoare and G. Nowell Smith (New York: International Publishers, 1971).

Gruen, E.S. 'Diaspora and Homeland', in H. Wettstein (ed.), *Diasporas and Exiles: Varieties of Jewish Identity* (Berkeley: University of California Press, 2002), 18–46.
Haebich, A. 'Imagining Assimilation', *Australian Historical Studies* 33(118) (2002), 61–70.
Hage, G. *White Nation: Fantasies of White Supremacy in a Multicultural Society* (Annandale, NSW: Pluto Press, 1998).
———. *Against Paranoid Nationalism: Searching for Hope in a Shrinking Society* (Annandale, NSW: Pluto Press, 2003).
Halbwachs, M. *On Collective Memory*, trans. Lewis A. Coser (Chicago, IL: University of Chicago Press, 1992).
Hall, C. 'Gender, Nations and Nationalisms', in E. Mortimer (ed), *People, Nation and State: The Meaning of Ethnicity and Nationalism* (London: I.B. Tauris Publishers, 1999), 45–55.
Hall, S. 'The State in Question', in G. McLennan, D. Held and S. Hall (eds), *The Idea of the Modern State* (Milton Keynes: Open University Press, 1987), 1–28.
Hall, S., B. Lumley and G. McLennan. 'Politics and Ideology: Gramsci', in University of Birmingham Centre for Contemporary Cultural Studies (ed.), *On Ideology* (London: Hutchinson & Co., 1977), 45–76.
Hansen, M.B. '"Schindler's List" is Not "Shoah": The Second Commandment, Popular Modernism and Public Memory', *Critical Inquiry* 22(2) (Winter 1996), 292–312.
Healy, C. *From the Ruins of Colonialism: History as Social Memory* (Cambridge: Cambridge University Press, 1997).
———. *Forgetting Aborigines* (Sydney: UNSW Press, 2008).
Heineman, E.D. 'Sexuality and Nazism: The Doubly Unspeakable?' *Journal of the History of Sexuality* 11(1/2) (January/April 2002), 22–66.
Herbermann, N. *The Blessed Abyss: Inmate #6582 in Ravensbrück Concentration Camp for Women*, trans. H. Baer, ed. H. Baer and E.R. Baer (Detroit, MI: Wayne State University Press, 2000).
Hershatter, G. and W. Zheng. 'Chinese History: A Useful Category of Gender Analysis', *American Historical Review* 113(5) (December 2008), 1404–421.
Herzl, T. *Diaries*, edited by M. Lowenthal (New York: Dial Press, 1956).
Heschel, S. 'Jewish Studies as Counterhistory', in D. Biale, M. Galchinsky and S. Heschel (eds), *Insider/Outsider: American Jews and Multiculturalism* (Berkeley: University of California Press, 1998), 101–15.
Hilberg, R. *The Destruction of the European Jews* (New York: New Viewpoints, 1973).
Hing, B.O. *To Be an American: Cultural Pluralism and the Rhetoric of Assimilation* (New York: New York University Press, 1997).
Hirsch, M. *Family Frames: Photography, Narrative and Postmemory* (Cambridge, MA: Harvard University Press, 1997).
Hirsch, M. and L. Spitzer. '"We Would Not Have Come Without You": Generation of Nostalgia', in K. Hodgkin and S. Radsteon (eds), *Constested Pasts: The Politics of Memory* (London: Routledge, 2003), 79–95.
———. 'Testimonial Objects: Memory, Gender, and Transmission', *Poetics Today* 27(2) (Summer 2006), 353–83.
Hobsbawm, E. 'The Revival of Narrative: Some Comments', in G. Roberts (ed.), *The History and Narrative Reader* (London: Routledge, 2001), 299–304.
Hogan, J. *Gender, Race and National Identity: Nations of Flesh and Blood* (New York: Routledge, 2009).
hooks, b. *Black Looks: Race and Representation* (Boston, MA: South End Press, 1992).
Horowitz, S.R. 'Gender, Genocide, and Jewish Memory', *Prooftexts: A Journal of Jewish Literary History* 20(1–2) (Winter/Spring 2000), 158–90.

Hyman, P.E. *Gender and Assimilation in Modern Jewish History: The Roles and Representation of Women* (Seattle: University of Washington Press, 1995).

———. 'Gender and the Shaping of Modern Jewish Identities', *Jewish Social Studies* 8(2–3) (2002), 153–61.

Iggers, G.G., and Q.E. Wang. *A Global History of Modern Historiography* (Harlow, U.K: Pearson Education Limited, 2008).

Janiewski, D. 'Gendering, Racializing and Classifying: Settler Colonization in the United States, 1590-1990', in D. Stasiulis and N. Yuval-Davis (eds), *Unsettling Settler Societies: Articulation of Gender, Race, Ethnicity and Class* (London: SAGE Publications, 1995), 132–60.

Jay, M. 'Of Plots, Witnesses, and Judgements', in S. Friedländer (ed.), *Probing the Limits of Representation: Nazism and the 'Final Solution'* (Cambridge, MA: Harvard University Press, 1992), 97–107.

Jupp, J. *From White Australia to Woomera: The Story of Australian Immigration* (Cambridge: Cambridge University Press, 2002).

Kahane, C. 'Dark Mirrors: A Feminist Reflection on Holocaust Narrative and the Maternal Metaphor', in E. Bronfen and M. Kavka (eds), *Feminist Consequences: Theory for the New Century* (New York: Columbia University Press, 2001), 161–88.

Kaplan, D.E. *American Reform Judaism: An Introduction* (New Brunswick, NJ: Rutgers University Press, 2003).

Kaplan, M.A. *The Making of the Jewish Middle Class: Women, Family, and Identity in Imperial Germany* (New York: Oxford University Press, 1991).

———. 'Keeping Calm and Weathering the Storm: Jewish Women's Responses to Daily Life in Nazi Germany, 1933-1939', in D. Ofer and L.J. Weitzman (eds), *Women in the Holocaust* (New Haven, CT: Yale University Press, 1998), 39–54.

Kaplan, M.M. *Judaism as a Civilization: Toward a Reconstruction of American-Jewish Life* (Philadelphia: The Jewish Publication Society of America and the Reconstructionist Press, 1981).

Kaplan, T. 'Reversing the Shame and Gendering the Memory', *Signs* 28(1) (Autumn 2002), 179–99.

Karon, T. 'Can the Jewish People Survive without an Enemy?', *Time* (1 January 2009). Retrieved 1 June 2009 from http://www.time.com/time/printout/0,8816,1869325,00.html.

Katz, E. and J. Ringelheim (eds). *Proceedings of the Conference on Women Surviving the Holocaust* (New York: Institute for Research in History, 1983).

Katz, J. *Out of the Ghetto: The Social Background of Jewish Emancipation, 1770-1870* (Cambridge, MA: Harvard University Press, 1973).

Katz, S.T. 'The Uniqueness of the Holocaust: The Historical Dimension', in A.S. Rosenbaum (ed.), *Is the Holocaust Unique? Perspectives on Comparative Genocide* (Boulder, CO: Westview Press, 1996), 19–38.

Kaufman, D.R. 'Post-Holocaust Memory: Some Gendered Reflections', in J.T. Baumel and T. Cohen (eds), *Gender, Place and Memory in the Modern Jewish Experience: Re-Placing Ourselves* (London: Vallentine Mitchell, 2003), 187–96.

———. 'Post-Memory and Post-Holocaust Jewish Identity Narratives', in J.M. Gerson and D.L. Wolf (eds), *Sociology Confronts the Holocaust: Memories and Identities in Jewish Diasporas* (Durham, NC: Duke University Press, 2007), 39–54.

Kaye/Kantrowitz, M. *The Colors of Jews: Racial Politics and Radical Diasporism* (Bloomington: Indiana University Press, 2007).

von Kellenbach, K. 'Reproduction and Resistance During the Holocaust', in E. Fuchs (ed.), *Women and the Holocaust: Narrative and Representation* (Lanham, MD: University Press of America, Inc., 1999), 19–32.

Kellner, H. '"Never Again" Is Now', in B. Fay, P. Pomper and R.T. Vann (eds), *History and Theory: Contemporary Readings* (Malden, MA: Blackwell Publishers, 1998), 225–44.

Khazzoom, L. (ed.). *The Flying Camel: Essays on Identity by Women of North African and Middle Eastern Jewish Heritage* (New York: Seal Press, 2003).

Klein, K.L. 'On the Emergence of Memory in Historical Discourse', *Representations* 69 (Winter 2000), 127–50.

Kramer, L. (ed.). *The Multicultural Experiment: Immigrants, Refugees and National Identity* (Paddington, NSW: Macleay Press, 2003).

Krauss, N. *The History of Love* (New York: W.W. Norton & Company, 2005).

———. *Great House* (Camberwell: Viking Books, 2010).

Kugelmass, J. and J. Boyarin. *From a Ruined Garden: The Memorial Books of Polish Jewry* (New York: Schocken Books, 1983).

Kushner, T. 'Holocaust Testimony, Ethics, and the Problem of Representation', *Poetics Today* 27(2) (Summer 2006), 275–95.

LaCapra, D. *History and Memory after Auschwitz* (Ithaca, NY: Cornell University Press, 1998).

Lake, M. and H. Reynolds. *Drawing the Global Colour Line: White Men's Countries and the Question of Racial Equality* (Carlton: Melbourne University Publishing, 2008).

Langer, L.L. *Holocaust Testimonies: The Ruins of Memory* (New Haven, CT: Yale University Press, 1991).

———. *Using and Abusing the Holocaust* (Bloomington: Indiana University Press, 2006).

Laska, V. (ed.). *Women in the Resistance and in the Holocaust: The Voices of Eyewitnesses* (Westport, CT: Greenwood Press, 1983).

Lavie, S. 'Academic Apartheid in Israel and the Lillywhite Feminism of the Upper Middle Class', *Women in Judaism: A Multidisciplinary Journal* 3(1) (2002). Retrieved 15 March 2014 from http://wjudaism.library.utoronto.ca/index.php/wjudaism/article/view/205/183.

———. *Wrapped in the Flag of Israel: Mizrahi Single Mothers and Bureaucratic Torture* (New York: Berghahn Books, 2014).

Lazar, A., J. Chaitin, T. Gross and D. Bar-On. 'Jewish Israeli Teenagers, National Identity, and the Lessons of the Holocaust', *Holocaust and Genocide Studies* 18(2) (Fall 2004), 188–204.

Lebel, U. 'Exile from National Memory: Memory Exclusion as Political', *National Identities* 11(3) (September 2009), 241–62.

Lemon, M.C. 'The Structure of Narrative', in G. Roberts (ed.), *The History and Narrative Reader* (London: Routledge, 2001), 107–29.

Lentin, R. 'A *Yiddishe Mame* Desperately Seeking a *Mame Loshn*: Toward a Theory of the Feminisation of Stigma in the Relations between Israelis and Holocaust Survivors', *Women's Studies International Forum* 19(1/2) (April 1996), 87–97.

———. 'Re-Occupying the Territories of Silence: Israeli Daughters of Shoah Survivors between Language and Silence', in E. Fuchs (ed.), *Women and the Holocaust: Narrative and Representation* (Lanham, MD: University Press of America, Inc., 1999), 47–62.

———. *Israel and the Daughters of the Shoah: Reoccupying the Territories of Silence* (New York: Berghahn Books, 2000).

———. 'Introduction: Postmemory, Unsayability and the Return of the Auschwitz Code', in R. Lentin (ed.), *Re-Presenting the Shoah for the Twenty-First Century* (New York: Berghahn Books, 2004), 1–24.

Levenson, A.T. 'Contemporary Jewish Thought', in M.L. Raphael (ed.), *The Columbia History of Jews and Judaism in America* (New York: Columbia University Press, 2008), 406–32.

Levi, N. and M. Rothberg. 'General Introduction: Theory and the Holocaust', in N. Levi and M. Rothberg (eds), *The Holocaust: Theoretical Readings* (Edinburgh: Edinburgh University Press, 2003), 1–22.

Levi, N. '"No Sensible Comparison"? The Place of the Holocaust in Australia's History Wars', *History and Memory* 19(1) (Spring/Summer 2007), 124–56.

Levi, P. *Survival in Auschwitz: The Nazi Assault on Humanity*, trans. Stuart Woolf (New York: Touchstone, 1996).

Linenthal, E.T. *Preserving Memory: The Struggle to Create America's Holocaust Museum* (New York: Viking Penguin, 1995).

Linn, R. *Escaping Auschwitz: A Culture of Forgetting* (Ithaca, NY: Cornell University Press, 2004).

Lorde, A. *Sister Outsider: Essays and Speeches* (Berkeley, CA: The Crossing Press, 1984).

Lowenstein, A. *My Israel Question* (Melbourne: Melbourne University Press, 2007).

Lubin, A. '"We Are All Israelis": The Politics of Colonial Comparisons', *South Atlantic Quarterly* 107(4) (Fall 2008), 671–90.

Lyotard, J.-F. *The Differend: Phrases in Dispute* (Minneapolis: University of Minnesota Press, 1988).

Maier, C.S. 'A Surfeit of Memory? Reflections on History, Melancholy and Denial', *History & Memory* 5(2) (Fall/Winter 1993), 136–51.

Mamdani, M. 'The Politics of Naming: Genocide, Civil War, Insurgency', *London Review of Books* (8 March 2007).

Mann, B. 'Modernism and the Zionist Uncanny: Reading the Old Cemetery in Tel Aviv', *Representations* (69) (Winter 2000), 63–95.

Marrus, M.R. *The Unwanted: European Refugees in the Twentieth Century* (New York: Oxford University Press, 1985).

———. *The Holocaust in History* (Toronto: Lester & Orpen Dennys Limited, 1987).

Massad, J. 'The "Post-Colonial" Colony: Time, Space, and Bodies in Palestine/Israel', in F. Afzal-Khan and K. Seshadri-Crooks (eds), *The Pre-Occupation of Postcolonial Studies* (Durham, NC: Duke University Press, 2000), 311–46.

Mayer, T. 'From Zero to Hero: Masculinity in Jewish Nationalism', in T. Mayer (ed.), *Gender Ironies of Nationalism: Sexing the Nation* (London: Routledge, 2000), 282–303.

———. 'Nation and Gender in Jewish Israel', in D. Cowen and E. Gilbert (eds), *War, Citizenship, Territory* (New York: Routledge, 2008), 327–44.

Memmi, A. *The Colonizer and the Colonized* (London: Earthscan Publications, 1990).

Mendes, P. 'Lifting the Lid on Poverty in the Jewish Community', in M. Fagenblat, M. Landau and N. Wolski (eds), *New under the Sun: Jewish Australians on Religion, Politics & Culture* (Melbourne: Black Inc., 2006), 357–65.

Meyer, M.A. 'The Emergence of Modern Jewish Historiography: Motives and Motifs', in A. Rapoport-Albert (ed.), *Essays in Jewish Historiography* (Atlanta, GA: Scholars Press, 1991), 160–75.

———. 'Reflections on Jewish Modernization', in E. Carlebach, J.M. Efron and D.N. Myers (eds), *Jewish History and Jewish Memory: Essays in Honor of Yosef Haim Yerushalmi* (Hanover, NH: Brandeis University Press, 1998), 369–77.

Meyerowitz, J. 'A History of "Gender"', *American Historical Review* 113(5) (December 2008), 1346–356.

Milton, S. 'Women and the Holocaust: The Case of German and German-Jewish Women', in R. Bridenthal, A. Grossmann and M. Kaplan (eds), *When Biology Became Destiny: Women in Weimar and Nazi Germany* (New York: Monthly Review Press, 1984), 297–333.

Mintz, A. *Hurban: Responses to Catastrophe in Hebrew Literature* (New York: Columbia University Press, 1984).
Morgensen, S.L. 'Settler Homonationalism: Theorizing Settler Colonialism within Queer Modernities', *GL* 16(1–2) (2010), 105–131.
———. *Spaces Between Us: Queer Settler Colonialism and Indigenous Decolonization* (Minneapolis: University of Minnesota Press, 2011).
Moreton-Robinson, A. 'The Possessive Logic of Patriarchal White Sovereignty: The High Court and the Yorta Yorta Decision', *borderlands* 3(2) (2004), retrieved 12 January 2008 from http://www.borderlands.net.au/vol3no2_2004/moreton_possessive.htm.
———. (ed.). *Sovereign Subjects: Indigenous Sovereignty Matters* (Crows Nest, NSW: Allen & Unwin, 2007).
———. 'Writing Off Treaties: White Possession in the United States Critical Whiteness Studies Literature', in A. Moreton-Robinson, M. Casey and F. Nicoll (eds), *Transnational Whiteness Matters* (Lanham, MD: Lexington Books, 2008), 81–96.
Morgenstern-Leissner, O. 'Hospital Birth, Military Service and the Ties That Bind Them: The Case of Israel', *Nashim: A Journal of Jewish Women's Studies and Gender Issues* 12 (October 2006), 203–41.
Moses, A.D. 'Genocide and Historical Consciousness in Australia', *History Compass* 1 (2003), 1–13.
Mosse, G.L. *The Image of Man: The Creation of Modern Masculinity* (New York: Oxford University Press, 1996).
Nahshon, E. (ed.). *From the Ghetto to the Melting Pot: Israel Zangwill's Jewish Plays. Three Playscripts by Israel Zangwill* (Detroit, MI: Wayne State University Press, 2006).
Neumann, K. *Refuge Australia: Australia's Humanitarian Record* (Sydney: UNSW Press, 2004).
Neumann, K., N. Thomas and H. Ericksen. 'Conclusion', in K. Neumann, N. Thomas and H. Ericksen (eds), *Quicksands: Foundational Histories in Australia and Aotearoa New Zealand* (Sydney: UNSW Press, 1999), 238–42.
Neusner, J. *The Reformation of Reform Judaism* (New York: Garland Publishing, Inc., 1993).
Neusner, J. (ed.). *The Alteration of Orthodoxy* (New York: Garland Publishing, Inc., 1993).
———. *Israel and Zion in American Judaism: The Zionist Fulfillment* (New York: Garland Publishing, Inc., 1993)
Nimni, E. 'From *Galut* to *T'futsoth*: Post-Zionism and the Dis><Location of Jewish Diasporas', in E. Nimni (ed.), *The Challenge of Post-Zionism: Alternatives to Israeli Fundamentalist Politics* (London: Zed Books, 2003), 117–52.
Nora, P. 'Between Memory and History: Les Lieux De Memoire', *Representations* 26 (Spring 1989), 7–24.
Novick, P. *The Holocaust and Collective Memory: The American Experience* (London: Bloomsbury, 1999).
Nutkiewicz, M. 'Shame, Guilt, and Anguish in Holocaust Survivor Testimony', *Oral History Review* 30(1) (Winter/Spring 2003), 1–22.
Obenzinger, H. 'Naturalizing Cultural Pluralism, Americanizing Zionism: The Settler Colonial Basis to Early-Twentieth-Century Progressive Thought', *South Atlantic Quarterly* 107(4) (Fall 2008), 651–69.
Ofer, D. and L.J. Weitzman (eds). *Women in the Holocaust* (New Haven, CT: Yale University Press, 1998).
Ophir, A. 'The Identity of the Victims and the Victims of Identity: A Critique of Zionist Ideology for a Post-Zionist Age', in L.J. Silberstein (ed.), *Mapping Jewish Identities* (New York: New York University Press, 2000), 174–200.

Oz, A. *Under This Blazing Light* (Cambridge: Cambridge University Press, 1995).
Papastergiadis, N. *Dialogues in the Diasporas: Essays and Conversations on Cultural Identity* (London: Rivers Oram Press, 1998).
Pappé, I. 'Zionism as Colonialism: A Comparative View of Diluted Colonialism in Asia and Africa', *South Atlantic Quarterly* 107(4) (Fall 2008), 611-33.
Patraka, V.M. 'Situating History and Difference: The Performance of the Term *Holocaust* in Public Discourse', in J. Boyarin and D. Boyarin (eds), *Jews and Other Differences: The New Jewish Cultural Studies* (Minneapolis: University of Minnesota Press, 1997), 54-78.
Pellegrini, A. 'Whiteface Performances: "Race," Gender, and Jewish Bodies', in J. Boyarin and D. Boyarin (eds), *Jews and Other Differences: The New Jewish Cultural Studies* (Minneapolis: University of Minnesota Press, 1997), 108-49.
Piterberg, G. *The Returns of Zionism: Myths, Politics and Scholarship in Israel* (London: Verso, 2008).
Podeh, E. 'History and Memory in the Israeli Educational System: The Portrayal of the Arab-Israeli Conflict in History Textbooks (1948-2000)', *History & Memory* 12(1) (Spring/Summer 2000), 65-100.
Pozzetta, G.E. (ed.). *Assimilation, Acculturation, and Social Mobility* (New York: Garland Publishing, 1991).
Prager, D. and J. Telushkin. *Why the Jews? The Reason for Antisemitism* (New York: Touchstone, 2003).
Prell, R-E. *Fighting to Become Americans: Jews, Gender, and the Anxiety of Assimilation* (Boston, MA: Beacon Press, 1999).
———. 'Triumph, Accommodation, and Resistance: American Jewish Life from the End of World War II to the Six-Day War', in M.L. Raphael (ed.), *The Columbia History of Jews and Judaism in America* (New York: Columbia University Press, 2008), 114-41.
Presner, T.S. *Muscular Judaism: The Jewish Body and the Politics of Regeneration* (London: Routledge, 2007).
Radford, J. 'The Woman and the Jew: Sex and Modernity', in B. Cheyette and L. Marcus (eds), *Modernity, Culture and 'the Jew'* (Cambridge: Polity Press, 1998), 91-104.
Ragoné, H. and F. Winddance Twine (eds). *Ideologies and Technologies of Motherhood: Race, Class, Sexuality, Nationalism* (New York: Routledge, 2000).
Raider, M.A. *The Emergence of American Zionism* (New York: New York University Press, 1998).
Raphael, M.L. 'Introduction', in M.L. Raphael (ed.), *The Columbia History of Jews and Judaism in America* (New York: Columbia University Press, 2008), 1-17.
Reading, A. *The Social Inheritance of the Holocaust: Gender, Culture and Memory* (Hampshire: Palgrave, 2002).
Reinharz, S. 'Women's Names and Place(s): Exploring the Map of Israel', in J. Tydor Baumel and T. Cohen (eds), *Gender, Place and Memory in the Modern Jewish Experience: Re-Placing Ourselves* (London: Vallentine Mitchell, 2003), 240-51.
Renan, E. 'What Is a Nation?' in H.K. Bhabha (ed.), *Nation and Narration* (London: Routledge, 1993), 8-22.
Reynolds, H. *Why Weren't We Told? A Personal Search for the Truth About Our History* (Melbourne: Penguin, 1999).
———. *An Indelible Stain? The Question of Genocide in Australia's History* (Ringwood, NJ: Viking Press, 2001).
Rich, B.R. 'In the Name of Feminist Film Criticism', in D. Carson, L. Dittmar and J.R. Welsch (eds), *Multiple Voices in Feminist Film Criticism* (Minneapolis: University of Minnesota Press, 1994), 27-47.

Richardson, T.R. and E.V. Johanningmeir. *Race, Ethnicity, and Education: What Is Taught in School* (Greenwich, CT: Information Age Publishing, 2003).
Ricoeur, P. *Time and Narrative: Volume I*, trans K. McLaughlin and D. Pellauer (Chicago, IL: University of Chicago Press, 1984).
Riley, D. *'Am I That Name?': Feminism and the Category of 'Women' in History* (London: Macmillan, 1988).
Ringelblum, E. *Diary and Notes from the Warsaw Ghetto, September 1939-December 1942*, cited in S.R. Horowitz. 'Gender, Genocide, and Jewish Memory', *Prooftexts: A Journal of Jewish Literary History* 20(1–2) (Winter/Spring 2000), 11.
Ringelheim, J. 'Women and the Holocaust: A Reconsideration of Research', in C. Rittner and J.K. Roth (eds), *Different Voices: Women and the Holocaust* (New York: Paragon House, 1993), 373–418.
———. 'The Split between Gender and the Holocaust', in D. Ofer and L.J. Weitzman (eds), *Women in the Holocaust* (New Haven, CT: Yale University Press, 1998), 340–50.
Rittner, C. and J.K. Roth. 'Prologue: Women and the Holocaust', in C. Rittner and J.K. Roth (eds), *Different Voices: Women and the Holocaust* (New York: Paragon House, 1993), 1–19.
Roberts, G. 'Introduction: The History and Narrative Debate, 1960-2000', in G. Roberts (ed.), *The History and Narrative Reader* (London: Routledge, 2001), 1–21.
Roediger, D.R. *The Wages of Whiteness: Race and the Making of the American Working Class*, revised edition (London: Verso, 1999).
———. *Working Towards Whiteness: How America's Immigrants Became White. The Strange Journey from Ellis Island to the Suburbs* (New York: Basic Books, 2005).
Roskies, D.G. *The Jewish Search for a Usable Past* (Bloomington: Indiana University Press, 1999).
Rose, D.B. 'Hard Times: An Australian Study', in K. Neumann, N. Thomas and H. Ericksen (eds), *Quicksands: Foundational Histories in Australia and Aotearoa New Zealand* (Sydney: UNSW Press, 1999), 2–19.
Rose, G. 'Beginnings of the Day: Fascism and Representation', in B. Cheyette and L. Marcus (eds), *Modernity, Culture and 'the Jew'* (Cambridge: Polity Press, 1998), 242–56.
Rose, J. *The Question of Zion* (Carlton: Melbourne University Press, 2005).
Rothberg, M. *Traumatic Realism: The Demands of Holocaust Representation* (Minneapolis: University of Minnesota Press, 2000).
———. *Multidirectional Memory: Remembering the Holocaust in the Age of Decolonization* (Stanford, CA: Stanford University Press, 2009).
Roy, S. 'Living with the Holocaust: The Journey of a Child of Holocaust Survivors', in T. Kushner and A. Solomon (eds), *Wrestling with Zion: Progressive Jewish-American Responses to the Israeli Palestinian Conflict* (New York: Grove Press, 2003), 170–77.
Rubinstein, H.L. *Chosen: The Jews in Australia* (Sydney: Allen & Unwin, 1987).
Rubinstein, H.L., D. Cohn-Sherbok, A.J. Edelheit and W.D. Rubinstein. *The Jews in the Modern World: A History since 1750* (London: Arnold, 2002).
Rubinstein, W.D. *The Jews in Australia* (Melbourne: AE Press, 1986).
Ruffins, F.D. 'Culture Wars Won and Lost: Ethnic Museums on the Mall, Part I: The National Holocaust Museum and the National Museum of the American Indian', *Radical History Review* 68 (1997), 79–100.
Rutland, S.D. *Edge of the Diaspora: Two Centuries of Jewish Settlement in Australia*, 2nd revised edition (Sydney: Brandl & Schlesinger, 1997).
———. *The Jews in Australia* (Melbourne: Cambridge University Press, 2005).
Said, E.W. 'Invention, Memory, and Place', *Critical Inquiry* 26(2) (Winter 2000), 175–92.

Saidel, R.G. *The Jewish Women of Ravensbrück Concentration Camp* (Madison: University of Wisconsin Press, 2004).
Saidel, R.G. and S.M. Hedgepeth (eds). *Sexual Violence Against Women During the Holocaust* (Waltham, MA: Brandeis University Press, 2010).
Santner, E.L. 'History Beyond the Pleasure Principle: Some Thoughts on the Representation of Trauma', in S. Friedländer (ed.), *Probing the Limits of Representation: Nazism and the 'Final Solution'* (Cambridge, MA: Harvard University Press, 1992), 143–54.
Sax, D. 'Rise of the New Yiddishists', *Vanity Fair* (8 April 2009). Retrieved 16 April 2009 from http://www.vanityfair.com/culture/features/2009/04/yiddishists200904.
Schamp, J. 'Beyond Assimilation: Difference and Reconfiguration in the Works of Irena Klepfisz, Jyl Lynn Felman, and Rebecca Goldstein', *ZAA* 47(3) (1999), 229–43.
Schmidt, N. 'Art Spiegelman: Walking Gingerly, Remaining Close to Our Caves', in J. Witek (ed.), *Art Spiegelman: Conversations* (Jackson: University Press of Mississippi, 2007), 220–22.
Scholem, G. *On Jews and Judaism in Crises: Selected Essays*, ed. and trans. Werner J. Dannhauser (New York: Schocken Books, 1976).
Schroeter, D.J. 'A Different Road to Modernity: Jewish Identity in the Arab World', in H. Wettstein (ed.), *Diasporas and Exiles: Varieties of Jewish Identity* (Berkeley: University of California Press, 2002), 150–63.
Scott, J.W. 'Review of *Heroes of Their Own Lives: The Politics and History of Family Violence* by Linda Gordon', *Signs* 15(4) (Summer 1990), 848–52.
———. 'Response to Gordon', *Signs* 15(4) (Summer 1990), 859–60.
———. 'The Evidence of Experience', *Critical Inquiry* 17 (Summer 1991), 773–97.
———. 'Introduction', in J.W. Scott (ed.), *Feminism and History* (Oxford: Oxford University Press, 1996), 1–13.
———. *Gender and the Politics of History*, revised edition (New York: Columbia University Press, 1999).
———. 'Unanswered Questions', *American Historical Review* 113(5) (December 2008), 1422–430.
Seidman, N. 'Lawless Attachments, One-Night Stands: The Sexual Politics of the Hebrew-Yiddish Language War', in J. Boyarin and D. Boyarin (eds), *Jews and Other Differences: The New Jewish Cultural Studies* (Minneapolis: University of Minnesota Press, 1997), 279–305.
Seltzer, R.M. 'Introduction: The Ironies of American Jewish History', in R.M. Seltzer and N.J. Cohen (eds), *The Americanization of the Jews* (New York: New York University Press, 1995), 1–16.
Seth, S. *Subject Lessons: The Western Education of Colonial India* (Durham, NC: Duke University Press, 2007).
Shabi, R. 'The Fight to Not Fight', *The Guardian* (17 April 2006).
Shohat, E. 'Sephardim in Israel: Zionism from the Standpoint of Its Jewish Victims', *Social Text* 19/20 (Autumn 1988), 1–35.
———. 'Antinomies of Exile: Said at the Frontiers of National Narrations', in M. Sprinkler (ed.), *Edward Said: A Critical Reader* (Oxford: Blackwell, 1993), 121
———. *Taboo Memories, Diasporic Voices* (Durham, NC: Duke University Press, 2006).
Short, G. 'The Holocaust Museum as an Educational Resource: A View from New York City', *The Journal of Holocaust Education* 9(1) (Summer 2000), 1–18.
Silverstein, J. '"We're Dealing with How Do We Live and Work with This Memory and What Are We Supposed To Do About It": Making use of Jewish Liminality', *Borderlands e-journal*, 9(1) (2010). Retrieved 15 March 2014 from http://www.borderlands.net.au/vol9no1_2010/silverstein_liminality.htm.

Simpson, G. *Law, War and Crime: War Crimes Trials and the Reinvention of International Law* (Cambridge: Polity Press, 2007).
Solomon, A. 'Viva la Diva Citizenship: Post-Zionism and Gay Rights', in D. Boyarin, D. Itzkovitz and A. Pellegrini (eds), *Queer Theory and the Jewish Question* (New York: Columbia University Press, 2003), 149–65.
Sorin, G. *Tradition Transformed: The Jewish Experience in America* (Baltimore, MD: Johns Hopkins University Press, 1997).
Spiegel, G.M. 'Memory and History: Liturgical Time and Historical Time', *History and Theory* 41(2) (May 2002), 149–62.
Spiegelman, A. *The Complete Maus: A Survivor's Tale* (New York: Pantheon Books, 1996).
Stannard, D.E. *American Holocaust: Columbus and the Conquest of the New World* (New York: Oxford University Press, 1992).
———. 'Uniqueness as Denial: The Politics of Genocide Scholarship', in A.S. Rosenbaum (ed), *Is the Holocaust Unique?: Perspectives on Comparative Genocide* (Boulder, CO: Westview Press, 1996), 163–208.
Stone, D. *Constructing the Holocaust: A Study in Historiography* (London: Vallentine Mitchell, 2003).
———. 'Biopower and Modern Genocide', in A.D. Moses (ed.), *Empire, Colony, Genocide: Conquest, Occupation, and Subaltern Resistance in World History* (New York: Berghahn Books, 2008), 162–79.
Stratton, J. *Race Daze: Australia in Identity Crisis* (London: Pluto Press, 1998).
———. 'The Color of Jews: Jews, Race, and the White Australia Policy', in S.L. Gilman and M. Shain (eds), *Jewries at the Frontier: Accommodation, Identity, Conflict* (Urbana: University of Illinois Press, 1999), 309–34.
———. *Coming out Jewish: Constructing Ambivalent Identities* (London: Routledge, 2000).
———. *Jewish Identity in Western Pop Culture: The Holocaust and Trauma through Modernity* (New York: Palgrave Macmillan, 2008).
Sturken, M. 'The Remembering of Forgetting: Recovered Memory and the Question of Experience', *Social Text* 57 (Winter 1998), 103–25.
Sullam Calimani, A.-V. 'A Name for Extermination', *The Modern Language Review* 94(4) (October 1999), 978–99.
Taussig, M. 'Culture of Terror-Space of Death. Roger Casement's Putumayo Report and the Explanation of Torture', *Comparative Studies in Society and History* 26(3) (July 1984), 467–97.
Tavan, G. *The Long, Slow Death of White Australia* (Melbourne: Scribe Publications, 2005).
Taylor, C. 'Nationalism and Modernity', in R. McKim and J. McMahan (eds), *The Morality of Nationalism* (New York: Oxford University Press, 1997), 31–55.
Terdiman, R. *Present Past: Modernity and the Memory Crisis* (Ithaca, NY: Cornell University Press, 1993).
Thompson, E.P. 'Time, Work-Discipline, and Industrial Capitalism', *Past & Present* 38 (December 1967), 56–97.
Tinsman, H. 'A Paradigm of Our Own: Joan Scott in Latin American History', *American Historical Review* 113(5) (December 2008), 1357–374.
Trask, H.-K. *From a Native Daughter: Colonialism and Sovereignty in Hawai'i*, revised edition (Honolulu: University of Hawai'i Press, 1999).
Troen, S.I. 'Frontier Myths and Their Application in America and Israel: A Transnational Perspective', *The Journal of American History* 86(3) (December 1999), 1209–230.
United Nations, *Convention on the Prevention and Punishment of the Crime of Genocide*. Retrieved 18 December 2014 from https://treaties.un.org/doc/Publication/UNTS/Volume%2078/volume-78-I-1021-English.pdf.

Veracini, L. 'The Evolution of Historical Redescription in Israel and Australia: The Question of the "Founding Violence"', *Australian Historical Studies* 34(122) (October 2003), 326-45.

———. *Israel and Settler Society* (London: Pluto Press, 2006).

Wake, C. 'Regarding the Recording: The Viewer of Video Testimony, the Complexity of Copresence and the Possibility of Tertiary Witnessing', *History and Memory* 25(1) (Spring/Summer 2013), 111-44.

Waxman, Z. 'Testimony and Representation', in D. Stone (ed.), *The Historiography of the Holocaust* (Hampshire: Palgrave Macmillan, 2004), 487-507.

Weissman, G. *Fantasies of Witnessing: Postwar Efforts to Experience the Holocaust* (Ithaca, NY: Cornell University Press, 2004).

Weitzman, L.J. and D. Ofer 'Introduction: The Role of Gender in the Holocaust', in D. Ofer and L.J. Weitzman (eds), *Women in the Holocaust* (New Haven, CT: Yale University Press, 1998), 1-18.

Wettstein, H. 'Coming to Terms with Exile', in H. Wettstein (ed.), *Diasporas and Exiles: Varieties of Jewish Identity* (Berkeley: University of California Press, 2002), 47-59.

White, H. *Metahistory: The Historical Imagination in Nineteenth Century Europe* (Baltimore, MD: Johns Hopkins University Press, 1973).

———. 'Historical Emplotment and the Problem of Truth', in S. Friedländer (ed.), *Probing the Limits of Representation: Nazism and the 'Final Solution'* (Cambridge, MA: Harvard University Press, 1992), 37-53.

———. 'The Historical Text as Literary Artifact', in B. Fay, P. Pomper and R.T. Vann (eds), *History and Theory: Contemporary Readings* (Malden, MA: Blackwell Publishers, 1998), 15-33.

Wisse, R.R. 'Jewish Writers on the New Diaspora', in R.M. Seltzer and N.J. Cohen (eds), *The Americanization of the Jews* (New York: New York University Press, 1995), 60-78.

Wolf, D.L. 'Holocaust Testimony: Producing Post-Memories, Producing Identities', in J.M. Gerson and D.L. Wolf (eds), *Sociology Confronts the Holocaust: Memories and Identities in Jewish Diasporas* (Durham, NC: Duke University Press, 2007), 154-75.

Wolfe, P. *Settler Colonialism and the Transformation of Anthropology: The Politics and Poetics of an Ethnographic Event* (London: Cassell, 1999).

———. 'Logics of Elimination: Colonial Policies on Indigenous Peoples in Australia and the United States', *University of Nebraska Human Rights and Human Diversity Initiative Monograph Series* 2 (2000), 2.

———. 'Land, Labor, and Difference: Elementary Structures of Race', *American Historical Review* 106(3) (June 2001), 866-905.

———. 'Settler Colonialism and the Elimination of the Native', *Journal of Genocide Research* 8(4) (December 2006), 387-409.

———. 'Palestine, Project Europe and the (Un-)Making of the New Jew: In Memory of Edward W. Said', in N. Curthoys and D. Ganguly (eds), *Edward Said: The Legacy of a Public Intellectual* (Melbourne: Melbourne University Press, 2007), 313-37.

———. 'Structure and Event: Settler Colonialism, Time, and the Question of Genocide', in A.D. Moses (ed.), *Empire, Colony, Genocide: Conquest, Occupation, and Subaltern Resistance in World History* (New York: Berghahn Books, 2008), 102-32.

Woodcock, S. 'Romania and EUrope: Roma, Rroma and Țigani as Sites for the Contestation of Ethno-National Identity', *Patterns of Prejudice* 41(5) (2007), 493-515.

Yad Vashem. *Yesterdays and Then Tomorrows: Holocaust Anthology of Testimonies and Readings* (Jerusalem: The International School for Holocaust Studies, 2002).

Yerushalmi, Y.H. *Zakhor: Jewish History and Jewish Memory* (Seattle: University of Washington Press, 1982).

Young, J.E. *Writing and Rewriting the Holocaust: Narrative and the Consequences of Interpretation* (Bloomington: Indiana University Press, 1988).
———. *The Texture of Memory: Holocaust Memorials and Meaning* (New Haven, CT: Yale University Press, 1993).
———. 'Toward a Received History of the Holocaust', *History and Theory* 46(4) (December 1997), 21–43.
Yuval-Davis, N. 'Front and Rear: The Sexual Division of Labor in the Israeli Army', *Feminist Studies* 11(3) (Autumn 1985), 649–75.
Zeitlin, F. 'New Soundings in Holocaust Literature: A Surplus of Memory', in M. Postone and E. Santner (eds), *Catastrophe and Meaning: The Holocaust and the Twentieth Century* (Chicago, IL: University of Chicago Press, 2003), 173–208.
Zertal, I. 'The Sacrificed and the Sanctified: The Construction of a National Martyrology', *Zemanim* 12(48) (Spring 1994), 38.
———. *Israel's Holocaust and the Politics of Nationhood*, trans. Chaya Galai (Cambridge: Cambridge University Press, 2005).
Zertal, I. and A. Eldar. *Lords of the Land: The War Over Israel's Settlements in the Occupied Territories, 1967-2007* (New York: Nation Books, 2007).
Zerubavel, Y. 'The Historic, the Legendary, and the Incredible: Invented Tradition and Collective Memory in Israel', in J.R. Gillis (ed.), *Commemorations: The Politics of National Identity* (Princeton, NJ: Princeton University Press, 1994), 105–23.
———. *Recovered Roots: Collective Memory and the Making of Israeli National Tradition* (Chicago, IL: University of Chicago Press, 1995).

Index

Agamben, Giorgio, 11, 84, 105
Alba, Avril, 153–54
Alcalay, Ammiel, 7, 99
ambivalence, 3, 8–9, 23–24, 26, 44, 100, 114, 133n29, 139, 147, 162, 166, 199–200. *See also under* anxiety; diaspora; the Holocaust
antisemitism, 13, 38, 45, 47–48, 51, 65, 72, 103, 132n10, 151, 156, 207
    discrimination, 13, 38, 42, 46, 61, 66, 151, 156
    marginalisation, 13, 51, 135n56
    the Holocaust, 66, 151, 156, 161
anxiety, 2–3, 7–8, 31n51, 88, 208
    ambivalence, 39, 44, 209–10
    belonging, 12–14, 31n47, 37–38, 41, 43–44, 47–49, 52, 89, 100, 118–19, 124, 127, 131, 144, 147, 160, 163–64, 166, 168, 200, 209–10
    chronology, 62–63, 70–71, 74, 87, 90–91, 188, 200
    definition, 12, 31n40
    feminization, 4, 15, 26, 53–54, 179–80, 184, 187
    gender, 15, 113, 123, 128, 179, 184
    haunting, 131, 156, 167
    masculinization, 4, 15–16, 26, 53, 106, 128
    memory/forgetting, 4, 12–13, 74, 84–85, 144–45, 156, 160–1, 163, 165–6, 187, 210
    mimicry, 23–24, 25, 71, 102, 111, 123–24, 168
    nation-building, 2, 23, 106, 124
    power/powerlessness, 14–15, 160
    testimony, 74, 87–88
    the uncanny, 110–12
    uniqueness, 145

Zionism, 17, 101–2, 106
    See also under diaspora; the Holocaust; settler colonialism
Arabs, 45–46, 59n39, 111, 160
Arendt, Hannah, 105
Aryan, 32n61, 54, 162
Ashkenazi, 5, 7, 12, 28n16, 40, 114–15, 136n68
    hegemony, 8, 115
assimilation, 15, 72, 101, 112, 124, 141n139, 167
    Australia, 38, 50–51, 163, 176n106
    Jewishness, 31, 41, 44, 101, 131, 138n89
    history, 21, 40–42, 58n21, 71
    Holocaust education, 117–21
    United States, 38, 40–41, 130, 163
Auschwitz, 1, 48, 59n40, 75, 81, 84, 95n60, 105, 109, 110, 136n59, 139n112, 181, 186, 191, 197, 199, 206n90
authority, 9, 10, 81, 95n68, 112–13

Babi Yar, 66, 83
Bauer, Yehuda, 158–59
Ben Gurion, David, 104, 108
Bergen-Belsen, 86
Berman, Judith, 153–54
Biale, David, 13–14, 31n51, 40–43, 119–20, 131n2
Bialik, Chaim Nachman, 53, 137n73
Birch, Tony, 144, 175
Boyarin, Daniel, 17–18, 24, 32n61, 34n99, 139n110, 141n137, 141n139
Boyarin, Jonathan, 8–9, 17–18, 94n53, 139n110, 141n139
Brodkin, Karen, 40, 57n15
Butler, Judith, 1–2, 14, 188–89, 203n42, 207, 210
bystanders, 67, 77, 83–84, 157

categorization of gender, 21, 185, 188–89, 201n5, 210
   See also gender; feminization; masculinization
centre and periphery model of historiography, 2, 15–17, 129, 131n1, 163–64
   See also home
Cheyette, Bryan, 18–19
chronology/chronological narrative, 25, 63–74, 78–79, 85, 87–91, 91–2n15, 93n30, 93–4n45, 94n46
   pedagogy, 25, 64–71, 78, 85, 87–91, 91n11, 103
citizenship, 36–37, 49, 63, 104, 106, 108, 119
   racialized, 37–38, 49–50, 106
"The City of Slaughter," *See* Bialik, Chaim Nachman
Clark, Anna, 9–10, 165
Cole, Tim, 149–51
concentration camps, 30n33, 39, 65–66, 73, 75, 82–84, 86, 96n90, 97n97, 117, 125, 149–50, 178–79, 186–87
   in curriculum, 91n11, 92n16
   men's experiences, 186–87, 194
   pedagogy, 88–90
   women's experiences, 186–87, 190, 192, 194–97, 204n59
   See also death camps; *names of individual camps*
Cowie, Elizabeth, 14, 180

Dalsheim, Joyce, 9, 94n49, 133–34n31
death camps, 30n33, 39, 66, 89–90, 96n90, 108, 178, 186, 192, 204n59. *See also* concentration camps; *names of individual camps*
diaspora, 1–36, 99–141, 142–78
   anxiety, 2, 8, 14–17, 23, 25–26, 37, 54–55, 99–131, 163, 179–80, 184–85, 187–88, 200, 208–10
   ambivalence, 4, 8, 14, 16, 23–24, 26, 37, 55, 100, 102, 112–13, 119–21, 128, 129–31, 210
   definition, 17, 27n4, 131n1
   Diaspora Jew, 2, 15, 32n58, 53, 136, 141
   feminization, 15, 25, 53–54, 108, 111, 122–23, 127, 130, 178–200

   gender, 15–16, 25–6, 52–5, 100, 108, 111–12, 121–31, 141n136, 179–85, 187–88, 197, 200
   the Holocaust, 1–26, 37, 53–55, 99–131, 138n107, 146, 179–87, 200, 207–11
   homeland binary, 2, 16–17, 19, 37, 112, 120–23, 127–31, 163, 210
   Israel, 34n99
   masculinization, 26, 123, 179, 182, 187–88, 197, 200
   narrative, 2, 15, 25, 19, 25, 54–55, 100, 105–10, 123, 129–31, 135n56, 200, 208, 210
   New Jew, 53, 124–26,
   power/powerlessness, 14, 54
   Zionism, 2, 15, 19, 25–26, 53–55, 99–131, 131n1, 135n56, 136n107, 141n139, 184–85, 200
diasporic excess, 26, 207, 210
difference, 10, 13–14, 22–25, 31n47, 31n50, 36–56, 59n38, 117–18, 123, 143–45, 147, 152–53, 157–59, 163–67, 169n16, 192, 203n42, 209–10
disempowerment, 14–15, 32n59, 54, 112, 128
Docker, John, 17
Dreyfus Affair, 128

Eichmann, Adolph, 104
Eisen, Arnold, 21, 34n87
Eurocentrism, 114–15
Evian Conference, 120
   Australia's response, 49

feminization, 15, 82, 108, 122–23, 127, 130, 138n102, 179–80, 201
   Holocaust victims, 81–82, 130, 190, 196–98
   See also diaspora: feminization; maternal metaphor; Zionism: feminity
Felman, Shoshana, 77
Final Solution, 65–66, 85–86
film, 65, 85, 97n108, 148
   Playing for Time, 192
   Schindler's List, 105–6
   Shoah, 97n108
forgetting, 4, 8–9, 25, 142–68, 168n4, 182
   disremembering, 143, 151, 154, 159, 171n50

the Holocaust, 25, 96n87, 145–46, 151, 154, 155–56
narrative, 68, 143, 152
nation-building, 8–9, 148, 163–64, 166, 170n36
screen memory, 146, 154–55, 171
settler colonialism, 4, 50, 55, 142–68, 170n36
uniqueness, 25, 148, 155–62
violence, 144–45, 150, 155, 160, 162–66, 170n36
Frank, Anne, 198–99
Freud, Sigmund, 12, 32n61, 65, 101, 110–12, 123, 146, 154–55
screen memory, 146, 154–55, 171n54
the uncanny, 101, 110–13, 127–28, 131, 136n61
Funkenstein, Amos, 72, 92, 93n28

gender, 7, 14–15, 21, 52–55, 81–82, 100–101, 111–13, 121–29, 137n73, 138n102, 140n127, 141nn136–37, 179–80, 183, 185–89, 206n88, 210–11. *See also* anxiety: gender; diaspora: gender; feminization; Jewish women; masculinity; patriarchy
genderqueer, 183
genocide, 30n33, 42, 150, 155–68, 170n37, 172nn59–60, 173n77, 173n79, 174n88, 185. *See also* the Holocaust; violence
Gestapo, 66
ghettos, 20, 65, 67, 71, 75, 77, 79, 82–83, 90, 91n11, 92n16, 96n90, 116–17, 125–26, 133n31, 181, 190, 194–95, 197–98. *See also* Lohamei Hagatteot (Ghetto Fighters Museum); Warsaw Ghetto Uprising
Gilman, Sander, 11, 42, 129, 205n80
Gilroy, Paul, 19
Goldenberg, Myrna and Amy H. Shapiro, 187

Hage, Ghassan, 13, 22–23, 31n45, 38, 40
Halbwachs, Maurice, 10
Hall, Catherine, 36
haunting, 99, 104, 112–13, 131, 142–68, 169n14, 210
Healy, Chris, 30n26, 156, 164–65
Heschel, Susannah, 43–44
Herzl, Theodore, 24, 34, 124, 126, 128, 199
Hyman, Paula, 21, 34n87

history, 8–10, 13–14, 17, 22–23, 25, 64, 73–74, 78, 81, 207–11
assimilation, 42, 44, 71–73, 117
truth, 4, 25, 63–65, 69–70, 73–74, 78–81, 92n28, 93n45, 95n69, 200, 207
as objective/known, 4–5, 9–10, 22, 25, 63, 65, 68–71, 74
writing, 14, 17–18, 24, 43, 64–65, 70–71, 78, 81, 83–85, 117, 129, 179–85, 200, 209–10
See also chronology/chronological narrative; narrative; memory
historiography, 1–23, 49, 69–74, 84, 92n28, 93n30, 93n45, 180, 201n17
the Holocaust, 1–23, 69–73, 84, 100, 129, 149–200
Western methodologies, 117–18, 145, 181, 183, 188, 200
Zionism, 7, 93n30, 100, 129, 200
Hitler, Adolf, 65, 67, 103, 148
home, 2, 12, 15, 16–23, 32n63, 34n99, 37–38, 41, 75, 84–86, 100–102, 105–10, 112, 119–23, 127–31, 143–45, 147, 163, 197, 210
homelessness, 130
homeliness, 12, 16, 23, 31n45, 38, 112, 120–21, 123, 145
See also diaspora
the Holocaust
ambivalence, 14, 79, 86, 87, 100, 102, 109–10, 116, 119, 121, 149, 176–77n109, 184, 195, 209
anxiety, 4, 13, 38, 43–44, 47, 52, 55, 133n26, 164, 210
children, 83, 125, 159, 161, 181, 186, 190–91, 195–96
chronologies, 25, 63, 64–74, 78, 79, 85, 87–91, 91–92n15, 93n30, 93–94n45, 94n46
definition, 10–11, 65
gender, 7–8, 14, 52–55, 82, 100–101, 112–13, 178–200
Israel, 9–10, 14–15, 23–25, 38, 46, 85, 100, 102–4, 105–10, 114, 120–23, 124–28, 131, 134n41, 161, 173n77, 176n109
Jewish women, 4, 7, 8, 25–26, 53, 81, 99, 125, 138n102, 178–200, 207–8, 209, 210

the Holocaust, *continued*
  memory, 3, 12–13, 47–48, 62, 91, 100, 104, 115, 133n26, 133n31, 143, 149–51, 153–55, 185, 210
  museums, 10, 12, 30n30, 40, 60n50, 129, 149–50, 153 (*see also names of individual museums*)
  Nuremberg Trials, 67, 94n53, 102–5, 107
  survivors, 6, 85, 90, 109, 119–20, 131–34, 149, 173n77, 194–95
  testimony, 25, 52, 61n68, 62–91, 95n60, 95nn68–69, 95n75, 96n80, 96n87, 105–6, 116, 156
  uniqueness, 18, 68, 100, 117, 142–68, 173n77, 174n81
  victims, 11, 15, 46, 56n11, 83, 88, 90, 116, 119, 135n57, 145, 155, 157–62, 167, 171n57, 173n73, 182, 185, 191–94
  See also under diaspora; rape; reproduction; resistance; Zionism
homogenization of Jews, 7, 19, 36–38, 68, 113–16, 120, 161
homosexuality, 78, 127, 139n114, 141nn136–37, 161–62, 171n57

intersex, 136n65, 183
Israel
  creation of, 4, 6, 65, 93n30, 101–10, 114, 119–20, 131, 134n41, 176–77n109
  gender, 15–16, 25, 52–55, 101, 106, 108, 110–12, 121–30, 141n136
  narrative, 9, 15–16, 25, 65, 85, 100, 103, 105–10, 114, 129, 131
  sovereignty, 104, 106, 108, 110, 112, 120, 135n49
  See also under the Holocaust

Janowska Road Camp, 76
Jewish Community Councils, 36
Jewish Holocaust Museum and Research Centre (Melbourne), 61n68, 94n53
Jewish Women, 4, 7, 8, 25–26, 53, 81, 99, 125, 138n102, 178–200, 207–10
  abortion, 194–95
  hair cutting, 192
  menstruation, 178–79, 196
  as mothers, 81–82, 104, 125, 139n117, 181, 183–86, 189–91, 194, 199
  nakedness, 192–93
  pregnancy, 186, 191–92, 194–96, 204n55
  resistance, 182, 185–86, 196–99
  sexual violence, 53–54, 191, 193–94, 204n64, 205n66
  as victims, 81–82, 181–82, 185, 191–94, 196, 199
  See also under the Holocaust; rape
Judenrat, 116, 181
Jupp, James, 49–50

Kahane, Claire, 14, 179, 190–91
Kapo, 84
Katz, Jacob, 20
Kaye/Kantrowitz, Melanie, 15, 114, 123
Kindertransport, 66, 190
Kristallnacht, 39–40, 66–67, 77, 103
  and women, 185–86

language, 14, 68–69, 80, 84–85, 123, 127, 165, 178–79, 186–89, 193, 200, 203n42, 205n66, 209, 211
Lauenburg camp, 86
Lentin, Ronit, 127, 130
Levi, Primo, 84, 86, 88
liberation, 73, 82, 85–6, 110, 135n57, 196
lieux de mémoire, 9, 168n4
Lohamei Hagatteot (Ghetto Fighters Museum), 126, 206n90

March of the Living, 52, 61n67, 89–90, 107–8, 109, 133–34n31, 137n73, 157, 211n3
masculinity, 4, 15–16, 25–26, 100, 106, 108, 110–12, 121–24, 128–30, 139nn114–15, 140n127, 179–80, 182, 184, 199, 201n5, 203n42, 210
  emasculation, 53–54, 124, 126–28, 130, 141n136, 187–88, 197, 200
maternal metaphor, 82, 190, 204n53
Maus, 91–92n15, 105–6
Memmi, Albert, 167
metropole, 163–64
Meyer, Michael, 21–22
Meyer, Tamar, 124, 127
memory, 3, 10, 12–13, 17–18, 30, 48, 72, 74, 85–87, 100, 104–5, 108, 115, 148–49, 153–68, 168n4, 171n54, 187, 190, 207, 210

Americanization of, 149–51
Australianization of, 153–54
collective memory, 10, 133n26, 134n31, 154, 173n79
commemoration, 48, 153–54, 171n57
deep memory, 85–87, 91n15, 97n98
memorialisation, 39, 96n87, 143, 146, 153, 168n4, 174n79
multidirectional memory, 18, 33n77, 171n54, 173n79
nativization, 146, 148–49, 152
postmemory, 29n20
screen memory, 146, 154–55, 171n54
split memory, 185
See also anxiety: memory/forgetting; the Holocaust: memory; national memories; nativization of memory; screen memory; survivor testimony
menstruation, 178–79, 194–96
Middle-East, 28n16, 46, 114. *See also* Arabs
Milton, Sybil, 185–86
mimicry, 8, 15, 23–25, 31n47, 71, 100–102, 105, 110–13, 123–24, 127–28, 131, 145, 166–67, 210
Mizrahi, 7, 19, 28n16, 39n59, 111
modernity (Western), 4, 13, 15–16, 19–24, 26, 37–38, 43, 102, 106–7, 111–12, 113n28, 137n71, 139n112, 142, 208, 210
Moreton-Robinson, Aileen, 57n15, 106
Morgensen, Scott Lauria, 144
multiculturalism, 2, 31n51, 41–44, 152
Museum of Jewish Heritage: A Living Memorial the Holocaust, 150

narrative, 3, 8, 9–10, 15–16, 19, 24, 41, 43, 54–55, 63–74, 78, 80, 85, 87–88, 90, 90n45, 92n28, 93n30, 100–109, 113–18, 129, 130–31, 133n31, 135n56, 143, 150, 163–68, 181–86, 190–91, 200, 208, 210
   closure/ resolution, 68, 85–87, 97n108, 100, 102–5, 105–110, 200
   group identity, 9–10, 43, 109, 115, 150, 165, 182
   truth, 4, 25, 64–65, 69, 70, 74–91
narrative fetishism, 64–65
national memories, 8–9, 39, 115, 143, 145–46, 149–50, 154, 166
nation-state, 2, 4, 6, 8, 12, 16, 19–23, 25, 37–38, 51, 55, 102–3, 106, 108–9, 111, 113, 121–22, 128–29, 133n28, 135n49, 137n89, 138n89, 143, 155, 162–64
nativization of memory, 146, 148–49, 152
Nazis, 11, 39, 45–46, 52, 54, 65–67, 82, 92n16, 102–5, 107–8, 116–17, 120, 122, 125, 132n10, 138n107, 150, 161–62, 182–83, 186, 191–96, 199, 205n66. *See also* Hitler, Adolph; Aryan; SS; Gestapo
New Jew, 53, 124–27
Nora, Pierre, 9, 143, 168n4
Novick, Peter, 42–43, 150–51
Nuremberg Trials, 67, 94, 103–5, 107

Ofer, Dalia and Lenore Weitzman, 186, 205n66
outsiderness, 17, 31, 37, 41, 44, 46, 49, 58n26

Palestine (Mandate Palestine), 115, 120, 138n107, 199
Palestinians, 9, 108, 142, 160, 173n77
patriarchy, 7, 106, 110, 113, 129, 133, 168n6, 182–83, 186. *See also* masculinity
Pearl, Gisella, 195–96
power, 1, 7, 10, 14, 28–29n19, 54, 69, 76–77, 125, 204n53
   whiteness, 22
   antisemitism, 48, 92n16, 103
   gendered, 7, 21, 123, 180–83, 189, 199
   institutional, 36, 104
   powerlessness, 14–15, 32n59, 54, 112, 128
   settler colonial, 166
   state, 123, 141n139
   See also authority; patriarchy; racialization; resistance

racialization, 13, 31n51, 38, 43, 45–51, 55, 57n18. *See also* whiteness
rape, 181, 191, 193, 204n64, 205n66
   Bialik's poem, 53–54
   Holocaust testimony, 82, 96n87, 193–94, 204n64, 205n65
   Jewish men in the Holocaust, 194, 205n65
   Jewish women in the Holocaust, 53–54, 191, 193–94, 204n64, 205n66
Ravensbrück, 181–82, 186–87

The Reader (novel), 105
Renan, Ernest, 142
reproduction and the Holocaust, 181, 186–87, 191–96
revolt, 197–99. *See also* resistance; Warsaw Ghetto Uprising
resistance, 19, 36, 67, 155
    the Holocaust, 14, 24, 65–66, 100, 109, 116, 122–23, 125–26, 135n57, 182, 185–86, 196–99, 206n84, 206n88
    settler colonialism, 6
    See also Warsaw Ghetto Uprising
Rich, Adrienne, 178
Ringelblum, Emmanuel, 178, 185
Ringelheim, Joan, 185
Rittner, Carol and John K. Roth, 186
Rosenberg, Ethel and Julius, 40
Roth, John K. and Carol Rittner, 186
Rothberg, Michael, 18–19, 33, 160, 173–74n79. *See also* memory
rule of law, 102–5, 131, 133n26, 163–64,

Said, Edward, 115, 207
Santner, Eric, 64–65, 70
screen memory, 146, 154–55, 171n54
Scott, Joan, 62, 64, 77–78, 80–81, 91n4, 188–89
self-determination, 16, 53–54, 110, 119
settler colonialism, 4, 6–7, 25, 99, 106, 142–168, 169n14, 170n37, 171n54, 172n60, 174n84, 209–10
    ambivalence, 144–45, 162, 166–68, 210
    anxiety, 4, 6, 25, 106, 144–45, 163–66, 209–10
    belonging, 144–45, 163, 166–67, 209–10
    forgetting 4, 25, 142–68
    historiography, 4, 7, 25, 143, 145–46
    nation building, 4, 6, 25, 106, 143–46, 150–51, 155, 163, 166, 209–10
    structure, 6–7, 142–44, 164–66, 209
    violence, 144–45, 155, 159–60, 162–64, 166, 209
Shapiro, Amy H. and Myrna Goldenberg, 187
Shabbat, 26, 39, 183–84
Shohat, Ella, 7, 19, 61n69, 173n73
Simon Wiesenthal Center (SWC), 47–48
St Louis (ship), 120

survivor testimony, 62–91, 94n53, 95n60, 95n69, 96n87
    anxiety, 63, 88
    diaries, 75, 79–80, 204n64
    Fortunoff Institute, 73–74, 94n53
    language, 80, 84–85
    memory, 74, 85–87
    pedagogy, 64, 74–91
    story books, 75–76
    truth, 63–65, 73–78, 80–81, 88, 95n69
    unspeakability, 81–87
sovereignty. *See under* Israel; Zionism
Spiegelman, Art, 91–92n15, 105–6
Stannard, David, 156, 160, 173n79
Stratton, Jon, 12, 15, 22, 31n40, 34n99, 37, 51, 123
SS, 65, 76, 84, 94n60, 105, 186, 191–92, 206n88
Sydney Jewish Museum, 153–54
Szenes, Hannah, 197, 199, 206n89
The Shoah Teaching Alternatives in Jewish Education (STAJE), 90

Terdiman, Richard, 74, 91–92n15
trauma, 13, 29, 64–65, 70, 81–87, 100, 104, 109, 130, 155, 190–91, 195, 204n53, 208–9
testimony. *See* survivor testimony
transgender, 183

the uncanny, 99–131, 136n61
United States Holocaust Memorial Museum (USHMM), 10, 30n30, 39–42, 56–57n11, 83, 136–37n57, 149–50, 157
uprisings. *See* revolt; resistance; Warsaw Ghetto Uprising

violence, 3, 29, 39–40, 111–12, 134n41, 143–46, 150, 155, 158–68, 168–9n9, 170n106, 191–94, 209. *See also* genocide; the Holocaust; rape; revolt; settler colonialism

Warsaw, 79, 125–26, 133–34n31, 166, 178
Warsaw Ghetto Uprising, 24, 124–26, 140n127, 198–99, 206n90
Weitzman, Lenore and Dalia Ofer, 186, 205n66
White Australia Policy, 49–51
White, Hayden, 64, 68–70, 88, 92–93n28

whiteness, 34n98, 44, 57n15, 144–45
    assimilation, 13, 41, 49
    Australia, 22, 49–51
    class, 40, 57n18
    race, 42, 49, 50, 57n18
    United States, 31n51, 42
    See also racialization
Wissenschaft des Judentums, 22, 43–44, 71, 93n41

Yad Vashem, 10, 30n30, 60n50, 67, 94n53
Yad Vashem Law (1953), 104
Yerushalmi, Yosef, 22, 29n25, 63, 71–72
Yiddish, 12, 24, 36, 41–42, 130
    cultural organizations, 36
    New Yiddishists, 41–42, 58n28
Yom Ha'atzmaut, 52, 101, 122
Yom Hashoah, 52, 82, 153–54, 192
Young, James E. 80, 85, 90

Zionism
    assimilation, 15, 101, 117–21, 123–24, 130–31, 141n139
    diaspora, 2, 15, 19, 25, 26, 53–55, 99–131, 131n1, 135n56, 136n107, 141n 139, 184–85, 200
    femininity, 15, 108, 111, 123, 127, 180
    gender, 15, 21, 52–54, 99–131
    the Holocaust, 3, 6–7, 17, 19, 23–26, 38, 45, 52–55, 61n68, 87–88, 99–131, 151, 209–10
    masculinity, 15, 25, 53, 100, 108, 110–12, 122, 123–30, 140n131, 141n136, 199
    memory/memorialisation, 52, 100, 101–2, 105, 107, 110, 115, 122, 126, 210
    positive ending, 100, 105–10
    sovereignty, 106, 108, 110, 112–13, 120, 131n2
    youth groups, 36, 52, 124–27, 206n90

www.ingramcontent.com/pod-product-compliance
Lightning Source LLC
Chambersburg PA
CBHW072150100526
44589CB00015B/2167